WOMEN AND WRITING IN MEDIEVAL EUROPE

Carolyne Larrington has gathered together a uniquely comprehensive collection of writing by, for and about medieval women, spanning one thousand years and Europe from Iceland to Byzantium. The extracts are arranged thematically, dealing with the central areas of medieval women's lives and their relation to social and cultural institutions. Each section is contextualized with a brief historical introduction, and the materials span literary, historical, theological and other narrative and imaginative writing. The writings here uncover and confound the stereotype of the medieval woman as lady or virgin by demonstrating the different roles and meanings that the sign of woman occupied in the imaginative space of the medieval period.

Larrington's clear and accessible editorial material and the modern English translations of all the extracts mean this work is ideally suited for students. *Women and Writing in Medieval Europe: A Sourcebook* also contains an extensive and fully up-to-date bibliography, making it not only essential reading for undergraduates and postgraduates but also a valuable research tool for scholars.

Carolyne Larrington is Lecturer in Medieval English at Lady Margaret Hall, Oxford. Her main research interests are in Old Icelandic literature and mythology, and in women's history and writing. Previous publications include *The Feminist Companion to Mythology* and *A Store of Common Sense*.

WOMEN AND WRITING IN MEDIEVAL EUROPE

A sourcebook

Carolyne Larrington

London and New York

First published 1995
by Routledge
11 New Fetter Lane, London EC4P 4EE

Simultaneously published in the USA and Canada
by Routledge
29 West 35th Street, New York, NY 10001

Typeset in Garamond by
Solidus (Bristol) Limited

Printed and bound in Great Britain by
Biddles Ltd, Guildford and King's Lynn

British Library Cataloguing in Publication Data
A catalogue record for this book is available from the British Library

Library of Congress Cataloguing in Publication Data
Larrington, Carolyne
Women and Writing in Medieval Europe : A sourcebook / Carolyne
Larrington.
p. cm.
Includes bibliographical references (p.) and index.
1. Literature, Medieval–History and criticism. 2. Women in
literature. I. Title.
PN682.W6L37 1995
809'.89287'0902–dc20 94-30485

ISBN 0–415–10684–2 (hbk)
ISBN 0–415–10685–0 (pbk)

For Vicky Licorish and for Louise Elkins

CONTENTS

ILLUSTRATIONS

ACKNOWLEDGEMENTS

Thanks are owed to very many people who have contributed ideas, suggested texts, discussed the difficulties of reading medieval literary texts and their relation to history. John Blair, Katy Cubitt, Julia Smith and Frédérique Lachaud have all shown the historian's tolerance for the bizarre questions asked by someone trained in a different discipline. John and Sarah Blair, Suzanne Bobzien and Frédérique Lachaud have also been of great assistance in the pursuit of illustrations, while Ivona Ilic and Oliver Gutman have kindly provided translations.

A great debt of gratitude is owed to St John's College, Oxford which has supported me throughout this project and granted me valuable writing time in the form of a sabbatical term in Michaelmas 1993. Thanks are due to all at the Gender and Medieval Studies Conference in Leeds in January 1994, in particular Mark Chinca, Simon Gaunt, Jane Taylor, Ivona Ilic, Ruth Evans, Rosalynn Voaden and Lesley Johnson.

Talia Rodgers at Routledge, and Tricia Dever, her indefatigable assistant, have made the process of publication extraordinarily painless. Sarah-Jane Woolley was a wonderfully efficient Desk Editor. Maureen Pemberton at the Department of Western Manuscripts, Bodleian Library gave generously of her time and enthusiasm in finding illustrations. Sîan Williams indexed with her usual enthusiasm.

The students of the Advanced Studies in England Program in Bath – especially Hue Le, Annette Thompson and Sarah Thumm, the first guinea-pigs on whom this book was tested – have been enthusiastic and inventive in their responses, and I thank all of them for the suggestions, reactions and ideas which they have contributed during the 'Women in Pre-Renaissance Europe' courses. Thanks are due also to Don Nunes and Barbara White of ASE for their encouragement in the development of the course.

And thanks to John Davis, as usual, for everything.

ACKNOWLEDGEMENTS

PERMISSIONS

The author and publishers gratefully acknowledge permission from the following to quote from copyright material: Elspeth Benton and the Medieval Academy of America for material from J. F. Benton, *Self and Society in Medieval France: The Memoirs of Abbot Guibert of Nogent*, Medieval Academy Reprints for Teaching, published by the University of Toronto Press in association with the Medieval Academy of America, 1984; Boydell and Brewer Ltd for Aldhelm, *The Prose Works*, transl. M. Lapidge and M. Herren, Cambridge, D. S. Brewer, 1989, Saxo Grammaticus, *A History of the Danish People*, transl. P. Fisher and H. Ellis-Davidson, Woodbridge, Suffolk, Boydell Press, 1980 and J. Jesch, *Women in the Viking Age*, Woodbridge, Suffolk, Boydell Press, 1991; Professor Peter Dronke for *Medieval Latin and the Rise of European Love Lyric*, Oxford University Press, 2nd edn 1968; Professor Peter Dronke and Cambridge University Press for extracts from *Women Writers of the Middle Ages*, 1984; The Council of the Early English Text Society for material from *The Book of the Tour Landry*, EETS SS 2, and *The Book of Margery Kempe*, EETS OS 212; Everyman's Library Ltd for William Langland, *The Vision of Piers Plowman: A Complete Edition of the B-Text*, ed. A. V. C. Schmidt, London, Everyman, 1978; Exeter University Press for Julian of Norwich, *A Revelation of Love*, ed. Marion Glasscoe, 2nd edn 1986; Garland Press for Mechthild of Magdeburg, *Flowing Light of the Divinity*, transl. C. Mesch Galvani, ed. S. Clark, Garland Library of Medieval Literature Series B Vol. 72, New York and London, Garland, 1991; Gomer Press for *Dafydd ap Gwilym: Poems*, ed. and transl. Rachel Bromwich, Welsh classics series, Gomer Press, 1982; Manchester University Press for material from J. Snow, 'The Spanish Love Poet: Florencía Pinar' and K. M. Wilson, 'Hrotsvit' in *Medieval Women Writers*, ed. K. M. Wilson, Manchester University Press, 1984; Medieval Academy of America and Toronto University Press for *Marie de France, Fables*, ed. and transl. H. Spiegel, Medieval Academy Reprints for Teaching, published by the University of Toronto Press in association with the Medieval Academy of America, 1994; Oxford University Press for G. Boccaccio, *The Decameron*, transl. G. Waldman, 1993, 'A Letter on Virginity' in *Medieval English Prose for Women*, ed. and transl. B. Millett and J. Wogan-Browne, 1990, A. Blamires, *Woman Defamed and Woman Defended*, 1992 and *Paston Letters*, ed. N. Davis, 1958; Dr Christopher Page, Sidney Sussex College, Cambridge for translations of Hildegard of Bingen, 'Ave generosa' and 'O Ecclesia'; Paulist Press Mahwah for material reprinted from *Hadewijch: The Complete Works*, translated by Mother Columba Hart, O.S.B. © 1980, and from *Francis and Clare: The Complete Works*, translated by Regis J. Armstrong, O.F.M. Cap. and Ignatius C. Brady, O.F.M. © 1982

xiii

by the Missionary Society of St Paul the Apostle in the State of New York, used by permission of Paulist Press; University of Pennsylvania Press for S. F. Wemple, *Women in Frankish Society*, 1981; Penguin Books Ltd for material from *The Lais of Marie de France*, transl. G. S. Burgess and K. Busby, 1986, Chrétien de Troyes, 'Erec and Enide' and 'Yvain' in *Arthurian Romances*, transl. C. W. Carroll and W. W. Kibler, 1991, Christine de Pizan, *The Treasure of the City of Ladies*, transl. S. Lawson, 1985, *The Letters of Abélard and Héloise*, transl. B. Radice, 1974, Dante Alighieri, *La Vita Nuova*, transl. B. Reynolds, 1969, Gregory of Tours, *The History of the Franks*, transl. L. Thorpe, 1974, E. Ladurie, *Montaillou*, transl. B. Bray, 1980, Bede, *History of the English Church*, transl. L. Sherley-Price, 1955, Anna Comnena, *The Alexiad*, transl. E. R. A. Sewter, 1969, Gottfried von Strassburg, *Tristan*, transl. A. T. Hatto, 1960 and St Augustine, *Confessions*, transl. R. S. Pine-Coffin, 1961; Persea Press for Christine de Pizan, *The Book of the City of Ladies*, transl. Earl Jeffrey Richards, 1982; Princeton University Press for P. Strohm, *Hochon's Arrow*, 1992; Scholars' Facsimiles and Reprints for Boncompagno da Signa, *Rota Veneris*, ed. and transl. J. Purkart, 1975; State University of New York Press for J. Ruiz, Archpriest of Hita, *The Book of Good Love*, transl. R. Mignani and M. A. di Cesare, Albany, N.Y., State University of New York Press, 1980; Tafol Press for *Canu Maswedd yr Oesoedd Canol/Medieval Welsh Erotic Poetry*, ed. and transl. D. Johnston, 1991; University of Toronto Press for material from J. M. Pizarro, *A Rhetoric of the Scene*, 1989; Weidenfeld and Nicolson for M. Warner, *Joan of Arc*, 1981; Yale University Press for *Three Medieval Views of Women*, ed. and transl. G. K. Fiero, W. Pfeffer, M. Allain, © Yale University 1989.

Every effort has been made to trace copyright holders, although that has not been possible in every case.

ILLUSTRATION ACKNOWLEDGEMENTS

The author and publishers would like to thank the following for their kind permission to use the following illustrations: The Master and Fellows of Balliol College: cover; The Bodleian Library: Figs 1, 7, 8, 11, 12; Augustiner Museum, Freiburg: Fig. 2; The British Museum: Figs 3, 4; Keith Barley, Barley Studio, Dunnington, York: Fig. 5; Bildarchiv der Österreichischen Nationalbibliothek, Vienna: Fig. 6; The Fellows of Corpus Christi College, Cambridge: Fig. 9; The Provost and Fellows of The Queen's College, Oxford: Fig. 10; Inventaire Général/SPADEM 1974: Fig. 13; Bibliothèque Nationale de France, Paris: Fig. 14.

INTRODUCTION

Reading the writing of women

The difficulty of interpretation lies in the delicate relation of figurative imagery to literary and intellectual representations and to reality, a difficulty that is compounded when the images are intended to be 'realistic' or 'naturalistic'.

(Klapisch-Zuber 1992: 321)

The appeal to 'history' so commonly made in current critical discourses of all varieties is necessarily always to a reconstruction fabricated according to processes of interpretation that are identical to those applied to the 'not-history' of the literary text.

(Patterson 1987: 44)

This is not a history, but a 'not-history', book. It contains many facts which can be understood as historical, but those facts are subordinate to the texts by, for, and about medieval women which are presented here. The facts give a context, a sufficient anchorage in the past to diminish the anachronistic expectations which the modern reader might bring to the text, but they cannot explain it in its entirety. Rather the historical is in dialogue with the 'not-historical', in juxtaposition to it, querying it, and suggesting tangents. Though some of these texts purport to be history – that is, they are composed by medieval writers who intended to write history – the modern reader needs to revise her own definition of history as 'fact' in order to interpret them. This is not only because they contain non-historical material: miracles, divine interventions, and supernatural happenings, but also because, for the medieval chronicler, history is the working out of God's will in the world. The telling of events conforms to certain patterns and expectations on the writer's part: he structures his narrative to reflect them.

Bias, prejudice, preconception, subtext, political agenda all shape the language and argument of the writer for or, especially, about women. 'Woman' may only be, as Christiane Klapisch-Zuber asserts, 'a creation of the male gaze' (1992: 7), but the

1

concept of 'Woman' nevertheless exists for the male medieval writer as a sign, bearing meanings which have little to do with the actual social roles of individual women. A nun who is heavily pregnant is miraculously restored to virginity, an event which is interpreted as a sign of God's power and benevolence, even towards the most wretchedly sinful of creatures. The physical and social dimensions of the story – where did the baby go? how did the mother feel at the loss of her child? what happened then to the errant woman? – are ignored by the clerical author in favour of the theological and symbolic significance. Meaning is interpreted within a quite different discourse.

If history as 'fact' bears a problematic relation to reality, how much more so does the literary or narrative text, holding a more or less distorting mirror up to contemporary reality, or looking deliberately away from it towards an ideal version, or a diabolical inversion, of what should be. Although we read texts from the past knowing that we cannot recapture or recreate the women we encounter there in their historical actuality, yet we persist in trying to do so – or else why should we read such texts at all, if not in the belief that we may come to touch the minds of writers like Hildegard of Bingen, or to understand the complex motivations of Joan of Arc?

This is a book of representations and self-representations, meant to display the variety and range of female experience as imagined in the medieval period. Some imaginings may, as Klapisch-Zuber warns, have pretensions to naturalism, but here we must be at our most wary as readers. Which medieval woman, real or otherwise, could be as lifelike as Chaucer's Wife of Bath? And which other medieval woman has generated as much uncertainty as to how she may be interpreted: as a feisty proto-feminist, as a fully realized psychological character, at once brave and pathetic, or as a nightmare of misogynist stereotyping? So too with our texts: the women we shall encounter in what follows are equally susceptible of different interpretations.

Historians of women for a long time pursued the myth of the Golden Age, drawing up a kind of league table of historical periods when it was bad to be a woman (the nineteenth century) and when good (Anglo-Saxon England). Only recently have scholars begun to argue that the concept of 'the status of women' is so dependent on age, class, occupation, economic circumstances, political and intellectual freedom as to be impossible to construct for any one period and society. Similarly, literary scholars have trawled the literatures of the past seeking 'positive' and 'negative' images of women, and reinterpreting the societies that originated such images through the prism of the literary text. Thus the figuring of the *domna* in twelfth-century Provençal troubadour poetry as powerful and all-commanding was held to represent a real improvement in the lives of the noble women of southern France; more broadly the pervasiveness of misogynistic writing throughout the period has been thought to show how women in the High Middle Ages were held in little esteem. Medieval women are constantly shown by later interpreters as trapped within the stereotypes of misogynistic discourse: gateways of the Devil or brides of Christ as Howard Bloch terms the dichotomy (Bloch 1991). Yet the sign of woman in the period is packed with many further and more complex meanings, and the historical women who lived in the Middle Ages faced choices between a wide range of roles and functions.

The Middle Ages

The Middle Ages is a term invented by the eighteenth century in the course of its own construction of the past, positioning the period as a long and rather unsatisfactory age of transition between the brilliance of the Roman Empire and the rebirth of the Renaissance. But for the most part the people who lived in those thousand years knew little of Rome, and still less of Greece. They looked towards, not the dawn of humanism, but the coming of Judgement Day, and did not see themselves as being in the middle of anything except ordinary lived experience: 'No more than a fish can understand the water in which it swims can a medieval man understand his medievalness,' writes Lee Patterson (1987: 28). Yet, as historians are increasingly aware, in western Europe, and in the parts of the world colonized by Europeans after the end of our period, the social institutions which structure our lives originated in the Middle Ages and were formed by them. Romantic love, western marriage, the banking system, the parliament, the university, to name only the most obvious, are medieval legacies. Hence how the medieval writer understood the place and operations of these institutions in his or her culture is crucial to a full appreciation of how they shape our lives today.

To characterize the Middle Ages is an impossible task: the texts in this book span a thousand years and range geographically from Wales to Byzantium, from Iceland to Italy. The period which the book spans – 500–1500 – is both arbitrary and 'the most banal of textbook periodizations' (Klapisch-Zuber 1992: 5). In 500 the Roman Empire's slow retreat from the West was complete, England and France were converting to Christianity, the German tribes were living much as they had for centuries, and the citizens of Constantinople, the rump of the empire, were the most civilized people in Europe. By 1500 humanism was well established in Italy, Constantinople was lost to the Turks, complex social systems had developed in the western states, and colonization of the New World was already under way. Although in Italy the medieval period was over by the early fourteenth century, further east in Serbia and Romania, or north, in Iceland and the remoter parts of Scandinavia, the Middle Ages lasted well into the nineteenth century. However, for the greater part of western Europe, the area with which this book is principally concerned, once we have accepted the arbitrariness of any two dates, the time-span 500–1500 is usually recognized as significantly different enough from what preceded it and what followed it to function as a useful analytical category.

The texts

The organization of a body of texts which span the chronological and geographical expanses of early Europe offers different choices. They might have been presented chronologically (as they are within chapters), at the risk of seeming to present a meta-narrative: a story of women's mounting achievement or gradual degradation, or they might have been ordered geographically, providing a kind of snapshot of each culture or region. I have chosen, however, to present the texts in groups arranged by theme, by a relationship to a central idea, the implications of which are worked out in the texts in widely different ways.

The book begins with marriage: the central experience in the lives of around 90 per cent of women, both in medieval times and today. Romance, sex and affection follow marriage, a connection which the modern reader sees as inevitable, but which was by no means so regarded for the greater part of the medieval period. What was inevitable for the medieval wife was work, and usually motherhood; in contrast, chapter 4 presents imaginative explorations of the alternatives available to the woman who rejected the secular for the religious life. The autonomy which the medieval woman as subject is usually perceived to lack underpins chapter 5, where the problematic relation of women and power is analysed. Here the exceptional 'real' woman (Eleanor of Aquitaine, Joan of Arc), the semi-legendary (Sigrid the Strong-minded) and the imagined (Alvild the Pirate) flesh out medieval cultural beliefs about powerful women. How women can aspire to learning, how they use traditional knowledge, their difficult entry into textuality, their awareness of rhetoric and convention, and their own self-representations figure in the last two sections. Thus the written subject becomes herself a writing subject, constructing versions of a domestic reality which can include the writer's mother calling her to supper, the author's feelings when her husband becomes senile and incapable of caring for himself, and the wife's annoyance when she is blamed for letting water get into the verjuice, as well as an imaginative reality in which the soul is lifted into ecstasy by God, where bold and ingenious morals are drawn from talking animals, and where Christ is figured as a mother labouring in agony to give rebirth to mankind.

The texts are written by men, and by unknown authors, as well as women. Women's own writings, even where, inevitably, they are heavily influenced by prevailing masculine rhetorical codes, provide perhaps the surest grounding upon which we can construct their experiences. Yet to use women's writings alone in a sourcebook which aims to trace the complexities of the relationship between women and writing would be to offer distorted representations of that relationship. Much of medieval women's own writing is religious or mystical in content; literacy was initially the province of the nun, while the noble lady had little time to write imaginatively and other classes were disbarred from literacy entirely. Moreover, women lived alongside men and the ways in which they regarded men, in which they were regarded by men, and in which they regarded themselves, all determined the quality of women's lives and its textual expression.

The range of texts in this book reflects the availability of relevant material: thus England and France are well represented since literacy arrives early and much writing has been preserved. Eastern Europe, on the other hand, provides fewer examples of writing by, for and about medieval women, since literacy (particularly lay literacy) was far less widespread, even by the end of the period, while my own interests have led me to include more Norse material than is usual in books centring on western Europe. I have tried to select texts which are seldom reproduced elsewhere, or which are difficult to find, but a few well-known texts beg nevertheless to be included; I hope they take on new freshness when juxtaposed with others engaging with a similar theme. I have steered clear of myth and legend: though some writing – for example the depiction of Sigrid the Strong-minded – is clearly influenced by mythical motifs, the problems of interpretation which myth, legend and folktale offer are distinct from those of literary texts. Nor, for reasons of accessibility and space, have I been able to include literary material concerning women from minorities, Jewish and Muslim women, whose lives and whose significance when they were written into texts were very different from those of ordinary Christian women. One exception is the Mooress who rebuffs the advances of the Archpriest of Hita in chapter 2 below, who is figured as more virtuous and single-minded than her Christian sisters. Amt, mentioned below, documents the experiences of Jewish and Muslim women (1993: 277-304).

Documents which are resolutely non-literary or non-narrative – law codes, wills, charters, court records and the like – have also been omitted. These offer their own problems of interpretation, but they are not susceptible of the kind of literary analysis – analysis precisely as 'not-history' – which the texts presented here demand. The documentation of medieval women's lives and an unproblematized relation of such texts to 'history' is the subject of Emilie Amt's *Women's Lives in Medieval Europe* (1993), a book which shuns literary and artistic sources. The present volume in some ways complements that of Amt by restoring the literary to the range of materials which form our view of the 'medieval', while attempting to give a theoretical and methodological orientation to that restoration.

The study of women from anthropological, historical, geographical and literary perspectives has grown exponentially over the last twenty years. The magisterial Italian–French project, *A History of Women in the West*, is nearing completion; neglected writers such as Mechthild of Magdeburg or Beatrijs of Nazareth are being re-edited, collections of essays about women and anthologies of women's writing from every period are published for academic and general readerships alike. It is no longer necessary to apologize for an interest in women and their complex relations to culture; rather, with the opening up of so many different terrains, the difficulty is finding appropriate methods of analysis. This book tries to bring together literature and history in a conjunction which makes clear the contingent and uncertain nature of the text as witness to lived reality, and of history as an interpretative key to literary texts.

1

MARRIAGE

INTRODUCTION

I think it would please you to have me there with the whole household,
and yet you leave the choice to me. This you do for your courtesy, and
I am not worthy of so much honour. I have resolved to go not only to
Pisa, but to the world's end, if it pleases you.

(Origo 1959: 162)

You bid me make merry and be of good cheer. I have naught in the
world to make me merry; *you* could do so if you would, but you will
not .... Each night, when I lie abed, I remember that you must wake
until dawn. And then you bid me be of good cheer.

(Origo 1959: 164)

Margherita Datini's letter to her husband, a merchant from the small Italian town of
Prato, cited first above, was dictated by her in 1382; the second, rather tarter
missive to the same recipient dates from a few years later. Francesco Datini was
about 42 when he married his 16-year-old wife from the lesser Florentine nobility in
Avignon in 1377, a marriage which was to last thirty-three years. Margherita was
taught to read and write by a family friend only at the age of 30, but her letters,
together with the fifteenth-century English Paston letters, are among the few
writings by ordinary married women in our period. Although the great majority of the
female population were married at some point in their lives, the writings by women
which survive are overwhelmingly those of monastic women, who had never been, or
were no longer, married. Yet the universality of marriage in one form or another is
such that there are many texts which serve to flesh out a conception of the
changing institution emerging in law codes and theological writing throughout the
period. Marriage customs varied by region: in some places women were married
when very young to men some ten to fifteen years older than they were (a pattern
associated with southern Europe), or they married men of like age at roughly the
same age as women now marry in the West (a northern European pattern). These

patterns were heavily modified by class: the lower the class, the more choice the partners might have. (Goldberg 1992 and Smith 1992 give full summaries of the debates surrounding European marriage patterns.)

Marriage as institution

At the most general level marriage is a social mechanism designed to regulate the distribution of women between male members of society and to formalize the links between a man and his offspring. In western Europe men have tended to have only one wife at a time: serial monogamy, or marriage to a (legal) wife with a number of concubines ensured variety in the man's sexual life. In the early period, the concubine might co-exist with the wife, or – a pattern frequent in early France – the young nobleman might take an official concubine in his youth, replacing her with a wife of rank equal to his, who would bear him legitimate children. Separation from the concubine, who might also have borne children and have been a partner for many years, was not always easy, as demonstrated by the case of Lothar and Waldrada outlined below. Saint Augustine records his misery when, as his marriage to a young heiress approached, he was forced to give up the woman with whom he had been living for many years:

> The woman with whom I had been living was torn from my side as an obstacle to my marriage and this was a blow which crushed my heart to bleeding, because I loved her dearly. She went back to Africa, vowing never to give herself to any other man, and left with me the son whom she had borne me ... the wound I had received when my first mistress was wrenched away showed no signs of healing. At first the pain was sharp and searing, but then the wound began to fester, and though the pain was duller there was all the less hope of a cure.
>
> (Augustine 1961: 133)

Augustine does not record the fate of his discarded mistress; similar women who have lived in non-marital arrangements tend to disappear from the record when the relationship is terminated. Charlemagne did not allow his daughters to marry, lest the alliances thus formed with other families should weaken his own and his sons' positions. However, he tolerated his daughters taking sexual partners outside marriage. Their brother, Louis the Pious, was less broad-minded: on his accession to the throne the sisters were packed off to the convent of Chelles where their aunt Gisela was abbess. The most famous of all the marital wrangles of the early French kings was occasioned by the passion of Lothar of Lotharingia (roughly eastern France, west Germany and north Italy) for the concubine Waldrada, with whom he had lived before his marriage to Theutberga. Lothar married Theutberga for political reasons; although Waldrada came from the lower nobility she unfortunately 'did not have a brother who could guarantee the defence of the Alpine passes for

Lotharingia' (Wemple 1981: 90). From 858 to 869 the clergy of Lotharingia, and chiefly the redoubtable Bishop Hincmar of Reims, were occupied with the question of Lothar's divorce from Theutberga. The political advantages of alliance with Theutberga's family had now passed, and Lothar wanted to marry his former concubine. Lothar's great-grandfather, Charlemagne, had easily repudiated one of his wives and lived with several concubines in his old age, but Lothar was driven to accusing his wife of incest, of conceiving through femoral intercourse and of procuring an abortion without damaging her virginity, and was still unable to get rid of her. The case was still in progress when he died (Bishop 1985: 53–84; Wemple 1992: 180).

In early medieval Europe divorce seems to have been relatively easy to obtain. The Icelandic sagas suggest that a husband or wife simply had to declare before witnesses that they were divorcing their spouse, as Thrain does (p. 27 below). Anglo-Saxon laws allowed a wife to keep half of the couple's joint property if she had custody of the children (Fell 1984: 64). But by the tenth century marriage had changed from an essentially private arrangement between a man and a woman and their respective families into a Christian and lifelong monogamous partnership. It was a difficult ideal to impress upon the male members of the ruling classes: the wife had to have useful kindred to cement political alliances, be able to provide sons and heirs in sufficient numbers to ensure inheritance, and, increasingly, to be a companion to her husband. The ninth-century writer Christian of Corbie warns:

> [Be she] gluttonous, quarrelsome or sickly, a wife must be kept until the day of her death, except if by mutual agreement both partners withdraw from the world. Therefore, before he accepts a wife, a man must get to know her well, both with regard to her character and health. He should not do anything rash that may cause him sorrow for a long time. If all decisions are to be made with advice, this one even more so; in matrimony a man surrenders himself. Most men, when they choose a wife, look for seven [sic] qualities: nobility, wealth, looks, health, intelligence, and character. Two of these, intelligence and character, are more important than the rest. If these two are missing, the others might be lost.
>
> (cited from Wemple 1981: 88)

Marriage, then, had come to be for life, save in exceptional circumstances. Incest was one of these. By the 1060s, in the course of the Gregorian reforms, the theologian Peter Damian extended the consanguinity prohibitions to marriages within the sixth degree of kinship. However, few people, even among the nobility, were able to reckon up their fifth cousins accurately, and over time the European aristocracy had become very closely connected. This had its advantages: a marriage could be contracted apparently in all innocence only for the true kinship relation to emerge some time later if one or other of the partners no longer wished to be married. A case in point is that of Louis VII and Eleanor of Aquitaine. The two parties in the marriage were related in the fourth and fifth degrees, but it was not until they had been married for twelve years, during which time Eleanor had produced only two children, both daughters, that the consanguinity issue was raised. Eleanor and Louis were divorced, and Louis married two subsequent wives, the third of whom was his son-in-law's sister. As a hindrance to marriage consanguinity could be overlooked if the need arose. By the thirteenth century, overwhelmed by the number of annulment cases which the extended consanguinity laws had brought about, the Church had to retreat and the restrictions were eased (Brooke 1991: 134–6).

Adultery by the female partner (male adultery was rarely considered significant) provided another ground for divorce; however, the Church did not allow the parties to remarry in this instance. Laws concerning adultery varied: some codes permitted the aggrieved man to kill both wife and lover if he caught them *in flagrante*. One Anglo-Danish law made under Knut condemns the adulterous wife to having her nose cut off, while an earlier law simply requires the lover to provide a new wife for the outraged husband, presumably making himself responsible for the payments to the new wife's kin (Fell 1984: 64).

Making a marriage

Even though the Church became increasingly concerned in promoting the ideal of lifelong monogamy and constructing theories of marriage, it had little part to play in the actual ceremony. Broadly speaking, a marriage had three stages: *petitio* (negotiations), *desponsatio* (betrothal) and *nuptae* (wedding). The sequence is clearly illustrated in excerpt 4 below. The families concerned would make contact, either directly or through intermediaries, and negotiate the financial arrangements. At a private, though legally binding, ceremony involving an oral or written contract, the parties would pledge themselves, and at some subsequent time, the public celebration, often, though not necessarily, including a nuptial mass, would take place and the marriage be consummated.

When did the couple *actually* become married during this process? According to the Roman jurist Ulpian, 'consent makes the marriage', and thus the betrothal came to be regarded as binding. Ulpian had in mind the consent of the families, arrived at after the negotiations, not the consent of the parties themselves, though over time the consent of the husband and wife was seen to be what mattered. After betrothal the parties could not extricate themselves from the match without incurring penalties. Consummation might also occur after betrothal without moral disapproval; in the Spanish frontier towns of Castile and Léon in the twelfth and thirteenth centuries, records show an assumption that the betrothed couple would sleep together, though problems would arise in the case of subsequent repudiation (Dillard 1984: 57).

Betrothal involved consent in one of two ways. In the 1150s Peter Lombard had elaborated the distinction between consent made *per verba de futuro*, words in the future tense, which constituted a promise to marry at some future date, and a promise *per verba de praesenti*, words in the present tense (i.e. I, N, marry you, M), which constituted an indissoluble union. Consent *per verba de futuro* only constituted a marriage after consummation. Marriages *per verba de praesenti* in fact remained legal in England until the Hardwick Marriage Act of 1753. In 1215 the Fourth Lateran Council moved to require ecclesiastical participation in weddings, but clandestine marriages were not invalidated by this, despite the difficulties attendant upon proving that such marriages had taken place if one or other party should change their mind. The Sarum Ritual dating from 1085 makes clear that, in England at least, the expectation was of a public betrothal 'at the church door,' where the whole community could establish that there was no impediment to the marriage and witness the exchange of vows and ring (Conway 1993; Amt 1993: 83–9). The ceremony did not move inside the church until after the Reformation (Fig. 1).

What was marriage for? According to Augustine's influential analysis, the goods of marriage were: *fides, proles, sacramentum* (mutual sexual fidelity, children and the function of marriage as a sign of the union between Christ and the Church). Thus marriage was to be exclusive, all sexual acts were to be open to the possibility of conception, and the union was indissoluble (Payer 1993: 70–1). In the thirteenth century, in the writings of Thomas Aquinas and thereafter, marriage was analysed

Figure 1 A bride, accompanied by her male kin, maidens, musicians, and a married woman at the rear approach the church door, where the priest, the bridegroom, his kin (one of whom is listening out for the musicians) wait. From a fourteenth-century Flemish manuscript, MS Bodl 264 fol. 105v, Bodleian Library, Oxford.

in terms of intentions (*causae*): what was marriage intended for? First, marriage was intended for procreation, second to pay the marriage debt (see below, p. 16), third to avoid fornication, and finally for pleasure. The first two reasons were morally straightforward, while the second two caused innumerable problems for the Church in the later medieval period as theologians tried to determine how sinful sexual acts undertaken primarily, or partly, for pleasure might be (Payer 1993: 111–31).

Thus, in philosophical and theological terms, marriage seemed to require consummation; an unconsummated marriage fulfilled none of the *causae* above, and negated one of Augustine's goods. The Church therefore became troubled by its failure to include consummation in its formal definition of marriage. Early in the period unconsummated marriages had been regarded as meritorious, an assessment stemming in part from Augustine's pronouncement that the marriage of the Virgin Mary and Joseph, though unconsummated, was nevertheless a true marriage (Clark 1991: 23). Thus Bede celebrates Queen Ætheldred of Northumbria, who kept her virginity through two marriages, much to the annoyance of her second husband Ecgfrith. Henry III of Germany (1017–56) and his wife Cunégonde were believed by later chroniclers to have had a *mariage blanc* – at all events no children were born and Henry was canonized some hundred years after his death (Duby 1983–4: 57–8). By the late twelfth century Pope Alexander III (1159–81), deeply conscious of the significance of the biblical phrase 'una caro' (one flesh) in describing the nature of marriage, came to see consummation as an essential part of the sacrament (as it had now been defined) (Brooke 1991: 132–3). Failure to consummate thus became a ground for annulment; a ground which stored up as much trouble for the papal courts as the consanguinity rules. Consummation *and* consent now made the marriage (Amt 1993: 79–83).

Marriage and property

The disposition of property at a wedding changed greatly over the medieval period. At the beginning of the period, in the parts of Europe under non-Roman law, the bride-price was paid by the groom to the bride's family (later the bride herself), and the wife would receive a 'morning-gift' on the morning after the marriage was consummated. Some Germanic law codes limited the amount of the morning-gift, others were more generous: Chilperic of the Franks gave his Visigothic queen, Galswinth, the cities of Bordeaux, Limoges, Cahors, Lescar and Cieutat. These were inherited from Galswinth, whom Chilperic subsequently had garrotted, by her sister Brunhild (Gregory of Tours 1974: 505). Gradually, the bride-price came to be paid to the wife herself, often in the form of a dower which would form the woman's financial security when she became a widow.

In the 1140s the Roman dowry system was instituted, probably because there were now more young women of marriageable age than young men, and because marriage patterns were changing in southern Europe. Men now tended to marry girls who were ten years or more younger than they were, and thus the pool of marriageable women was enlarged (Hughes 1978). The new system was found first in Italian towns, from where it spread rapidly across Europe. Now property passed on marriage from wife's family to husband's; Dante himself, in the *Paradiso*, refers to the fear which a father felt at the birth of a daughter as he anticipated her future dowry expenses (Dante 1971: 219). By the end of the period dowry inflation in Italy had reached such a peak that the Florentines established the Monte del Doti, a bank into which an anxious father could pay a deposit at the birth of his infant daughter. This would mature into her dowry payment when she became marriageable, or would provide a settlement for entry to a convent (Brooke 1991: 15–16).

Early historians of Anglo-Saxon and Germanic societies argued that the bride-price system meant that Germanic women must have lacked status since they were 'bought' at marriage (Fell 1984: 16); other historians ascribe women's gradual loss of power through the medieval period to the institution of the dowry system (Stuard 1987: 161). Neither contention gives the whole picture, however, for women's status depended far more on their capacity to own, and to buy and sell property in their own right, and to inherit property from parents and husbands. These rights varied enormously in both time and place. The Merovingian queen had control over the royal treasury at the death of her husband, thus, as Pauline Stafford writes, 'the masterplan of a sixth- or seventh-century usurper had three stages: murder the king, get the gold-hoard, marry the widow. Since the widow usually sat on the gold the two went together' (Stafford 1983: 50). Anglo-Saxon women might buy and sell property independently of their husbands, and bequeath it away from their children back to their own kin, if they wished (Amt 1993: 130–6). Royal women were able to use their lands for monastic foundations, a development which was popular with the Church, if not always with the royal family (see p. 157 below). Under the dowry system, daughters usually received their portion of the family inheritance at marriage, instead of at the parents' death, when they might expect to inherit nothing further. The dowry was meant to be held in trust for the wife's support after her husband's death, but very often the wife was in no position to prevent her husband from selling or mortgaging her property.

In Castile the townswomen benefited from egalitarian legislation (the law of acquisitions) which held that all property jointly acquired, such as the profits from a husband-and-wife business partnership, were owned in common, and there were efficient checks on a husband's right to dispose of family property (Dillard 1984: 68). The law of acquisitions thus 'acknowledged [wives'] importance in the accumulation and management of family assets and strengthened perceptions of marriage as a cooperative team rather than a hierarchical partnership' (Dillard 1984: 215).

In peasant households, evidence from wills shows that marriage may also have been regarded as a partnership, with both partners contributing their separate skills to the household economy. The buying of stock and seed, tools and household implements would be matters for joint discussion where husband and wife were trying to make most efficient use of limited resources. Thus 'many of the decisions that would have to be made during the course of the marriage would be ones in which mutual expectations or mutual needs would determine the course of action' (Hanawalt 1986a: 154, though see Bennett 1992: 155). Fabliaux and ballads often suggest a power imbalance in peasant marriages with one spouse (often the wife) tyrannizing the other; even Marie de France, who sympathized with the unhappily married lady in her *Lais*, zestfully recounts tales of cantankerous and contrary peasant wives and stupid husbands in her *Fables* (Marie de France 1987: 238–45). Nevertheless, the harsh conditions of peasant existence must rather have demanded co-operation and teamwork to ensure survival. Peasants too were often freer to choose their marriage partners than the nobility; young people would meet while working in the fields or at the community's feasts and festivities. Couples might also become unofficially betrothed, only going to church when a child was on the way and the bride's fertility thus proven (Hanawalt 1986a: 188–204).

Widows and second marriages

The Church felt that women should not marry more than once. Even though Christ said that in heaven 'they neither marry nor shall be given in marriage' (Matthew 22: 30), there was an apprehension that the relationship between man and wife was not simply a matter for this world. At the death of Peter Abélard, Abbot Peter the Venerable of Cluny writes to Abélard's former wife, the abbess Héloise, in these terms:

> God fosters him, my venerable dear sister in the Lord – him to whom you have been attached, first in carnal union, then in the stronger, higher bond of divine love; under whom you have long served the Lord – God fosters him, I say, in your place, as your other self, in his bosom; and keeps him to be restored to you, by his grace, at God's trumpet call.
>
> (Brooke 1991: 103)

Many husbands were anxious that their wives should not marry again: Francesco Datini, the recipient of the letters with which this chapter opened, stipulated in his will that his wife should have one hundred gold florins a year, as long as she remained 'a widow and chaste'. Margherita also had the use of a house, a plot of land, and household goods, under the same conditions. As the couple had no children, Francesco left the bulk of his possessions to a charitable foundation. Hence Margherita was not the type of wealthy widow who would appeal to fortune-hunters, especially since she was 51 at Francesco's death (Origo 1959: 337).

Younger widows might be extremely desirable, if their dowers were large enough and they were capable of bearing children. Christiane Klapisch-Zuber charts the dilemma which the young Florentine widow frequently found herself in at her elderly husband's death. On the one hand her own natal family would be anxious for her to return to the parental dwelling so that her dower could be used to marry her off again, forging a new alliance with another patrician family, on the other her husband's kin would be eager to keep her and the dower in her husband's family, especially where there were young children, who might inherit the dower from their mother (Klapisch-Zuber 1985: 117–31). Stanley Chojnacki analyses the growth of bequests to wives in Venetian wills of the fifteenth century partly in terms of securing the wife's loyalty – and dower entitlement – to her new family (Chojnacki 1988); however, as we shall see below, wives are increasingly valued as friends and companions as the medieval period comes to a close.

At one level, then, social forces tended to urge widows into further marriages, yet a certain ambivalence remained. Second marriages were not celebrated with as much festivity as first marriages: there would be no procession from the bride's house to the groom's house, nor lavish banqueting. Some communities practised 'rough music' or the charivari: groups of young men would assemble outside the new couple's house, jeering, singing obscene songs and banging pots and pans together, to signal social disapproval of the second marriage. Disapproval was especially strong if there was a marked disparity in the couple's ages: January–May marriages of the sort pilloried in Chaucer's *Merchant's Tale* and in Boccaccio's *Decameron*. The bridegroom would have to buy off the disgruntled youths in order to enjoy his wedding night in peace (Klapisch-Zuber 1985: 262–82). Though the charivari was normally a town or village practice, in 1393 even the French king and his courtiers dressed as savages and rampaged through the palace on the occasion of a remarriage (Rossiaud 1988: 171).

Being a wife

Only where husband and wife are separated for long enough to make correspondence between them worth while, as in the case of the Datini and Paston letters, do we see how married women viewed themselves and their husbands. How far we can use the brisk demands of Margaret Paston for cross-bow bolts and almonds (see p. 158 below) or the aggrieved response of Margherita Datini when her husband blames her for letting water get in the barrels of verjuice (a sour juice used for making vinegar) as evidence for the quality of their marriages is highly debatable (Origo 1959: 173). As Iris Origo points out of the Datini correspondence, 'a great many things which, if the couple had lived together, would no doubt merely have been said in moments of exasperation, were … put down on paper' (Origo 1959: 14).

When so many marriages were arranged without the partners having met, or when there was a great disparity in ages, it is difficult for the modern reader to imagine romantic or sexual passion fuelling the actual wedding celebrations. Some marriages, undoubtedly, were torment, a theme sympathetically explored in literary works. Marie de France's *Lais* frequently take up the figure of the cruel husband, as in *Laüstic* (p. 20 below), while a tradition of women's lyrics, songs of the *malmariée* (unhappily married woman), sprang up, though whether such songs were actually composed by women, or by men adopting a feminine persona is impossible to determine. Could love exist within marriage at all? Andreas Capellanus, writing in the late twelfth century, even puts the following observation into the mouth of his fictionalized Countess Marie de Champagne:

> We declare and we hold as firmly established that love cannot exert its powers between two people who are married to each other. For lovers give each other everything freely, under no compulsion of necessity, but married people are in duty bound to give in to each other's desires and deny themselves to each other in nothing.
>
> (Andreas Capellanus 1941: 107)

Andreas here touches on the concept of the marital debt, a concept rooted in St Paul's formulation in I Corinthians 7: 3–4: 'The wife hath not power of her own body, but the husband: and likewise also the husband hath no power of his own body, but the wife.' Each partner has the right to ask the other for sex, and each has the duty to respond favourably to the partner's requests. Although Pierre Payer argues that discussing sexual relations in marriage in terms of the debt 'does not reduce those human relations to justice and obligation' (Payer 1993: 89), the idea of constraint, as opposed to the freedom which lovers have to grant or withhold their favours, is clear in Marie's analysis. If he was a priest himself, Andreas would have been thoroughly familiar with the notion of the debt, and his treatise is, in part, a *reductio ad absurdum* of the complex set of behaviours which constituted 'courtly love'. Nevertheless, the contrast between married and unmarried love is one which Chaucer explores in the *Franklin's Tale*, while the coercive possibilities of the notion of marriage debt are ramified in other *Tales*: notably the *Merchant's*, *Wife of Bath's* and *Shipman's Tales*.

Yet, as the couple lived together and children were born, strong partnerships developed in which the couples cherished and respected one another. The Knight of the Tour-Landry, whose alarming encounter with a forward young woman when his father was negotiating a possible marriage is related below, speaks with measured respect and affection of the wife whom he did marry, holding her up as an example, and even teasing her a little, in the treatise he writes for his daughters, setting himself up against her as devil's advocate in an argument about paramours (Knight of the Tour-Landry 1971: 163–76 and see below p. 27). The Ménagier of Paris wrote an instructional treatise for his young wife between 1392 and 1394. He was well over 60 when he married his 15-year-old bride, an orphan who had thus not benefited from a mother's training for the role which awaited her, and who had asked him for instruction in the art of being a wife. The Ménagier complied both with moral teaching and with practical advice, ranging from recipes to the hiring of reliable servants to how best to rid a room of fleas:

> I have heard tell that if you have at night one or two trenchers of bread covered with birdlime or turpentine and put about the room with a lighted candle set in the midst of each trencher, they will come and get stuck thereto.
>
> (Power 1986: 112)

The Ménagier addresses his wife affectionately as 'sister' throughout, and part of his avowed reason for writing the book is so that she will do him credit when she marries her next husband. Despite Andreas Capellanus, the Ménagier believes that love between husband and wife drives all other loves away: 'all their special pleasure, their chief desire and their perfect joy is to do pleasure and obedience one to the other, if they love one another' (Power 1986: 105) – a formulation which confirms the ending of Chaucer's *Wife of Bath's Tale*.

Over the thousand years of the medieval period, marriage as an institution was theorized in different ways. Augustine asserts that God must have intended procreation from the first, since, if Adam were simply lonely, he would have been far better off with a male companion to talk to: 'How much more agreeably could two male friends, rather than a man and woman, enjoy companionship and conversation in a life shared together' (cited from Blamires 1992: 79). Augustine does emphasize the social and companionate aspects of marriage in *The Good of Marriage* (401), but he fails to develop the notion in his last treatise (Clark 1991: 28). By the time of Aquinas, however, theologians recognized marital affection and companionship in terms to which the Ménagier of Paris would have assented:

> Now there seems to be the greatest friendship between husband and wife, for they are united not only in the act of fleshly union, which produced a certain gentle association even among beasts, but also in the partnership of the whole range of domestic activity.
>
> (Aquinas 1956: 148)

Once marriage had become established as a sacrament, renewed attention was paid to it by thirteenth-century intellectuals – a new doctrine of marriage, aimed especially at wives, began to evolve (Vecchio 1992).

Marriage also becomes a topic for literary exploration in the later part of the period. Although most English vernacular romances conclude with the hero's marriage, Chrétien de Troyes lays bare the conflict between passionate love of one's wife and the knightly duty to bear arms in 'Erec et Enide', while in 'Yvain' he illustrates the converse. The knight Yvain is so absorbed by tournaments and knightly prowess that he forgets to return to his wife within the year she has specified. Her consequent rejection of him causes him to go mad; only after he has learned maturity and moderation is he reconciled with his lady, through the devoted efforts of her handmaiden, Lunete (below p. 24) (Fig. 2).

Marriage, then, was the fate of almost every woman in medieval Europe. Whether she married a boy she had played with on the village green, or an elderly stranger, a woman's marriage was the single most important event in her life, determining her future social status, personal development (Christine de Pizan owed much of her learning to her husband's encouragement), and sense of self-fulfilment. Although

Figure 2 A detail from the Malterer Tapestry *c.* 1310–20, illustrating the story of Iwein (Yvain). Lunete, the faithful maiden, persuades her lady Laudine to marry Iwein, the knight who has just defeated and killed Laudine's first husband. Augustiner Museum, Freiburg.

medieval life expectancies were comparatively low – David Herlihy calculates that a woman's average life expectancy in early fifteenth-century Florence would have been around 29.54 years (Herlihy 1975: 13), this figure, as Herlihy shows, is misleading, for the figures are skewed by the enormously high rate of infant mortality. Investigations of medieval English burials show that 10 per cent of the dead were over 50, while in fourteenth- and fifteenth-century rural Tuscany between 6 to 15 per cent of the population were over 60 (Hanawalt 1986a: 229; Herlihy and Klapisch-Zuber 1978: 374–8). A woman who survived to marriageable age could expect to share a good twenty years with a husband of a similar age, a longer period than many modern western marriages last.

The staunch words of Bergthora, wife of Njal, hero of the Icelandic *Njals saga*, could stand as an epigraph to the experience of most medieval wives. The farmhouse Bergthorshval is surrounded by the enemies of Njal's sons, and set on fire. Flosi, the leader of the burners, offers passage out to Njal, who refuses, and then to Bergthora, who answers simply: 'I was married young to Njal, and I promised him then that the same fate would overtake us both.' She and Njal lie down in their bed, with their little grandson, and they die together (*Njals saga* 1954: 330). Truly, ''till dethe us departhe' (cited from Hanawalt 1986a: 203) was the medieval wife's expectation.

1 THE GOOD WIVES

Text from: G. Krapp and E. V. K. Dobbie (1936) *Anglo-Saxon Poetic Records* III, 'The Exeter Book', London: Routledge. *Maxims I* b, ll. 83b–106. Transl. C. Larrington.

Almost all the Old English poetry which survives is anonymous, and without any title. *Maxims I* is found in the Exeter Book, which was compiled around 1000. The *Maxims* is a wisdom poem which details ideal human and natural behaviour. The portrait of the lady in this extract matches the queens whom we see in poems such as *Beowulf*; the Frisian's wife is interesting particularly because this is one of the few glimpses which we have of non-aristocratic women in Old English literature.

War-skills are fitting for a warrior, he should grow in battle-knowledge, and his wife should prosper, dear to her people, be cheerful of spirit, keep secrets, be open-hearted with horses and treasure; when there is a mead-feast she must always, on every occasion, first salute the leader of the war-band in front of the company of kinsmen, first swiftly offer the cup to the lord's hand, and she should give him advice, both of them together ruling over the fortress.

A ship should be stoutly nailed, a shield of light linden wood bound together. A dear welcome guest comes to the Frisian's wife when the ship is moored. His boat has come in and her man is home, her own provider; she invites him in, washes his dirty clothes and gives him new garments; on the land she gives him what his love demands. A woman should keep her promises to a man. Often people say shameful things about them. Many are staunch-hearted, many are rather more inquisitive, they make love with a strange man when the other one has gone far away. A sailor is away journeying for a long time, but always one should look forward to the beloved's return, put up with what cannot be changed. When he can, he will come home again, if he survives, unless the sea prevents him, the ocean seizes his raiding-ship.

2 THE MALMARIÉE

(a) Marie de France's *Laüstic*

Text from: *The Lais of Marie de France* (1986), transl. G. S. Burgess and K. Busby, Harmondsworth: Penguin, pp. 94–6.

Marie is one of the earliest known women writers in Europe. She wrote in French, often translating from Latin, or from Breton. As well as the *Lais*, a collection of romances, she also composed a book of fables and the *Purgatory of St Patrick*, a translation of an account of a visit to hell. Marie wrote in the 1180s, but nothing more is known of her. She must have lived in England for some time, for she knew English, as well as French, Breton and Latin, and her surname suggests that she must have been of French birth, as opposed to being of French descent – a member of the Anglo-Norman aristocracy.

I shall relate an adventure to you from which the Bretons composed a lay. *Laüstic* is its name, I believe, and that is what the Bretons call it in their land. In French the title is *Rossignol*, and *Nightingale* is the correct English word.

In the region of St Malo was a famous town and two knights dwelt there, each with a fortified house. Because of the fine qualities of the two men the town acquired a good reputation. One of the knights had taken a wise, courtly and elegant wife who conducted herself, as custom dictated, with admirable propriety. The other knight was a young man who was well known amongst his peers for his prowess and great valour. He performed honourable deeds gladly and attended many tournaments, spending freely and giving generously whatever he had. He loved his neighbour's wife and so persistently did he request her love, so frequent were his entreaties and so many qualities did he possess that she loved him above all things, both for the good she had heard about him and because he lived close by. They loved each other prudently and well, concealing their love carefully to ensure that they were not seen, disturbed or suspected. This they could do because their dwellings were adjoining. Their houses, halls and keeps were close by each other and there was no barrier or division, apart from a high wall of dark-hued stone. When she stood at her bedroom window, the lady could talk to her beloved in the other house and he to her, and they could toss gifts to each other. There was scarcely anything to displease them and they were both very content except for the fact that they could not meet and take their pleasure with each other, for the lady was closely guarded when her husband was in the region. But they were so resourceful that day or night they managed to speak to each other and no one could prevent their coming to the window and seeing each other there.

For a long time they loved each other, until one summer when the copses and meadows were green and the gardens in full bloom. On the flower-tops the birds sang joyfully and sweetly. If love is on anyone's mind, no wonder he turns his attention towards it. I shall tell you the truth about the knight. Both he and the lady made the greatest possible effort with their words and with their eyes. At night, when the moon was shining and her husband was asleep, she often rose from beside him and put on her mantle. Knowing her beloved would be doing the same, she would go and stand at the window and stay awake most of the night. They took delight in seeing each other, since they were denied anything more. But so frequently did she stand there and so frequently leave her bed that her husband became angry and asked her repeatedly why she got up and where she went. 'Lord,' replied the lady, 'anyone who does not hear the song of the nightingale knows none of the joys of this world. This is why I come and stand here. So sweet is the song I hear by night that it brings me great pleasure. I take such delight in it and desire it so much that I can get no sleep at all.'

When the lord heard what she said, he gave a spiteful, angry laugh and devised a plan to ensnare the nightingale. Every single servant in his household constructed some trap, net or snare and then arranged them throughout the garden. There was no hazel tree or chestnut tree on which they did not place a snare or bird-lime, until they had captured and retained it. When they had taken the nightingale, it was handed over, still alive, to the lord, who was overjoyed to hold it in his hands. He entered the lady's chamber. 'Lady,' he said, 'where are you? Come forward and speak to us. With bird-lime I have trapped the nightingale which has kept you awake so much. Now you can sleep in peace, for it will never awaken you again.' When the lady heard him she was grief-stricken and distressed. She asked her husband for the bird, but he killed it out of spite, breaking its neck wickedly with his two hands. He threw the body at the lady, so that the front of her tunic was bespattered with blood, just on her breast. Thereupon he left the chamber.

The lady took the tiny corpse, wept profusely and cursed those who had betrayed the nightingale by constructing the traps and snares, for they had taken so much joy from her. 'Alas,' she said, 'misfortune is upon me. Never again can I get up at night or go to stand at the window where I used to see

21

my beloved. I know one thing for certain. He will think I am faint-hearted, so I must take action. I shall send him the nightingale and let him know what has happened.' She wrapped the little bird in a piece of samite, embroidered in gold and covered in designs. She called one of her servants, entrusted him with her message and sent him to her beloved. He went to the knight, greeted him on behalf of his lady, related the whole message to him and presented him with the nightingale. When the messenger had finished speaking, the knight, who had listened attentively, was distressed by what had happened. But he was not uncourtly or tardy. He had a small vessel prepared, not of iron or steel, but of pure gold with fine stones, very precious and valuable. On it he carefully placed a lid and put the nightingale in it. Then he had the casket sealed and carried it with him at all times.

This adventure was related and could not long be concealed. The Bretons composed a lay about it which is called *Laüstic*.

(b) A malmariée song

Text from: R. Lemaire (1989) 'The Semiotics of Private and Public Matrimonial Systems and their Discourse', in K. Glente and L. Winther-Jensen (eds) *Female Power in the Middle Ages: Proceedings from the Second St Gertrud Symposium, Copenhagen, August 1986*, Copenhagen: C. A. Reitzel, p. 84.

It seems likely that this sort of song was sung when women gathered together, perhaps on their doorsteps or in their homes, to weave or spin. Such friends were called 'gossips' in Middle English (from *godsib* meaning those related to one other through god-parenting). 'Gossip' was beginning to acquire its current pejorative and female connotations in the medieval period (see p. 51 below).

> I hope I will not want
> to love my husband
> as long as I have a friend
> as I have chosen him
> brave, valiant and handsome
> attractive, gallant and wise.
> But my husband is furious
> about the shame brought upon him
> And he wants to know to whom
> I have promised my love.
> I have answered:
> 'You bad husband with your stupid face
> You won't know now
> whose friend I am.'

3 MARRIAGES IN ROMANCE

(a) Text from: Chrétien de Troyes (1991) 'Erec and Enide', in *Arthurian Romances*, transl. C. W. Carroll, Harmondsworth: Penguin, pp. 67–8.

Chrétien de Troyes wrote the five earliest known Arthurian romances in the second half of the twelfth century. He attended the court of Marie de Champagne, daughter of Eleanor of Aquitaine, for whom he specifically wrote 'The Knight of the Cart', and may have spent part of his youth in England. In the two romances from which excerpts are given here, Chrétien examines the conflict between uxorious domesticity and the desire for honour and adventure which drives the knight from home. In the first extract, Erec and Enide are newly married; in the second Yvain has been given permission by his wife to go adventuring for a year. He promises to return 'eight days after the feast of John the Baptist' – at the end of June. When the extract begins, it is now August.

But Erec was so in love with her [Enide] that he cared no more for arms, nor did he go to tournaments. He no longer cared for tourneying; he wanted to enjoy his wife's company, and he made her his lady and his mistress. He turned all his attention to embracing and kissing her; he pursued no other delight. His companions were grieved by this and often lamented among themselves, saying that he loved her far too much. Often it was past noon before he rose from her side. This pleased him, whoever might be grieved by it. He kept very close to her, but still continued to provide his knights with arms, clothing, and deniers [money]. Wherever there was a tournament he sent them there, most richly apparelled and equipped. He gave them fresh chargers to tourney and joust with, regardless of the cost.

All the nobles said that it was a great shame and sorrow that a lord such as he once was no longer wished to bear arms. He was so blamed by everyone, by knights and men-at-arms alike, that Enide heard them say among themselves that her lord was becoming recreant with respect to arms and knighthood, because he had profoundly changed his way of life. This weighed upon her, but she dared not show it, for her husband might have taken it ill had she mentioned it.

The matter was hidden from him until one morning, when they were lying in the bed where they had enjoyed many a delight: in each other's arms they lay, their lips touching, like those who are deeply in love. He slept and she lay awake; she remembered what many people throughout the land were saying about her lord. As she began to recall this, she could not refrain from weeping; she felt such pain and sorrow that by mischance she happened to make a remark for which she later counted herself a fool, though she meant no evil by it. She began to contemplate her lord from head to foot; she saw his handsome body and fair face and wept so violently, that as she wept, her tears fell upon his chest.

'Wretch,' she said, 'unhappy me! Why did I come here from my land? The earth should truly swallow me up, since the very best of knights – the boldest and the bravest, the most loyal, the most courteous that was ever count or king – has completely abandoned all chivalry because of me. Now have I truly shamed him; I should not have wished it for anything.' Then she said to him: 'My friend, what misfortune for you!' Then she fell silent and said no more.

But he was not deeply asleep: he had heard her voice as he slept. He awoke upon hearing her words and was greatly astonished to see her weeping so bitterly. Then he questioned her, saying: 'Tell me, dear sweet lady, why are you weeping in this way? What causes you anguish or sorrow? Truly, I will find out – I insist. Tell me, my sweet lady; take care that you don't conceal from me why you called me unfortunate. You referred to me and no other; I heard your words clearly.'

> Enide tells Erec what is being said about him. He is furious to be so shamed and takes up his arms again, making Enide journey ahead of him as a kind of bait to attract evil-doers. Enide's love for him remains undiminished, and after Erec has recovered his honour by further brave deeds, he comes to appreciate the loyalty and courage of his wife.

> (b) Text from: Chrétien de Troyes (1991) 'Yvain', in *Arthurian Romances*, transl. W. W. Kibler, Harmondsworth: Penguin, pp. 329–30.

King Arthur was seated in their [Yvain and his companions'] midst when Yvain suddenly began to reflect; since the moment he had taken leave of his lady he had not been so distraught as now, for he knew for a fact that he had broken his word to her and stayed beyond the period set. With great difficulty he held back his tears, but shame forced him to repress them.

He was still downcast when they saw a damsel coming straight towards them, approaching rapidly on a dappled black palfrey. She dismounted before their tent without anyone helping her, and without anyone seeing to her horse. And as soon as she caught sight of the king, she let fall her mantle and without it she entered the tent and approached the king. She said that her lady sent greetings to the king and my lord Gawain and all the others except Yvain, that liar, that deceiver, that unfaithful cheat, for he had beguiled and deceived her. She had clearly seen through his guile, for he had pretended to be a true lover, but was a cheat, a seducer and a thief....

'Her complaint is not unreasonable, nor is it premature. I am not mentioning it to publicly humiliate, but am simply stating that the one who married you to my lady has betrayed us. Yvain, my lady no longer cares for you, and through me she orders that you never again approach her and keep her ring no longer. By me, whom you see here before you, she orders you to send it back to her: return it, for return it you must!'

Yvain could not answer her, for he was stunned and words failed him. The damsel stepped forward and pulled the ring from his finger; then she commended to God the king and all the others, except the man whom she left in great anguish. And his anguish grew constantly, for everything he saw added to his grief and everything he heard troubled him; he wanted to flee entirely alone to a land so wild that no one could follow or find him, and where no man or woman alive could hear any more news of him than if he had gone to perdition. He hated nothing so much as himself and did not know whom to turn to for comfort now that he was the cause of his own death. But he would rather lose his mind than fail to take revenge upon himself, who had ruined his own happiness. . . .

Then such a great tempest arose in his head that he went mad; he ripped and tore at this clothing and fled across fields and plains, leaving his people puzzled and with no idea of where he could be. They went in search of him right and left among the knights' lodgings and through the hedgerows and orchards; but where they were seeking he was not to be found.

And he ran on and on until, near a park, he encountered a youth who had a bow and five barbed arrows, whose tips were broad and sharp. Yvain approached the youth and took from him the bow and arrows he was holding; yet afterwards he did not remember anything he had done. He stalked wild animals in the forest and killed them and ate their raw flesh.

4 A RASH WOOING: UNUSUAL EVENTS AT A WEDDING FEAST

Text from: *Njals saga* (1954), ed. E. O. Sveinsson, Islenzk Fornrit 13, Reykjavík: Hid Islenzka Fornritafelag, pp. 85–90. Transl. C. Larrington.

Njals saga was composed in Iceland in the thirteenth century. It is the story of two men, Gunnar and Njal. Gunnar is the hero of the first part of the saga; the events which bring about the death of Njal and his family occupy the second part. Gunnar is renowned for his physical courage and endurance. Njal is his best friend, wise and resourceful. Just before the events related here, Njal has advised Gunnar how to use trickery to recover the dowry of one of his female relatives who is Hrut's estranged wife. Hallgerd is the daughter of Hoskuld, Hrut's brother; she is strong-willed and beautiful. By this stage in the saga she has already had two husbands, one whom she did not love and one whom she did. Both husbands have met violent deaths at the hands of Hallgerd's foster-father, now dead himself. As a widow Hallgerd has a degree of independence: she wears her hair loose to signify her unmarried status and is allowed to betroth herself, yet the marriage arrangements are still concluded between husband and bride's kin. The action takes place at the Assembly, an annual meeting of all the Icelandic chieftains. They gather at Thingvellir to resolve law-cases, do business and meet one another. The chieftains encamp in booths, turf structures which were tented over during the Assembly.

One day Gunnar left the Law-rock; he was walking below the booths of the men from Mosfell when he saw some very well-dressed women coming towards him. The best turned-out one was in the lead. When they met, she greeted Gunnar. He accepted her greeting and asked who she was; she said she was Hallgerd, daughter of Hoskuld Dala-Kollsson. She spoke confidently to him, and asked him to tell about his travels, and he said he could not refuse to speak to her; they sat down and talked.

She was dressed like this: she was wearing a red kirtle and it had a great deal of brocade work on it; over it she wore a scarlet cloak, decorated on either side with lace, her hair hung down over her breast, thick and beautiful. Gunnar was in his best clothes, which King Harald Gormsson [of Norway] had given him, and he had the ring, Hakons-treasure, on his hand. They talked for a long time. Then it came to the point that he asked if she were not married. She said that this was the case – 'and there aren't many who would risk it,' she said. 'Do you not think anyone is good enough for you?' he said. 'It's not that,' she said, 'but I am choosy about men.' 'How would you answer then, if I were to ask for you?' said Gunnar. 'You can't be thinking that way,' she said. 'That's not the case,' said Gunnar. 'If you do have it in mind,' she said, 'then go and see my father.' After that the conversation came to an end.

From there Gunnar went to the booth of the Dalamen and found some men outside in front of the booth, and asked whether Hoskuld were inside or not, and they said that he was; then Gunnar went inside. Hoskuld and Hrut greeted Gunnar warmly; he sat down between them, and you could not tell from their conversation that there had previously been some bad feeling between them. Then Gunnar brought the conversation round to asking how the brothers might respond if he were to ask for Hallgerd. 'Favourably,' said Hoskuld, 'if that's what you really want.' Gunnar said that he was serious about it – 'though the way we parted last time, most people would think it rather unlikely that we should ever enter into such a relationship.' 'What do you think about it, Hrut, my kinsman?' said Hoskuld. Hrut answered, 'This doesn't seem a suitable match to me.' 'What's the matter with it?' asks Gunnar. Hrut said: 'I have to tell you the truth: you are a handsome man with a good reputation, but she is very mixed in temperament, and I don't want to deceive you.' 'That does you credit,' says Gunnar, 'but I would think that it was rather our former enmity that weighed with you if you didn't let the match take place.' 'That's not it,' said Hrut, 'but more importantly I can see that you won't be denied in this. But even if the match doesn't come off, then we would still want to be your friends.' 'I've talked to her, and it's not totally out of the question for her,' said Gunnar. 'I know what is the matter: you are both smitten with one another, and, however it turns out, you are the ones who have most at stake.' Without being asked, Hrut told Gunnar all about Hallgerd's character, and it seemed to Gunnar that there was quite a lot which was not pleasant, but in the end they agreed the match. Then Hallgerd was sent for, and the matter discussed in her hearing. Now they did as they had before, they let Hallgerd declare her own betrothal. The wedding-feast was to be at Hlitharendi [Gunnar's home], and it was to be kept secret at first, though it soon happened that everyone knew about it.

Gunnar rode home from the Assembly and went to Bergthorshvol, and told Njal about his match. He reacted rather gloomily to it. Gunnar asked what the objection was if he thought it was so inadvisable. 'Everything that goes wrong will be caused by her if she comes out east here,' said Njal. 'She will never ruin our friendship,' says Gunnar. 'It will come pretty close to that,' says Njal, 'but you will always have to pay compensation for what she does.' Gunnar invited Njal to the feast and as many as he wanted to bring with him; Njal promised to come. Afterwards Gunnar went home and rode around the district inviting people.

There was a man called Thrain; son of Sigfus, son of Sighvat the Red. He lived at Grjota in the Fljothlid district; he was a kinsman of Gunnar, and a greatly respected man. He was married to Thorhild the Poet; she was free with her words and given to mockery; Thrain did not love her very much. He was invited to the feast at Hlitharendi, and his wife was to help with the serving, along with Bergthora Skarphethins-daughter, the wife of Njal....

Hoskuld and Hrut came to the feast with a large following. Hoskuld's sons Thorleik and Olaf were there. The bride [Hallgerd] came with them and Thorgerd, her daughter, and she was the most attractive of women; she was then fourteen years old. Many other women were there too....

Thorhild was on her feet serving, and she and Bergthora were taking food to the table. Thrain Sigfusson was goggling at Thorgerd; his wife, Thorhild noticed this; she got angry and said this couplet to him:

> 'Ogling is not good
> there's lust in your eyes

Thrain,' she said. Then he strode forward over the table, and named witnesses and declared himself divorced from her: 'I am not going to put up with her mockery and her scornful words to me.' And he was so aggressive in this matter that he would not stay at the feast, unless she were driven away; and so it came about that she went away. And now each man sat in his place and drank and enjoyed himself.

Then Thrain began to speak: 'I shan't keep secret what's in my mind; this I want to ask you, Hoskuld Dala-Kollsson: will you marry your kinswoman, Thorgerd, to me?' 'I don't know about that,' he said. 'It seems to me that you've only just separated from the other one that you had before – what sort of man is this, Gunnar?' Gunnar answered, 'I don't want to answer as the man is closely related to me – you speak about him, Njal, for everyone will believe what you say.' Njal said, 'One can say this about the man, that he is wealthy and accomplished in everything, and a splendid, high-ranking man, and so you should make the match with him.' Then Hoskuld said, 'How does the match seem to you, Hrut my kinsman?' Hrut answered, 'You should make the match, it's a suitable one for her.' Then they talked about the terms and everything was agreed. Then Gunnar stands up and so does Thrain and they go to the dais; Gunnar asks the mother and daughter whether they will accept the match; they say they have no objections. Hallgerd betroths her daughter. Then the women change round a second time; Thorhalla [the highest-ranking woman there] now sat between the brides. The feast proceeded in good order. And when it was over, Hoskuld and his men rode westwards, and the men from Ranga went home. Gunnar gave gifts to many men, and they were valuable ones. Hallgerd took over running the household and was extravagant and demanding. Thorgerd took over the household at Grjota and was a fine housekeeper.

Njal's forebodings prove correct: Hallgerd begins to feud with Bergthora, Njal's wife, and the quarrel escalates. Gunnar slaps Hallgerd for stealing cheese from Njal's farm; a blow for which she will never forgive him. Gunnar becomes involved in another feud and is sentenced to outlawry; since he refuses to leave Iceland his enemies surround the house and eventually kill him. In his final moments, his bow-string breaks, and Hallgerd, who is with him, remembers the slap and refuses to give him a lock of her hair to use as a bow-string. Gunnar is killed; Hallgerd becomes infamous in Icelandic literature.

5 THE DISOBEDIENT WIFE

Text from: G. Boccaccio (1993) *The Decameron*, transl. G. Waldman, Oxford: Oxford University Press, pp. 590–2.

Giovanni Boccaccio (1313–75) was born the illegitimate son of a businessman in Certaldo, and educated in Florence. He was sent to Naples to study law, but abandoned law for literature and wrote a number of courtly works and romances there before he returned to Florence, where he witnessed the Black Death. In 1349 he began work on the *Decameron*, a collection of one hundred stories told by a group of nobles who have fled from the plague. Many of the stories in the *Decameron* treat the relationship between the sexes. Each day of storytelling has a theme, but on the ninth day the queen for that day (Emilia) decrees a free choice, and tells this story herself. Thus Boccaccio defuses the misogyny of the story by putting it in a woman's mouth.

Joseph has had wife trouble, and has gone to wise King Solomon for advice. Told to go to Goose Bridge, he travels home over this bridge and sees a mule-driver beating a recalcitrant mule. Joseph suggests treating it kindly, but the muleteer says that he knows his animal, and beats it until it goes onwards. With his friend Melissus, Joseph reaches home.

Some days later they reached Antioch, where Joseph detained his friend for a few days' rest. Joseph's wife extended him an indifferent welcome, but he told her to prepare supper the way Melissus would like it. As this was Joseph's wish, Melissus described in a few words what he would like. The lady, however, followed her usual habit and supper came not as Melissus asked for it but the very opposite in just about every respect.

This irritated Joseph, who said to her: 'Were you not told precisely how this meal was to be prepared?'

His wife drew herself up and remarked with a sniff: 'What are you going on about? Get on and eat if you want to eat. Maybe I was told differently but this is the meal I've chosen. Like it or lump it!'

Melissus was surprised by the wife's retort and roundly told her so, while Joseph, on hearing it, said: 'You're still no different from before, woman, but I'm going to alter your manner, believe you me.' Then he turned to Melissus. 'We'll soon see what Solomon's advice is worth, my friend. Pray don't mind witnessing this; imagine that what I'm going to do is mere playfulness. Before you try to stop me, just remember what the muleteer said to us when we took him to task over the mule.'

'I'm in your home, and have no intention of crossing you.'

Joseph found himself a round stick cut from an oak sapling; he went into the bedroom, whither his wife had withdrawn, muttering, after leaving the table in a huff. He grabbed her by the hair, threw her down at his feet, and started belabouring her with this stick. She yelled to begin with, and uttered threats, but when she saw that none of this topped him, she quite crumpled and begged for mercy, pleaded with him for God's sake not to murder her, for she would never again disregard his wishes. Joseph never laid off all this while, but thrashed her with ever-increasing ferocity, getting her in the ribs one moment, on the hips the next, then across the shoulders, hammering her into shape and never letting up until he was dog-tired. In fact the good woman was not left with a single bone, not an inch of her back, that was not reduced to pulp.

When he was done, he went over to Melissus and observed; 'We shall see tomorrow how effective has been the advice to go to Goose Bridge.' He took a few moments' rest, washed his hands, sat down to supper with Melissus, and in due course they went to bed.

The wretched woman struggled to her feet, threw herself into bed, and got such rest as she could. The next morning she was up very early and sent to ask Joseph what he would like for lunch. He placed his order as he and Melissus had a good laugh. They came back at lunch time to find everything prepared to perfection and exactly as he had instructed. So they had only praise for the advice that at first they had failed to grasp. . . .

The tale of the queen's [Emilia, who is in charge of the storytelling for the day] had the ladies muttering somewhat, and the young men chuckling.

6 A FORWARD YOUNG WOMAN

Text adapted from: *Book of the Knight of the Tour-Landry* (1971), transl. William Caxton, ed. M. Y. Offord, Early English Text Society (hereafter EETS) SS2, Oxford: Oxford University Press, pp. 27–8.

The Knight of the Tour-Landry wrote his manual for his daughters around 1371. It was one of the earliest printed books translated and published by William Caxton in 1484. The author is Geoffroy de la Tour-Landry IV. His date of birth is not known, but he appeared as a young soldier at the siege of Aiguillon in 1346 and died between 1402 and 1406. He married twice; the lady referred to in his writings is his first wife Jeanne de Rougé, who came from a powerful Breton family. A fuller account of his *Book* is given in chapter 6 below (p. 208).

In this extract the Knight warns against forward behaviour. Whether the young woman is attracted to the young knight on sight and thus responds to his gallantries with too much enthusiasm, or whether the 'one she has seen lately' is a third person is not clear.

And yet my fair daughters, I shall say to you of a fact that happened to me in this matter. It happened to me once that I was spoken to of marriage, of marrying with a noble woman who had a father and mother. And my lord my father led me thither to see her. When we were there, there was made to us great cheer and joyous. And I beheld her of whom I was spoken to. And I set myself in communication with her of many things, for to know the better her maintaining and governance and so we fell in speaking of prisoners. And then I said to her: 'Damoiselle, I wish well and had rather be your prisoner than any other's, and I think that your prison should not be so hard nor cruel as is the prison of English men.' And she answered me that she had lately seen such a one that she wished well that he were her prisoner and I demanded of her if she would give him evil prison and she answered me nay, but that she would keep him as precious as her own body, and I said to her that, whoever he was he was very lucky and fortunate to have so sweet and noble a prison.

Shall I say to you she loved him enough, and had a quick and light eye, and she was full of words and when we had to part she took me aside, for she asked me two or three times that I should not leave, but come to see her, however it went, but I kept all quiet for I had never seen her before, and she knew well that there was spoken of marriage of her and of me.

And when we were departed my lord my father demanded of me what I thought of her that I had seen and bade me to tell him my views and I answered him and said that she was good and fair, but 'I shall never be nearer to her than I am, if it please you' and told him what I thought of her and her behaviour, and then he said that he also would not want me to have her, and thus the over-great forwardness and the light manner that I thought I saw in her discouraged me so that I married not with her, whereof I have thanked

God since many times, for it was not a year and a half later that she was blamed, but I don't know whether it was rightly or wrongly and soon after she died.

7 DUTIES OF THE BOURGEOIS HOUSEWIFE

Text from: Christine de Pizan (1985) *The Treasure of the City of Ladies*, transl. Sarah Lawson, Harmondsworth: Penguin, pp. 145–9.

Christine de Pizan was born in 1365 in Venice. Shortly after her birth, her father was invited by Charles V of France to become his court astrologer. The family fortunes flourished, and Christine, as she describes below, gained an unusual education as a result of her father's standing at court. Christine married at the age of 15, and, by her own account, seems to have had an exceptionally happy marriage, for her husband encouraged her literary activity. Widowed only ten years later, left with three young children and very little property as a result of the machinations of her husband's kin, Christine decided to earn her living with her pen. She became a court poet of considerable standing, the biographer of Charles V, and wrote an enormous number of works on subjects as diverse as politics, knightly training, classical mythology and the contemporary debate on the morality of the acclaimed *Roman de la Rose*. Her best-known work today is the *Book of the City of Ladies* (1404), to which the *Treasure of the City of Ladies* (1405) is a kind of sequel. The *Book of the City of Ladies* is an attack on the misogynist tradition, utilizing stories of virtuous, wise and enterprising women of past and present to show the emptiness of the anti-feminist argument. The *Treasure* 'part etiquette book, part survival manual' (Christine de Pizan 1985: 21) is a guide to the practicalities of life for women, ranging from the royal court to the brothel and peasant hut. This extract depicts the duties of the married townswoman. As for the Anglo-Saxon women of the first extract of this section, provision of food and clothing and maintaining the husband's social position are still, at the end of the period, the wife's primary responsibilities.

We three Virtues therefore repeat what we said before to you women of rank and dwellers in cities and fine towns: please lend an ear to the teachings that pertain to you. There are four principal teachings, although they have been mentioned elsewhere. Your duty to be good and devout towards God goes without saying, but as for what concerns Worldly Prudence: the first of the four pertains to the love and faith that you ought to have for your husbands and how you ought to conduct yourselves towards them. The second point is the matter of the government of your household. ...

As for the first, which has to do with the love and fidelity that you owe to your spouses and your conduct towards them, whether your husbands be old or young, good or bad, peaceable or quarrelsome, unfaithful or virtuous: so that we need not repeat ourselves, we refer you to the twelfth chapter of the first part of this book, where the matter is set out plainly. But besides this, so that you may find those attitudes more agreeable, we will remind you of three blessings that can come to you conducting yourselves well and wisely towards them, whoever they are, and keeping your promise to be faithful and loyal to them and holding your peace and in all things doing your duty. The first is the great merit to the soul that you acquire by doing your duties; the second is great honour in the world; and the third is, as one has often seen, that although many rich men of many and varied positions are and have always been remarkably cruel to their wives, when the hour of death comes their conscience pricks them and they consider the goodness of their wives, who have endured them with such a good grace, and the great wrong that they have committed against their wives, and they leave them in possession of their whole fortune.

The second point of our teaching and doctrine that we have said is necessary to you touches on the subject of the household. You ought to devote very great care and diligence to giving wisely, sharing out intelligently and using to the best advantage all the goods and provisions that your husbands by their labour, business or income gather or obtain for the home. It is the duty of the man to acquire all the necessary provisions and to have them brought into the house. Likewise the woman ought to manage and allocate them with good discretion and right priorities without too much parsimoniousness, and equally she ought to guard against foolish generosity, for that is what empties and flattens the purse and impoverishes a person. She should understand that nothing must be wasted, and she should expect all her household to be frugal. She herself must be in overall charge and, always watchful, she must ask for everything to be accounted for.

This wise lady or housewife ought to be very familiar with everything pertaining to the preparation of food so that she may know how best to organize it and give orders to her serving-men or women; in this way she may always be able to keep her husband contented. If he sometimes invites important people to the house, she herself (if need be) ought to go into the kitchen and supervise the serving of the food. She ought to see that her home is kept clean and everything in its place and in order. She should see that her children are well taught and disciplined, even if they are small, and that they are not heard whining or making a lot of noise. They should be kept tidy and established in their own routine. Neither the wet-nurses' swaddling clothes nor anything else that belongs to them should be left lying around the house. She ought to ensure that her husband's garments and other things are kept clean, for the good grooming of the husband is the honour of the wife. She should ensure that he is well served and his peace and quiet are uninterrupted. Before he comes home for dinner everything should be ready and in good order, with tables and sideboards according to their means.

If she wants to act prudently and have the praise of both the world and her husband, she will be cheerful to him all the time, so that if he should be in any way troubled in his thoughts, perhaps by property, she may be able by her gracious welcome to get him to put them somewhat out of his mind. It is undoubtedly a great refreshment for a man of substance when he comes into his house with some troubling thought and his wife wisely and graciously welcomes him. It is quite right that she should do this, for the man who is occupied with the burden and care of earning a living can at least be warmly welcomed in his own home. The wife ought not to quarrel with the other members of the household nor nag them nor make a fuss at the table, but if there is something that they have done wrong, she ought to correct them at the time in a few calm words, but at meals which ought to be taken happily, this kind of thing strikes a very harsh note. If her husband is bad or quarrelsome, she ought to appease him as much as she can by soothing words. She should not ask him about his business affairs or other confidential things at table or in front of the household, but only when they are alone together and in her chamber.

The wise housewife will be careful to rise early in the morning. When she has heard Mass and said her devotions and returned home, she will issue orders to her people for whatever is necessary. Then she will take up some useful work, whether spinning or sewing or something else. When her chambermaids have done their housework, she will want them to do some other work. She will not want to see either girls or women or even herself tolerate any idle hours. She will buy flax cheaply at fairs; she will have it spun in town by poor women (but she will be careful not to take advantage of them deceitfully or by her superior rank, for she would damn herself, and there would be no advantage in it for her). She will have fine wide cloth, table-cloths, napkins and other linen made. She will be most painstaking about this, for it is the natural pleasure of women and not odious or sluttish, but upright and proper. In the end she will have very fine linen – delicate, generously embroidered and well made. She will keep it white and sweet smelling, neatly folded in a chest; she will be most conscientious about this. She will use it to serve the important people that her husband brings home, by whom she will be greatly esteemed, honoured and praised.

This wise woman will take great care that no food goes bad around her house, that nothing goes to waste that might help the poor and indigent. If she gives them to the poor, she will ensure that the left-overs are not stale and that the clothes are not moth-eaten. But if she loves the welfare of her soul and the virtue of charity, she will not give her alms only in this way, but with the wine from her own cellar and the meat from her table, to poor women in childbed, to the sick, and often to her poor neighbours. She will do this with pleasure if she is wise and has the means, for these acts are all the laid-up treasure she will take with her, nor will she ever be the poorer for it. She ought, however, to be careful and have discretion about all her charity.

This woman will be wise and gracious, that is, of pleasant expression, modest, with restrained language; she will welcome and receive the friends and acquaintances of her husband. She will speak nicely to everyone. She will cultivate the friendship of her neighbours; she will offer them companionship and friendship if they need it and she will not refuse to lend little things. To her household staff she will be neither mean, sharp-tongued, nor spiteful, nor will she nag them all day about trifles, but reprimand them properly when they do something wrong and threaten to dismiss them if they do not mend their ways. But she will do this without raging or making a noisy fuss that can be heard in the next street, as some foolish women do who imagine that by being quite disagreeable and quarrelling vehemently about nothing with their husbands and their household servants, and making a lot of work out of only a small job, and finding things everywhere to complain about, and always gossiping, they will be regarded as good and wise housewives. But that kind of housewifery has nothing to do with our teaching, for we want our adherents to be wise in all their actions. There can be no sensible behaviour without moderation, which does not require malice or anger or shouting – all things that are most unseemly in a woman.

8 CARING FOR A SICK HUSBAND

Text adapted from: Margery Kempe (1940) *The Book of Margery Kempe*, ed. H. E. Allen and S. Meech, EETS 212, Oxford: Oxford University Press, pp. 179–81.

Margery Kempe was an Englishwoman, born around 1373 in the East Anglian town of Lynn, now called King's Lynn. She was of a bourgeois family, her father being Mayor of Lynn, and married John Kempe who was slightly beneath her in class terms. After the birth of her first child, Margery had a period of madness, from which she recovered through Christ's miraculous intervention. After many years in which she frequently saw visions of Jesus and spoke with him, she persuaded her husband to take a vow of chastity, and she travelled around the country meeting other holy people, an activity which caused her to be arrested on more than one occasion. She visited Julian of Norwich for advice about her visions. Margery visited Jerusalem and the shrine of St James at Compostela, and spent many months in Rome. At certain periods of her life she was afflicted with the gift of tears: uncontrollable sobbing and weeping at the mention of Christ or at the thought of the Crucifixion, which brought much public disapproval. Her *Book* is the first autobiography to be composed in English; with much difficulty she dictated it to a priest (see p. 254 below). Notable is the lack of self-consciousness with which Margery speaks, her honesty, and her sensitivity to the opinions and views of other people. As a woman who was trying to live a holy life in the world, instead of retreating to a convent, she faced unique difficulties.

In this extract, Margery and her husband had agreed to a vow of chastity, and to live separately from one another, although they still remained fond of each other.

It happened on an occasion that the husband of the aforesaid creature [Margery's habitual way of referring to herself], a man of great age, over 60 years old, as he was coming down from his chamber, barefoot and barelegged, slipped, or else lost his footing and fell down to the ground from the steps and his head was under him, and was grievously broken and bruised in so much that he had five bandages on his head for many days while his head was healing. And, as God wished it, some of his neighbours knew that he had fallen down the stairs, probably through the noise and the rushing of his fall. And so they came to him and found him lying with his head under him, half alive, all streaked with blood, never likely to speak to a priest or a clerk again, except by grace and a miracle. Then the said creature [Margery], his wife, was sent for and so she came to him. Then he was taken up and his head was sewn up and he was sick for a long time after, and people thought that he was going to die. And then the people said that if he died, his wife deserved to be hanged for his death, for she could have stayed with him and did not. They did not live together, nor did they sleep together, for, as was written earlier, they had both, with one assent and with the free will of both of them, made a vow to live chaste, and therefore, to avoid all perils, they lived in different places where there could be no suspicion of their lack of chastity, for first they had lived together after they had made their vow, and then people slandered them and said that they used their lust and their pleasure as they did before their vow-making. And when they went out on pilgrimage, or to see and speak with other spiritual people, many evil folk, whose tongues were their own hurt, lacking the fear and the love of our Lord Jesus Christ, judged them and said that rather they went to woods, groves or valleys to use the lust of their bodies so that people should not spy it or know it. . . .

Margery is reluctant to nurse her husband, as she feels it will leave her less time for her devotions to Christ, but Jesus orders her to look after her husband, as he has fulfilled Jesus's will by taking the vow of chastity.

Then she took her husband home with her and kept him years after, as long as he lived, and had very much labour with him, for in his last days he turned childish again and lacked reason, so that he could not manage his own easement of the bowels by going to the privy, or else he would not, but, like a child voided his natural digestion in his linen cloths, there as he sat by the fire, or at the table, wherever it was, he spared no place. And therefore she had much more labour in washing and wringing, and the expense of firewood and it hindered her much from her contemplation so that many times her labour would have irked her, except she thought about how, in her youth, she had had many delectable thoughts, fleshly lusts, and an inordinate love of his body. And therefore she was glad to be punished with the same body and accepted it much more easily and served him and helped him, it seemed to her, as she would have done for Christ himself.

9 A CLANDESTINE MARRIAGE

Text from: *Paston Letters* (1958), selected and ed. N. Davis, Oxford: Clarendon Press, pp. 74–6.

The Paston letters are a series of over one thousand documents, mostly letters, dating from *c.* 1420–1500, dealing with the affairs of the Paston family of East Anglia. John Paston I had studied law at Cambridge, but spent much time away from home in London. He was married to the heiress Margaret Mautby, by whom he had several sons (one of whom is John II, recipient of this letter), and a daughter, Margery. Margery had fallen in love with Richard Calle, the family's bailiff, and they had married without the family's permission. The letter shows Margaret writing to her son, Margery's brother, explaining the steps she had taken to try to recover the situation.

Letter from Margaret Paston to John Paston II, 1469
c. 10 September

I greet you well, and send you God's blessing and mine, letting you know that on Thursday last, my mother and I were with my Lord [the Bishop] of Norwich, and desired him to do no more in the matter concerning your sister until you and my brother, and the others who were your father's executors could all be here together; for they had rule over her as well as me. And he said plainly that he had been asked so often before to examine her that he could not, nor would he, delay any longer, and charged me on pain of excommunication that she should not be put off, but that she should appear before him the next day. And I said plainly that I would neither bring her nor send her; and then he said that he would send for her himself and charged that she should be at liberty to come when he sent for her. And he said by his troth that he would be as sorry for her if she had not acted well as he would be if she were closely related to him, both for my mother's sake and mine, and other of her kinsmen; for he knew well that her behaviour had pierced our hearts sorely.

My mother and I informed him that we could not make out, from what she said, by any conversation that she had had with him, that either of them were bound to the other, but that they were both free to choose. Then he said that he would speak to her as well as he could before he examined her, and so I was told by various people that he acted as well and as openly as if she had been closely related to him, which would be too long to write at this time. Hereafter you shall know who were the workers in this; the chancellor [an officer on the family's estate] was not as guilty as I thought he was.

On Friday the bishop sent for her at Ashfield and others who are very sorry about her behaviour. And the bishop spoke to her very plainly and reminded her of her birth, and who her friends and kin were, and how she should have more, if she would be ruled and guided by them; and if she did not, what rebuke and shame and loss it would be to her if she were not guided by them, and it would be the cause of them forsaking her, for any good or help or comfort that she should have had of them. And he said that he had heard say that she loved such a one that her friends were not pleased that she should have him, and therefore he warned her to be very cautious in what she did, and said that he wanted to hear the words which she had said to him [Calle] so that he could see whether it constituted matrimony or not. And she rehearsed what she had said, and said if those words did not make it sure, she said boldly that she would make it surer still before she went from there; for she said she thought in her conscience she was bound, what ever the words might be. These wicked words grieved me and her grandmother as much as everything else. Then the bishop and the chancellor both said that neither I nor any kin of hers would take her in.

And then Calle was examined separately [to see] if her words and his accorded, and the time and the place where it was supposed to have happened. And then the bishop said that he supposed that other things might be found against him which could cause a hindrance to the marriage, and so he said he would not be too hasty to give judgement, and said he would wait until the Wednesday or Thursday after Michaelmas [29 Sept.], and so it is delayed. They wanted to get their way quickly, but the bishop said that he would not do anything other than what he said.

I was with my mother at her place when she was examined, and when I heard tell what her attitude was I ordered my servants that she should not be received in my house. I had given her warning, she might have taken note of it before if she had been so disposed. And I sent to one or two others to say that they should not receive her if she came there. She was brought back to my place, to be taken in, and Sir James told those who brought her that I ordered them all that she should not be received; and so my Lord of Norwich has left her at Roger Best's, to be there until the day mentioned above, God knows very much against his [Roger's] will, and his wife's, if they dared do otherwise. I am sorry that they are encumbered with her, but yet I am better pleased that she should be there for the time being, than in some other places, because he and his wife are serious and of a good disposition, and she shan't be allowed to play the whore there.

I pray you and require you that this should not make you too sad, for I know that you take this matter to heart, and so do I, and other people; but remember, as I do, that in losing her we have lost a whore, and so take it not so much to heart; for if she had been virtuous, whatever she might have been, things would not stand as they do, and if he [Calle] were to drop dead this hour she should never be in my heart as she used to be.

As for the divorce you wrote to me about, I understand what you meant, but I charge you by my blessing that you should not do, nor cause anyone else to do, what would offend God and your conscience, for if you do, or cause someone to do so, God will take vengeance for it, and you will put yourself and others in great jeopardy; for believe me, she will sorely repent her wickedness later, and I pray God she does.

The marriage was declared valid. Margery seems never to have been reconciled to her family (though her mother did leave a bequest to Margery's daughter in her will, Margery was probably dead when the will was made). Richard continued in the Pastons' service for some years. Margery died c. 1479.

2

LOVE, SEX AND FRIENDSHIP

INTRODUCTION

The passion and sorrow of love were an emotional discovery of the
French troubadours and their successors.

(Curtius 1953: 588)

'I've been in love with you for weeks.' 'There's no such thing,' she says.
'It's a rhetorical device. It's a bourgeois fallacy.' 'Haven't you ever been
in love then?' 'When I was younger,' she says, 'I allowed myself to be
constructed by the discourse of romantic love for a while, yes.'

(Lodge 1988: 210)

The 'discourse of romantic love' has become an unquestioned part of western life,
a social force shaping the lives of millions of women and men in modern culture. If,
as Curtius and others have claimed, romantic love was essentially invented by the
French in the twelfth century, then it represents the most enduring social phenomenon to emerge in the medieval period. Indeed, the type of romantic love known as
'courtly love', 'amour courtois' or 'fin'amors' is one of the principal constituents of
most modern readers' visions of the Middle Ages, produced in part by the
stereotypical image of the troubadour serenading the lady in the tower, and in part
by the enduring interest in Arthurian myth. Yet, though the notion of courtly love
drives the popular imagining of the Middle Ages, the concept itself is notoriously
slippery. Unlike the social institution of marriage, which, as we saw in the last
section, can be recovered from theological and legal writings, evidence for the
existence of courtly love is drawn almost exclusively from imaginative literature,
whose relationship to 'reality' is both complex and elusive.

Curtius overstates the case when he claims that passionate love had not existed
in western Europe before the eleventh century. As Peter Dronke shows in his
influential book (Dronke 1965), lyric poetry expressing sentiments very similar to
those found in the songs of the southern French troubadours existed in Ancient
Egyptian, Georgian, Mozarabic Spanish and a number of other literatures. These

sentiments include the idea that the lover is unworthy of his goddess-like lady, that love of her improves his character, and that his love inevitably involves suffering which he gladly bears (Dronke 1965: 4–7). Lyrics expressing passionate, apparently (hetero)sexual, love have survived from well before the eleventh century: 'Wulf and Eadwacer' (excerpt 1 below) – certainly dating from before the year 1000 – is only one of a number of women's songs from all over Europe which precede, or are unaffected by, the register of 'courtly love'. That men might also compose love-poetry in the early period is less easy to prove, since the poetry preserved tends to be heroic or religious, but early Icelandic law legislated against the singing of *mansöngvar* (love-songs) about women (Mundal and Steinsland 1989: 114), and possibly tenth-century skaldic verses in praise of women are preserved in the thirteenth-century Icelandic poets' sagas: *Kormáks saga*, *Hallfreds saga* and *Gunnlaugs saga* (Sørensen 1993b: 88–9).

In reading these early love-lyrics we have to be constantly aware of the unknowable gap between experience and reality. The composers of these verses are usually anonymous; although they strive for an impression of sincerity and deeply felt passion, there is no necessary identity between poetic persona or poetic voice on the one hand and the actual poet or lived experience on the other (Boffey 1993: 169–71). In the past the belief that women had no social role as composers of poetry in the early Middle Ages has led to analysis of 'women's lyrics' as the work of male poets adopting a female voice; the critical history of the Old English poems known as 'The Wife's Lament' and 'Wulf and Eadwacer' demonstrates an anxiety on the part of some scholars to deny the feminine gender of the poems' speakers, precisely because they can neither imagine a male poet impersonating a female speaker in performance nor envisage the possibility of a female poet (Bambas 1963). More recently critics have tended to blur the line between (unknown) poet and the 'I' of the poem, assuming an authenticity of felt experience in the text which it often does not bear. As the troubadour Elias Carel makes clear in this verse, to say, or sing, is not always to mean in the way the reader or listener might believe:

> but if I praised you for them [your virtues]
> in my songs, I didn't speak out of love
> but for the honour and gain that I thought I'd get for it,
> just as any joglar [troubadour] does with a noble lady.
> (Rieger 1992: 275)

Not every poet composed for mercenary motives (even Elias Cairel retracts the above statement a few verses later), but the sincerity of medieval love poetry, courtly or otherwise, must not be taken for granted.

'Courtly love'

Peter Dronke's parallels notwithstanding, the majority of critics and readers recognize a particular linguistic register, a set of motifs and themes, and system of conventions occurring in medieval literature, which, since the French scholar Gaston Paris coined the term in 1883, have been identified with 'courtly love'. The poetry of 'courtly love' begins with the troubadours of southern France, spreads to the north, east and west, influencing Dante and Petrarch in Italy, the Minnesänger of Germany, the courts of northern France and English courtly circles.

Duke William IX of Aquitaine (1071–1127), grandfather of Eleanor, is regarded as the first of the troubadours; many of the most common motifs, such as the belief that love ennobles a man, are found in his poetry. Tradition holds that William underwent a conversion from the composition of comic and scabrous verse to the poetry of the 'religion of love', so the poetic art itself is held to have been made virtuous and courtly by the adoption of courtly love as a theme. As Howard Bloch shows, however, there is no textual evidence that William changed his themes and styles so dramatically; the vigorously obscene and the delicately chivalrous were most likely to have been composed at the same time. Such is the force of the 'courtly love' myth that the poet's life has been reshaped to reflect a much more modern theory of poetic evolution and refinement (Bloch 1991: 156–61).

'Courtly love' is epitomized by the poetry of the southern French troubadours. It is underpinned by the idea of the lover's unworthiness, the educative and ennobling effects of love, the need for secrecy, and the pain that the lover feels. Often the love is characterized as hopeless: the lady is stony-hearted or far away (*amor de lonh*). Conventional dramatis personae also appear: as well as the lover and his lady, there is often a jealous husband, a confidante, and a cast of *lozengiers* (gossips/slanderers) who jeopardize the secrecy of the love affair. These generic traits recur most fully in Andreas Capellanus's *De Arte Honeste Amandi* (c. 1185), a tract which purports to be a guide to courtly love (see below p. 45), and in certain romances, most notably those of Chrétien de Troyes, and the German *Tristan*. Many other works, such as the poetry of the Minnesänger, Chaucer's *Troilus*, Boccaccio's *Teseida*, and in a spiritualized and intellectualized form, Petrarch's Sonnets and Dante's *La Vita Nuova*, draw on the language and some of the conventions of 'courtly love', without subscribing to all the assumptions which inhere in the Provençal tradition.

Even if scholars are in agreement as to the main features of 'courtly love', no disagreement in medieval scholarship is more profound and more varied than the debate as to what 'courtly love' was for and how it can be related to contemporary attitudes towards women (Boase 1977 is a wide-ranging survey). Did 'courtly love' have any existence at all, apart from a textual one? Was it an elaborate game played by courtiers who did not take it particularly seriously (Huizinga 1949)? Did it signal a real change in women's status – and how did it square with the institution of marriage which was examined in chapter 1 (Gold 1985: 145–52)? What did the Church make of the use of religious language for profane purposes, and the apparent disregard of prohibitions against fornication, adultery and immoderate sexual desire (Robertson 1973)? Did 'courtly love' serve a social function, educating and civilizing the young courtier, channelling his erotic thoughts into poetry to console him for the lateness of marriage, as Duby suggests (Duby 1978; 1992)? And what roles were available to women within the terms of 'courtly love'? It is possible to see them as objectified and silenced; given voice only by male authors who manipulate their utterances (Moi 1986). Thus Andreas Capellanus has his fictional 'Marie de Champagne' pronounce that love is impossible in marriage, women in male-authored troubadour poetry remain unmoved by their lovers' sufferings, and Guinevere, in the 'Chevalier de la Charrette', refuses to acknowledge Lancelot because he hesitated for a fraction of a second before enduring disgrace for her sake (Chrétien de Troyes 1991: 256, 262).

C. S. Lewis identified 'courtly love' closely with adultery. Taking literally the dictum of Marie de Champagne in *De Arte Honeste Amandi*, that love could not exist within marriage (see p. 16 above), Lewis asserted that medieval love must therefore be adulterous, a contention which, though fundamentally untenable, has preoccupied many critics for a number of years (Lewis 1965: 13; Robertson 1973; Benton 1973). Adultery and illicit love are certainly to be found in romances of 'courtly love', such as the 'Chevalier de la Charrette' and *Tristan*. Nevertheless, as many historians have pointed out, the aim of the aristocratic marriage was primarily the production of heirs. The chastity of the wife had to be beyond suspicion, or the family inheritance might be passed to a child with no blood tie to the paternal line. Adultery was punishable by death: in particular the adultery of a vassal with his lady was accounted treason, and could be punished cruelly. In the reign of Philip the Fair (1268–1314) two young nobles accused of adultery with the wives of two French princes were castrated, dragged to the gallows by wild horses and hanged (Benton 1973: 27). Thus illicit sex with a nobleman's wife was risky in the extreme.

Georges Duby argues that the practices of 'courtly love' are psycho-social in origin. Noble boys would leave their families at the age of 7 or so to be raised in another noble household. Separated from their own mothers, the youths were likely to become emotionally attracted to the lady of the household, often much younger than her husband. As they matured, the young men's feelings might change from the filial to the erotic. To please the lady and gain her attention they applied themselves to courtly arts: singing, dancing, jousting and the composition of poetry. 'Courtly love' thus acted as a civilizing influence on the aggressive, hypermasculine behaviour of the young men, particularly necessary since they were unlikely to be able to marry until they had an estate of their own. Sexual frustration was sublimated into adoration of the female. 'Courtly love' was simply 'worldly rituals of social intercourse – and everyone knew that they were no more than that' (Duby 1978: 14) (Fig. 3).

Figure 3 Ivory writing tablets in diptych form, depicting a pair of lovers hawking and exchanging roses for a wreath. From Paris *c.* 1300: M&LA 56, 5–9, 2 (BM Ivories 360). Copyright British Museum.

The model of 'courtly love' as an elaborate game of behaviour and language, subject to rules and role-playing, is a persuasive one. It sidesteps the question of whether men could really aspire to adulterous affairs with married ladies without risking their husbands' wrath, and how the Church could apparently ignore a prevalent culture of eroticism and adultery. To Duby's model of 'domestication' must be added considerations of status and honour. In the aristocratic circles in which 'courtly love' is rooted, courtiers were continually jockeying for the lord's favour and for advancement. Eloquence and rhetorical skill were among the qualities which brought the suitor to the lord's notice; facility of speech was appropriate, even necessary to, lovemaking. Stephen Jaeger cites the story told of the cleric Gervase of Tilbury, who, riding through the countryside, sees a beautiful woman in a vineyard. He approaches her and speaks to her 'in the courtly way of wanton love'. The terms of her rebuff reveal her to be a Cathar, and Gervase is instrumental in having her burned as a heretic (Jaeger 1985: 158). To woo women is part of the successful courtier's role: the nobler the woman, the greater the honour of the suitor. Since a woman's rank is determined first by her birth, but also by her marriage, the husband must be included in the courtly lover's assessment of his lady's worth. Marchello-Nizia (1981) suggests that the 'courtly love' triangle of lover, lady and husband is fundamentally homosexual in orientation; while the lover praises the lady his eyes are fixed on the lord whose power enhances the lady and whose attention is captured by the praise-songs made in his wife's honour. Kay's more nuanced analysis identifies the impulse rather as 'homosocial' (as in Sedgwick 1985). In a culture where the profoundest bonds are those between men what is at stake in the public performance of the troubadour's song is the social relationship between men (Kay 1990: 236 n.16).

Women as poets of 'courtly love'

'Courtly love', then, was predominantly an institution serving male interests: the acquisition of honour and status. Yet women were necessarily implicated in the tradition, primarily as textual objects. Thus we should not be surprised to find that women, too, experiment with the genre. Poems, apparently written by women troubadours (*trobairitz*), survive from southern France. Little information survives about any of them, and in some cases the gender of the poet is a simple extrapolation from the narrative voice of the lyric. We must therefore be wary of assuming, as with the early lyrics discussed above, that all the texts ascribed to the *trobairitz* are historical productions of real women. The *trobairitz* were composing in a tradition which was not of their making, and often seem to subscribe uncritically to the conventions of gender which men employ in their poetry. Kay finds two versions of women in troubadour poetry: the 'feminine', a misogynistic imagining of the bad woman as cruel, fickle and undiscriminating, and the *domna* or lady to whom much of the poetry is addressed. The *domna* is of 'mixed' gender. She is often represented by a masculine disguised name (*senhal*), and possesses the normally male attributes of power and rank in comparison with her lover (Kay 1990: 86–100). Knowing that certain of the texts are composed by women tells us nothing new about the way women regarded themselves within Provençal culture: 'only if [women] use this gender system ironically, or attempt to reform it, will their status as subjects be distinguished from the masculine model' (Kay 1990: 102). The castigated 'feminine' role is an unattractive subject position for the woman poet to adopt, but, despite the power which the rhetoric of the genre ascribes to the *domna*, in practice she finds herself powerless against her lover. The *domna* role is essentially passive and reactive; the lady has no recourse if her lover abandons her, even if she conforms perfectly to the value system which male poetry sets up (Kay 1990: 101–11). The pain of abandonment is the theme of many of the *trobairitz* songs. The Countess of Dia (born *c.* 1140) complains:

44

> My worth and noble birth should stand me in good stead
> my beauty and more so my true thoughts;
> so I'm sending to you, there on your estate,
> this song as to be my messenger
> for I want to know, my handsome noble friend,
> why you are so hard and cruel to me.
> I don't know if it's pride or hatred for me that causes it.
>
> (Rieger 1992: 592–3)

Some *trobairitz* do depict themselves as taking the initiative. Castelloza (born *c.* 1200) states openly that she does not fear shame in addressing her lover:

> I know very well that I enjoy it –
> even if everyone says it isn't decent,
> that a lady should woo a knight on her account,
> keep him for a long time in conversation;
> but whoever says that, doesn't know how to enjoy love.
>
> (Rieger 1992: 520)

And the Countess of Dia is frank about her sexual longing: 'How much I'd like to hold my knight / for an evening naked in my arms' (Rieger 1992: 600). Nevertheless, Castelloza's poem is composed for a man who has been 'wicked and cruel and false':

> if you won't let me have the slightest joy,
> and if you let me die;
> you'll be committing a sin,
> and I'll be the one who suffers,
> and everyone will blame you villainously.
>
> (Rieger 1992: 520)

Assertiveness and self-expression are harnessed to express grief and powerlessness: the *trobairitz*'s experience of love is seldom happy or fulfilled.

The 'code of courtly love' and Andreas Capellanus

It is Andreas Capellanus's treatise *De Arte Honeste Amandi* (*c.* 1180) which has been primarily responsible for the idea that medieval court circles aspired to imitating the behaviours described by the troubadours. Andreas tells us that he is writing a handbook to the details and practices of 'courtly love' at the request of one Gualterus. In the Author's Preface, Andreas expresses some doubts about the pursuit of courtly love:

> Therefore, although it does not seem expedient to devote oneself to
> things of this kind or fitting for any prudent man to engage in this kind

of hunting, nevertheless, because of the affection I have for you I can
by no means refuse your request.

(Andreas Capellanus 1941: 27)

Books 1 and 2 set out scholastic definitions of love, offer sample dialogues
between men and women of different classes and warning visions about those who
love falsely, list the rules of love, and deal with questions as to the propriety of
various courses of action. In the dialogues the idealism of true love is tempered
both by a mistrust of women's words – as Toril Moi points out: 'if the deceitful
woman's language is indistinguishable from an honest woman's, the lover will never
know whether he is listening to truth or deceit' (Moi 1986: 29) – and by the rigidity
of the social hierarchy. Absent too is a sense of the woman's desire: like the
Provençal *domna*, she reacts, parries, refuses or assents: 'her desire seems either
to be non-existent or entirely cultural, inextricably caught up, as it must be, in a
series of mundane considerations of wealth and social prestige' (Moi 1986: 22).
Book 3 unequivocally warns Gualterus against love:

> Now for many reasons any wise man is bound to avoid all the deeds
> of love and to oppose all its mandates. The first of these reasons is one
> which it is not right for anyone to oppose, for no man, so long as he
> devotes himself to the service of love, can please God by any other
> works, even if they are good ones.

(Andreas Capellanus 1941: 187)

What follows is an argument against love, drawing on the usual medieval
misogynist stereotypes, warning that Gualterus should devote himself rather to
making himself ready for the Divine Bridegroom than to the 'vanities of the world'.
The relationship of Book 3 to Books 1 and 2 has puzzled scholars for decades
(see Moi 1986: 14 for a table of possible relationships). A. Karnein's research into
the *Arte*'s reception in the decades after it was first composed has suggested
that the work was initially understood as critical of the 'courtly love' ethic. The
author, identified by Karnein with a cleric in the chancellory of the court of King
Philip Augustus in Paris, and quite unconnected with the circle of Marie de
Champagne at Troyes, wrote for the son of his immediate superior, Gautier 'le
jeune', giving him, as the Author's Preface states, a learned and often satirical
analysis of love, as requested, and a theologically grounded coda, giving advice
which the young man had not requested (Karnein 1985). The *Arte* represents 'the
learned reaction of an intellectual cleric to the culturally and literarily already
conspicuous new system of secular values that vigorously challenged the
established universal system of literary and cultural Latinity' (Wierschin 1987:
962). It is only in the fourteenth century, with Jean de Meung's uncritical use of
the *Arte* in the *Roman de la Rose* that it comes to be read outside its original
scholastic and intellectual context as a systematic treatise elaborating

favourably a code of beliefs and behaviour thought to be widespread in twelfth-century court circles. Andreas was not writing anthropology, however, but rather exercising a university-trained brain on the assumptions of the rhetoric of a literary vernacular which he found uncongenial. Andreas makes use of exaggeration and *reductio ad absurdum* to demonstrate the oppositional nature of 'courtly love' to orthodox Christian belief. Topical satire is also employed: Eleanor of Aquitaine, who is made in *De Arte* (p. 176) to comment that the 'embraces and solaces of young men' are to be preferred to those of older men, had divorced Louis VII of France, who was about her own age, to marry Henry II of England, eleven years younger than she. Most recently, Peter Dronke has suggested that 'Andreas Capellanus' is a *nom de plume*, drawn from a lost romance 'Andreas and the Queen of France' (Dronke forthcoming). The *Arte* may reflect, distortedly, the ideals of romantic love, but, as Howard Bloch suggests:

> antifeminism and courtliness stand in a dialectical rapport, ... woman is placed in the overdetermined and polarized position of being neither one nor the other but both at once, and thus trapped in an ideological entanglement whose ultimate effect is her abstraction from history.
>
> (Bloch 1991: 164)

The rhetoric and practices of courtly love, existing in circumscribed contexts, and as we have seen, inseparable, both in the troubadours and in Andreas, from misogynist assumptions about the 'real' nature of the feminine, did nothing to raise the status of women in the regions where 'courtly love' flourished. If idealization of the feminine became culturally widespread, there were no tangible benefits to actual women in terms of individual autonomy (Fig. 4). It is arguable that the chief beneficiary of this cultural development was the Virgin Mary, who combined the roles of virgin, mother and bride in a way impossible for any other woman. The cult of Mary developed in tandem with the rhetoric of courtly love: as Marina Warner points out, to suggest, as has been traditional, that the cult of the Virgin is both cause and effect of courtly love is to amalgamate two quite distinct social currents, originating in different circles (Warner 1976: 134). Both the cult of the Virgin and the ideology of courtly love were evolved by men intent on working out their own ideas of what women should be, ideologies which fulfilled their own emotional needs and desires (Gold 1985: 73–4).

In later medieval lyric and in mystical writing Mary is favoured by men, where, as Caroline Bynum suggests (and as we shall see in chapter 4), women tend to be attracted rather by Christ in his humanity (Bynum 1982: 18). Yet Mary was not without appeal to women: in miracle collections she often appears to help the anxious mother (for example, Herolt 1928) or, in a tale from the *Cantigas de Santa Maria* by King Alfonso the Wise of Castile, she protects a nun, who, although devoted to the Virgin, cannot resist the allure of a knight and runs away with him. Before she goes, she puts herself, and her keys, in Mary's keeping:

Figure 4 Shield of Parade: late fifteenth century Flemish. The shield is wooden with painted gesso. A knight kneels in homage to his lady under an inscription 'vous ou la mort'. Death himself waits behind the knight. M&LA 63, 5–1, 1. Copyright British Museum.

'Ah, Mother of God!' she then
said within her thoughts,
'I'll leave you these to care for,
and with all my heart
put myself in your care.'

When the nun repents, after having borne the knight several children, she returns to the convent only to find that no one has missed her. For the years she had been away the Virgin had assumed her place and carried out her duties. The nun confesses all to the sisters who are convinced of the miracle (Dronke 1968: 71–2). Here then we see the Virgin helping a woman who has been ensnared by the values of romance, even to the point of concealing her delinquency. How actual women relate to images and ideologies of the feminine created by men is often problematic, but we should not assume that they have no relevance to women.

Pastoral

Against the courtly ambience of the troubadour lyric, and the writings of Chrétien we can set the pastoral. The French pastourelle, its German equivalent and many of the English lyrics are set out in the countryside, where the relationship between man and woman is apparently untrammelled by the artifice of court, and an Edenic simplicity seems to prevail. In some lyrics with female speakers the illusion of joyful and reciprocal sexual pleasure is maintained: Walther von der Vogelweide's most famous lyric (below, p. 55) epitomizes this sort of carefree encounter. In English secular lyrics the love affair is usually with a cleric who wins the girl over with his seductive language and promises: 'Thou semest well to ben a clerk, / For thou spekest so stille' (it suits you well to be a cleric for you speak so softly) says one girl, on the verge of surrendering in 'My deth I love, my lif ich hate' (Davies 1963: 62). The setting is often in the village rather than out in the woods and fields as in continental lyrics; the lovers meet in church or at a village dance. The affair is sometimes regretted when the girl finds herself pregnant, 'my gurdel aros, my wombe wax out', but often the girl's tone is defiant. She does not blame her lover but rather fears social obloquy.

In French pastourelle the encounter is usually between a knight and a shepherd girl, a far more pronounced class discrepancy than in the English lyric. The characters often discuss the class difference with wit and irony. Sometimes the girl may be wooed by a gift of clothing or even promises of marriage. Just as Andreas Capellanus recommends in *De Arte* (Andreas Capellanus 1941: 150), if a lower class woman is unwilling to make love with a nobleman, the use of force is often found effective. Kathryn Gravdal (1991: 104–21) demonstrates how the discourse of class serves to mask the sexual violence at the heart of many pastourelles. However witty the wordplay between knight and shepherdess, if he cannot defeat

49

her on verbal terms, he can defeat her by physical force. Comedy may be used to deflect the reader's attention from the sexual violence: the motif of the girl's 'real' enjoyment of the encounter despite her initial screams of pain and fear. The pastourelles, long thought to be a non-courtly genre, were in fact composed by courtly poets, demonstrating once again the complex relation of courtliness and misogyny:

> the powerful muse of courtly lyric is manageable only as the speechless *domna*. In the pastourelle, where the female is given a voice, she can be disempowered in yet another way. In a drama set far from the court, yet played before the court audience, the poet finds a convenient discursive place in which to challenge the courtly discourse of female power.
>
> (Gravdal 1991: 119)

Women and sex

Medieval medical writers and natural philosophers, as opposed to theologians, viewed sex as necessary to both men and women. Without a regular outlet for sexual desire both sexes were likely to become ill. 'No one who does not have intercourse will be healthy. Intercourse is truly useful and promotes health,' states the eleventh-century medical writer and Benedictine monk, Constantine the African (Cadden 1993: 273). Hildegard of Bingen writes that men whose disposition is sanguine, and 'dry' women can abstain safely from sex, but those in whom the humours are differently balanced are not likely to thrive if abstinent. Male seed, and the female equivalent which many writers believed to exist and to be discharged by the woman during orgasm, had to be eliminated from the body periodically, just as other discharges such as phlegm, saliva and menstrual fluid did. Retention of seed could be dangerous, and some medical treatises prescribed massage and application of poultices to the female genitals to discharge seed. Some versions of Trotula's *On the Care of Women* even give instructions for 'restoring' lost virginity, either by constricting the vulva (said to promote conception) or by the insertion of a small sac of membrane filled with animal blood which would rupture during intercourse (Cadden 1986: 164).

Sexual pleasure on the part of the woman was regarded by many writers as a precondition of conception: an early fourteenth-century writer urges the importance of foreplay: 'the husband ... should stroke smoothly the breasts and belly of his lady and excite her to intercourse' (Cadden 1993: 252). Without orgasm, it was thought, ejaculation of the 'female seed' would not occur and conception could not take place. The corollary of this belief, that a pregnancy could only result from pleasurable and consensual intercourse, would have repercussions for rape cases for centuries to come (Laqueur 1990: 161–2).

Women then were expected to take pleasure in sex. It was a commonplace of misogynist writing that women were naturally more lustful and voracious in their sexual appetites than men, and that they could easily exhaust and destroy their husbands' health with their importunacies. Nor was women's sexual activity always heterosexual; although women were unlikely to write openly about same-sex erotic encounters – one poem is, however, included below – some evidence of lesbian practices has survived in legal records and in the penitentials, manuals to help priests assess the sins revealed to them in confession and the due punishments (Payer 1984: 43, 68–9). In a text written between 1063 and 1072 Peter Damian recounts the vision of a woman in Rome who sees her dead godmother appear. The godmother confesses that in her youth she committed 'shameful acts with girls of my age'. After a year of punishment after death, the erring woman is only now being admitted to heaven (Le Goff 1984: 178). Cadden notes a French case of 1405 in which a married woman and her female work companion were prosecuted for having a number of sexual encounters; the married woman, who is importuning for a royal pardon, casts her friend Jehanne as aggressor in the incidents under discussion. Repeated transgression was a capital crime, though, because female sexuality tended to be cast as passive by male authors and legislators, and because all-women households, beguinages and convents provided relative privacy for lesbian acts (see Brown 1986 for an early modern, but well-documented, case of lesbianism in an Italian convent), very few women, in comparison to homosexual men, were ever brought to trial (Cadden 1993: 224; Crompton 1980/1: 11–25).

Friendship

Male friendship was theorized in the twelfth century by Ælred of Rievaulx in his *De Spirituali Amicitia* (On Spiritual Friendship) written between 1150 and 1165, partly based on Cicero's *De Amicitia*. Friendship, even between members of the same sex, might be passionately expressed, as the letters of St Anselm or St Bernard of Clairvaux show (Morris 1987: 96–107). Far fewer letters between women survive from the medieval period: correspondence between Hildegard of Bingen and Elisabeth of Schönau and Clare of Assisi and Agnes of Prague (see p. 149 below) tends to be concerned with spiritual matters (Cherewatuk and Wiethaus 1993; Wiethaus 1993). We may surmise that women's friendships with one another, even if undocumented, must have sustained and comforted them: the warmth of female friendship within the convent is shown by the affectionate references to various nuns in the writings of Gertrude the Great (Gertrude 1993). In villages and towns women were linked across the generations by the godparent relationship; god-daughters are often mentioned in wills while women who were godmothers to the same siblings formed close relationships with one another and with the parents. Riddy (1993) gives a convincing account of Middle English evidence for this, and other forms of 'feminine subculture'. Although the modern, pejorative term 'gossip', used almost exclusively of women (Coates 1988), is derived from 'god-sib' (one in a godparent or -child relationship), the mixture of anxiety and contempt felt by men about women communicating and sharing their knowledge with one another is far older than the word 'gossip' (Dalarun 1992: 40–1). Chaucer satirizes women's friendship in his treatment of the Wife of Bath and her 'gossip' Alison (Chaucer 1988: 112), while Figure 5 shows a devil who was detailed to collect women's talk, designated idle and trivial by moralists, to add to their other sins when judgement came, figuring 'the endless "cackle" of women, the disorder it is supposed to engender and the dangers of possession' (Régnier-Bohler 1992: 430) (Fig. 5).

The romance and 'romance'

The medieval romance is pre-eminently about identity and self-discovery. The hero moves from ignorance, complacency or immaturity to enlightenment, knightliness and full adulthood. Women are often instrumental in the hero's quest, helping him, as Lunete does Yvain, or tempting him, as Bercilak's Lady tempts Gawain in *Sir Gawain and the Green Knight*. She may do all she can to hinder his setting out, as does Parzifal's mother, or be the reward for his endeavours, as in Marie de France's *Sir Landevale*. The one role which the woman can never play in French romance is that of the hero – even a woman as resourceful as Nicolette in 'Aucassin and

Figure 5 Devils lurk near gossiping women, waiting to carry off their idle words to weigh against them on Judgement Day. Stained-glass window from Stanford-on-Avon, Northants, *c.* 1325–40. Photograph by K. C. Barley.

Nicolette'. The hero is not yet complete at the beginning of the romance: he finds himself by casting off some values and acquiring new ones. He discovers his own capabilities and learns how to hold in balance the public world of renown and knightly deeds with the private world of emotion. 'Women ... cannot be at its [sc. romance's] center, as they act only in the private personal realm – they cannot themselves experience a conflict between public and private' (Gold 1985: 41). Women's essential identity is never in doubt. It is enough to know whether a woman is good or bad; the finer details of women's characters hold no interest. The nature of the feminine is established for women through the different discourses which describe them. Though medieval women seem, like their modern sisters, to have been keen consumers of romance – in England the Arthurian romances of Tristan and Lancelot figured largely among books owned by women (Meale 1993: 139–42) – the stories they read were fantasies, imparting stereotypical and often contradictory views of the nature of women.

Medieval women were by no means immune to the discourse of romantic love, as the extracts below demonstrate, but it is unlikely that they allowed themselves to be defined by it. The realities of marriage and childbearing, the social penalties for extramarital affairs and the fear of the next world were more compelling arguments against the ideology of romance than they are in modern western society, where we have come to ascribe to it a near-unlimited power. The longevity of this discourse is remarkable, outlasting even as powerful an ideology as Christianity in the West, for its importance as a shaping value in our society remains more or less unchallenged.

1 AN EARLY WOMAN'S SONG

Text from: G. Krapp and E. V. K. Dobbie (1936) *Anglo-Saxon Poetic Records* III, 'The Exeter Book', London: Routledge. 'Wulf and Eadwacer' pp. 179–80. Transl. C. Larrington.

This Old English poem, usually known as 'Wulf and Eadwacer', is without any title in the manuscript. We cannot be sure of its date, but it is earlier than 1000. The speaker's gender is assured only by a feminine ending in one line, and her situation is confusing. It is usually assumed that Wulf is her outlaw-lover and Eadwacer her husband, though who the father of the 'cub' may be is uncertain. The apparent reference to Matthew 19: 6: 'What therefore God hath joined together, let not man put asunder' in the final lines suggests the context is that of a failed marriage. The lexis of the poem is extremely ambiguous. In the translation I have given alternatives where the word is capable of more than one meaning.

For my people, it is as if someone is giving them a present/booty/sacrifice
they wish to receive/devour him, if he comes among an armed troop.
We are separated/our fates are different.
Wulf is on an island, I on another.
Secure is that island, surrounded by fens.

There are cruel men there on that island;
they wish to receive/devour him, if he comes among an armed troop.
We are separated/our fates are different.
I endured with hope the wide-ranging of my Wulf
when it was rainy weather and I sat grieving
then the warrior laid his arms around me
I took delight in that, yet it was also hateful to me.
Wulf, my Wulf, the hope of you
has made me ill, your rare visits,
a mourning spirit, not at all lack of food.
Do you hear, Eadwacer? Our miserable cub
Wulf/the wolf is carrying to the wood.
That may easily be torn asunder, what was never in harmony/joined,
Our relationship/song together.

2 SEXUAL PASSION RECALLED

Text from: *The Letters of Abélard and Héloise* (1974), transl. Betty Radice, Harmondsworth: Penguin, p. 133.

Héloise, whose full story is told below (pp. 204–7) recalls in a letter to her former lover
and husband, Abélard, the pleasures which they shared before they both took monastic
vows. When Héloise's uncle had Abélard castrated (the wound referred to in the
passage) he lost his sexual appetites, but Héloise herself finds that time and separation
have not dimmed her desire for her lover.

In my case, the pleasures of lovers which we shared have been too sweet – they can never displease me, and can scarcely be banished from my thoughts. Wherever I turn they are always there before my eyes, bringing with them awakened longings and fantasies which will not even let me sleep. Even during the celebration of the Mass, when our prayers should be purer, lewd visions of those pleasures take such a hold upon my unhappy soul that my thoughts are on their wantonness instead of on prayers. I should be groaning over the sins I have committed, but I can only sigh for what I have lost. Everything we did and also the times and places are stamped on my heart along with your image, so that I live through it all again with you. Even in sleep I know no respite. Sometimes my thoughts are betrayed in a movement of my body, or they break out in an unguarded word. In my utter wretchedness, that cry from a suffering soul could well be mine: 'Miserable creature that I am, who is there to rescue me out of the body doomed to this death?' Would that in truth I could go on: 'The grace of God through Jesus Christ our Lord.' This grace, my dearest, came upon you unsought – a single wound of the body by freeing you from these torments has healed many

54

wounds in your soul. Where God may seem to you an adversary he has in fact proved himself kind: like an honest doctor who does not shrink from giving pain if it will bring about a cure. But for me, youth and passion and experience of pleasures which were so delightful intensify the torments of the flesh and longings of desire, and the assault is the more overwhelming as the nature they attack is the weaker.

3 TWO LATER LOVE-LYRICS

(a) Text from: *Die Gedichte Walthers von der Vogelweide* (1965), ed. H. Kuhn, Berlin: De Gruyter, pp. 52–3. Transl. C. Larrington.

Walther von den Vogelweide (c. 1170–1230) was the greatest lyric poet in Germany in the medieval period. This is one of his most famous poems. The refrain 'tandaradei' is the song of the nightingale, the 'little bird' who will not betray the speaker's secret. Spearing (1991) gives a lively account of the interrelationship between poet, speaker and audience in this lyric.

'Unter den Linden'

Under the linden tree
on the heath
that's where we two had our bed.
There you'll find
crushed flowers and grass
in a glade in the wood.
Tandaradei!
How beautifully the nightingale sang!
I came walking over the meadow:
my lover had already come there,
there he greeted me:
'Noble Lady!'
That will always make me glad.
Did he kiss me? Thousands of times
tandaradei! – see how red my mouth is!
For he had fashioned
very splendidly a couch of flowers.
Anyone who comes on the same path
will laugh to himself.
By the roses he may well –
tandaradei! – work out where my head was.
If anyone knew
that he lay with me

(God forbid) I'd be so ashamed,
how he played with me.
Never will anyone
find out,
except him and me
and a little bird.
Tandaradei!
and he'll keep faith with me.

(b) Text from: K. Meyer, *Zeitschrift für celtische Philologie* 13 (1921), p. 18. Translation from R. P. M. Lehmann (1981) 'Women's Songs in Irish 800–1500', in J. Plummer (ed.) *Vox Feminae: Studies in Medieval Woman's Song*, Kalamazoo, Mich.: Medieval Institute Publications.

This song is unusual in that verse two seems to imply that the speaker's lover has left her for a man. 'Ochone' in v. 3 is a cry of distress.

Woe, I am away too long
from one I love, gone is he;
though it serve as fate this way,
each day seems longer to me.

With him I'm not without cheer,
though his smiles here briefly hang;
two stories go not with me:
be he woman, be she man.

I am my comrade till doom.
I'll not have room to love so;
though it were she or were he,
pity me, God, ochone woe.

4 THE *TROBAIRITZ*

Texts translated from: A. Rieger (1992) *Trobairitz: Der Beitrag der Frau in der altokzitanischen höfischen Lyrik*, Tübingen: Max Niemeyer Verlag, pp. 600–1, 539–40, 204–5.

The *trobairitz* flourished in Provence in the twelfth century. They were of noble family and composed verse, just as the male troubadours did. They often speak explicitly of sexual desire, though, undoubtedly, some of their lyrics are likely to be elaborately conventional compositions. Very little is known of any of these women's lives.

(a) The Countess of Dia (born *c.* 1140). Her *vida* (the brief biographical note attached to her poems) says: 'The Countess of Dia was the wife of Guillems de Peitieus, a good and beautiful lady, and she fell in love with Lord Raimbaut d'Aurenga and made many good songs about him.' Floris and Blanchefleur, mentioned in the song below, are a famous pair of lovers in romance.

'Estat ai en greu cossirier'

I've lately been lost in anguish
for a knight who was mine once,
and I want everyone to know for all time,
that I loved him beyond reason;
but now I see I've been betrayed,
because I wouldn't give him my love;
and that I see was a great mistake
when I'm lying in bed and when I'm dressed.

I'd gladly hold my knight
one evening naked in my arms,
for he would be in transports of joy
if I served him as a pillow,
for I find more happiness with him
than Floris did in Blancaflor.
To him I give my heart and my love,
my mind, my eyes, my life.

Handsome friend, dear and kind,
when shall I hold you in my power?
and spend a night with you,
and give you loving kisses –
you know, I have a great desire
to hold you in place of my husband,
if only first you'd promise me,
to do everything I wanted of you.

(b) Castelloza was born *c.* 1200. For a thoughtful analysis of her poetry see Dronke (1984b).

'Mout avetz faich long estatge'

You've stayed away a long time,
my friend, since you parted from me
and it's cruel and heartrending for me,
for you swore to me and you promised
that, all the days of your life,
you'd have no lady but me;
if now you care about another
you've killed and betrayed me,
for of you I had great hopes
that you'd love me unconditionally.

Handsome friend, with all my heart
I loved you, since I fell for you
now I know I've been a fool,
for that estranged you from me,
that I never tried to entrap you,
but you gave me evil for good;
I love you so, and I won't give up,
for love has seized me so violently,
that I don't think any good thing
can come to me, without your love.

I must be a poor example
to other women in love,
for it's the man who should bring messages
in carefully chosen words,
and then I'd be cured and satisfied:
dear friend, by my faith,
when I woo you
it gives me pleasure;
for the noblest woman becomes richer
if you give her kisses or attention.

May I be cursed, if ever an inconstant heart
I showed, or a changeable one
or if I ever, no matter who it was,
felt love for any other.
No, rather am I thoughtful and downcast,
that you don't remember my love,
and if you won't grant any of love's joys to me,
soon you'll find me gone:
for from a little unhappiness
a woman dies, unless her man drives it off.

All the misery and condemnation
which has come upon me because of you
has made you loved in my family
and by my husband most of all;
and if you ever acted wrongly towards me
I forgive you in all good faith
and pray you to come back to me
as soon as you hear my song:
for it tells you,
that here you'll find a warm welcome.

(c) Garsenda de Forcalquier was born c. 1170. She was the wife of Alphonse II, lord of Provence and brother of the king of Aragon; Garsenda held sovereignty over Provence after his death. This is a *tenson*, a form in which two speakers, often male and female, exchange alternate verses. The identity of the male speaker is unknown.

'Vos que.m semblatz dels corals amadors'

You, who seem to me to be among the true lovers,
I wish you wouldn't be so uncertain;
yet it pleases me that love for me torments you
for I'm in just as much pain because of you,
and it's you who's suffering by your reticence,
since you don't dare to take my heart as an avowal;
and you do yourself and me a great wrong,
for a lady doesn't dare – for fear of being mistaken –
to uncover all her desires.

Noble lady, your honour and your worth
makes me timorous, so great is it;
and no other fear holds me back
from declaring my love to you,
for first I wished to serve you so completely
that no outrage should come of it
for I knew that then I'd dare to woo you;
and I wished that deeds would form my message
and you took my service instead of my pleading,
for a noble deed must outweigh a word.

5 ABOUT LOVE

Text from: Andreas Capellanus, *De Arte Honeste Amandi*, translated (1941) as *The Art of Courtly Love*, transl. J. J. Parry, New York: Columbia University Press, pp. 28–9, 31–2.

The identity of Andreas Capellanus is not known for certain, nor is the provenance of *De Arte*. It is now thought to have been composed by a Parisian cleric at the late twelfth-century royal court, and to be ironic in its approach to the rituals of courtly love. The extracts below come from Book 1, in which the author, treating his subject as a serious topic susceptible of strict formal analysis, sets out the definitions and signs of love.

(a) What love is

Love is a certain inborn suffering derived from the sight of and excessive meditation upon the beauty of the opposite sex, which causes each one to wish above all things the embraces of the other and by common desire to carry out all of love's precepts in the other's embrace.

That love is suffering is easy to see, for before the love becomes equally balanced on both sides there is no torment greater, since the lover is always in fear that his love may not gain its desire and that he is wasting his efforts. He fears, too, that rumours of it may get abroad, and he fears everything that might harm it in any way, for before things are perfected a slight disturbance often spoils them. If he is a poor man, he also fears that the woman may scorn his poverty; if he is ugly, he fears that she may despise his lack of beauty or may give her love to a more handsome man; if he is rich, he fears that his parsimony in the past may stand in his way. To tell the truth, no one can number the fears of one single lover. This kind of love, then, is a suffering which is felt by only one of the persons and may be called 'single love'. But even after both are in love the fears that arise are just as great, for each of the lovers fears that what he has acquired with so much effort may be lost through the effort of someone else, which is certainly much worse for a man than if, having no hope, he sees that his efforts are accomplishing nothing, for it is worse to lose the things you are seeking than to be deprived of a gain you merely hope for. The lover fears, too, that he may offend his loved one in some way; indeed he fears so many things that it would be difficult to tell them.

That this suffering is inborn I shall show you clearly, because if you will look at the truth and distinguish carefully you will see that it does not arise out of any action; only from the reflection of the mind upon what it sees does this suffering come. For when a man sees some woman fit for love and shaped according to his taste, he begins at once to lust after her in his heart; then the more he thinks about her the more he burns with love, until he comes to a fuller meditation. Presently he begins to think about the fashioning of the woman and to differentiate her limbs, to think about what she does, and to pry into the secrets of her body, and he desires to put each part of it to the fullest use. Then after he has come to this complete meditation, love cannot hold the reins, but he proceeds at once to action; straightway he strives to get a helper and to find an intermediary. He begins to plan how he may find favour with her, and he begins to seek a place and a time opportune for talking; he looks upon a brief hour as a very long year, because he cannot do anything fast enough to suit his eager mind. It is well known that many things happened to him in this manner. This inborn suffering comes, therefore, from seeing and meditating. Not every kind of meditation can be the cause of love, an excessive one is required; for a restrained thought does not, as a rule, return to the mind, and so love cannot arise from it.

(b) Where love gets its name

Love gets its name (*amor*) from the word for hook (*amus*), which means 'to capture' or 'to be captured', for he who is in love is captured in the chains of desire and wishes to capture someone else with his hook. Just as a skilful fisherman tries to attract fishes by his bait and to capture them on his crooked hook, so the man who is a captive of love tries to attract another person by his allurements and exerts all his efforts to unite two different hearts with an intangible bond, or if they are already united he tries to keep them so forever.

(c) What the effect of love is

Now it is the effect of love that a true lover cannot be degraded with any avarice. Love causes a rough and uncouth man to be distinguished for his handsomeness; it can endow a man even of the humblest birth with nobility of character; it blesses the proud with humility; and the man in love becomes accustomed to performing many services gracefully for everyone. O what a wonderful thing is love, which makes a man shine with so many virtues and teaches everyone, no matter who he is, so many good traits of character! There is another thing about love that we should not praise in few words: it adorns a man, so to speak, with the virtue of chastity, because he who shines with the light of one love can hardly think of embracing another woman, even a beautiful one. For when he thinks deeply of his beloved the sight of any other woman seems to his mind rough and rude.

I wish you therefore to keep always in mind, Walter my friend, that if love were so fair as always to bring his sailors into the quiet port after they had been soaked by many tempests, I would bind myself to serve him forever. But because he is in the habit of carrying an unjust weight in his hand, I do not have full confidence in him any more than I do in a judge whom men suspect. And so for the present I refuse to submit to his judgement, because 'he often leaves his sailors in the mighty waves'. But why love, at times, does not use fair weights I shall show you more fully elsewhere in this treatise.

6 THE WRITING OF LOVE LETTERS

Text from: Boncompagno da Signa (1975) *Rota Veneris*, ed. and transl. J. Purkart, Scholars' Facsimiles and Reprints, New York: Delmar, pp. 77–8, 83–4.

Boncompagno da Signa (*c.* 1170–*c.* 1250) was an Italian professor of rhetoric, who studied at the University of Bologna, then travelled widely in Italy and abroad. Boncompagno claimed to be the first doctor of the *ars dictaminis* (the art of composition) in the University of Bologna, and composed numerous guides to the new more practical rhetoric which was needed by the legal profession and the civil service. The *Rota Veneris*

(Wheel of Venus) is a collection of letters for all occasions, demonstrating the use and effectiveness of rhetoric for both men and women. The first extract gives a letter suitable to send to any lady as the first move in a courtship. The imagery of the letter draws heavily on the Song of Songs, while the catalogue structure, praising the lady's charms, starting at the head and working downwards, was the prescribed method for describing a person, and corresponds closely to the second stage of meditation in love described by Andreas Capellanus above. The second extract presupposes that a lady has refused to marry her lover, who has taken another as wife, only for her to have second thoughts when she realizes her predicament.

(a) The commendation of women

'When I saw you the day before yesterday among the glorious entourage of maidens with my corporeal eyes, a certain spark of love took hold of my heart and, in an instant, made me another person. Nor am I what I had been, nor could I be anything else. No wonder; for to me and to the entire world it seemed far from doubt that you shone forth from amongst all like the morning star which, like a herald, seems to promise the dawn of day. And while I intently examined how much glory Nature had bestowed upon you, my spirit, in enrapturement, was overwhelmed. For the strands of your hair flowed down like braided gold over your most delicately reddened ears; your forehead was noble, and your eyebrows like gem-encrusted hinges; like two stars, your eyes were shining forth most brightly, and through their splendour all parts of your body were lent radiant light. Your straight nostrils, your sensuous and ruby lips vied with your ivory teeth; your smooth neck and whitest throat doubled, for the beholder, a beauty which, I think, could never have been intended more for Helena [of Troy]. Your bosom rose above your body like a garden of paradise, in which lay two apples like bundles of roses, from which wafted the sweetest perfume. Your shoulders rested like sockets of gold, into which your arms, like boughs of cedar, were fitted naturally. Your long hands, your slender fingers, your well-shaped knuckles, and your nails, resplendent as crystal, enhanced the seemliness of your whole figure. But in truth, since he who praises is more likely to be lacking than is the immensity of beauty he is praising, I shall turn my pen towards the magnitude of your wisdom, for which I cannot but have admiration. For there are men who, although they enjoy the convenience of beauty, are not, however, adorned with wisdom; and then there are others to whom Nature has granted the endowment of wisdom, but has denied the beauty of appearance; but in you everything has mingled without flaw, so that time and time again my mind has led me to this conclusion: that I should deem you in possession of divine quality. But nevertheless, I humbly submit myself to your greatness, that you might deign to instruct me, your servant, because I am willing to entrust my very self and all my own to your every wish.'

And keep in mind that, by changing one phrase, this letter may be altered in such a way that it can be sent to any virgin, married woman, widow, nun, and deflowered female; only that where, in the beginning, it states 'of maidens', it should read 'of ladies'. For nuns, too, should be addressed as ladies in the salutations no less than in all parts of the letter, since, if you were to call them nuns or sisters, it would more than likely redound to their disgrace than to their honour.

(b) An awkward situation

Suppose that, before the man weds [another], she becomes pregnant; thus she shall write to her lover as follows:

'I was safe in the house of my father, and most pleasing in the sight of both my parents, when, through entrapping flatteries of adulation, you dragged me all too carelessly into the noose of deception. Now, however, I dare not divulge to anyone the cause of my suffering. And nonetheless it is known in the streets what in secret we have done: the complexion pales, the belly swells, the gates of chastity stand open; rumour vaunts abroad, I am torn asunder without remission. I am subject to lashings, I long for death. There is no grief like unto my grief, for I have lost my reputation and honour with the flower of my virginity. And, in addition to my unspeakable torments, you have become a complete stranger to me; nor are you in the least mindful of her, to whom you used to promise seas and mountains of gold and all else that is contained within the circuit of the sky. With like snares a birdcatcher deceives birds, and the fish is drawn out of the sea with such a hook. But nothing I put forth in writing profits me; for he who falls from on high falls irremediably, and in vain seeks remedy where danger preceded. Come aid me, finally, I beseech you; and, even if you are unwilling to offer assistance, at least behold how I die for you – and would that I could die! For it would be a lesser evil to die than to live for all time in disgrace.'

The man's response:

'Before I took a wife, you consistently refused to have me as a husband; now, however, how could I possibly condescend to your wishes, since I have a most elegant wife, adorned with abundant beauty? So desist from such ways and examine within yourself those words again. For I think another is responsible for making your ship dock in the port of disgrace.'

7 LOVE BETWEEN WOMEN

Text from: MS München, Clm 19411, fols. 69r–70r, no. VII, 12th/13th century, from Tegernsee. Translation from: P. Dronke (1966) *Medieval Latin and the Rise of European Love Lyric*, vol. II, Oxford: Oxford University Press, p. 481.

This poem is clearly written from a woman to a woman and, as Dronke says, 'seems to presuppose a passionate physical relationship' (1966 II: 482).

To G———, her one-and-only rose,
from A——— the bond of precious love.
What strength have I, that I may bear it,
that I may have patience while you are gone?
Is my strength that of stones
that I should wait for your return,
I who do not cease to ache night and day,
like one who lacks both hand and foot?
Without you all that is joyous and delightful
becomes like mud trodden underfoot,
instead of rejoicing I shed tears,
my spirit never appears joyful.
When I remember the kisses you gave,
and with what words of joy you caressed my little breasts,
I want to die
as I am not allowed to see you.
What shall I, unhappiest [of women], do?
Where shall I, the poorest [of women], turn?
Oh if my body had been consigned to the earth
till your longed-for return,
or if Habakkuk's trance-journey came upon me,
that I might once come to see
my lover's face –
then I'd not care if in that hour I should die!
For in the world there is no woman born
so lovable, so dear,
one who loves me
without feigning, with such deep love.
So I shall not cease to feel the endless pain
till I win the sight of you again.
Indeed, as a certain wise man says, it is a great misery
for a man not to be
with him without whom he cannot be.
While the world lasts,
you'll never be effaced from the centre of my heart.
Why say more?
Return, sweet love!
Do not delay your journey longer,
know that I cannot bear your absence longer.

Farewell,
remember me!

8 THE ARCHPRIEST OF HITA

Text from: Archpriest of Hita (1970) *The Book of Good Love*, transl. R. Mignani and M. A. di Cesare, Albany, N.Y.: State University of New York Press, pp. 287–8, 205–7.

Il Libro de Buen Amor is a narrative poem of 1728 lines written some time in the fourteenth century by Juan Ruiz, the Archpriest of Hita, a town to the northeast of Madrid. Juan is the protagonist of the work, which recounts his amours, and a number of fables and moral tales. In this extract, an affair with a nun has come to an end when the lady dies. The Archpriest asks his go-between, Trotaconventos (Convent-hopper) to assist. The Mooress answers the importuner in Arabic.

(a) The Archpriest and the Mooress

To forget my grief and sorrow, I asked my old woman to try to find a mistress for me. She spoke to a Mooress, who did not want to listen to her. She acted wisely, and I wrote many songs.

Trotaconventos said to the Mooress on my behalf: 'Hello my friend! How long is it since I saw you last? Nobody can get to see you. Why are you this way? A new love greets you.'

The Mooress said, 'lês nedrí' (I don't know).

'Daughter, a man from Alcalá sends you many greetings and a robe together with this note. God is with you, because this man is very well-to-do. Accept it, my child.'

The Mooress said, 'lâ wah llâh' (Be quiet!)

'Daughter, may the Creator give you peace and health! Do not disdain it, for I could not carry more. I bring you a good gift; speak to me kindly; do not send me away without an answer.'

The Mooress said, 'uskut' (Be quiet!)

When the old woman saw that she could not accomplish anything there, she said, 'I see that I have wasted my words; since you will not say anything else to me, I will go away.'

The Mooress nodded and said, 'imâsí' (Go away!)

(b) The Archpriest and the mountain girl

The Archpriest is travelling over the mountains where he meets a succession of ugly and sexually voracious shepherdesses. His description is a fine example of the 'Loathly Lady' motif which appears widely in medieval literature; Bloch (1991) discusses the interconnectedness of courtly and misogynistic discourse. Here it is important to note that the Archpriest's views are as much rooted in town–country and class antagonisms as gender hostility.

Hills and mountains are always harsh; either it's snowing or the ground is icy; it is never warm. At the top of this pass, an icy wind was blowing the hail and snow. Since one doesn't feel as cold when one is running, I trotted down the slope, saying, 'If you hit the tower, the stone falls, not the falcon. I am lost if God doesn't help me.'

Never in my whole life had I been in such danger from the cold. I descended the pass and found at the bottom of it a strange monster, the most fantastic thing I had ever seen – a muscular shepherdess, a horrible creature to look upon. But in my fear of the weather and the bitter cold, I asked her for a day's lodging. She said she would put me up if I paid her well. I thanked God for that, and she took me to Tablada.

She had a figure and limbs that were fantastic, I tell you; she was built like a mare. Wrestling with her couldn't possibly come off well; one could hardly lay her against her will either. In his Apocalypse, St John the Evangelist never envisioned such a prodigious creature. She could tumble with, or beat off, a whole crowd, though I cannot imagine what devil would lust after such a monster.

Her head was huge and shapeless; her hair was short, black and straight as a magpie's; her eyes sunken and red, and shortsighted. She left a footprint bigger than a bear's and had the ears of a yearling donkey. Her short, thick neck was dark and hairy. Her nose was long, like the bill of a whimbrel; and she could have drunk her way through a large pool of water in a few days. She had the mouth of a hound-dog set in a fat, dumpy face, with great long teeth, irregular and horsy. Listen to me, anyone who has marriage in mind! She had thick eyebrows, blacker than those of a thrush, and a heavy growth of beard around her mouth. I saw no more, but if you dig deeper you will find many more strange qualities. I am sure though you would be better off minding your own business.

In fact I did see her legs, up to the knees: large bones, huge shanks, all scarred and burned; ankles thicker than those of a full-grown calf. Her wrist was broader than my hand. Her hand was covered with long, coarse hair, and was always wet. Her loud hoarse voice would deafen anyone; her speech was slow and harsh, hollow and graceless. Her little finger was larger than my thumb; imagine what the others were like! If she should ever try to delouse you, your scalp would think her fingers were tree-trunks. Her breasts hung down over her dress to her waist, even though they were folded over; otherwise they would have reached her hips. They would keep time to the guitar without lessons. Her ribs protruded so far out of her black chest that I could count them two and three times even from a distance.

Now I tell you that I saw nothing else; and I will say no more, for an evil-tongued young man is no good as a messenger. I wrote three songs about what she said and how ugly she looked, but I could hardly do justice to her.

9 *IL DOLCE STIL NUOVO*

(a) Petrarch: *Rime*

Text from: *Sonnets for Laura* (n.d.), transl. G. R. Nicholson, London: Autolycus Press, pp. 18, 20.

Francesco Petrarca was born in Arezzo, Italy, in 1304. His parents were exiles from Florence, and moved to Avignon, at the time the seat of the papacy, in 1312. Petrarca studied law in Montpellier and Bologna, returning to France at the age of 22. It was in 1327 that Petrarca first saw Laura (possibly Laure de Noves, wife of Hugues de Noves) and, apparently, fell immediately in love. Although she rejected his advances, he remained faithful until her death twenty-one years later. Petrarca wrote 297 sonnets, most of which are about his lady, both before and after her death. Some have doubted whether Laura ever existed, or, if she did, whether Petrarca knew her any more intimately than Dante did Beatrice. The two sonnets reproduced here were well known to contemporaries: 132 is the source of Troilus's love-song in Book 1 of Chaucer's *Troilus and Criseyde*; 159 draws on neoplatonic diction for its effect.

Sonnet 132

If love it be not, what is this I feel?
If love it be, it is what kind of thing?
If good, then why so deadly is its sting?
If ill, why sweet to suffer on its wheel?
If willingly I burn, is my pain real?
If not, what use is all my murmuring?
O living death, O pains that pleasure bring!
How, unconsenting, am I brought to heel?
If I consent, I have no right to curse.
Amid such adverse winds in barque so slight
Without a helm, I sail on stormy seas,
Burdened with error, but of wisdom light,
So that I know not what desires I nurse,
I burn in winter and in summer freeze.

Sonnet 159

In what Idea, where in the firmament
Did Nature find the model whence she made
That lovely face, and here on earth displayed

Such handiwork as is heaven's ornament?
What fountain nymph, what woodland sylph unpent
Such golden locks as hers, freed from their braid?
When were such virtues in one heart arrayed?
Although the highest one my doom has meant.
He who has never gazed upon her eyes
Can never see heaven's beauty here below,
For in no other's glance such sweetness lies.
How love can cure and kill he cannot know
Who has not heard the music of her sighs,
Heard her sweet voice and her sweet laughter flow.

(b) Dante: from *La Vita Nuova*

Text from: Dante Alighieri (1969) *La Vita Nuova*, transl. B. Reynolds, Harmondsworth: Penguin, pp. 76, 99.

Dante (1265–1321) was 9 years old when he first saw Beatrice Portinari, who was just 8 years old. Dante sought her out to gaze at during his boyhood, but it was not until nine years later that Beatrice greeted him when she met him one day in the street. Dante was so overcome by this that he retreated to his room to meditate on Beatrice. He continued to love her from afar until her death in 1290, at the age of 24. *La Vita Nuova*, probably composed *c*. 1294 is a poetic treatise presenting and explaining the poems which Dante wrote for Beatrice. The information about Dante's love for Beatrice is drawn from *La Vita Nuova*; much may be fictional. The imagery of both Sonnets 15 and 25 (the last in the *Vita*) looks forward to Beatrice's role in the *Paradiso*.

Sonnet 15

So deeply to be reverenced, so fair,
My lady is when she her smile bestows,
All sound of speaking falters to a close
And eyes which would behold her do not dare.
Of praises sung of her she is aware,
Yet clad in sweet humility she goes.
A thing from Heaven sent, to all she shows
A miracle in which the world may share.
Her beauty entering the beholder's eye
Brings sweetness to the heart, all sweets above:
None comprehends who does not know this state;
And from her lips there seems to emanate
A gentle spirit, full of tender love,
Which to the soul enraptured whispers: 'Sigh!'

Sonnet 25

Beyond the widest of the circling spheres
A sigh which leaves my heart aspires to move.
A new celestial influence which Love
Bestows on it by virtue of his tears
Impels it ever upwards. As it nears
Its goal of longing in the realms above
The pilgrim spirit sees a vision of
A soul in glory whom the host reveres.
Gazing at her, it speaks of what it sees
In subtle words I do not comprehend
Within my heart forlorn which bids it tell.
That noble one is named, I apprehend,
For frequently it mentions Beatrice;
This much, beloved ladies, I know well.

10 AN *ALBA* (DAWN-SONG)

Text from: Dafydd ap Gwilym (1982) *Poems*, ed. and transl. R. Bromwich, Llandysul, Dyfed: Gomer Press, pp. 146–8.

Little is known about Dafydd ap Gwilym. He came from the area of Dyfed in Wales, though he travelled widely throughout the country. Most of his poems seem to date from the middle of the fourteenth century. Dafydd succeeded in integrating the elements of continental courtly-love poetry into traditional Welsh bardic forms. This poem takes the form of the courtly *alba* (dawn-song) in which the girl has to urge her reluctant lover to depart now the sun is up and discovery likely. Confusion between the sun and moon, and the lark and the nightingale, are traditional: less so are the fighting dogs and croaking ravens depicted here. The briskness of the girl's tone and the discussion of the poet's ability to run faster than savage dogs suggests a parody of the well-known genre.

Parting at dawn (Y wawr)

I sighed deeply [at the thought of it]:
so long a night the night that was before the last;
that night, my modest brilliant love,
a single night, my darling, was a week;
and yet, a judge would say, a maid
shortens the night, who utters no word of denial.

Last night, I was in strange perplexity:
[with] fair Nia, [lighted by] the heaven's candle,
insisting on repayment for my sleeplessness,
with complete respect on the side of the girl.

When my grip was at its strongest,
my mettle at its best – she had dark brows –
the coverlet above [us], and my zest most eager –
alas! good God, behold the dawn of day.

'Get up,' the maid said, in her brightly-coloured robe,
'hide this; see there the lively sign –
your love brings grievous weeping;
be off with you to the devil – see, it is now day.'

[HE]: 'Good maiden, tall and stately, slender, perfect beauty,
that is not true: better [interpret] thus,
it is the moon which the Lord God has given,
and stars there are surrounding her.
If indisputably I lay this down,
[only] imagination is it that it's dawn.'

[SHE]: 'Assuredly, if that were true,
why is the raven croaking up above?'

[HE]: 'Vermin are attempting there
to kill her – keeping her from sleep.'

[SHE]: 'Hounds are baying in the hamlet yonder,
and others too are fighting with each other.'

[HE]: 'Believe me, my denial [comes] near [the mark],
it is the Hounds of Night cause this distress.'

[SHE]: 'Cease your excuses, lad of poetry,
a shallow mind puts pain afar,
it is now high time for you to start
[and] to set forth on some adventurous raid today.
For Christ's sake, get up quietly,
and open yonder heavy door.
Take very large strides with both your feet,
the hounds are most importunate; run off to the wood.'

[HE]: 'Alas, the thicket is not far,
and I run quicker than a hound;
unless a sly one sees me, I shall not be caught,
if God allows it so, on that [short] space of ground.'

[SHE]: 'Tell me, good devoted poet,
for God's sake, shall you come here [again]?'

[HE]: 'I am your nightingale, and I shall come
assuredly my dear, when the night comes.'

11 A WOMAN POET CELEBRATES THE FEMALE GENITALS

Text from: D. Johnston (1991) *Medieval Welsh Erotic Poetry*, Cardiff: Tafol, pp. 41–3.

Little is known about Gwerful Mechain except that she seems to have been born around 1460–3 and have died around 1500 (Lloyd-Morgan 1993: 191). Gwerful's poetry has been excluded from many anthologies of Welsh verse on the grounds that it is salacious; certainly the viewpoint in her work is indisputably female. This poem seems to be a counterpart to Dafydd ap Gwilym's well-known poem to his penis, except that, unlike Dafydd's poem, it does not brag about sexual voracity, but is rather celebratory in tone.

The female genitals (Cywydd y cedor)

Every foolish drunken poet,
boorish vanity without ceasing
(never may I warrant it,
I of great noble stock),
has always declaimed fruitless praise
in song of the girls of the lands
all day long, certain gift,
most incompletely, by God the Father:
praising the hair, gown of fine love,
and every such living girl,
and lower down praising merrily
the brows above the eyes;
praising also, lovely shape,
the smoothness of the soft breasts,
and the beauty's arms, bright drape,
she deserved honour, and the girl's hands.
Then with his finest wizardry
before night he did sing,
he pays homage to God's greatness,
fruitless eulogy with his tongue:
leaving the middle without praise
and the place where children are conceived,
and the warm quim, clear excellence,
tender and fat, bright fervent broken circle,
where I loved, in perfect health,
the quim below the smock.
You are a body of boundless strength,
a faultless court of fat's plumage.
I declare, the quim is fair,
circle of broad-edged lips,

71

it is a valley longer than spoon or a hand,
a ditch to hold a penis two hands long;
cunt there by the swelling arse,
song's table with its double in red.
And the bright saints, men of the church,
when they get the chance, perfect gift,
don't fail, highest blessing,
by Beuno, to give it a good feel.   [Beuno: a Welsh saint]
For this reason, thorough rebuke,
all you proud poets,
let songs to the quim circulate
without fail to gain reward.
Sultan of an ode, it is silk,
little seam, curtain on a fine bright cunt,
flaps in a place of greeting,
the sour grove, it is full of love,
very proud forest, faultless gift,
tender frieze, fur of a fine pair of testicles,
a girl's thick grove, circle of precious greeting,
lovely bush, God save it.

12 THE DANGERS OF COURTLY LOVE

Text adapted from: *Book of the Knight of the Tour-Landry* (1971), transl. William Caxton, ed. M. Y. Offord, EETS SS2, Oxford: Oxford University Press, pp. 164–5, 167, 172.

The Knight and his lady are discussing the practices of courtly love for the benefit of his daughters, for whom the *Book* was written. Here the Knight plays devil's advocate, advancing an extreme version of the literary 'code of courtly love'; arguing that women should take lovers and thus they would encourage men to glorious and knightly deeds, a notion which his wife firmly rejects on both moral and pragmatic grounds.

Then your mother answered me, 'Sire, I marvel me not if among you men, [some] sustain and hold this reason that all women ought to love paramours. But since this debate and strife has come before our own daughters, I will answer according to my views and intention, for from our children we must hide nothing. You say, and so do all other men, that a lady or demoiselle is the better worth when she loves paramours, and that she shall be the more gay and of fair manner and countenance, and how she shall do great charitable acts in making a good knight. These words are but sport and amusement for lords and for men, and very common in language. For they that say that all the honour and worship which they get and have is coming to them by their paramours, and that their love encourages them to go on voyages and in order to please them they take up arms. But these words cost them but little to say for to get the better and sooner the grace and good will of their paramours, for such words and other very marvellous ones, many a man uses very often, but in the end they [the men] say that it is for them [the ladies] and their love that they have done it. In good faith, they have only done it to enhance themselves and to draw to them the grace and vainglory of the world. Therefore I charge you my fair daughters that in this matter you do not believe your father, but I pray you that you hold yourselves cleanly and without blame and that you be not amorous for many reasons which I shall rehearse unto you.

First, I say not but that every woman of age may love well and better, the one rather than the other, that is to say folk of worship and honour. And them also that shall counsel her for her own health and worship. And men ought to love in this way, one more than other. But as for being so far enamoured, to such an extent that this love is master of her and makes them fall into some foul and shameful delight, sometimes with right and sometimes with wrong – men have put a watch on this shameful deed or feat for it causes such dishonour and scandal which is not soon put out. And by the false watches and backbiters which never cease to talk of some evil rather than some good, whereby they take away and defame the good renown of the good women and many a good lady. And therefore all women who are not wedded should keep and hold themselves from it.

And so that you should not be deceived keep yourselves away from talking with them, and someone begins to argue and to talk with you of such matter [i.e. of love] leave him alone or else call to you somebody else to hear him say what he will. And thus you shall void and break his talking. And know this for certain that if you do thus once or twice he shall no more speak to you thereof, but in good faith at the last he shall praise and dread you and shall say "This woman is assured and firm". And by this way of behaving, you shall not be put in their janglery and talking and will not have blame or defame of the world.'

The Knight has suggested having lovers after marriage.

LADY: And therefore there is great peril to every wedded woman to put her lord and his estate and the wealth and joy of her marriage in this balance and in such perilous adventure, wherefore I counsel not to any good woman that she have any paramour, nor be amorous in so much that she be subject to another than to her lord, for by such a cause many good marriages have been left and forgotten and for one [good] word that is come thereof, a hundred evils come of it, I shall tell you one example of those who are dead and have ended their lives by the perils which be in foolish love. The lady of Coussy and her paramour died thereof, as did the Castellaine of the Verger, and after her the Duchess.

> The Chatelain of Coucy was a knight who died in the crusades. He had his heart sent home to the lady he loved, thus revealing the affair to her husband. He has the heart served to his wife, who, after eating it and learning the truth, starves herself to death. The Chatelaine of Vergi and the Duchess of Burgundy are characters in the romance *La Chatelaine de Vergi*. The chatelaine loves and is loved by a knight; if he reveals their secret he will lose her love. The chatelaine sends a little dog to signal their rendezvous. The duchess tries to seduce him unsuccessfully then denounces him to the duke. The knight reveals his secret to the duke, who swears not to tell; the duke tells the duchess who then tells the chatelaine. The chatelaine dies of a broken heart while the knight kills himself. The duke murders the duchess and goes into exile. The two stories are classic love tragedies, thoughtfully discussed in Bloch 1991: 114–42.

13 A THWARTED AFFAIR

Text from: Margery Kempe (1940) *The Book of Margery Kempe*, ed. H. E. Allen and Sanford Meech, EETS, Oxford: Oxford University Press, pp. 14–15.

See p. 34 above for Margery's life. This extract comes from a period in Margery's life where she is being subjected to temptations to test her faith. As always, Margery refers to herself in the third person, as 'this creature'.

In the second year of her temptations it fell so that a man which she loved well said to her on St Margaret's eve before evensong that for anything he would lie with her and have his lust of her body, and she should not resist him, for, if he could not have his will that time, he said, he should else have it another time, she should not choose. And he did it to test her to see what she would do, but she thought that he meant it quite seriously at that time, and she said very little to him. So they parted for the occasion and went both to hear evensong, for her church was of St Margaret.

This woman was so laboured with the man's words that she could not hear her evensong, nor say her Paternoster, or think any other good thought, but was more laboured than ever she was before. The Devil put in her mind that God had forsaken her, and else she should not be so tempted. She believed the Devil's persuasions and began to consent because she could not think any good thoughts. Therefore she thought that God had forsaken her. And, when evensong was done, she went to [say to] the man aforesaid that he should have his lust, as she thought he desired, but he made such dissimulation that she could not know his intent, and so they parted asunder for the night. This creature was so laboured and vexed all that night that she had no idea what she should do. She lay with her husband and to have sex with him was so abominable to her that she could not bear it, and yet it was permitted to her as being a lawful time, if she had wanted to. But ever she was concerned with the other man to sin with him, inasmuch as he had spoken to her. At last through the inopportunity of temptation and lacking of discretion she was overcome and consented in her mind, and went to the man to know if he would consent to her then.

And he said that he would not for all the goods in this world; he had rather be chopped up as small as meat for the pot. She went away all ashamed and confused in herself, seeing his stableness and her unstableness.

14 A VALENTINE LETTER

Text adapted from: *Paston Letters* (1958), selected and ed. N. Davis, Oxford: Clarendon Press, pp. 105–6.

For an account of the Paston Letters, see p. 36 above. Here Margery Brews writes to John Paston III, son of Margaret and John Paston I. Marriage negotiations are in train between the two families, and the Pastons are making difficulties over the size of Margery's dowry. Margery writes encouragingly to her future husband, sending Valentine greetings. The letter is written by a clerk, a trusted family retainer who was also involved in the marriage negotiations, and the date is February 1477. Through the uncooperative behaviour of John's brother, John II, and the meanness of Margery's father the match nearly came to grief, but the couple did in fact finally marry.

Unto my right wellbeloved Valentine, John Paston, Esquire, be this bill delivered.

Right reverent and worshipful and right well beloved Valentine, I recommend myself unto you full heartily, desiring to hear of your welfare, which I beseech Almighty God long to preserve unto his pleasure and your hearts desire. And if it please you to hear of my welfare, I am not in good health of body nor of heart, nor shall be till I hear from you;

For there knows no creature what pain I endure,

And for to be dead, I dare not disclose it.

And my lady mother has laboured the matter to my father very diligently, but she can get no more than you know of, for which God knows I am full sorry.

But if you love me, as I trust verily that you do, you will not leave me on this account; for if you had not half the livelihood which you have, to do the greatest labour that any woman alive could do, I would not forsake you.

And if you command me to keep true wherever I go,

Certainly I will do all my might to love you and never no mo[re].

And if my friends say I do amiss, they shall not hinder me so to do,

My heart bids me ever more to love you

Truly above all earthly things.

And however angry they may be, I trust it shall be better in times coming.

No more to you at this time, but the Holy Trinity have you in safekeeping.

And I beseech you that this bill be not seen by any earthly creature, save only yourself etc. And this letter was endited at Topcroft with a full heavy heart. By your own M. B.

15 A SPANISH WOMAN POET

Text from: J. Snow (1984) 'The Spanish Love Poet: Florencía Pinar', in K. M. Wilson (ed.) *Medieval Women Writers*, Manchester: Manchester University Press, p. 330.

Florencía Pinar is thought to have lived in the late fifteenth century at the court of Ferdinand and Isabella. She is obviously well-educated. Two other songs by her survive in song collections.

Song by Florencía Pinar

Love wields so many artful ruses
that all who 'gainst them are not clever
find Love's subtle subterfuges,
once in the heart, are there forever.

Love, when clearly, rightly seen,
resembles most that cancerous form
of nature, the snaking delving worm,
ravager of all that's whole and clean.
Of his tricks and of his rages,
the storms of protest never lessen.
(Lovers learn): Love's subterfuges
once in the heart, are there forever.

3

MOTHERHOOD AND WORK

INTRODUCTION

A second reason why,
As is known both far and wide,
One should honour women all
Is that men, both great and small,
Of humble rank or high,
Were born of women – that's no lie!
('Le Bien des Fames', ll.19–24)

Women work so many marvels
That I could only tell you half,
Unless I laboured at the task.
With women we are blessed,
By their work we are dressed;
They spin, weave, and prepare
The clothes that people wear.
('Le Bien des Fames', ll.80–6)

Motherhood

Why did God create women? Not to keep men company, for, as Augustine observed (see above p. 17), that objective could have been better achieved by giving Adam a male companion, but rather so that the earth should be populated with souls for God. Procreation might have been differently arranged before the Fall; sexual intercourse would have proceeded in a sinless and rational fashion, unaccompanied by the dangerous stirrings of will and desire, as Augustine held (Pagels 1988: 110–12), but there was no doubt that procreation, through the union of a man with a woman, was God's intention from the start. 'I do not see in what sense the woman was made as a helper for the man if not for the sake of bearing children,' Augustine comments (cited from Blamires 1992: 79). Previously Saint Paul had made it clear in the First Epistle to Timothy that the primary function of the woman is to give birth to and nurture children: 'Notwithstanding she shall be saved in childbearing, if they continue in faith and charity and holiness with sobriety' (I Timothy 2: 14).

Women expected, and were expected, to be mothers; the Dominican Nicholas of Gorran (d. 1295) said that a wife should 'generate children continually until her death' (Vecchio 1992: 121). However, as a popular misogynist trope first found in Jerome and endlessly repeated in medieval writing has it, wives had to be accepted faults and all:

If she has a bad temper or is a fool, if she has a blemish or is proud, or has bad breath, whatever her fault may be – all this we learn after marriage. Horses, asses, cattle, dogs, even slaves of the smallest worth, clothes, kettles, wooden seats, cups, and earthenware pitchers, are first tried and then bought: a wife is the only thing that is not shown before she is married, for fear that she may not give satisfaction.

(*Adversus Joviniam* I.47, cited from Blamires 1992: 71)

The demand for virginity in a bride in order to ensure that the family's property would be inherited in the paternal line meant that, in most cases, a bride's fertility could not be tested before the commitment to marriage – and childlessness was not considered a ground for annulment or divorce unless it could be shown that consummation had never taken place. This provision was a concern of the noble and bourgeois classes rather than the peasantry, however; Barbara Hanawalt suggests that there was little concern among prospective husbands in rural communities about marrying a virgin; studies of later peasant communities have even suggested that, since children were vital to the peasant household economy, proof of the woman's fertility might have been necessary for a marriage to take place at all (Hanawalt 1986a: 196).

Bearing healthy children was the ambition of the medieval married woman. Fertility could be problematic: in times of famine women might be too malnourished, overworked or anaemic to ovulate properly. Recipes and charms for getting children were abundant, if not always effective or pleasant. Margherita Datini's sister, Francesca, living in Florence, offers advice to her childless sister:

Many women here are with child. . . . I went to inquire and found out the remedy they have used: a poultice, which they put on their bellies. So I went to the woman and besought her to make me one. She says she will do so gladly, but it must be in winter. . . . She has never put it on any woman who did not conceive, but she says it stinks so much, that there have been husbands who have thrown it away. So discover from Francesco if he would have you wear it. The cost is not great.

(Origo 1959: 160)

We do not know whether Margherita tried the evil-smelling poultice or not, but she remained childless. In the case of the Datinis, the problem in fertility was Margherita's for her husband fathered a number of illegitimate children by his household slaves and servants. One of these, Ginevra, was eventually taken into the household and brought up as the couple's daughter; she was given a dowry at marriage, but did not inherit any of her father's estate.

Although medical writers were well aware that fertility problems could lie with both husband and wife – John of Gaddesden's *Rosa Anglica*, an early fourteenth-century survey of medical topics, defines sterility as 'a certain ill disposition by reason of which a man may not generate or a woman may not conceive' – in practice it was the woman who was held to be defective. In addition to the malnutrition mentioned above, women were likely to sustain injuries and infections in previous childbirths which might damage their fertility. Not insignificant in the social construction of sterility is the ancient tradition of gynaecological writing; such treatises, in the act of problematizing women's reproductive functions, defined giving birth as the work which women did, the counterpart of men's labour in economic activity (Cadden 1993: 249). Failure to bear a son was almost tantamount to sterility for many women. Charms and medical recipes for procuring a son were abundant: 'So that a woman may conceive a male; let her take and eat the testicles of a cock' runs one prescription from a Viennese miscellany (Cadden 1993: 257). Other aids to giving birth to a son may have been more successful: a desperate Spanish woman who wanted a son promised her child to St Dominic. When she gave birth to a girl she complained to the saint and the girl miraculously became a boy (Shahar 1992: 45).

When conception was successful, the care of the mother during pregnancy and parturition was essentially women's work (though see Green 1989). Midwives advised and attended the expectant mother; female friends and relatives would arrive for the birth, their entertainment constituting a considerable expense for the new father. Being a midwife was a high-status occupation for women: in late medieval Nuremberg a midwife earned as much as a male craftsman or journeyman. She was assumed to be literate too: the influential midwife's manual *Den Swangern frawne und hebammen Roszgarten* (The Rosegarden for Pregnant Women and Midwives) was first published in Nuremberg in 1513. This gives detailed information about normal and abnormal pregnancies, signs of labour, how to ease the birth, and courses of action for when the child appears to be dead inside the mother, or, in cases where the mother is dead, but the child alive, how to perform a Caesarean section. Mothers in Nuremberg gave birth on a birthing stool, a chair with back support and a hollowed-out seat, and the midwife would normally sit in front ready to catch the baby (Wiesner 1986: 99–105) (Fig. 6). In most depictions of childbirth the mother is shown in bed, recovering after the event, while the midwives wash the child, so we cannot be sure which other positions were used. Childbirth, and the immediate postnatal period, was highly dangerous for both mother and infant. As Merry Wiesner observes, 'no matter how skilled the midwife, the basic techniques and anatomical knowledge were the same as those used 1500 years earlier' (Wiesner 1986: 104). Twenty per cent of all married women who died in Florence in 1424 between the ages of 25 and 30 died in childbirth (Shahar 1992: 35).

If mother and child survived the birth, the next decision was how the child should be nursed. In southern Europe, in aristocratic, and, increasingly, bourgeois families the child was given to a wet-nurse. In the very richest families the nurse would live in the family home, but in the majority of cases the child lived in the nurse's own home for the first couple of years of its life. Why did mothers not nurse their babies

Figure 6 A pregnant woman undergoing treatment with coriander. *Above*: one woman prepares a potion to administer to a baby while another pregnant woman looks on enquiringly. From Pseudo-Apuleius, *De Herbarium Virtutibus*, Codex Vindobonensis 93, fol. 102v, Bildarchiv der Österreichischen Nationalbibliothek, Vienna.

themselves? Some were incapable of providing enough milk to nourish them, while others may have wished to be free of the messiness of looking after a very small child. Most importantly, however, breast-feeding offers partial contraceptive protection: the quicker a woman's milk dried up the sooner she would be ready to conceive again. Conversely, when a new pregnancy began, breast-milk would cease anyway, and a nurse would need to be found for any infant who was too young to be weaned – feeding with animal milk was both unhygienic and held to be barbaric. Having a wet-nurse was a mark of status, and, in the disease-ridden cities of late medieval Italy and France, sending the child out into the countryside to get milk from a well-nourished and healthy young woman may have increased its chances of survival. Sending the child away thus did not imply that the parents did not care for it. The ideal nurse was young and healthy, having recently given birth, preferably to a child that had died. In theory, the nurse's morals were also important: the Church was equivocal about wet-nursing, believing that the child partook of the nurse's characteristics through the milk. So well-established was the custom, however, and such the difficulty in finding nurses, that Florentine fathers, who were usually responsible for negotiating the nurse's services with her husband, do not seem to have worried too much about the nurse's morals, provided the milk was 'young' (Klapisch-Zuber 1985: 141). In northern Europe there seems to have been a general assumption that women of all classes would nurse their children themselves (Biller 1992: 80–1).

We have relatively good evidence for wet-nursing practices, because of the documentary evidence involved in hiring the nurse and paying her salary. However, the majority of medieval women breast-fed their own children for as long as they could; parents from the peasant and lower bourgeois classes could not afford the alternative. The mother was held legally responsible for the child for the first seven years of its life; she was the primary carer while the father was at work outside the family home and yard (Shahar 1992: 116). However, the mother could not always watch the child throughout its infancy: her domestic responsibilities, other economically productive activities notwithstanding, meant that child-minding was often delegated to the baby's siblings. Babies were swaddled after christening and sometimes tied to their cradles to prevent them from straying. While this may have preserved them from some kinds of accidents, many peasant babies died from fires in their cradles, often caused by the chickens who pecked around the hearth, picking up burning twigs or straw and dropping them in the cradle, placed nearby for warmth. Other accidents happened at harvest-time: the importance of getting the crop in meant that all pairs of hands were occupied in the fields and even less attention than usual was paid to very small children (Hanawalt 1986a: 175–6).

Some scholars have supposed that the high rate of infant mortality in the medieval period meant that parents could not afford the emotional investment in each child which modern parents make: 'parents did not treat the child as an individual but erected emotional barriers against any attachment to the tiny creatures whose chances of survival were very slim', as Shahar summarizes these arguments (Shahar 1992: 2). Certainly there does not seem to have been the degree of sentimentalization of childhood in the medieval period that characterizes the modern western construction of childhood with its notions of childish innocence and marked difference from adulthood, yet a notion of childhood as a distinct category is found very early in the West (Cramer 1993: 131–6). Philosophical and scientific writers recognized childhood as a distinct phase of life, during which a child was to be treated with tenderness: as a little child Clare of Montefalco was allowed by the Virgin Mary to play with the infant Jesus to obviate her misery at being separated from her family (Frugoni 1992: 407–8). The age of 7 was the time for discipline and training to begin, although younger children, especially in peasant households, might already be entrusted with such tasks as fruit-picking, herding geese and ducks, fetching water and learning to sew and spin. It was important to discipline children: the proverb 'Spare the rod and spoil the child' was elaborated in the English early thirteenth-century *Proverbs of Alfred*:

A wise child is his father's joy – if it so happens that you have a child – while it is little teach it virtues befitting men. When it is grown it will follow them; ... better a child unborn than disobedient. The man who spares the rod and the young child, and lets it do as it likes and have the mastery will sorely repent it in his old age.

(*Proverbs of Alfred* 1904: 40)

Those parents who let their children go to wet-nurses must have had more difficulty bonding with them than the parents who saw their children grow up in the parental home. When Francesco Datini takes back his illegitimate daughter from her foster-parents at the age of 6, the foster-father warns that little Ginevra is very fearful of the change to come, 'and we love her dearly, and therefore we beseech you, be gentle with her'. Despite the strictures of contemporary moralists about the education of children, Francesco's account-book later records the purchase of a tambourine (which took up a whole day of his business partner's time looking for it in Florence) for Ginevra and his wife's niece, who was also living with them (Origo 1959: 186–7). In medieval writings there is an expectation that the birth of a child is a joy for both mother and father: Giovanni Morelli, a late medieval Tuscan, reports in his family records the day that he was able to feel his child kicking in his wife's belly (Herlihy and Klapisch-Zuber 1978: 533–4). Francesco di Barberino recommended that after the foetus has quickened, the mother should 'eat and drink with moderation and live happily as God's friend so that the new spirit within her takes on a gentle aspect' (Vecchio 1992: 122) while Francesco Datini arranged for his illegitimate son by one of his maidservants to be buried at the foot of his own tomb (Origo 1959: 167). Klapisch-Zuber suggests that the advent of humanism encouraged an interest in child psychology, in particular in the child's individuality, while contemporary iconography, focussing its attention on the Christ child, rather than the Virgin who displays him, shows him behaving like a real baby: 'playful, laughing, and hungry' (Klapisch-Zuber 1985: 113–15).

Mothers were thought to have a special bond with their children, a bond so powerful that it becomes a central trope for describing divine love, as in the excerpt from Julian of Norwich below. Though fathers surely felt grief at the death of their children, their sorrow seems to have been expressed privately – in Florentine *ricordanze* (family chronicles) for example. Public displays of grief were unmanly: in the Old Norse *Flóamanna saga*, the open grief of a father at his young son's death is interpreted by his companions as the result of the father's special relationship with this child. Marooned in Greenland with the child after its mother had been murdered, the father had sliced his nipples and tugged on them 'until there was milk and then he fed the child on it' (*Flóamanna saga* 1987: 750). The 'unmanliness' of the father's grief was excused by the womanly bond he had with his child 'for they love the children they have nursed more than others' (*Flóamanna saga* 1987: 759). Women's tenderness and affection is found less in their letters to their children – for the medieval letter was often a semi-public document, written by scribes – but rather in incidental descriptions or analogies. The 'Motherhood of Christ' topos has already been mentioned (Bynum 1982); mystical texts sometimes compare God's testing of the human soul with a mother's play with her children: God is like a mother who 'suffers the child to weep and cry and busily to seek her with sobbing and weeping. But then comes the mother suddenly with merry cheer and laughing, embracing her child and kissing, and wipes away the tears' (*Chastising of God's Children* 1957: 98). Gertrude the Great compares God's exaltation of the humble soul to a mother engaged in embroidery who involves her toddler in the task by putting her child 'in a higher place to hold the thread of pearls or help her in some other way' (Gertrude 1993: 160). The joy which a mother takes in her children in these texts contrasts with the misery they can cause her. In the years 841–3 the Frankish noblewoman Dhuoda wrote her *Manual of Instruction* for the son she had scarcely seen since infancy:

> Having noticed that most women in this world are able to live with and enjoy their children, but seeing myself, Dhuoda, living far away from you, my dear son William, filled with anxiety because of this, and with the desire to be of aid to you, I am sending you this little manual.
>
> (Marchand 1984: 12).

Similarly the popular medieval lyric subgenre, the lament of the Virgin over the body of Christ, epitomizes the depth of maternal love.

Dhuoda's two sons had been taken from her by her husband Bernard of Septimania, who had sent the elder as a kind of hostage to King Charles the Bald. The widespread tale of 'Patient Griselda', best known in the versions of Boccaccio in the *Decameron*, of Petrarch and of Chaucer's *Clerk's Tale*, in which a woman of humble birth promises absolute obedience to her noble husband, even to the extent of allowing him apparently to take away and murder her children, provides a happy resolution – the children were not really killed, and Griselda's obedience is exalted. Chaucer's version shows uneasiness with the cruelty of the story: the Clerk claims that the tale is not to be read as naturalistic, but rather as an allegory of the soul's obedience to God (Chaucer 1988: 152). Nevertheless, the absolute authority of a father over his children which underpins the tale reflects the imbalance of power between medieval parents in this regard.

In widowhood, however, a woman might find herself solely responsible for her children's welfare. Barbara Hanawalt shows how medieval English wills often entrusted children to their mothers' guardianship, even to the extent of allowing her to disinherit the children if she saw fit (Hanawalt 1986a: 222–3). The only reference to the curiously named Astralabe, son of Abélard and Héloise, in Héloise's writing comes after the death of Abélard when she writes to her old friend Peter the Venerable, asking for his assistance in finding the young man ecclesiastical office (*Letters* 1974: 43). Christine de Pizan, left widowed with three young children, exerted considerable energy in getting her daughter admitted to the prestigious royal convent at Poissy, where Christine herself probably retired. Her elder son was taken into the service of the English Duke of Salisbury, who greatly admired Christine's poetry. When Salisbury was killed in the events surrounding the deposition of Richard II, the new king Henry IV favoured the young man and tried to attract Christine to the English court. However, Christine was unhappy at the developments in England and had to use cunning to get her son back to France, a strategy which, she says wryly, cost her the patronage for a number of poems (Willard 1984: 42–3, 165–6).

Medieval mothers may have lacked authority, in comparison with their husbands, but the power which they exercised over their sons was by no means negligible. In her widowhood a woman might gain or increase status through her sons, as we shall see in chapter 5; where correspondence between mothers and sons survives, as in the Paston letters, or the fifteenth-century letters of Alessandra Macinghi degli Strozzi, a member of an influential Florentine family (Uitz 1990: 146–7), the sons show a great deal of deference to their mothers' views. Even where the mother was not involved in maintaining the family estates or position, but had retired from public life to the convent, her psychological hold over her child might still be powerful: the French monk Guibert de Nogent (*c.* 1064–1123) gives an account of his mother in his memoirs, a woman whom John Benton describes as 'a censorious mother who had nearly destroyed the potency of her husband' (Benton 1984: 14). Guibert himself blames his mother for retiring from the world in a little house near the Abbey of St Germer when he was aged 12: 'she knew that I should be utterly an orphan with no one at all on whom to depend … she was a cruel and unnatural mother' (Benton 1984: 74). Nevertheless, Guibert himself soon entered the Abbey, and it was not until he was about 40 that he left this house, and his mother, for the first time.

Guibert's attitude towards his mother is as susceptible of psychological interpretation as any modern autobiography. In most medieval writings the view of
motherhood was very much simpler, corresponding with the lines from the 'Bien des
Fames' cited at the head of this chapter: mothers gave birth to men. In this they
were blessed; in this lay both despair and their salvation.

Work

Medieval medical writers may have liked to suggest that women's work in
reproduction was the counterpart of men's economic activity, but this would be to
give a wholly false picture of the division of labour in medieval society. Women's
work had to fit around the childbirth and child-rearing roles which occupied a large
part of their twenties and thirties, but the weeks that they spent in bed recovering
from childbirth were probably the only ones in which they had no other responsibilities. Labour tended to be divided into complementary sex-determined roles;
evidence for sex-specific tasks exists from Carolingian manuals (Ennen 1989:
92–3; Amt 1993: 179–80), and the division remains remarkably constant throughout the period. In the countryside men went out to plough and work the fields and
took the produce to the market towns. Women's sphere was the house, croft (the
land immediately surrounding the house) and village. Here they prepared food,
brewed, baked, tended poultry and pigs, cultivated vegetables – onions, leeks, peas,
beans, and herbs – and fruits: apples, pears and cherries; made butter and cheese,
spun wool and made clothes for the family (Bennett 1987: 116–19; Hanawalt
1986a: 141–55). Where they produced excess, they would sell or exchange goods
with other families in the village. Brewing, for example, was a time-consuming and
laborious business. Ale was the staple drink of the household, for water was unsafe,
but it did not keep for long, and thus ale had to be brewed very frequently. Most rural
households alternated the production of ale with the purchase of ale from other
households: few women seem to have brewed on a commercial scale but rather
sold off their occasional excess for profit (Bennett 1987: 120–9; though also
Graham 1992: 136–44). By the fourteenth century in most English villages clothing
production, brewing and baking had become more or less commercial enterprises.
Women might still spin – the distaff is a central symbol of femininity, evidenced by
John Ball's famous tag 'When Adam delved and Eve span / Who then was the
gentleman?' and the lines from 'Le Bien des Fames' cited above – in their idle
moments, but the making up of yarn into cloth and then into clothing had become
a specialized role. However, such activity did not necessarily improve the woman
producer's public standing; she still needed to be represented by her husband in the
manorial court (Bennett 1986: 28).

Although women mostly worked from and around the home, at certain times of
the year they were needed in the fields to work alongside the men. Women (and
young children) were delegated to weed, pick out stones, goad the oxen, plant and

glean after harvest. During the harvest itself all hands were needed to bring in the crop (Hanawalt 1986a: 126–8).

In the towns, women were able to find work particularly at times when the population had declined; they were the first to be excluded from the labour market in times of demographic increase. As well as the household tasks outlined in advice books such as those of the Ménagier de Paris, the late medieval Italian Alberti or Christine de Pizan, women also engaged in a range of other occupations. 'The notion that urban women of the late Middle Ages functioned exclusively or chiefly as "housewives" is a misconception, at least for regions north of the Alps,' writes Claudia Opitz (Opitz 1992: 283). Townswomen often worked alongside their husbands in artisanal trades, though guild regulations often restricted their capacity to continue the trade after their husbands' deaths, by forbidding them to take on apprentices. Parisian records show that widows might practise as butchers, fishmongers, bakers, hat-, bag- and belt-makers, cutlers, leatherworkers, tailors and dyers among others (Uitz 1990: 52). Very few female workers formed themselves into guilds: the exceptions are found in Rouen, Cologne and Paris, where the silk-ribbon makers formed all-female guilds (Kowaleski and Bennett 1989: 18–21; Amt 1993: 194–6). While the silk makers, gold-thread spinners and yarn makers of Cologne were organized into guilds, the women who did the work tended to be related to the merchants of the city as wives, sisters or daughters. They were subordinate to male guild-masters; the two guild-mistresses of the silk-makers' guild were solely responsible for overseeing the technical standards of the work (Howell 1986: 210–11). Artisanal work in the cities was organized as a family business; married women would not draw a wage, while women employees were often paid less. In Alcalá in Castile women working in the carpet industry earned considerably less than men, although they may have had lighter duties or have been working part-time (Dillard 1984: 157).

Women might work in production, but the distribution and trade of the products was the prerogative of the men. Women were restricted by their domestic responsibilities, by considerations of physical and moral danger, and by the general and widely held cultural expectation that a woman's place is in the home. 'A woman should be at her embroidery,' the Old English poem Maxims I tells us, 'word goes round about a woman who wanders, often she is slandered, men say contemptuous things about her' (Anglo-Saxon Poetic Records 1936: 66). In the Italian maritime towns wealthy women could speculate in long-distance trading; in 1206 a Genoese lady is recorded as signing a contract with one Galetta to sell a large amount of linen for her in Sicily. Even the wives of Venetian doges were not above lending money to traders – in 1209 Maria Ziani lent 120 Venetian pounds to a sea captain. Italian women were involved in trade with cities as distant as Alexandria, Constantinople and Ceuta in Morocco (Uitz 1990: 24, 37), but they did not journey themselves. Yet by the end of the period, businesswomen were making trips on their own account: one woman from Danzig had to make several trips to England because her agent there was unreliable, while the Cologne female silk-makers were to be found at trade fairs in Frankfurt, Antwerp and the Netherlands (Uitz 1990: 46–7). Cologne women possessed civic rights equal to those of men if they were wives or widows of Cologne citizens, or, like men, they could pay for admission and swear an oath of citizenship (Ennen 1989: 174–5).

One form of work which suited women well was the retail trade. Women could work from home, supervising their children and servants at the same time as serving their customers. Some would specialize in dry goods: the town regulations of Erfurt in 1486 permitted the sale of luxury goods only on the shopkeepers' bridge, while traders throughout the town could sell, *inter alia*: juniper berries, dyes, raisins, millet, brimstone, wooden jugs, Flemish yarn, sandalwood, corals, silk bonnets, Frankfurt and Nuremberg ribbon (Uitz 1990: 44–5). In twelfth-century Castile markets developed early, and women shopkeepers set up trade in perishable commodities which had to be easily available for everyone to buy: wine, cheese, vegetables, fish and meat (Dillard 1984: 157).

In literary works women shopkeepers are often depicted as dishonest and grasping: in the Chester mystery play 'The Harrowing of Hell' a female alewife is left behind in Hell by Christ, as she confesses to using false measures, adulterating her ales and beer and encouraging dicing, swearing and other 'tavern sins' (*Chester Mystery Cycle* 1974: 337–9). Judith Bennett speculates that distrust of those who traded in basic foodstuffs, combined with popular misogyny, and Church ambivalence towards the selling of alcohol with its potential for encouraging disorderly and sinful behaviour, produced a satirical tradition which may have been instrumental in discouraging women from continuing in the ale trade (Bennett 1991: 66–88). Amt (1993: 201–5) reproduces London records of women trading fraudulently: bakers selling lightweight loaves, a woman giving short measure of ale, Margery Hore, put in the pillory for selling rotten fish, and Katherine Duchewoman who had tried to pass off a tapestry woven of inferior materials (Fig. 7).

Other townswomen might work in relatively skilled occupations, such as midwifery and other healing trades. With the growth of the university medical faculties, women healers came under increasing pressure to abandon their practices. The case of Jacoba, a woman healer in early fourteenth-century Paris who came into contention with the University for practising medicine without a licence, is well documented (Green 1989; Amt 1993: 108–12). For some women only lower status jobs, as nurses, domestic servants or even slaves were available. Susan Stuard shows that in late thirteenth-century Ragusa (modern Dubrovnik) 87.9 per cent of the slaves sold were women, usually from the city's mountainous hinterland. Female slaves were more tractable and less prone to violence than males; moreover, the mountain women were so strong and sturdy that they could usually perform the heavy work of male slaves, in addition to traditional female tasks (Stuard 1986: 44–5). Women servants might sometimes augment their earnings by prostitution. In England prostitution appears to have been mostly undertaken on a casual basis;

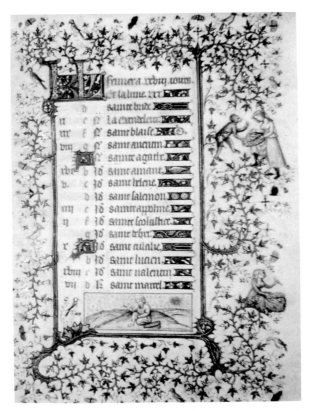

Figure 7 Woman selling fish from a basket: MS Douce 62 fol. 4r, Bodleian Library, Oxford.

although Karras documents the organization of the stews and brothels of London (Karras 1989), few other English towns had the kinds of highly regulated municipal brothels evidenced in northern Italy and southern France (Rossiaud 1988; Otis 1985). Maryanne Kowaleski shows that in late fourteenth-century Exeter most women who were fined for prostitution also worked in other trades. They tended to be untrained and unmarried, often recent immigrants from the countryside augmenting their meagre wages as servants (Kowaleski 1986: 153–7). Depending on the relative demand and supply, servants need not always be badly paid: in some frontier towns in twelfth-century Castile women domestic servants were earning more than male agricultural labourers (Dillard 1984: 157).

It was not only peasant and bourgeois women who worked. Noble women too were expected to fill their hours productively. A noble girl would be taught by her mother how to spin and sew, sometimes in addition to literacy skills. Francesco da Barberino, author of an early fourteenth-century Florentine conduct book, suggests that this will keep the young girl from boredom and depression while she waits to get married. However, the prospective bride rarely learned the details of household management, and often had to be taught by her husband how to oversee her servants (Klapisch-Zuber 1986: 58–9). Other work undertaken by noble women included overseeing an absent husband's estates, or sewing vestments and linen for the church. In *Piers Plowman* the classes are neatly distinguished by their handiwork; noble ladies embroider, peasant women sew sacks for the harvest and bourgeois women make clothing:

'What should we women do meanwhile?'
'Some should sew the sacks,' said Piers, 'to [stop] the shedding of the
    wheat;
And you lovely ladies with your long fingers,
[See that] you have silk and sendal to sew when you have time
Chasubles for chaplains to honour churches.
Wives and widows, spin wool and flax;
Make cloth, I advise you, and so teach your daughters.
                                            (Langland 1978: 66)

Women's work was a matter of expediency. The poor woman, untrained in any craft, had to piece together temporary money-making enterprises: selling surplus produce, brewing, working as a domestic servant, sometimes prostituting herself. All these activities would have to be fitted around pregnancy, birth and child-care. The married woman's work, in addition to her domestic chores, was usually undertaken in partnership with her husband. Again her participation in the household economy would vary at different times of her life; as Barbara Hanawalt writes, essentially 'women were dabblers'. Although the 1363 reissue of the English Statute of Labourers demanded that all men choose a trade and stick to it, women were allowed to continue in the piecemeal work they had always done (Hanawalt 1986b: xii–xiii). Women's work was indispensable to the household economy, but they did not necessarily have a say in profit or expenditure. It was in widowhood, or in the cases in cities such as London where women could trade as 'femmes soles' (as legally independent of their husbands), that they could truly reap the rewards of their labours (Bennett 1992). Being a 'femme sole' had its disadvantages: the institution had developed as early as the first half of the thirteenth century in Lübeck to ensure that business confidence could be maintained; thus women could incur debts and be bankrupted, even to the extent of losing their dowries (Ennen 1989: 168–9).

MOTHERS

1 FREDEGUND AND RIGUNTH

Text from: Gregory of Tours (1974) *The History of the Franks*, transl. L. Thorpe, Harmondsworth: Penguin, pp. 521–2.

A full account of Fredegund (*d.* 597), and how she came to rise from the position of slave to the queen of Chilperic, king of the Franks, is given in chapter 5, p. 164. Rigunth was Fredegund's only daughter, and had been intended as a bride for Recared, prince of the Visigoths. Rigunth set out for Spain with a huge dowry, fifty cartloads of precious objects, but when she reached Toulouse word came of her father's assassination and the treasure was pillaged by Duke Desiderius. Fredegund was enraged when she heard of her daughter's mistreatment, and arranged for her to be brought home from the church where she had taken refuge. Baulked of her marriage and subject now to her mother's control, Rigunth showed little gratitude towards her mother.

Rigunth, Chilperic's daughter, was always attacking her mother [Fredegund], and saying that she herself was the real mistress, whereas her mother ought to revert to her original rank of serving-woman. She would often insult her mother to her face, and they frequently exchanged slaps and punches. 'Why do you hate me so, daughter?' Fredegund asked her one day. 'You can take all your father's things which are still in my possession and do what you like with them.' She led the way into a strongroom and opened a chest which was full of jewels and precious ornaments. For a long time she kept taking out one thing after another, and handing them to her daughter, who stood beside her. Then she suddenly said: 'I'm tired of doing this. Put your own hand in and take whatever you find.' Rigunth was stretching her arm into the chest to take out some more things, when her mother suddenly seized the lid and slammed it down on her neck. She leant on it with all her might and the edge of the chest pressed so hard against the girl's throat that her eyes were soon standing out of her head. One of the servant-girls who was in the room screamed at the top of her voice: 'Quick! Quick! Mistress is being choked to death by her mother!' The attendants who had been waiting outside for them to emerge burst into the strongroom, rescued the princess from almost certain death and dragged her out of doors. The quarrels between the two were even more frequent after this. There were never-ending outbursts of temper and even fisticuffs. The main cause was Rigunth's habit of sleeping with all and sundry.

2 OLD ENGLISH PREGNANCY CHARMS

Text from: G. Storms (1948) *Anglo-Saxon Magic*, The Hague: Martinus Nijhoff, pp. 197–9. (Ms Harley 585, f. 185 a, b.)

The spell consists of a series of actions to be taken by a woman who has already lost one child. It is not clear whether the spell is for miscarriages or against stillborn children for the term *afedan*, here translated as 'bring to maturity' could mean either.

(a) Against miscarriage

The woman who cannot bring her child to maturity must go to the grave of a dead man, step three times over the grave and say these words three times:

> This as my help against the evil late birth,
> this as my help against the grievous dismal birth,
> this as my help against the evil lame birth.

And when the woman is with child and she goes to bed to her lord, then she must say:

> Up I go, I step over you
> with a live child, not with a dying one,
> with a full-born child, not with a doomed one.

And when the mother feels that the child is alive, she must go to church, and when she comes in front of the altar, then she must say:

> I have said that by Christ it is manifested.

The woman who cannot bring her child to maturity must take part of the grave of her own child, wrap it up in black wool and sell it to merchants. And then she must say:

> I sell it, you must sell it,
> This black wool and the seeds of this grief.

The woman who cannot bring her child to maturity must take the milk of a cow of one colour in her hand, sip up a little with her mouth, and then go to running water and spit the milk into it. And then with the same hand she must take a mouthful of water and swallow it. Let her then say these words:

> Everywhere I carried with me this great powerful strong one,
> strong because of this great food;
> such a one I want to have and go home with.

When she goes to the stream she must not look round, nor again when she goes away from there, and let her go into another house than the one from which she started, and there take food.

(b) To know whether the child will be a boy or girl

MS Cotton Tiberius A II f. 40b.

Methods to find out whether a pregnant woman will bear a boy or a girl. If she walks slowly and has hollow eyes she will bear a boy; if she walks quickly and has swollen eyes, she will bring forth a girl.

Take two flowers, namely a lily and a rose, put them before the pregnant woman and bid her take either. If she chooses the lily she will bear a boy; if she chooses the rose she will bring forth a girl.

Observe how the woman walks. If she touches the ground more with her heels she will bear a boy; if she touches the ground only with her toes she will bring forth a girl.

If the woman's belly is high up she will bear a boy; if it is sunk down she will produce a girl.

(c) To conceive a boy or a girl

Leechbook III, xxxvii.

On the left thigh, up against the matrix one may bind either the lower part of henbane or twelve grains of coriander seed, and that shall produce either a boy or a girl.

3 TAKING IN AN ORPHAN CHILD

Text from: J. F. Benton (ed.) (1984) *Self and Society in Medieval France: The Memoirs of Abbot Guibert of Nogent*, Medieval Academy Reprints for Teaching 15, Toronto: University of Toronto Press, pp. 93–7.

Guibert (*c.* 1064–1123) was for much of his life abbot of Nogent in northern France. Besides his memoirs (*De Vita Sua*). from which this extract is taken, he also wrote a treatise on virginity and an account of Frankish participation in the Crusades. Guibert's mother plays a central part in his account of his early years, for his father died when Guibert was eight months old. Guibert's mother was a pious and determined woman who staved off attempts to remarry her and who concerned herself solely with her son and his education until he reached the age of 12, when she withdrew from the world, much to Guibert's annoyance. Guibert's parents had been unable to consummate their marriage for a period of three years. 'It was said that their marriage drew upon them the envy of a stepmother, who had some nieces of great beauty and nobility and who was plotting to slip one of them into my father's bed. Meeting with no success in her designs, she is said to have used magical arts to prevent entirely the consummation of the marriage' (p. 64). Eventually the magic is countered. However, during this time Guibert's father was able to have sex with other women; the result is chronicled below.

Guibert's mother and the vision in purgatory

One summer night, for instance, on Sunday after matins, after she had stretched out on her narrow bench and had begun to sink into sleep, her soul seemed to leave her body without her losing her senses. After being led, as it were, through a certain gallery, at last she issued from it and began to approach the edge of a pit. After she was brought close to it, suddenly from the depths of that abyss men with the appearance of ghosts leaped forth, their hair seemingly eaten by worms, trying to seize her with their hands and to drag her inside. From behind the frightened woman, who was terribly distressed by their attack, suddenly a voice cried out to them, saying, 'Touch her not.' Compelled by that forbidding voice, they leaped back into the pit. Now, I forgot to say that as she passed through the gallery, as she knew she had left her mortal being, her one prayer to God was to be allowed to return to her body. After she was rescued from the dwellers in the pit and was standing by its edge, suddenly she saw that my father was there, appearing as he did when he was young. When she looked hard at him and piteously asked of him whether he was called Evrard (for that had been his name), he denied that he was....

Although he denied that he was called by that name, and yet nonetheless she felt that it was he, she then asked him where he was staying. He indicated that the place was located not far away, and that he was detained there. She also asked how he was. Baring his arm and his side, he showed both of them so torn, so cut up with many wounds, that she felt great horror and emotional distress as she looked. The figure of a little child was also there, crying so bitterly that it troubled her greatly when she saw it. Moved by its cries, she said to him, 'My lord, how can you endure the wailing of this child?' 'Whether I like it or not,' said he, 'I endure it.' Now, the crying of the child and the wounds on his arm and side have this meaning. When my father in his youth was separated from lawful intercourse with my mother through the witchcraft of certain persons, some evil counsellors appealed to his youthful spirit with the vile advice to find out if he could have intercourse with other women. In youthful fashion he took their advice, and having wickedly attempted intercourse with some loose woman unknown to me, he begat a child which at once died before baptism. The rending of his side is the breaking of his marriage vow; the cries of that distressed voice indicate the damnation of the evilly begotten child. Such, O Lord, O Inexhaustible Goodness, was Thy retribution on the soul of Thy sinner, who yet lives by faith. But let us return to the orderly narrative of the vision.

When she asked him whether prayer, almsgiving, or the mass gave him any relief (for he was aware that she frequently provided these things for him), he replied that they did, adding, 'But among you there lives a certain

Liégarde.' My mother understood that he named this woman so that she would ask her what memory of him she had. This Liégarde was very poor in spirit, a woman who lived for God alone apart from the customs of the world.

Passage omitted in which Guibert's mother also sees in purgatory a knight who was in fact killed on the very day on which she had the vision.

My mother drew her conclusion about the cries of the infant, of whose existence she had been aware, from the exact way in which the vision agreed with the facts, when she put them together, and from the immediate prophecy of the impending slaying of the knight, whom she had seen assigned to the place of punishment below. Having no doubt about these things, she devoted herself wholly to bringing help to my father. Setting like against like, she chose to take on the raising of a little child only a few months old that had lost its parents. But since the Devil hates good intentions no less than faithful actions, the baby so harassed my mother and all her servants by the madness of its wailing and crying at night – although by day it was very good, by turns playing and sleeping – that anyone in the same little room could get scarcely any sleep. I have heard the nurses whom she hired say that night after night they could not stop shaking the child's rattle, so naughty was he, not through his own fault, but made so by the Devil within, and that a woman's craft failed entirely to drive him out. The good woman was tormented by extreme pain; amid those shrill cries no contrivance relieved her aching brow, nor could any sleep steal over her sorely tried and exhausted head, since the frenzy of the child goaded from within and by the Enemy's presence caused continual disturbance. Although she passed her sleepless nights in this way, she never appeared listless at the performance of the night offices. Since she knew that these troubles were to purge away those of her husband, which she had seen in her vision, she bore them gladly, because she rightly thought that by sharing his suffering herself she was lessening the pains of the other sufferer. Yet she never shut the child out of her house, never appeared less careful of him. Indeed, the more she perceived that the Devil was cruelly blazing against her to destroy her resolve, the more she chose to submit with equanimity to any inconvenience rising from it; and the more she happened to experience the eagerness of the Devil in the irritation of the child, the more she was assured that his evil sway over the soul of her husband was being countered.

4 *TROBAIRITZ* LYRIC ON CHILD-BEARING

Text translated from: A. Rieger (1992) *Trobairitz: Der Beitrag der Frau in der altokzit-anischen höfischen Lyrik*, Tübingen: Max Niemeyer Verlag, p. 155.

The meaning of the poem is difficult to determine: some critics have seen two speakers 'Alais' and 'Yselda' in the alternating verses (Bogin 1976: 144–5; Dronke 1984a: 101–3); some have interpreted 'crowned with wisdom' in v. 2 as referring to Christ and advocating virginity. This translation follows Rieger.

'Na Carenza al bèl còrs avenenz'

Lady Carenza with the lovely, gracious body,
give us two sisters your advice,
and since you know best how to tell what's best,
advise me according to your own conviction:
should I take a husband – one whom you know of?
should I stay a virgin? and even if that did happen to me
I don't think it would be good to have children,
and without a husband it would be very hard.

Lady Alaisina Yselda, I know you have learning,
virtue and beauty, youth, a fresh complexion,
courtly manners and rank,
higher than all other educated women;
so I advise you to plant a good seed,
to take a husband who is crowned with wisdom,
through whom you'll bear fruit in a famous son.
Such a man knows how to keep the virgin he weds.

Lady Carenza, to be married would please me
but making babies seems a huge penitence:
then your breasts hang down limp
and your belly's wrinkled and horrible.

Lady Alaisina Yselda, keep me in your memory,
in the shadow of protection [of a marriage?]
when you are far away, ask your glorious lord,
if, at parting, I may be with you.

5 MOTHERS IN MONTAILLOU

Text from: E. Ladurie (1980) *Montaillou*, transl. B. Bray, Harmondsworth: Penguin, pp. 211–12 and P. Dronke (1984) *Women Writers of the Middle Ages*, Cambridge: Cambridge University Press, p. 210.

According to Cathar belief, a child could only be introduced into the highest rank of the sect once it had attained the age of reason. However, in this case a little girl, Jacotte, less than a year old, is seriously ill. The parents decide to have her hereticated, so that when she died she would be guaranteed salvation, and Prades Tavernier, a *parfait* (a kind of Cathar priest), undertakes to perform the ceremony. Once Jacotte is hereticated, she may eat only fish and vegetables: since she was probably not weaned, this is tantamount to a sentence of death by starvation. Jacotte's mother takes up the story:

The baby Jacotte

When my husband and Prades Tavernier had left the house, I could not bear it any longer. I couldn't let my daughter die before my very eyes. So I put her to the breast. When my husband came back, I told him I had fed my daughter. He was very grieved and troubled, and lamented. Pierre Maury [a Cathar shepherd who worked for the family] tried to console his master. He said to my husband, 'It is not your fault.'

And Pierre said to my baby, 'You have a wicked mother.'

And he said to me, 'You are a wicked mother. Women are demons.'

My husband wept. He insulted and threatened me. After this scene, he stopped loving the child; and he also stopped loving me for a long while, until later, when he admitted that he had been wrong. My daughter Jacotte survived this episode for a year; and then she died.

Mengarde's child

When my mother-in-law became a Cathar, I had a sick child, a boy two or three months old, and Guillaume Buscalh said to me: 'Would you like us to have one of those good men receive your child into their sect, if he begins to dwindle into death – for, if he's received by them and dies, he'd be an angel of God?' And when I asked him 'What should I do about the child after he's been received by the Cathars?' he told me that then I must not give the boy milk or anything else, just let him die like that. Hearing this, I said I'd never stop giving him my breast as long as he was alive. For, as he was a Christian, and had no sin except from me, I thought that if I lose him God would take him. . . . And because of this the boy was not received, though it would have pleased me if he had been, if only I could have suckled him afterwards.

6 THE HORRORS OF MOTHERHOOD

Text from: 'A Letter on Virginity' in *Medieval English Prose for Women* (1990), ed. and transl. B. Millett and J. Wogan-Browne, Oxford: Oxford University Press, pp. 29–35.

When should I have finished an account of everything that comes between those who are joined in this way [sc. married]? If she cannot have children, she is called barren; her lord loves her and honours her less, and she, as the one who has the worst of it, bewails her fate, and calls those women who do bear children full of happiness and good fortune. But now suppose that it turns out that she has all she wanted in the child that she longs for, and let us see what happiness she gets from it. In conceiving it, her flesh is at once defiled with that indecency, as has been shown before; in carrying it there is heaviness and constant discomfort; in giving birth to it, the cruellest of all pains, and sometimes death; in bringing it up, many weary hours. As soon as it comes into this life it brings more anxiety with it than joy, especially to the mother. For if it is born handicapped, as often happens, and one of its limbs is missing or has some kind of defect, it is a grief to her and shame to all its family, a reproach for malicious tongues, and the talk of everyone. If it is born healthy and seems to promise well, fear of its loss is born along with it, for she is never without anxiety lest it should come to harm until one of the two of them first loses the other. And often it happens that the child which is most loved, and paid for with most suffering, grieves and distresses its parents most in the end. Now what joy does the mother have, who feels great sorrow and shame as well for the handicapped child, and fear for the healthy one until she loses it?

By God, woman, even if it were not at all for the love of God, or for the hope of heaven, or for the fear of hell, you should avoid this act above all things, for the integrity of your flesh, for the sake of your body, and for your physical health. For as St Paul says, every sin that is committed is outside the body except this one alone. All the other sins are only sins; but this is a sin, and also disfigures you and dishonours your body, defiles your soul and makes you guilty in God's sight, and pollutes your flesh too. You offend on both sides: you anger the Almighty with that filthy sin, and do harm to yourself, mistreating yourself quite voluntarily in such a shameful way. Let us now go further, and see what happiness comes to you afterwards during pregnancy, when the child inside you quickens and grows, and how many miseries come into being at the same time, which cause you much unhappiness, assail your own flesh, and attack your own nature with many afflictions. Your rosy face will grow thin, and turn green as grass; your eyes will grow dull, and shadowed underneath, and because of your dizziness your head will ache cruelly. Inside, in your belly, a swelling in your womb which bulges you out like a water-skin, discomfort in your bowels and stitches in your side, and often painful backache; heaviness in every limb; the dragging weight of your two breasts, and the streams of milk that run from them. Your beauty is all destroyed by pallor; there is a bitter taste in your mouth, and everything that you eat makes you feel sick; and whatever food your stomach disdainfully receives – that is, with distaste – it throws up again. In the midst of all your happiness and your husband's delight, you are reduced to a wretch. Worry about your labour pains keeps you awake at night. Then when it comes to it, that cruel distressing anguish, that fierce and stabbing pain, that incessant misery, that torment upon torment, that wailing outcry; while you are suffering from this, and from your fear of death, shame added to that suffering with shameful craft of the old wives who know about that painful ordeal, whose help is necessary to you, however indecent it may be; and there you must put up with whatever happens to you. You should not see this as morally wrong, for we do not blame women for their labour pains, which all our mothers suffered for ourselves; but we describe them as a warning to virgins, so that they should be the less inclined towards such things, and understand the better through this what they ought to do.

After all this, there comes from the child born in this way wailing and crying, which will keep you up in the middle of the night, or the woman who takes your place, who is your responsibility. And all the filth in the cradle, and in your lap sometimes, so many weary hours in feeding and rearing it, and its development so late, and its growth so slow; and always being anxious, and anticipating after all this the time when it will go astray and bring all kinds of unhappiness to its mother. Though you may be rich and have a nurse, you must as a mother concern yourself with everything that she had to do.

... A virgin knows little of all this misery, of the unhappiness of a wife with her husband, or of the disgusting act they take part in together, or of the pain and misery in pregnancy and childbearing, of a nurse's vigils, or of her troubles in rearing the child, how much food she should put in its mouth at a single time, not to bespatter it or its baby-clothes; though these are trivial things to mention, all the more they show what slavery wives are in, who must endure such things, and what liberty virgins have, who are free from them all.

7 MARGERY AND HER CHILDREN

Text adapted from: Margery Kempe (1940) *The Book of Margery Kempe*, ed. S. Meech and H. E. Allen, EETS 212, Oxford: Oxford University Press, pp. 6–9, 221–5.

Margery Kempe had fourteen children by her husband. After the first one is born, she experiences something akin to postnatal depression and loses her sanity. The son who is portrayed in the second extract seems to contract a venereal disease from his loose living; Jacquart and Thomasset (1988: 177–88) discuss such diseases. Margery's son is also taken to task for wearing 'dagged' clothes, that is, with wide sleeves cut into zigzags. These were highly fashionable, but drew the opprobrium of moralists who deplored the waste of material; not only did the dags trail in the mud, but the material cut away could be used for nothing else.

When this creature [this is how Margery habitually refers to herself] was twenty years of age, or a little more, she was married to a worshipful burgess and was with child within short time, as nature intended. And, after she had conceived, she was laboured with great attacks of sickness until the child was born, and then, what with the labour she had in giving birth and for the sickness beforehand, she despaired of her life, thinking that she would not live. And then she sent for her confessor, for she had a thing on her conscience which she had never confessed before that time in all her life. For she was always hindered by her enemy, the Devil, evermore saying to her that, while she was in good health, she did not need to confess, but could do penance by herself, and everything would be forgiven for God is merciful enough.

And for that reason this creature often did great penance in fasting on bread and water and giving alms with devout prayers, only that she would not make confession. And whenever she was sick or diseased, the Devil said in her mind that she would be damned, for she was not confessed of that fault. Wherefore, after her child has born, she, not trusting to live, sent for her confessor, as I said before, in full intention to be shriven of all she had done in her lifetime, as near as she could. And when she came to the point to say that thing which she had concealed for so long, her confessor was a little too hasty and began sharply to reprove her before she had fully said all which was in her mind, and so she would say no more, despite anything he might do. And immediately, because of the fear she had of damnation on the one side and his sharp reproving on the other side, this creature went out of her mind and was wonderfully vexed and laboured with spirits half a year, eight weeks and odd days. And in this time she saw, as she thought, devils opening their mouths, all inflamed with burning flames of fire as if they were going to swallow her up, sometimes leaping at her, sometimes threatening her, sometimes pulling her and dragging her, both night and day during the aforesaid time. And also the devils cried upon her with great threats and said that she should forsake her Christianity and deny her God, his mother, and all the saints in heaven, her good deeds and all good virtues, her father, her mother and all her kinsmen. And so she did.

She slandered her husband, her kinsmen and her own self; she spoke many a word of reproof and many a spiteful word; she knew neither virtue nor goodness; she desired all wickedness; just as the spirits tempted her to say and do, so she said and did. She would have killed herself many a time at the spirits' promptings, and been damned with them in hell, and in witness of this, she bit her own hand so violently that it was seen all her life after. And also she tore her skin her body next to her heart with her nails, cruelly, for she had no other instruments, and she would have done worse except that she was tied up and kept by force both night and day so that she could not have her way.

A vision of Christ heals Margery of her madness.

And immediately the creature became stable in her wits and her reason as well as she ever was before, and she prayed her husband as soon as he came to her that she might have the keys of the buttery to take food and drink as she had done before. Her maidens and her keepers counselled him that he should not give her the keys, for they said she would only give away such goods as there were, for she did not know what she was saying, as they thought. Nevertheless, her husband, ever having tenderness and compassion for her, commanded they should deliver the keys to her. And she took food and drink as her bodily strength would permit her and recognized her kin and her household and all the others who came to her to see how our Lord Jesus Christ had wrought his grace in her.

Margery's son

The said creature had a son, a tall young man, living with a respectable burgess in Lynn, dealing in merchandise and selling overseas, whom she wished to have drawn away from the perils of this wretched and unstable world if her power could stretch to it. Nevertheless, she did as much as she could, and when she met with him at his leisure, many times she counselled him to leave the world and follow Christ, so much so that he fled her company and would not gladly meet with her. So one time it happened to the mother to meet with her son although it was against his will and his intention at that time. And as she had done before, so now she spoke to him again that he should flee the perils of this world and not rest all his study and his efforts so much upon it as he did. He did not agree but answered her sharply; she, somewhat moved with sharpness of spirit, said: 'Now since you will not leave the world at my counsel, I charge you by my blessing to keep your body clean at least from the company of women until you take a wife according to the law of the Church. And if you do not, I pray God chastise you and punish you for it.' They parted, and soon after the same young man passed over the sea in the business of merchandise, and then what through the evil enticing of other people and the folly of his own self-control, he fell into the sin of lechery. Soon after his colour changed, his face became full of pimples and pustules, as if he had become a leper. Then he came home again to Lynn to his master with whom he had been dwelling before. His master put him out of his service for no fault that he found in him, but supposing that he must be a leper, as he looked to be from his face. The young man told people wherever he felt like it how his mother had cursed him, through which, as he thought, God had so grievously punished him. A certain person, knowing about his complaint, and having compassion on his disease, came to his mother, saying that she had done very evilly, for through her prayer God had taken vengeance on her own child. She, taking little heed of his words, let it pass as if she did not care until he would come and ask for grace himself. So at last, when he saw there was no other remedy, he came to his mother, telling her of his misgovernance, promising that he would be obedient to God and to her and to amend his faults through the help of God, eschewing all misgovernance from that time forward as far as was in his power. He prayed his mother for her blessing, and especially he prayed her to pray for him that our Lord of his high mercy would forgive him that he had trespassed and would take away that great sickness for which men fled his company and his fellowship as they would a leper. For he supposed by her prayers our Lord had sent him that punishment, and therefore he trusted by her prayers to be delivered from it, if she would, of her charity, pray for him. Then she, trusting in his amending and having compassion of his infirmity, with sharp words of correction promised to fulfil his desire if God would grant it. When she came to her meditation, she did not forget the fruit of her womb, she asked forgiveness for his sin and for his release from the sickness which our Lord had given him if it were his pleasure and of profit to his soul. So long she prayed that he was clean delivered of the sickness and lived many years after and had a wife and a child, may God be blessed, for he married a wife in Prussia, in Germany....

In a few years after this young man had wed, he came home to England to his father and his mother all changed in his array and his conditions. For before his clothes were all dagged and his language was nothing but vanity; now he wore no dagged clothes, and his conversation was full of virtue.

The son goes on many pilgrimages to Rome and other holy places. Later he comes on a visit with his wife.

They came home on that Saturday in good health and on the next day, which was Sunday, while they were at table at noon with other good friends, he fell into great sickness. He rose from the table and laid himself on a bed, which sickness and infirmity occupied him about a month, and then in good life and right belief he passed to the mercy of our Lord.... In short time after, the father of the said person followed the son on the way which every man must go.

8 ON THE MOTHERHOOD OF CHRIST

Text adapted from: Julian of Norwich (1986) *A Revelation of Love*, ed. M. Glasscoe, Exeter: Exeter University Press, pp. 73–4.

At the age of 30, in response to her prayers, Julian (*c.* 1342–?1429) fell dangerously ill, and, at the point of death, experienced a series of sixteen revelations. These she wrote down soon afterwards in the 'Shorter Version' of her Revelations, but some twenty years later she produced a 'Longer Version' in which she meditated upon and elaborated more fully what she had seen. For part of her life Julian was an anchoress at the Church of St Julian in Norwich where Margery Kempe visited her. The conception of Jesus as mother is not original to Julian: Caroline Bynum (1982) explores the history and development of the topos. However, Julian's writing is perhaps the most fully worked-out exploration in medieval literature. Julian may have been particularly close to her own mother; she was certainly at her daughter's bed during the crucial illness.

How we are bought again and redeemed by mercy and grace of our sweet, kind and ever-loving mother Jesus, and of the properties of motherhood; but Jesus is our very mother, not feeding us with milk, but with himself, opening his side to us and challenging all our love.

But now it behoves to say a little more about this spreading forth, as I understand in the meaning of our Lord, how we are bought again by the motherhood of mercy and grace into our natural place where we were made by motherhood of natural love; which natural love never leaves us. Our natural mother, our gracious mother, for he wishes to become our mother completely in all things. He laid down the basis of his work very humbly and meekly in the maiden's womb. And that he showed in the first Revelation [earlier in the book] when he brought that meek maid before the eye of my understanding in the simple stature that she was when she conceived; that is to say, our high God is sovereign wisdom of all, in this low place he raised himself and made himself ready in our poor flesh, himself to do the service and the office of motherhood in all things.

The mother's service is nearest, readiest and surest, for it is most of truth. This office might not, nor could not, nor ever be, performed to the full, except by him alone. We know that all our mothers' bearing of us is only to pain and to dying; but to what does our true mother Jesus bear us, he who is all love, except to joy and endless living, blessed may he be? Thus he sustains us within himself in love, and he was in labour for the fullest length of time so that he wanted to suffer the sharpest agonies and the most grievous pains which ever were, or ever shall be, and he died at the last. And when he had done, and so born us all to bliss, yet all this could not give satisfaction to his marvellous love; and that he showed in these high and overpassing words of love: 'If I might suffer more, I would suffer more.' He could die no more, but he would not give up his work. Wherefore it behoves him to feed us, for the precious love of motherhood has put him in debt to us. The mother may give her child suck with her milk, but our precious mother Jesus can feed us with himself; and does so full courteously and full tenderly with the blessed sacrament that is the precious food of very life. And with all the sweet sacraments he sustains us very mercifully and graciously. And so he meant in this blessed word where he said: 'It is I that holy church preaches to you and teaches you'; that is to say: 'All the health and life of sacraments, all the virtue and grace of my word, all the goodness that is ordained in holy church for Lyon, it is me.'

The mother may lay the child tenderly to her breast, but our tender mother Jesus, he may intimately lead us into his blessed breast by his sweet open side, and show therein part of the Godhead and the joys of heaven, with spiritual assurance of endless bliss; and that was shown in the [tenth revelation] giving the same understanding in this sweet word, when he says 'Lo how I love thee', looking into his side and taking pleasure. This fair lovely word 'mother', it is so sweet and so natural of the self that it may not truly be said of anyone but of him, and of her that is the true mother of him and of all people. To the property of motherhood belongs natural love, wisdom and knowing, and it is good; for though it may be that our bodily bringing forth is but little, low and simple, in comparison with our spiritual bringing forth, yet it is he who brings it about in the creatures in which it happens. The kind loving mother who knows the needs of her child, keeps it very tenderly as the kind and condition of motherhood will. And as it grows older, she changes her method, but not her love. And when it has grown to a greater age, she allows it to beaten for the breaking down of vices to make the child receive virtues and graces. This working, along with all that is fair and good, our lord does it in those in whom it is done. Thus he is our mother in nature by the working of grace in the lower part, for love of the higher part. And he wants us to know it; for he will have all our love fastened on him. And in this I saw that all our debt which we owe, by God's bidding, by fatherhood and motherhood, for God's fatherhood and motherhood is fulfilled in true loving of God; which blessed love Christ works in us. And this was shown in all and namely in the high and plenteous words where he says: 'I am it that thou lovest.'

WORK

9 FREYDIS'S TRADING VENTURE

Text from: *Grœnlendinga saga* (1935), ed. E. O. Sveinsson and M. Thordarson, Islenzk Fornrit 4, Reykjavik: Hid Islenzka Fornritafelag, pp. 264–8. Transl. C. Larrington.

Freydis, most probably a fictional character, is depicted in *Grœnlendinga saga* (The Saga of the Greenlanders) as the daughter of Eric the Red, and sister of Leif Eriksson, the discoverer of America. In this extract, word has come back to the colony in Greenland of the riches of America (Vinland), most probably present-day Newfoundland. Freydis determines to profit from this.

Now it is told that Freydis Eriks-daughter left her home in Gardar [in

Greenland] and went to meet the two brothers Helgi and Finnbogi [two recently arrived Icelanders] and asked them to come to Vinland with their vessel, and to take a half-share with her in the cargo which they might get there. Now they agree to this. Then she went to see Leif, her brother, and asked him to give her those buildings which he had had built in Vinland. And he answered in the same way, said he would lend the buildings, but not give them. This was the agreement between the brothers and Freydis, that each should have thirty fighting men on each ship, and women as well. But Freydis broke the agreement immediately, and had five extra men and hid them, and the brothers did not find out about it until they came to Vinland.

Now they put out to sea, and they had said beforehand that they would sail in convoy if that were possible; and there was little in it, but the brothers got there slightly ahead and had carried their supplies up to Leif's buildings. And when Freydis landed, then they cleared their ship and took their things up to Leif's house. Then Freydis said: 'Why are you carrying your things in here?' 'Because we thought,' they said, 'that every promise made to us would be kept.' 'It was me Leif lent the buildings to,' she said, 'and not to you.' Then Helgi said, 'We brothers will not compete with you in wickedness.' They took out their supplies and built themselves a hall, and put it by the sea at the edge of the water, and they built it very well. And Freydis had timber cut for her ship.

Now winter came on, and the brothers decided that they would play some games and amuse themselves. This was done for a while, until the men started to fight with each other, and then they divided into factions and gave up the games and there was no coming and going between the halls, and this went on long into the winter.

It was early one morning that Freydis got out of bed, and didn't put on her shoes; the weather was such that a great deal of dew had fallen. She took her husband's cloak and put it on, then she went to the hall of the brothers, to the door. One man had gone out a little earlier and left the door ajar. She opened the door and stood for a while in the entryway and said nothing; and Finnbogi lay nearest in bed in the hall and he woke up. He said, 'What do you want here, Freydis?' She answered, 'I want you to get out and come outside with me as I want to talk to you.' So he did; they went to a tree which was lying next to the wall of the building and sat down on it. 'How do you like it here?' she said. He answered, 'The land seems good to me, but what doesn't seem good is this hostility between us, since I don't think I have caused it.' 'What you say is as it is,' she said, 'and that's how it seems to me; but this is what my errand was in coming to see you, that I want to exchange ships with you brothers, because you have a bigger ship than I, and I want to go away from here.' 'I can get that to happen,' he said, 'if that pleases you.' Now they part at this; she goes home, and Finnbogi goes back to bed. She gets back into bed with her cold feet, and this wakes up Thorvard and he asks why she is so cold and wet; she answers very vehemently, 'I went to those brothers,' she says, 'to ask for their ship, and I wanted to buy a bigger ship; and they were so angry at that that they struck me and mistreated me; but you, you wretched man, will neither avenge my shame nor yours, and I can now see that I am a long way from Greenland! I am going to divorce you unless you avenge this.' And now he couldn't stand her nagging and told his men to get up as quickly as possible and to get their weapons, and they did so and went to the brothers' hall and went in and took the sleepers and bound them and led each one of them outside when he was tied up; and Freydis had each one killed as he came out. Now all the men were killed, and the women remained, and no one wanted to kill them. Then Freydis said, 'Pass me an axe.' It was done. Then she struck the five women who were there, and left them dead. Now they go back to their hall after this wicked deed and everyone thought it remarkable that Freydis thought that things had gone very well. She said to her companions, 'If we have the good fortune to get back to Greenland, I shall kill any man who reveals what has happened here. Now what we will say is that they stayed behind when we went away.'

Now in the spring they filled up the ship which the brothers had owned with all the valuable cargo that they could get hold of and the ship could carry; they put out to sea and had good sailing weather and brought their ship into Eiriksfjord early in the summer. . . .

Freydis now went to her farm, as it had taken no harm in the meantime. She gave a great many presents to all the crew since she wanted to hide her wickedness. Now she sits at home on her farm. Not everyone was so reliable as to keep so silent about the crimes and the wickedness, so later it came out. Now Leif, her brother, got to hear about it and he did not like the story at all. Then Leif took three of Freydis's men and tortured them until they all told the same story about the events, and their accounts all agreed. 'I can't bear to punish Freydis, my sister, as she merits, but I can prophesy this of them, that their descendants will have very little success.' Now it happened that, from then on, no one thought anything but bad of them.

This is the last we hear of Freydis in this saga; in Eric the Red's Saga she heroically chases away marauding Native Americans by pulling out her breasts and slapping them (Jones 1986: 228).

10 WOMEN IN RETAIL

(a) Text from: John Gower (1992) *Mirour de l'Omme*, transl. W. B. Wilson, East Lansing, Mich.: Colleagues Press, p. 345. (b) Text from: William Langland (1978) *The Vision of Piers Plowman: A Complete Edition of the B-Text*, ed. A. V. C. Schmidt, London: Everyman, pp. 49, 53.

These passages belong to a popular satirical tradition which characterizes women in the retail trade as dishonest and grasping. Men are also depicted as fraudulent in their business methods, but, as Judith Bennett argues, the participation of women in the business of retailing essential foodstuffs and drinks tapped into a vein of misogyny (Bennett 1991). In the second extract Rose uses false weights in her cloth trade and gives people the best ale to taste while filling their barrels with poor quality stuff.

(a) But, to tell the truth, the retail shopkeeping trade belongs most rightly to women. If a woman does it, in her stinginess she connives and deceives more than a man. She will never give up the profit of a single crumb, which she will hold tightly from her neighbour. It is a waste of time to beg her for anything, for she does nothing from goodness of heart. This is known to everyone who patronizes her shop.

(b) Rose the Regrator

My wife was a weaver and woollen cloth made;
she spoke to spinners to spin it out.
The pound weight she paid by weighed a quarter more
Than my own steelyard when I weighed truly.
   I brought her barley – she brewed it to sell.
Penny ale and pudding ale she poured together;
[Meant] for labourers and low folk it stood apart by itself.
The best ale lay in my inner room or in my bedchamber,
And whoever tasted of it bought it afterwards
A gallon for a groat, God knows, no less,
When it came by the cupful – this craft my wife used.
Rose the Retailer was her right name;
She has held to retailing this eleven winters.

Beton the Brewster

Now Glutton begins to go to confession
And directs himself to the church to show his sin,
But Beton the Brewer bade him good morrow
And asked him with that, whither he intended.
'To holy church,' said he, 'for to hear mass,
And afterwards I will be shriven, and sin no more.'
'I have good ale, friend,' said she, 'Glutton, will you try it?'
'Have you,' said he, 'any hot spices?'
'I have pepper and peony seeds,' said she, 'and a pound of garlic,
A farthing's worth of fennel seed for fasting days.'

Then Glutton goes in, and great oaths go with him.
Cesse the female cobbler sat on the bench,
Wat the Warren-keeper and his wife both,
Tim the Tinker and two of his lads
Hick the Horse-hirer and Hugh the Needle-seller,
Clarice of Cock's Lane and the clerk of the church,
Sire Piers the priest and Pernelle of Flanders,
Davy the Ditcher and a dozen others –
A Fiddler, a Rat-catcher, a Scavenger of Cheapside,
A Rope-maker, a Lackey and Rose the Dish-seller,
Godfrey of Garlickhithe and Griffin the Welshman,
and a heap of oldclothes men, there early in the morning,
gave Glutton with good will good ale as a treat.

11 MARGERY'S BUSINESS VENTURES

Text adapted from: Margery Kempe (1940) *The Book of Margery Kempe*, ed. S. Meech and H. E. Allen, EETS 212, Oxford: Oxford University Press, pp. 9–11.

And when this creature had, through grace, returned to her mind she thought that she was bound to God and that she would be his servant. Nevertheless, she would not leave off her pride nor her pompous array which she had used before, neither for her husband, nor for any man's counsel. And yet she knew very well that men said many villainous things about her, for she wore gold pipes on her head and the tippets of her hoods were dagged [cut in zigzags]. Her cloaks were also dagged and lined with various colours between the dags so that it should be the more striking for men to see, and that she should be the more admired. . . .

And for sheer covetousness and to keep up her pride she began to be a brewer and was one of the greatest brewers of the town N. [Lynn] for three or four years until she had lost a lot of money, for she never had the hang of it. For, however good her servants and however knowledgeable they were about brewing, yet it would never ferment for them. For when the ale was standing as fair under the barm [yeast for fermenting] as any man might see, the barm would suddenly fall down so that the ale was lost, one brewing after another, so that her servants were ashamed and would not stay with her. Then this creature thought about how God had punished her before for not paying heed to him, and now this time through her losing her money, and she gave up and brewed no more. And then she asked mercy of her husband that she would not follow his counsel previously and she said that her pride and sin was cause of all her punishment and she would amend where she had trespassed with a good will. But yet she did not completely give up the world, for now she thought of a new housewifely scheme. She had a horse-mill. She got two good horses for herself and a man to grind people's corn and thus she thought she could earn her living. This provision did not last long, for a short time after, on the eve of Corpus Christi, this miracle occurred. This man was in good bodily health and his two horses very vigorous and they had been quite happy to draw [the millstones round] in the mill before. Now when he took one of these horses and put him in the mill as he had done before this horse would not draw at all for anything he could do. The man was very sorry and tried with all his wits to think how he should get this horse to draw. Sometimes he led him by the head, sometimes he beat him, and sometimes he petted him, and all availed not, for he would rather go backwards than forwards. Then this man put a sharp pair of spurs on his heels and rode on the horse's back to get him to draw and it was no better. When the man saw that it would not be, then he put his horse back in the stable and gave him food and ate well and keenly. And then he took the other horse and put him in the mill. And just as his fellow had done, so did he, for he would not draw for anything that the man might do. And then this man gave up his work and would no longer have anything to do with the aforementioned creature. As soon as this was noised about the town of [Lynn] neither man nor beast would work for the said creature, and some said she was cursed; some said God was taking public vengeance upon her; some said one thing and some said another. And some wise men, whose mind was more grounded in the love of our Lord, said it was the high mercy of our Lord Jesus Christ which entreated and called her from the pride and vanity of the wretched world. And then this creature, seeing all these adversities coming on every side, thought it was the scourges of our Lord who wanted to chastise her for her sin. Then she asked God for mercy and gave up her pride, her covetousness and the desire that she had for the admiration of the world, and did great bodily penance and began to enter the way of everlasting life, as shall be said afterwards.

12 THE DIVISION OF LABOUR

Text from: *Reliquiae Antiquae* (1845) vol. II, ed. T. Wright and J. Halliwell, London: John Russell Smith, pp. 196–9.

Wright and Halliwell record that this ballad was found in a manuscript dating from the reign of Henry VII, kept in Chetham's Library, Manchester. The ballad is incomplete, but it makes clear the division of labour between rural men and women. The men work in the fields, the women at home and around the yard and croft. The tasks of food preparation and raising domestic animals are hampered by small children; when the wife has a free moment she spins, threshes flax and cuts and twists tow for ropes. In order to preserve the rhyme, I have left some obsolete words. These are glossed at the right.

Ballad of the tyrannical husband

Jesu that art gentle, for joy of thy dame
As thou wrought all this wide world, in heaven is thy home,
Save all this company and shield them from shame
That will listen to me and attend to this game.

God keep all women that to this town belong
Maidens, widows and wives among;
For much they are blamed, and sometimes with wrong
I take witness of all folk that heareth this song.

Listen, good sirs, both young and old
By a good husband this tale shall be told;
He wedded a woman that was fair and bold,
And good enough to wend as they wolde.   [do as they wished]

She was a good houswife, courteous and hende   [skilled]
And he was an angry man and soon would be tende.   [annoyed]
Chiding and brawling and fared like a fiend
As they that often will be wroth with their best friend.

Till it befell upon a day, short tale to make,
The goodman would to the plough, his horse gan he take.   [began]
He called forth his oxen, the white and the black,
And he said 'Dame, dight our dinner betime, for God's sake.'   [prepare]

The goodman and his lad to the plough be gone
The goodwife had much to do, and servant had she none.
Many small children to keep beside herself alone,
She did more than she might within her own wone.   [dwelling]

Home came the goodman by the time of the day
To look that all thing were according to his pay.   [liking]
'Dame,' he said 'is our dinner dight?' 'Sir,' she said, 'Nay,
How would you have me do more than I may?'

Then he began to chide and said 'Evil mot thou thee,   [bad luck to you]
I would thou shouldst all day go to plough with me,
To walk in the clods that be wet and miry.
Then shouldst thou wit what it were a ploughman to be.   [know]

Then answered the goodwife and thus she gan say,
'I have more to do than I may;
And if you should follow me fully one day
You would be weary of your part, my head I dare lay!'   [wager]

109

'Weary! In the devil's name,' said the goodman,
'What hast thou to do but sit here at home?
Thou goest to thy neighbour's house, by one and one,
And sittest there jangling with Jack and with John.'   [chatting]

'Then,' said the goodwife, 'Fair may you befall!
I have more to do, whoever wist all.   [knew]
When I lie in my bed, my sleep is but small.
Yet early in the morning you will up me call.

When I lie all night waking with our child
I rise up in the morrow and find our house wild.
Then I milk our cows and turn them to field,
While you sleep full still, as Christ me shield.

Then I make butter further on in the day,
After I make cheese – these hold you a play.   [you like these]
Then will our children weep and up must they,
Yet will you blame me for our goods, if any be away.

When I have so done yet there come more even
I give our chickens food, or else they will be leyne.   [lost]
Our hens, our capons and our ducks bedene   [are seen to]
Yet tend I to our goslings which go on the green.

I bake, I brew, it will not else be well,
I beat and swingle flax, as ever I have heyll.   [good health]
I twist up the tow, I bind and I coil
I tease wool and card it and spin it on the wheel.'

'Dame,' said the goodman, 'the devil have thy bones!
Thou needst not bake and brew in a fortnight but once.
I see no good that thou dost within these wide wones   [rooms]
But ever thou excusest thee with grunts and with groans.'

'If a piece of linen and woollen I make once a year
For to clothe ourselves and our children in fere,   [altogether]
Else we should go to the market and buy it full dear.
I am as busy as I may [be] in every year.

When I have so done, I look at the sun,
I ordain food for our beasts against when you come home.
And food for ourselves before it be noon.
Yet I have not a fair word when I have done.

So I look to our goods without and within

That there be none away, neither more nor min. [bigger or smaller]
Glad to please you to pay, lest any bate begin [to your liking; quarrel]
And for to chide thus with me, in faith you be in sin.'

Then said the goodman in a sorry time [i.e. he would regret it]
'All this would a good housewife do before it were prime. [9 am]
And since the goods that we have is half-deal thine
Thou shalt labour for thy part as I do for mine.

Therefore, dame, make thee ready, I warn thee anon,
Tomorrow with my lad to the plough thou shalt gone,
And I will be housewife and keep our house at home
And take mine ease, as thou hast done, by God and St John.'

'I grant,' said the goodwife, 'as I understand
Tomorrow in the morning I will be walkand [walking]
Yet will I rise while ye be slepand
And see all things ready be laid to your hand.'

So it passed all to the morrow so that it was daylight.
The goodwife thought on her deeds, and she rose right.
'Dame,' said the goodman, 'I swear by God's might,
I will fetch home our beasts and help so that thou art dight.'
          [i.e. bring the plough-oxen in from their overnight grazing]

The goodman to the field hied him full yerne. [went eagerly]
The goodwife made butter, her deeds were full derne. [secret]
She took again the butter-milk and put it in the churn,
And said, 'Yet of one point our sire shall be to learn.'

Home came the goodman and took good keep
Of how the wife had put the meat for to steep. [soak, of salt meat]
She said, 'Sir, all this day you need not sleep.
Keep well our children, and let them not weep.

If you go to the kiln, malt for to make [malt-oven]
Put a small fire underneath, sir, for God's sake.
The kiln is low and dry, good tend that you take [take note]
For if it fasten on a fire, it will be evil to blake.
          [if it catches fire, it will become horribly blackened]

Here sit two geese abroad, keep them from woe,
If they may come to good, that ends sorrow enow. [enough]
'Dame,' said the goodman, 'hie thee to the plough,
Teach me not housewifery, for I can enough.'

111

Forth went the goodwife, courteous and hende, [skilled]
She called to her lad and to the plough they wend.
They were busy all day, a fitt here I find, [verse]
If I had a drink once, you will hear the best behind. [remaining]

The poem breaks off here, but it will clearly end with the vindication of the wife, as in the folktale analogues of the man and woman who exchange roles for the day, for example 'The Wife of Auchtermuchty' (Bannantyne MS 1928: 320–2). In our text the stage is set for the loss of the geese and the burning of the malt. The husband's burden is not helped by his wife's sabotage of the butter-churn; butter-milk, from which the curds have already been removed, will never churn into butter.

4

WOMEN AND CHRISTIANITY

INTRODUCTION

Out against me came an Egyptian, foul of aspect, with his seconds: he
was to fight with me. And some handsome young men came up beside
me: my own seconds and supporters. And I was stripped naked, and
became a man. . . . And I awoke. And I knew I should have to fight not
against wild beasts but against the Fiend; but I knew the victory would
be mine.

(Dronke 1984a: 4)

Perpetua (d. 203), aged about 22, here recounts a vision which she sees on the night
before she is to be martyred by wild beasts in the arena at Carthage; these are her
own words 'set down by her own hand,' says the author of her *Passio*. Dronke
explains Perpetua's 'unsexing' in her vision in terms of the ordeal that awaits her:
'Perpetua wants to strip herself of all that is weak, or womanish, in her nature'
(Dronke 1984a: 14).

Perpetua's assumption of masculinity probably reflects thinking prevalent even in
the early Church. Women needed to transcend their inherently flawed female
natures to win salvation, in a way which men, made in the image of God, did not.
Tertullian (c. 160–225) makes clear that the judgement of God falls particularly on
the female sex: 'You are the gateway of the devil; you are the one who unseals the
curse of that tree, and you are the first one to turn your back on the divine law'
(Blamires 1992: 51). For theological, economic and social reasons, salvation was
always going to be more difficult for women to achieve. Defined by her sexuality, it
was only by renouncing *mulieritas* (the capability of inspiring sexual desire in
others), a state that begins, inescapably, in puberty (Brown 1988: 81), and by
winning the battle for chastity that a woman could gain 'a masculine ... and
voluntary mind, one free from necessity, in order to choose, like masters, the things
which please us, not being enslaved to fate nor fortune' (Pagels 1988: 86).

113

Throughout the medieval period women tried to reach heaven by making different choices; opportunities to dedicate oneself to God varied by culture and by century. By the thirteenth century distinctively feminine forms of religious and mystical practice had begun to emerge (Bynum 1982: 172). Whether these constituted a recognizably feminist understanding of Christianity is debatable; most of the outstanding women of the period, dependent on male scribes and confessors to promote, and in some cases to approve, their unusual modes of devotion were orthodox in their theology and loyal to the institutions of the Church. For true 'feminist' alternatives to the Church's teachings it is necessary to turn to such heretical groups as the Italian Gugliemites, whose leader Gugliema proclaimed herself a female pope (Wessley 1978). Such cults, like the mysterious Brotherhood of the Free Spirit, were swiftly stamped out by the Church and often the only accounts we have of them are in hostile trial documents. Marguerite Porete, burned in Paris in 1310, is the only woman heretic whose own writing survives.

The overwhelming majority of medieval women had no religious vocation. As we have seen in preceding chapters, they grew up, married, gave birth and died with little more contact with the Church than baptisms, funerals, communion once a year at Easter, and attendance at church on Sundays to hear the Bible read in a language which they did not understand. Nevertheless, after the initial conversion period in western Europe, there was no real alternative to Christianity. Pagan superstitions might linger; often they were co-opted into Church ritual (in English and German the most important feast in the Church year, Easter, is named after a native goddess, while Celtic feasts became Lammas and All Saints' Day). Not to be a Christian becomes literally unthinkable: by the end of the period criticism of the Church's greed and corruption, and satire of the religious orders was commonplace, yet, as Jonathan Usher writes of Boccaccio's highly secular *Decameron*, 'religious attitudes and customs are so firmly anchored in his world-view that he, like many of his contemporaries, takes them for granted' (Boccaccio 1993: xxx).

Convents

Women's active participation in the religious life was always as a minority. Since women could not be priests or administer the sacraments, in the early period at least, the active religious life generally entailed entering a convent. However, even after the twelfth-century expansion of women's religious houses in England, only three thousand women out of a population of around three and a half million – or less than 0.02 per cent of the female population – were accommodated in convents (Elkins 1988: xiii, xx). Becoming a nun was not easy: convents demanded settlements as the price of admission which could rival in size the dowry which a marriage would require without the consequent benefit to the woman's kin of establishing an alliance with another family. Poor women might be taken into convents only as lay sisters; their manual labour freed the noble and bourgeois nuns for study, prayer and contemplation.

Girls were frequently educated in convents (see chapter 6 below). Some would leave and marry, others, like Hildegard of Bingen, were vowed to the convent from an early age. In the later period the acceptance of child oblates, as such girls were called, was often criticized. A young girl might choose to profess as a nun if the convent were the only home she had known, even if, like the Nun of Watton (see excerpt 2 below), she were manifestly unsuited for the religious life. Other women might be sent to the convent to get them out of the way – a frequent fate for discarded wives in Merovingian and Carolingian France. The famous (and violent) revolt of Clotild, who claimed to be the daughter of King Charibert, and Basina, daughter of King Chilperic, at the convent of the Holy Cross in Poitiers in 590, which Gregory of Tours recounts in the *History of the Franks* was in part motivated by the ringleaders' sense that, as royal women, they deserved more respect and better living conditions – in particular they resented having to share a bathroom with the servants (Gregory of Tours 1974: 571–2; Lucas 1983: 38–42).

Such scandals notwithstanding, for many women the convent life was a way of overcoming the disadvantages inherent in their sex: avoiding the tyranny of marriage and the dangers of childbirth, and achieving personal autonomy, even a measure of authority, within the institutions of the Church. They gained access to learning and the leisure and materials to write themselves. In the early period the Anglo-Saxon nun Hugeberc writes about the lives of her colleagues among the missionaries to Germany (*c.* 761), while at the same date another nun, Leoba, writes letters to Bishop Boniface, her mentor and kinsman (see below p. 196). The twelfth-century nun Hildegard of Bingen pours out medical treatises, plays, musical compositions and letters as well as her visionary writing. However, with the strict enforcement of enclosure rules (Schulenberg 1984), and the impoverishment of many nunneries, convent women's access to new learning and teaching became restricted. Herrad of Landsberg (or Hohenbourg), author of the *Hortus Deliciarum* (Garden of Delights) – an encyclopedic collection of Christian knowledge in prose and poetry composed between 1160 and 1170 – is the last nun to write anything other than mystical texts in the medieval period (Stuard 1987: 160). The convent writers who succeeded her were increasingly to seek within their own souls for the material about which they wrote, drawing on the Bible, the liturgy and the writings of the Fathers of the Church for the language they used: 'For women the only possible journey was within. Unable to learn, she could only burn with spiritual desire, and the singular, ineffable experience this brought her pointed up the inadequacy of the universal language of reason' (L'Hermite-Leclercq 1992: 249).

Merovingian France and Anglo-Saxon England had seen the formation of 'double monasteries', houses in which men and women lived and prayed side by side, ruled over by abbesses who were answerable only to God. The most famous is perhaps Hild's monastery at Whitby (see excerpt 1 below) where, according to Bede, five bishops were nurtured, and the tradition of English religious poetry originated

(Bede 1955: 242, 245–8). The abbesses of the double houses were often of royal blood; their ties with the reigning king added to their authority. Abbess Gerberga of Gandersheim in Germany was 'the head of a small kingdom with an army, courts of her own, a mint and representation to the imperial assembly', and, like certain other German abbesses, was entitled to be addressed as *Reichsfürstin* (princess) (Wemple 1992: 193). How far the English abbesses' spiritual remit ran is uncertain: Hollis suggests that the pastoral care which the abbesses exercised over their houses and local communities may have included the hearing of confession (Hollis 1992: 134–6), a privilege which holy women were not to retain for long. The founding of double houses was forbidden under the Second Council of Nice in 787, and those which continued were rigorously segregated (Hollis 1992: 102–3), even though the worst scandal that the double houses of Anglo-Saxon England seem to have produced is Bede's account of the nuns of Coldingham. These were guilty of excessive 'eating, drinking, gossip, or other amusements ... weaving fine clothes, either to adorn themselves like brides, or to attract attention from strange men' (Bede 1955: 251). Bede is not surprised when the convent burns to the ground. Late medieval nunneries were depicted as hotbeds of vice in satirical and popular literature (Daichman 1986). In the convents of the archdiocese of Rouen in the thirteenth century Archbishop Eudes uncovered scandalous behaviour ranging from the keeping of 'small dogs, squirrels and birds' to 'eat[ing] meat in the infirmary when there is no real need' to pregnancy: 'Jacqueline left the priory pregnant as a result of her relations with one of the chaplains, who was expelled because of this' (Amt 1993: 248–9).

Although scandals were uncovered by the visitations of bishops to the convents in their dioceses (Daichman 1986: 5–12), Roberta Gilchrist argues that such accounts are exceptional and partial; in reality nunneries were greatly valued by the communities which supported them: 'the wills of local gentry and merchants continued to bequeath gifts and money to the nuns even after monks had lost favour with benefactors' (Gilchrist 1994: 190–1; Oliva 1994).

Unlike most of the other new religious orders emerging in the wake of the eleventh-century Gregorian reforms (ending lay patronage and establishing clerical celibacy), the Cistercian order initially eschewed the foundation of any houses for women. As the Premonstratensians were to discover, women were best kept at a safe distance from monastic houses for they were awkward to supervise and a considerable drain on an order's economic resources. Enclosure meant that their communities were unlikely to be self-sustaining (Thompson 1978; Gold 1985: 76–93). Different solutions to the problem of maintaining convents were assayed: in England Gilbert of Sempringham's Gilbertine order returned to an arrangement something like the later Anglo-Saxon double house. Monks and nuns were kept firmly apart: lay brothers performed the heavy manual tasks, lay sisters domestic tasks, while the nuns communicated with the monks and the outside through small windows 'a finger length long and a thumb wide' (Elkins 1988: 143). Rotating 'turning windows' were used to pass things across without the parties catching sight of each other. Despite the scandal of the Nun of Watton (below, excerpt 2), Ælred of Rievaulx, who recounts the story, does not blame deficiencies in Gilbert's Rule for the catastrophe, rather the moral he draws is the inadvisability of admitting child oblates (Constable 1978; Elkins 1988: 108).

Elsewhere the competing demands of enclosure and self-sufficiency were resolved by the ideal of perfect poverty. In Italy Clare of Assisi founded her Order of Poor Ladies according to the ideals of her mentor, St Francis (Fig. 8). But while his order of friars could tramp the roads of Italy with staff and begging-bowl, taking the Gospel to the poor and needy, and accepting only such alms as they needed to live by, Clare's nuns could not safely or decently become mendicants. Clare's house at San Damiano survived by means of alms and a little gardening. After 1215, when the Fourth Lateran Council decreed that all religious orders should live according to an approved Rule, the battle to maintain the privilege of poverty became an ideological one for Clare. It was a marker of difference from all other orders, of a new kind of order for women, and Clare was prepared to allow the sisters at San Damiano to starve rather than lose it. Clare's version of her own Rule was finally confirmed two days before her death in 1251 (Brooke and Brooke 1978; Petroff 1986: 235). Amt (1993: 235–45) reproduces Clare's Rule.

Economic stability and physical security may appear to be a *sine qua non* for writing in the convent, but in fact the foundation at Helfta in Germany, brought under Gertrude of Hackeborn, abbess from 1251 to 1291, to 'the highest level of

Figure 8 A Franciscan nun has her hair shorn. From a manuscript belonging to a community of Franciscan tertiaries, Florence, late fifteenth century. MS Canon Liturg. 347 fol. 3r, Bodleian Library, Oxford.

feminine culture known to the Middle Ages' (Finnegan 1991: 3), was attacked on more than one occasion in the course of local aristocratic feuds, once by the abbess's close kinsman. Yet the novices in the community were educated in grammar, rhetoric and logic (the *trivium*) and many progressed to the *quadrivium* (arithmetic, music, geometry and astronomy). Nor was theological knowledge lacking: 'the nun who wrote [Gertrude the Great's] biography ... is evidently a scholar as well – she quotes Bede, Augustine, Jerome, Bernard, Gregory and Hugh of St Victor' (Finnegan 1991: 10). Three women writers are associated with Helfta: Mechthild of Magdeburg, Gertrude the Great and Mechthild of Hackeborn, sister of the abbess. Though Gertrude and Mechthild of Hackeborn were initially shy of writing down their visions, they encouraged each other, and had the support of the community in committing them to writing. Caroline Bynum suggests that the dissemination of Gertrude and Mechthild of Hackeborn's writing in particular reflects a 'conscious effort to establish and hand on to a next generation of sisters and to readers outside the cloister a spiritual teaching and a collective reputation' (Bynum 1982: 180).

Recluses and anchoresses

In the early Celtic Church, following the eastern practices of the desert mystics, women sometimes withdrew from everyday society to live apart in meditation: the obscure St Ita, for example, was friend and confidante to St Brendan (Hollis 1992: 135). For later women the eremitic life had many attractions: one did not have to pass the stringent entry criteria of the convent; rather the recluse could simply take up residence in a cave or hut secluded from the community, relying on her reputation for sanctity for enough alms to live on. However, in practice life as a hermitess was simply too dangerous for the custom to prevail for long: recluse women needed a support network for food and security. Christina of Markyate (*d. c.* 1160) inherited her hermitage from Roger, the hermit who had sheltered her when she had run away from husband and kin (Talbot 1959; Holdsworth 1978). The eleventh-century English nun Eve of Wilton left her convent, dissatisfied with the lack of asceticism she found there, and went to live at Angers in France, near another male recluse, Herveus, whose support network she could share, and who could guide her spiritual growth (Warren 1984: 202; Leclerq 1987: 72). Eventually, if paradoxically, the recluse became institution-alized as the anchoress: a woman who lived in a cell attached to a church or monastery. She was subject to the rules of enclosure: the burial service would be read over her as she was immured, and she was never to leave the anchorhold until she died (Fig. 9). Conditions in the anchorhold varied. The aristocratic anchoresses of the thirteenth-century *Ancrene Riwle* have servants to look after them, are permitted to keep a cat, and have a considerable amount of space at their disposal, since they may have women and children to stay (Millett and

Figure 9 The enclosure of an anchoress by the bishop. From the Pontifical of Richard Clifford, CCCC MS 79 fol. 96a (formerly 72a). Reproduced by kind permission of the Fellows of Corpus Christi College, Cambridge.

Wogan-Browne 1990: 134–5). Other anchoresses might literally have a single cell with a window giving onto the church in order to receive communion. Despite her desire for contemplative solitude, the anchoress was in demand as counsellor. She received visitors, as Julian of Norwich received Margery Kempe and advised her about her spiritual experience (Kempe 1940: 42–3). The vocation of anchoress was particularly popular in England from 1100 to 1500, both as an opportunity for the laywoman to leave the life of Martha for that of Mary, the active life for the contemplative – as the *Ancrene Riwle* has it – or, less frequently, as a form of advanced monasticism (Warren 1984: 197).

Beguines

A wave of religious enthusiasm swept across Europe in the wake of the late eleventh-century Gregorian reforms. Many more women than previously wished to lead a religious life and, with the restrictions on places in convents outlined above, alternative ways of achieving salvation had to be found. Some women were drawn to the various heretical sects (see below), while others, particularly in northern Europe, found a new way of living in the world. The first phase of the beguine movement, if it can be so characterized, seems to have been a number of women living independent religious lives within the city: the *mulieres sanctae* (holy women) in and around Liège in present-day Belgium, whose lives were recorded by Jacques de Vitry (Bolton 1978). In the next generation women congregated in non-hierarchical, independent communities, leading a life devoted to prayer and good works, while supporting themselves by their own manual work. Calling themselves 'beguines' (a name whose derivation is obscure), these women were especially an urban phenomenon; their way of living appealed to the new bourgeois and lower gentry classes. Other factors leading to the founding of 'probably the first "women's movement" in western history' (Bynum 1982: 14) were the revival of commerce, making living by trade possible, the growth of towns, affording a secure environment, and an increasing disillusion with the ostentatious wealth and worldliness of the established Church.

The beguines were, in the first instance, extremely successful: 'Like St Francis and his early followers, the beguines succeeded in living a virtuous apostolic life essentially by minding their own business, by providing example rather than criticism, [and] by remaining humble and obedient to church authority' (Devlin 1984: 185). In 1233 Pope Gregory IX gave the beguines quasi-legal recognition, with the provision that a closer eye be kept upon the movement; the inevitable result was that the beguinages came under episcopal control and a form of enclosure in the beguinage resulted. Women who identified themselves as beguines still lived at home or elsewhere in the city, however, bringing their inner lives under the direction of the spiritual advisers of the beguinage. Poor and indigent women took refuge in the beguinage, sustaining themselves by industrial work. Amt (1993: 263–7) gives a contemporary description of the way of life of the beguines of Ghent. Although the beguine movement survived in the Low Countries until the French Revolution, it did not cross the Channel: English women who wished to serve God and live in the world might join hospital orders where they looked after the sick, elderly and dying, while poor women were often accommodated in *maisons dieus*, where they were provided for by the community in return for their prayers (Gilchrist 1994: 172–6).

Despite the simplicity and apparent harmlessness of the movement, beguines made the Church anxious and aroused hostility in the community: 'Even in Liège, there were shameless men hostile to all religion who called these holy women by malicious names, howling like mad dogs over their devout practices and further damaging their reputations with disparaging "new names",' Jacques de Vitry reports (Bolton 1978: 255). Mechthild of Magdeburg, a beguine for most of her life, alludes several times to enemies who threatened her: 'I was warned about this book and was told by men/ that it should not be preserved/ but destroyed by fire' (Mechthild 1991: 55), though the supposition that she actually faced charges of heresy appears to be unfounded.

Heretic women

The name 'beguine' has been derived by some scholars from 'Albigensian' (McDonnell 1954: 435), and the beguine movement so warmly approved by Jacques de Vitry, who saw the *mulieres religiosae* as 'an impenetrable bulwark to the multiple threat of infidel and heretic' (McDonnell 1954: 4), had, in its early years, some practices in common with the anathematized southern sect. All across Europe new sects were forming. Some followed ancient traditions like the Waldensians of Lyons, or the Humiliati of northern Italy, others were wholly new manifestations of popular piety, like the flagellant sects who roamed the countryside in public penance or the followers of charismatic preachers who preached the crusades (Smith 1978). Given women's exclusion from authority or office in the established Church, it was hardly surprising that many turned to sects which promised more to women. Catharism offered guaranteed salvation for women who chose to become *perfectae* (the highest order in the Cathar hierarchy), though in practice they did not achieve exact equality with men, while some Waldensians consecrated female priests (Wessley 1978: 300). The thirteenth-century Gugliemites believed that a female incarnation of the Holy Spirit, Gugliema of Milan, would shortly establish a new church with a female pope and cardinals (Wessley 1978).

Southern France provides one female heretic whose testimony survives: Na Prous Boneta, a follower of the Spiritual Franciscans who preached apostolic poverty (the belief that the Gospels show that Christ owned nothing while on earth, and that his followers should do likewise). This doctrine was the most controversial of the thirteenth and fourteenth centuries. Acceptable in the moderate form in

121

which St Francis preached it, the radical social message which the Spiritual Franciscans promulgated was declared heretical in 1317, and persecutions followed. Na Prous, who lived with her sister in Montpellier, confessed herself a heretic in 1325 and was condemned to death (Petroff 1986: 284–90). Her confession reveals that she believed herself to be in some sense a container for the Holy Spirit: 'she said that it shall be necessary henceforth for whoever shall wish to save himself to believe in the works of the Holy Spirit given to Friar Peter John [Spiritual Franciscan leader, d. 1297] and to her speaking' (Petroff 1986: 289).

Marguerite Porete was a beguine whose book, *The Mirror of Simple Souls*, was widely circulated and translated, despite being declared heretical. Marguerite has been associated with the Brotherhood of the Free Spirit, who taught the soul's freedom from sin while still on earth, if it is joined to God through complete passivity of the will. Once the soul has reached the fifth state of the pious soul, 'she sees herself and knows divine Goodness, and this knowledge of divine Goodness causes her to see herself again; and these two sights take away her will and desire, and works of goodness, and for this reason she is wholly at rest' (Bryant 1984: 223–4). Though similar ideas are found in the writings of other Low Country beguines, Beatrijs of Nazareth and Hadewijch for example, Marguerite's visibility and fearless refusal to recant must have made her an obvious target for the Inquisition.

Saints and mystics

For most of the medieval period accession to the canon of the saints was not under central Church control. Thus an outstanding woman would gain a reputation for saintliness in her lifetime, by founding religious houses, by missionary activity, teaching or leading, or by living an exemplary life in some other respect. The performing of miracles was not a necessary condition of sainthood, but, almost inevitably, a holy woman's grave and body parts would be believed to have miraculous powers, and the saint's post-mortem reputation increased with a repertoire of miracle stories (Kleinberg 1992). Styles of sanctity among women changed over the thousand years we are considering: in the early period royal women achieved sainthood through converting their husbands and nations to Christianity, like the Frankish Clotild, and establishing monastic foundations and becoming abbesses – a category to which most Anglo-Saxon women saints belong. As inheritance laws changed, royal women had less opportunity to use their lands for religious purposes, and, as monogamous lifelong marriage became a norm, there were fewer repudiated royal wives to enter the cloister as abbesses (Schulenberg 1978: 123). Nevertheless, this pattern persisted until late for women in frontier areas of Europe: St Margaret of Scotland (d. 1093), St Elizabeth of Hungary (d. 1231) thus are among the last royal female saints of the period.

Coinciding with the Gregorian reforms, new styles of sainthood emerged for women. One was a new domestic ideal – 'holy housekeepers' as Schulenberg calls them. These might often be noblewomen, like St Hunna, whose humble washing of the clothes of the poor earned her the name 'the holy washerwoman' (Schulenberg 1988: 117–18). This privatized and domestic model of sanctity extended in the later period to include even lower-class women: the Italian servant-saint Zita of Lucca (?1218–72) gave alms from her meagre wages to the poor, gave up her bed to indigents, distributed food and deliberately scratched her face in order to make herself unattractive – a reaction to the widespread characterization of women servants as promiscuous. Numerous miracles occurred during Zita's funeral procession: cures of blindness, lameness, muteness and more, all attested to by a distinguished law professor at Pavia (Goodich 1985: 129).

After 1200 new female saints were often associated with the new religious orders: for example St Clare of Assisi and St Birgitta of Sweden. New manifestations of sanctity became widespread in the great upsurge in women's religious activity from the end of the twelfth century onwards. Coinciding with the new forms of devotion often associated with St Francis – extreme ascetic practices entailing deprivation of food and sleep, intense meditation on the humanity of Christ and the events of his Nativity and Passion in particular – holy women found signs of Christ literally written on their bodies. An extreme example is that of St Clare of Montefalco (d. 1308), who had often prayed that the Cross should be placed in her heart. After her death, the nuns of her convent found not only the Cross and the scourge of Christ, but the crown of thorns, the three nails, the spear and the pole with the sponge formed in the flesh of Clare's heart, and three globules, representing the Trinity in her gall-bladder (Camporesi 1988: 5–6, 200). Other women survived for many years without food, consuming only the communion host, or received the stigmata (the marks of Christ's wounds). Among the most remarkable must be Christina 'Mirabilis' of St Trond in Belgium, who, after apparently dying and seeing the terrors of hell and purgatory, returned to life in order to demonstrate the pains of purgatory in her own mortal body. Perching on steeples and treetops to flee the unbearable stench of humanity, she fed herself on milk from her own breasts, crept into lighted ovens, jumped into boiling water, immersed herself in icy rivers for days at a time, and even, in a state of divine contemplation, rolled up like a hedgehog (Petroff 1986: 184–6).

These pathologies are not without meaning: they work to prove the greater glory of God, his power over nature, and, as Caroline Bynum has argued, they establish the medieval connection between 'woman and flesh and the body of God.... Holy women imitated Christ in their bodies; and Christ's similar bleeding and feeding body was understood as analogous to theirs' (Bynum 1991: 101–2). For our secular age the more sensationalist accounts of late medieval female piety are difficult to accept, though we should note that most pious medieval women earned their place in heaven through service to neighbours and devotion to prayer, a fact often overlooked by male hagiographers, who are drawn to a physical construction of sanctity:

Because preachers, confessors and spiritual directors assumed the person to be a psychosomatic unity, they not only read unusual bodily events as expressions of soul but also expected body itself to offer a means of access to the divine ... because they associated the female with the fleshly, they expected somatic expressions to characterize women's spirituality.

(Bynum 1991: 235)

Other religious women had direct mental and spiritual experience of God. Visions of the Other World, common in the early period, though generally a male rather than female genre (see excerpt 4 below), became transformed into inner raptures in which the soul communed with Christ or God. Sometimes the visionary might see brilliantly vivid images which symbolized Christian truths, as Hildegard did; sometimes, like Margery Kempe, she chatted with the Virgin Mary and participated in events in Christ's life; sometimes her soul became united to God in an inexpressible ecstasy. The Flemish beguine Beatrijs of Nazareth tries to describe mystical union:

the blessed soul sinks down so deeply and softly in love, it is so mightily led in desire, that the heart fails and is within full of disquiet, the soul flows away and liquefies in love, the spirit is possessed with the violence of great longing.

(Petroff 1986: 204)

A great part of the women's writing we have from the years post-1000 is from mystics: Hildegard and Elisabeth of Schönau, Julian of Norwich, Margery Kempe, the women of Helfta, the beguines of the Low Countries, the Italians Umiltà of Faenza and Angela of Foligno, to name only a few. It is in their struggle with language, their attempts to express the inexpressible (epitomized below by Gertrude), dictating their words in a vernacular which their scribes, conscious of their own unworthiness, recorded in Latin, that we sense, perhaps, the beginnings of an *écriture féminine* in western writing: 'the emergence of a new linguistic order composed of words, laughter, tears, sleep, and dreams' (Régnier-Bohler 1992: 467).

Secular women

Alongside the developments in spirituality which gave rise to the beguine movement, the fourteenth and fifteenth centuries brought increased interest in religion among women in ordinary walks of life. While the Church was promoting virginity as the highest ideal for women, salvation for the married woman might seem problematic (Dalarun 1992: 30–1): Margery Kempe, mother of fourteen children, fretted over her lack of virginity, to be consoled by Jesus:

Oh Lord, now maidens are dancing merrily in heaven. Shall I not do so? For because I am no maiden, the lack of my maidenhead is a great sorrow to me: it seems to me that I wish I had been slain when I was taken from the font, so that I should never have displeased you, and then, blessed Lord, you would have had my maidenhead for ever.... [Christ replies]: 'Since you are a maiden in your soul, I shall take you by one hand in heaven and my mother by the other hand, and you shall dance in heaven with other holy maidens and virgins, for I may call you one dearly bought by me, and my own precious darling.'

(Kempe 1940: 51, 52)

Umiltà of Faenza (*b.* 1226) married and had children who died early. When her husband contracted a disease which imposed sexual abstinence upon him, she was able to recover her early vocation and both she and her husband took monastic vows. Angela of Foligno's husband and children died suddenly, freeing her for a life of sanctity (Petroff 1986: 236–7). Possibly the most influential of the married saints was Birgitta of Sweden (1303–73), who bore her husband eight children and held an important post at the Swedish court. After her husband died Birgitta began to experience revelations and she founded a new order of nuns at Vadstena (the Birgittines). In 1349 she journeyed to Rome, where she remained until her death, becoming influential in Church and international politics. Unlike the Italian saints mentioned above, Birgitta remained outside the cloister, anxious about her children, especially her son Charles, who was rumoured to have had an affair with Queen Giovanna of Naples (Obrist 1984; Holloway 1992: 1–20). When Margery visited Rome, she met a former servant of Birgitta, and heard about the saint's 'laughing cheer' and how 'she was ever intimate and good to all creatures that wanted to speak to her' (Kempe 1940: 94–5). Clearly Margery saw Birgitta as one model of sanctity which she could imitate, though, unlike Birgitta, Margery still had to contend with the problems of an existing marriage and a husband little inclined to chastity.

The exile of the papacy to Avignon between 1309 and 1377, and the subsequent schism which lasted until 1417, did much to shake the ordinary Christian's faith in the institutions of the Church. One of the major heretical movements which arose in the period was the Lollard or Wycliffite heresy in England. Lollards questioned the role of the clergy in the administering of the sacraments, and supported the translation of the Bible into the vernacular, enabling the individual to understand God's word for him- or herself, without ecclesiastical interpretation. To women, who had been systematically excluded from Church office over the previous thousand years, this bypassing of the clerical hierarchy must have had particular appeal. Lollardy was a family sect, and through their power within the family women became fully involved in its dissemination (Cross 1978: 360). In East Anglia, where court records document Lollardy fully in the 1420s, women took as vigorous a part as men; a hundred years later Agnes Pykas of Bury St Edmunds is recorded as sending for her son John, a baker in Colchester, and persuading him against belief in the sacraments: 'And she gave him a book of Paul's epistles in English, and bade him live after the way of the epistles and gospels, and not after the way the church teaches' (cited from Cross 1978: 374). Salvation had become too important a matter to be left to the Church.

1 THE LIFE AND DEATH OF ABBESS HILD

Text from: Bede (1955) *History of the English Church*, transl. L. Sherley-Price, Harmondsworth: Penguin, pp. 240–3.

Hild (or Hilda) of Whitby (*d.* 680) was the niece of King Edwin of Northumbria. Her royal connections enabled her to gain lands for the foundation of a number of nunneries. She was the most influential woman in England at the time, and is particularly remembered for her role in reconciling the Roman and Celtic churches at the Synod of Whitby (664). Hollis calls Bede's account of Hild 'an artifact of his own bias' (Hollis 1992: 243) and, indeed, Bede's lack of interest in Hild's life before she became a nun is noticeable, as is his stress on the achievements of her male pupils, rather than her own wisdom. Hild may well have been a widow when she took the veil, and the information which Bede has about her, probably based on a lost Life from the Whitby community, is short on the sensational miracle stories which conferred definitive proof of saintly status in Bede's eyes.

In the following year, that is the year of our Lord 680, Hilda, abbess of the monastery of Whitby, a most religious servant of Christ, passed away to receive the reward of the eternal life on the seventeenth of November at the age of sixty-six, after a life full of heavenly deeds. Her life fell into two equal parts, for she spent thirty-three years most nobly in secular occupations, and dedicated the remainder of her life even more nobly to our Lord in the monastic life. She was nobly born, the daughter of Hereric, nephew to King Edwin, with whom she received the Faith and sacraments of Christ through the preaching of Paulinus of blessed memory, first bishop of the Northumbrians, and she preserved this Faith inviolate until she was found worthy to see him in heaven.

When she decided to abandon the secular life and serve God alone, she returned to the province of the East Angles, whose king was her kinsman; for having renounced her home and all that she possessed, she wished if possible to travel on from there into Gaul, and to live an exile for our Lord's sake in the monastery of Cale [Chelles, near Paris]. In this manner she hoped the more easily to attain her eternal heavenly home, for her sister Hereswith, wife of Aldwulf, king of the East Angles, was living there as professed nun and awaiting her eternal crown. Inspired by her example, Hilda remained in the province a full year, intending to join her overseas; but when Bishop Aidan was recalled home, he granted her one hide of land on the north bank of the River Wear, where she observed the monastic rule with a handful of companions.

After this, Hilda was made abbess of the monastery of Heruteu [Hartle-pool], founded not long previously by Heiu, a devout servant of Christ who is said to have been the first woman in the province of Northumbria to take vows and be clothed as a nun, which she did with the blessing of Bishop Aidan. But soon after establishing the monastery she left for the town of Calcaria, which the English call Calcacestir [possibly Tadcaster], and settled there. Then Christ's servant Hilda was appointed to rule this monastery, and quickly set herself to establish a regular observance as she had been instructed by learned men; for Bishop Aidan and other devout men, who knew her and admired her innate wisdom and love of God, often used to visit and advise her.

When she had ruled this monastery for some years, constantly occupied in establishing the regular life, she further undertook to found or organise a monastery at a place known as Streaneshalch [Whitby], and carried out this appointed task with great energy. She established the same regular life as in her former monastery, and taught the observance of justice, devotion, purity, and other virtues, but especially in peace and charity. After the example of the primitive Church, no one there was rich or poor, for everything was held in common and none possessed any personal property. So great was her prudence that not only ordinary folk, but kings and princes used to come and ask her advice in their difficulties. Those under her direction were required to make a thorough study of the Scriptures and occupy themselves in good works, in order that many might be found fitted for Holy Orders and the service of God's altar.

Subsequently, five bishops were chose from this monastery – Bosa, Hedda, Oftfor, John, and Wilfrid – all of them men of outstanding merit and holiness. As already mentioned, Bosa was consecrated Bishop of York; Hedda became Bishop of Dorchester; and I shall tell in due course how John became Bishop of Hexham, and Wilfrid Bishop of York.

Here follows an account of the career of Oftfor who became bishop of the Middle Angles.

Christ's servant Abbess Hilda, whom all her acquaintances called Mother because of her wonderful devotion and grace, was not only an example of holy life to members of her own community, for she also brought about the amendment and salvation of many living far distant, who heard the inspiring story of her industry and goodness. Her life was the fulfilment of a dream which her mother Bregusyth had when Hilda was an infant, during the time that her husband Hereric was living in banishment under the protection of the British king Cerdic, where he was poisoned. In this dream she fancied that he was suddenly taken away, and although she searched everywhere, she could find no trace of him. When all her efforts had failed, she discovered a most valuable jewel under her garments, and as she looked closely, it emitted such a brilliant light that all Britain was lit by its splendour. This dream was fulfilled in her daughter, whose life afforded a shining example not only to herself, but to all who wished to live a good life.

When Hilda had ruled this monastery for many years, it pleased the Author of our salvation to try her holy soul by a long sickness, in order that, like the Apostle, her strength might be perfected in weakness. She was attacked by a burning fever that racked her continually for six years; but during all this time she never ceased to give thanks to her Maker, or to instruct the flock committed to her both privately and publicly. For her own example taught them all to serve God rightly when in health, and to render thanks to him faithfully when in trouble or bodily weakness. In the seventh year of her illness she suffered interior pains, and her last day came.

2 THE NUN OF WATTON

Text from: *Patrologia Latina* (1841–64), ed. J. P. Migne, Paris, vol. 195, cols. 791–6, transl. O. Gutman.

Ælred of Rievaulx (*d.* 1167) joined the Cistercian foundation of Rievaulx Abbey in north Yorkshire in 1134, later becoming its abbot. He wrote a number of works in Latin, including the earliest Rule for a female recluse (his sister) known in England (see chapter 6 below). The account below is taken from a letter of Ælred which survives in only one manuscript. The addressee is not known. The events related must have taken place in the early 1160s. Ælred gives his motive for writing this rather sensational account in the opening paragraph; he writes from first-hand knowledge since the abbot of Watton, a neighbouring foundation, had called him in for advice in the case. Ælred's tone changes from one of outrage and condemnation to one of charity and compassion in the course of the story, and he is quick to dissociate himself from the violence of the nuns, even if he thinks their zeal is praiseworthy. Nor does Ælred make clear what he imagines happened to the child; in a similar miracle story from a collection by Dominic of Evesham, dating to the early 1120s, the child is later recovered and eventually becomes a bishop (Constable 1978: 213). Thoughtful analyses of the story are Constable (1978) and Elkins (1988: 105–11).

To know and yet to hide marvels of the Lord and clear signs of the divine holiness is to commit sacrilege. That which may be a source of consolation for those alive at present, of edification for future generations, and of devotion for all, ought not to be withheld from the knowledge of others. But often the folly of the many frightens us off; many languish either with envy or lack of faith, scarcely believe their eyes when they read of things which are good, but by a mere touch of the wind are led to believe things which are evil.

It is recorded that during the reign of Henry at the church of York, a girl was brought to this same holy father, and received food in this same monastery. Soon she grew from a child. She acquired the lust that is common in girls of her age. There was no love in her for religion, no feeling for her order, nor any fear of God. She would walk clothed in the sacred garment, yet with wanton eyes, indecent language, and an inviting manner. And the worthiness of her habit was not reflected in her actions. She was chastised with lectures, but not reformed. With words they might exhort her, but could not correct her.

For hours she stole away from the eyes of her mistresses, so that she might indulge her laziness, or give herself over to vain decorations, or waste her time with stories, or persuade the others to do something foolish. She drew the discipline of her order down upon her, and she was compelled to maintain the standards of people outside the nunnery. All that she did, she did from fear, nothing from love.

The time arrived when she might be considered of marriageable age. She still preferred pleasures of the body to those of the soul, idleness to the quietude of the nunnery, lighthearted pastimes to those of serious intent. Now to certain brothers of the monastery was entrusted the care of those outside, and one of their tasks involved visiting the nunnery. On hearing of this, the girl approached them and gazed with curiosity upon their faces and at what they were doing. There was a young man among them, better looking than the rest, and in the first flush of youth. The wretched girl cast her eyes at him, and indeed he gazed back at her. They remained fixed in this way, each enticing the other. Before long, the slippery serpent, entering their hearts, injected its fatal poison into each.

At first, they simply beckoned to each other, but more explicit signs followed. At last they broke the silence, and their conversation was filled with the sweetness of love. Each scattered the seeds of desire over the other. As she claimed afterwards, he was planning her defilement, whilst she thought only of love. Their feelings for each other strengthened. In order that they might speak more freely together, and enjoy each other, they would agree upon a time and a place. As the sun receded, they welcomed the darkness. They would avoid public places, that they might have their pleasures in secret.

The wicked plunderer gave as a sign to her, his booty, the sound of a stone against the wall or onto the roof of the building in which he usually stayed. He promised the deluded girl that, when he threw it, it was safe for her to come to him. Then this maiden of Christ would arrive, and the two of them would surrender themselves to their adultery. She came, but, as a pigeon that has gone astray, she was quickly caught by hawks. By these hawks she was torn, cast down, and her mouth stopped lest she cry out. Her wicked lust compelled her to return to her adulterer. As this continued, the sisters heard the sounds more often, and wondered at this trickery of which she was suspected. A girl whose behaviour is frowned upon by all is especially open to suspicion. And this suspicion was increased by the flight of the young man. When he learned that her adultery had become known, fearing that he too would be discovered, he left the monastery and entered the world.

Then the wiser and more senior nuns summoned the girl. She, unable to hide her secret any longer, confessed her crime. Astonishment was the reaction of all who heard her. Their faces burned with their anger, and they rushed at her to beat her. They tore the veil from her head. Some thought that they should drag her to the flames, others that she should be torn limb from limb, others still that she should be tied to a stake and roasted on hot coals. The elders had perforce to restrain the fervour of the younger ones.

She was, however, stripped of her clothing and tied up. She suffered injury, even though she was spared the whip. She was bound with chains and thrown into a small cell, prepared for her. They placed shackles on both feet. To these were attached heavy chains, one of which was locked with a key to a large pole, the other fastened to the door. She received only bread and water, and contempt was heaped upon her daily.

The girl had conceived, and the swelling in her womb became visible. How great was the distress of all! The young girls of the nunnery lamented even more than the others. They feared that the crime of one might taint them all, and that they too might get pregnant. They felt as if they also were exposed to scornful eyes, as if it were they who were being torn by gnashing teeth. Each of them wept, and, in their anger, reproached their captive. Had the elder women not spared her on account of the pregnancy, there were times when they would not have refrained from beating her.

She patiently bore the taunts of all, and she declared that she deserved still greater torments, if only the others should not suffer for her infidelity. They pondered what ought to be done about all this. If she was expelled, her infamy might taint them all, but to retain her involved no small danger to their souls. Bereft of all comfort, and with a small child, there was a risk that she might die. Yet, as some pointed out, if they looked after her it would not be possible to conceal her.

Then one of them said: 'It would be best if the harlot, now heavy with the fruit of her adultery, be entrusted to that most wicked of young men, that she may be relieved of the responsibility for the product of her wicked consent.' To this, the poor girl replied: 'If this may be a solution for you, although I know that it will be the death of me, I do know the night and the hour at which the young man shall appear, just as he promised. May it be done as he in heaven wills.'

Immediately they seized upon these words. They planned revenge against the young man, and they sought from the girl all that she knew. She confessed, and promised that the truth was as she claimed.

Then the master of the congregation revealed the matter to an assembly of the brothers. And he ordered that, on that night, one of them should conceal his head with a veil and go and wait in the arranged place. He commanded that others should be hidden, and that they should show themselves only when he had arrived. Then they should drag him away, tie him up, and set upon him with cudgels. As the master said, so it was done. The young man arrived unawares. Not only his intention, but his garb was that of a layman. Burning with the poison of lust, he saw the veil. As a horse or a mule might act, lacking any intelligence, he rushed towards her whom he thought to be the girl. The emerging monks applied a harsh antidote to the poison. Hitting him with their staffs, they extinguished the fever that had been lit.

These events were conveyed to the young girls. Some of the more naive, burning with zeal for God, and desiring to be avenged for the injury done to virginity, asked that the young man be handed over for a short time by the brothers, that they might learn a certain secret from him. They agreed to give him up to the girls, who threw him to the ground and tied him up. She was led forth as a spectacle, the cause of all their woes. An instrument was given to her, and she was forced, with her own hands, to cut off the source of the poison. Then someone standing near seized the mutilated parts and, as if they were a convenant given in his blood, threw them into the mouth of the harlot.

You see by what zeal these defenders of chastity burned, the guardians against impurity, those who love Christ before all men. You see in what fashion he was mutilated, with what viciousness they avenged the injury done to Christ.... I praise the zeal but not the deed. I do not sanction the spilling of blood, but such outrage against those who tarnish holy virginity ought to be esteemed. Yet it is not clear why they acted thus out of revenge, when they had previously failed to act for the preservation of virginity.

But let us return to the story. The mutilated man was returned to his brothers. The perplexed girl was cast back into prison. Thus far, o miserable woman, I have concentrated upon the story of your wretchedness; henceforth I shall record with my pen in what manner the most compassionate piety of Christ was poured over you. For wherever sin had abounded, grace has superabounded. With the punishment exacted, and their anger cooling, the sacred maidens submitted themselves to the marks of Christ. They cried out and prayed that he might forgive the nunnery and that he might look after the shameful girl.

Indeed it was with daily prayers and tears that they managed to arouse divine mercy. The harlot, with sorrows and grievances, on top of the attacks which she had suffered, stirred that holy flesh of Christ. The just hear and exult in the sight of God, and they delight in their joy. Sinners hear that they might not despair of the goodness of that man, who balances judgement and mercy. O kindly Jesus, you have gazed at such hatred and fear from your maidens, and the affliction of a sinner among them. Now a child was alive in her womb, and milk flowed plentifully from her breasts. Her womb was visibly swollen, and it seemed that she would have twins. There were dark rings around her eyes, her face was pale, and her breasts looked drained of milk, though after a time they would be filled once more.

She was rarely in her small cell, because, of necessity, they prepared her for the birth. They cared for her as much as they were able, so that her bewailing should not induce the birth of the child. And behold, during a period of silence in a stormy night, when the wretched girl was asleep, she saw the prelate appear to her in a dream, through whose mercy she had originally been placed in that nunnery and given the habit of a nun. He looked at her with a severe gaze and asked her: 'Why is it that you curse me daily?' In great fear she denied this, but the saint replied: 'It is true, so why do you deny it?' The woman, recognising that she had been discovered, replied: 'Truly, o lord, because it was you who handed me over to this nunnery, in which such evils have befallen me.' To which the prelate replied: 'These sins, which you have not yet made public as you ought, remain upon your head. See that you swiftly confess as you should, and daily recite the following psalms to Christ. You shall be sustained by me in these commands.' Having indicated to her which psalms, he disappeared.

She awoke, now strengthened, and committed to memory the vision and the psalms. On the following night, she felt that she was about to give birth. She was filled with dread at the thought of what was to come. But, as her apprehension over the birth grew, the venerable prelate appeared once more to her as she slept. To the despairing girl he led two women, silent and beautiful. He approached the poor girl, and, with her head pressed against his knees, he covered her face with the cloth in which she was wrapped, and chided her saying: 'If only you were purged by confession, you would see clearly those things which are taking place. Indeed at present you feel the benefit, but you are not able to understand what is being done.'

After a little while she sat up, and she saw the women, as it seemed to her in her dream, wrap the infant in white linen and follow the departing prelate with the baby in their arms. As she awoke, she could feel none of the weight in her womb. With her hand she felt her body, and found that her stomach was flat. The midwives arrived, and, gazing at her, saw that her womb was no longer swollen, and that the face of the girl – I shall not say maiden – had grown beautiful, her eyes clear, rid of their dark rings.

As if they could not believe their own eyes, they asked: 'What is this? Have you added to your crimes by killing your child?' And immediately they ransacked the small chamber in which she was lying chained. It was clear that there was nothing lying hidden in the small space of her prison, neither in the mean furnishings nor the meagre straw that was her bed.

'O wretched girl,' they cried, 'surely you have not induced the birth?' She replied: 'I do not know.' She related her vision to them, and swore that she knew nothing more. They were still suspicious and did not trust this new development. They felt her womb, and, sure enough the large swelling had vanished, and she was thin. They touched her breasts, but no milk came forth from them. Not trusting this, they squeezed harder, but nothing was produced. They ran their fingers across every limb, and studied every part of her. But there was no indication that she had given birth.

Other women were called, and, after these, still more. All found the same thing. She was fully healthy, clean, and beautiful. Yet they did not dare pronounce judgement without the authority of the abbot. Until now, the girl had been held in chains, with her feet bound in irons. She beheld two ministers of divine mercy approach her. One of them, helped by his companion, broke the chain with which she had been tightly bound. When the nuns arrived the next morning, they were amazed that the chain had disappeared. They enquired how this had happened. She told them, but they refused to believe.

Ælred is consulted and visits the monastery.

When every detail had been related to me, I felt the fetter with my own hands, and I understood that none of these people, nor indeed any one could have broken it, without the aid of God.

Some of my audience were still fearful, and asked whether new chains ought to be placed upon her. I rejected this, declaring that it would not be suitable, but merely an indication of our lack of faith. We should rather expect, and indeed, hope, that he who freed her from the chains would remove that fetter by which she was still bound. Therefore they commended my company with their prayers, and we consoled them, as much as we were able, by the word of God. We returned to our monastery, praising and glorifying the Lord for all the things which we had heard and seen, and which the holy maidens had related to us. A few days passed, and a letter arrived for me from that venerable man, in which he told me that the remaining fetter had fallen off, and he asked me, in my unworthiness, what he ought to do next. Amongst other things, I included these few words: 'What God has cleansed, do not thou call common [Acts 11: 9] and she whom he has absolved do not thou bind.'

3 HILDEGARD'S VISION OF ECCLESIA, THE CHURCH

Text from: Hildegard of Bingen (1990) *Scivias*, transl. C. Hart and J. Bishop, New York, Mahwah, N.J.: Paulist Press, pp. 169–74.

For a full account of Hildegard, see chapter 6, pp. 200–1 below.

Vision III: The Church, Bride of Christ and Mother of the Faithful

After this I saw the image of a woman as large as a great city, with a wonderful crown on her head and arms from which a splendour hung like sleeves, shining from Heaven to earth. Her womb was pierced like a net with many openings, with a huge multitude of people running in and out. She had no legs or feet, but stood balanced on her womb in front of the altar that stands before the eyes of God, embracing it with her outstretched hands and gazing sharply with her eyes throughout all of Heaven. I could not make out her attire, except that she was arrayed in great splendour and gleamed with lucid serenity, and on her breast shone a red glow like the dawn; and I heard a sound of all kinds of music singing about her, 'Like the dawn, greatly sparkling'.

And that image spread out in splendour like a garment, saying, 'I must conceive and give birth!' And at once, like lightning, there hastened to her a multitude of angels, making steps and seats within her for people, by whom the image was to be perfected.

Then I saw black children moving in the air near the ground like fishes in water, and they entered the womb of the image through the openings that pierced it. But she groaned drawing them upward to her head, and they went out by her mouth, while she remained untouched. And behold, that serene light with the figure of a man in it, blazing with a glowing fire, which I had seen in my previous vision, again appeared to me, and stripped the black skin off each of them and threw it away; and it clothed each of them in a pure white garment and opened to them the serene light, saying to them one by one:

'Cast off the old injustice, and put on the new sanctity. For the gate of your inheritance is unlocked for you. Consider, therefore, how you have been taught, that you may know your Father Whom you have confessed. I have received you, and you have confessed Me. Now, therefore, behold the two paths, one to the East and the other to the North. If you will diligently contemplate Me with your inner vision as in faith you have been taught, I will receive you into My kingdom. And if you love Me rightly, I will do whatever you shall wish. But if you despise Me and turn away from Me, looking backward and not seeking to know or understand me, Who am recalling you by pure penitence though you are filthy with sin, and if you run back to the Devil as to your father, then perdition will take you; for you will be judged according to your works, since when I gave you the good you did not choose to know Me.'

But the children who had passed through the womb of the image walked in the splendour that surrounded her. And she, benignly gazing on them, said in a sad voice, 'These children of mine will return again to dust. I conceive and bear many who oppress me, their mother, by heretical, schismatic and useless battles, by robberies and murders, by adultery and fornication, and by many such errors. Many of these rise again in true penitence to eternal life, but many fall in false obduracy to eternal death.'

And again I heard the voice from heaven saying to me: 'The great edifice of living souls, which is constructed in Heaven from living stones, is adorned with the immense beauty of its children's virtues, encircling them as a great city encircles its immense throngs of people, or as a wide net does a multitude of fishes; and however much the work of the faithful thrives in the Christian name, by so much does it blossom with celestial virtues.'

Hildegard interprets the vision.

I
The building of the Church, who redeems her children by Spirit and water

Wherefore now you see the image of a woman as large as a great city; this designates the Bride of My Son, who always bears her children by regeneration in the Spirit and in water, for the strong Warrior founded her on a wide base of virtue, that she might hold and perfect the great crowd of His elect; and no enemy can conquer or storm her. She expels unbelief and expands belief, by which it should be understood that in the mortal world each of the faithful is an example to his neighbour, and so they do great works of virtue in Heaven. And when the just, one by one, shall come to join the children of light, the good they have worked will appear in them, which cannot be seen here among mortal ashes, concealed as it is by the shadow of trouble.

II
The Church in her origin was adorned by apostles and martyrs

She has a wonderful crown on her head; for at her origin, when she was raised up by the blood of the Lamb, she was fittingly adorned with apostles and martyrs, and thus betrothed with true betrothal to My Son, since in His blood she faithfully formed herself into a firm edifice of holy souls.

III
The Church is adorned by the priesthood and almsgiving

And from her arms a splendour hangs like sleeves, shining from Heaven to earth. This is the work of power done by priests, who with purity of heart and hands and in the strength of good works offer the holiest of sacrifices upon the holy altar in the sacrament of the body and blood of the Saviour. And the most glorious of their works is to show mercy, always offering generous help for every grief and distributing alms to the poor with a gentle heart while saying with their whole soul, 'This is not my property, but that of Him Who created me.' And this work, inspired by God, is before His eyes in Heaven, when by the teaching of the Church it is done among the faithful on earth.

IV
On the maternal kindness of the Church

Her womb is pierced like a net with many openings, with a huge multitude of people running in and out; that is, she displays her maternal kindness, which is so clever at capturing faithful souls by diverse goads of virtue, and in which the trusting peoples devoutly lead their lives by the faith of their true belief. But He Who casts the net to capture the fishes is My Son, the Bridegroom of His beloved Church, whom He betrothed to Himself in His blood to repair the fall of lost humanity.

V
The Church, not yet perfected, will be brought to perfection near the end

She does not yet have legs or feet, for she has not yet been brought to the full strength of her constancy or the full purity of her fulfilment; for when the son of perdition comes to delude the world she will suffer fiery and bloody anguish in all her members from his cruel wickedness. By this calamity, with bleeding wounds, she will be brought to perfection; then let her run swiftly into the heavenly Jerusalem, where she will sweetly rise anew as a bride in the blood of My Son, entering into life with ardour in the joy of her offspring.

VI
How the Church devoutly offers up her children in purity

But she stands balanced on her womb in front of the altar that stands before the eyes of God, embracing it with her outstretched hands; for she is always pregnant and procreating children of hers by the true ablution, and offering them devoutly to God by the purest prayers of the saints and the sweet fragrance of chosen virtues both hidden and manifest; which are plain to the clear understanding of the mind's eye when all stain of falsity and all noises of human praise are removed, as incense is purged of a noxious stench which corrupts its smell. This good work is in God's sight the sweetest sacrifice, at which the Church constantly labours, striving with her whole desire for heavenly things in bringing virtues to fruition, and by increase of such fruit thirtyfold, sixtyfold and a hundredfold building the high tower of the celestial walls.

VII
No wickedness of devilish art can obscure the Church

And she gazes sharply with her eyes throughout all of Heaven; for her purpose, which she devoutly keeps to in the heavenly places, can be obscured by no wickedness: no persuasion of devilish art, nor error of a wavering people, nor storms over the various countries in which madmen tear themselves to pieces in the fury of their unbelief.

VIII
The human mind cannot fully understand the secrets of the Church

You cannot make out her attire, which is to say that the human intellect, weighed down by fragile weakness, cannot fully understand her secrets; except that she is arrayed in great splendour and gleams with lucid serenity, for the True Sun shines everywhere around her by the bright inspiration of the Holy Spirit and her most becoming adornments of virtue.

IX
On the virginity of Mary

And on her breast shines a red glow like the dawn; for the virginity of the Most Blessed Virgin when she brought forth the Son of God glows with the most ardent devotion in the hearts of the faithful. And you hear a sound of all kinds of music singing about her, 'Like the dawn, greatly sparkling'; for, as you are now given to understand, all believers should join with their whole wills in celebrating the virginity of that spotless Virgin in the Church.

X
On the expansion of the sacrament of the true Trinity

And that image spreads out its splendour like a garment, saying that she has to conceive and give birth, which means that in the Church the sacrament of the true Trinity will more widely expand, for it is her garment in which to shelter the faithful peoples, through whom she grows by the building up of the living stones, who are washed white in the pure font; thus she herself affirms that it is necessary to salvation that she conceive children in blessing and bring them forth in cleansing, by regeneration in the Spirit and water.

XI
The ministry of angels is at hand for each of the faithful

And at once, like lightning, there hasten to her a multitude of angels, making steps and seats within her for people, by whom the image is to be perfected; because for each of the faithful there is at hand a fearsome and desirable ministry of blessed spirits; they are building stairs of faith and seats of sovereign quiet for those faithful souls, in whom that happy mother, the Church, will attain to her full beauty.

XII
Those regenerated by the Church their mother in the faith of the Trinity

Then you see black children moving in the air near the ground like fishes in water, and they enter the womb of the image through the openings that pierce it. This signifies the blackness of those foolish people who are not yet washed in the bath of salvation, but love earthly things and run about doing them, building their dwelling on their unsteadiness; they come at last to the mother of holiness, contemplate the dignity of her secrets and receive her blessing, by which they are snatched from the Devil and restored to God. Thus they enter the confines of the churchly order in which the faithful person is blessed by salvation, when he says within himself, 'I believe in God', and the rest of the articles of faith.

4 RANNVEIG'S VISION

Text from: *Gudmundar saga Biskups* (1983), ed. S. Karlsson, Editiones Arnamagnæeanæ, Series B vol. 6, Copenhagen: C. A. Reitzels Forlag, pp. 92–9. Transl. C. Larrington.

Bishop Gudmund Arason (d. 1237) was a charismatic figure who, after an exemplary early life, was elected bishop of northern Iceland. In this post he had numerous quarrels with local chieftains, mainly about the jurisdiction of ecclesiastical courts, and was driven from his bishopric on more than one occasion. The vision recounted below is contained in his Life, probably composed by Lambkár Thorgilsson, his chaplain, after Gudmund's death. The Life is no longer preserved, but it is the basis of the account cited below. Rannveig's historicity is somewhat suspect. She has no family or genealogy, and disappears from view. The details of her vision are similar to others of this type, though the genre is 'feminized' in that women's sexual relations with priests (a controversial question in contemporary Iceland as the Church tried to establish the principle of clerical celibacy) and women's vanity in clothing are pointed up. More important for the story-teller are the remarks by the saints about Gudmund's sanctity, especially the comparison with Thomas Becket (d. 1170), whose struggle with the apparatus of the state Gudmund was to experience in his own future episcopacy. Rannveig's vision occurred in 1198. The three saints who help her are Olaf, patron saint of Norway, Earl Magnus, patron saint of the Orkneys, and the obscure Hallvard, patron saint of Oslo.

There was a remarkable happening one winter in the eastern fjords: a woman there fell into unconsciousness. She is called Rannveig. She was the mistress of a certain priest called Audun and had been the mistress of another priest before that. Although she was not very scrupulous in this respect, she was otherwise a devout woman. This is what happened: early one morning she fell down in front of the hall on the way from the living room; she was alone and when people came and found her she had been lying there for a long time. She was carried into the living-quarters and people sat by her all day long, and saw that she was not dead, for sometimes she thrashed about violently as if something was hurting her very much. That was on a Saturday, before the first Sunday in Lent. And when she recovered consciousness in the evening, she sat up and blessed herself and asked God to help all of them. She said that many great things had happened to her, which she had to relate to the highest clergy, and she singled out Gudmund Arason, the priest, whenever she could let him know, and Broddi the priest who was in the Fljótsdal district. She had to tell everyone whom the vision concerned, although it seemed difficult to her. And we heard this, from those who were present to hear her very words, and when she related this vision to Gudmund Arason, the priest.

She said that demons came for her with great ferocity and seized her hands and led her roughly and mercilessly over rocky ground and brambles. And as they went along she saw many torments, and men in the torments, and they went with her until they came to where she could see before her what looked like a big cauldron or a deep and wide pit, full of boiling pitch and all around was burning fire. There she saw many men, both living and dead, and she recognised some people there. She saw there nearly all the secular chieftains who had misused their authority. Then the demons began to speak to her, saying: 'You shall go down into this, for you deserve it. You have lived in disgusting depravity, and you have committed the same sins as those who are down here, since you have slept with two priests and corrupted their ministry and have been arrogant and avaricious as well. Now you shall stay here since you would never cease to serve us and we shall torture you in many ways.' Then they dragged her forward to the pit and there was such a terrible surge that it splashed up over her legs and every part of her body that was bare. When she woke up she was burnt there. Then she was more frightened than can be described. She called upon the saints to intercede for mercy to God, first to Mary the queen and Peter the apostle. She called to holy King Olaf and Earl Magnus, the saint, and to Hallvard, for people invoked them a great deal then in this land. And at that moment a great light came upon her and she saw that some splendid men were in it, and yet it was rather terrifying. She was very glad at this sight, so much so that she dared ask who they were. And they said that they were King Olaf, and Earl Magnus and the holy Hallvard. They caught hold of her, and took her out of the hands of the demons and led her away. Then the demons lashed after her with a whip and it struck her on the shoulder and on the back and the loins, and they said this: 'Though now, as often happens, we have to abandon the conversation we were having, yet she shall have something for her wickedness.' The whip was red hot and she burnt everywhere that it touched her. And when the demons had gone, the men who were with her spoke to her. 'Now you have been shown your deserts, and those of many others who also would not listen to people's advice. And you must tell every man that you have seen here about his case. Now you were burned on the legs because you had embroidered stockings and black shoes and adorned yourself to attract men, and on the hands because you have sewn sleeves for yourself and for others on holy days, and on the back and shoulders because you have worn finery and rich linen, and dressed yourself up for men out of pride and spiritual weakness. And because God is mild and merciful and you invoked Mary the queen and Peter the apostle and us to intercede for you, they have sent us on their behalf, for otherwise you would have been destroyed, but they have obtained that boon from God that you shall return to life and atone for your misdeeds. And you shall come to see the rewards of the holy men who are here in your land, both living and dead, for in no other land are there proportionally as many of the saved as there are in Iceland and their prayers and ours maintain the land, otherwise it would be doomed.'

Then a great light came over her once again. In it was a tall man who was radiant and as bright as snow, as were his garments also. They told her that it was Peter the apostle. And when they had gone on with her for a while, then another light came over her once again, brighter than she had ever seen before. There was also a sweet perfume, and Mary the queen, Mother of God, was in this light and she was as bright as the sun, so that Rannveig could scarcely look at her. Before them there were delightful, smooth meadows, made beautiful with all kinds of flowers and perfumes. There she saw many beautiful mansions and many houses, high and gorgeous so that she thought she would never be able to comprehend their splendour, but they were not all equally splendid. Then they said to her, 'Now here you see the dwellings assigned to holy men, both living and dead, and here the houses are not all equally beautiful, for although they are all holy men, yet the most holy of them are Bishop Jon and Bishop Thorlak the Younger, and then next Bishop Björn and Bishop Isleif and Bishop Thorlak the Elder.

And likewise it is with these holy men who are alive now, enduring trials and bearing patiently the people's disobedience to them, for the holier the man, the greater his patience for God's sake. And the house that you see there which is high and beautiful, but from which no sound comes, that belongs to Björn, the hermit at Thingeyri. And the other house there which is high and magnificent, from which you can hear a great deal of splendid sounds and beautiful singing, that belongs to Gudmund Arason the priest, for his prayers maintain this land, just as our prayers maintain Norway and the Orkneys, and he will be the greatest upholder of this land, and he will not occupy any lower seat than Thomas [Becket], the archbishop of England.' Many wonderful things she saw and heard there. And when she awoke, she was so afraid that she could scarcely speak about them, and it was always the case afterwards that she trembled where she said anything about her experience. And many men benefited by this vision, for many hidden things were told them about their own conduct. And yet some men bore a grudge, because they were despised for their misdeeds, and yet they would neither give up, nor atone for their wrongdoing.

5 THE WOMEN OF HELFTA

Texts from: Mechthild of Magdeburg (1991) *The Flowing Light of the Divinity*, transl. C. Mesch Galvani, ed. S. Clark, Garland Library of Medieval Literature, New York and London: Garland Publishing; Gertrude of Helfta (1967) *Œuvres spirituelles* I, *Les Exercices*, ed. J. Hourlier and A. Schmitt, Sources Chrétiennes 127 and (1968) II, *Le Héraut*, Books I–II, ed. P. Doyère, Paris: Les Editions du Cerf. Transl. C. Larrington.

An important body of mystical, devotional and theological writings was produced by the group known collectively as the women of Helfta, who lived and worked in the scholarly and serene ambience created by Abbess Gertrude of Hackeborn in the convent of Helfta in Germany, founded in 1229. The three women writers associated with Helfta are: Mechthild of Magdeburg (1207–82), a former beguine, who spent the last twelve years of her life there; Mechthild of Hackeborn (1241–98/9), sister of Abbess Gertrude, and Gertrude of Helfta or Gertrude the Great (1255–1301?). These women's works were widely translated, and influential across Europe. Mechthild of Hackeborn's *Book of Special Grace* was known as far away as the Low Countries and translated into Middle English as the *Book of Gostly Grace*; Boccaccio and Dante may have known her work.

Mechthild of Magdeburg seems to have been brought up in a courtly environment: at all events she is familiar with courtly poetic styles. She had her first mystical experience at the age of 12, and began to compose her book in Low German in 1250. Mechthild lived in Magdeburg as a beguine; she seems to have suffered some persecution for her views. Books 1 to 6 of *The Flowing Light* were written in Magdeburg; Book 7 at Helfta, where Mechthild died around 1282.

Gertrude entered Helfta at the age of 5, and lived there until her death *c*.1301; at the age of 25 she experienced a 'conversion' and her mystical life begins. Gertrude's visionary imagination, as we see below, is less erotic than Mechthild's. Her images are often selected from the natural world, but the excerpts below are drawn partly from biblical imagery, and from a strong maternal sense. Although she wrote a great deal, in German and in Latin, all that remains is her book of spiritual *Exercises*, and the five volumes of the *Legatus Divinae Pietatis* (*The Herald of Divine Love*), of which only Book 2 was actually written by Gertrude herself.

(a) Mechthild of Magdeburg: *The Flowing Light of the Divinity*

(i) Now, I lack the German language, and I have no command of Latin, so if this has any merit to it, I cannot take the credit, for there was never such a worthless dog who did not readily come to his master when enticed with a white roll.

(p. 33)

(ii) *God is jubilant over the soul's vanquishing four sins*

In Heaven, Our Lord is jubilant over the loving soul He has on earth and He says:

> Behold, how she, who has wounded Me, ascends!
> She has thrown off the ape of the world.
> She has vanquished the bear of unchastity.
> She has trodden on the lion of pride.
> She has torn the belly of the wolf of greed.
> And she comes running like an exhausted stag
> To the well, which I am.
> She soars like an eagle
> Out of the depths to the heights.

(pp. 20–1)

(iii) *How a vision asks the loving soul about the seraphim and the lowest human being*

The soul points out that the angels are God's children and yet his servants. But the soul is daughter of the Father, sister of the Son, and Bride of Holy Trinity.

When the game comes to an end,
Look to the one who is the prime mover of it,
The worthiest angel, Jesus Christ,
Who soars above the Seraphim
Who must be God undivided with His Father;
That is whom I will take into my arms,
To eat and drink Him
And do with as I please.
That can never happen to an angel,
No matter how high above me he might be.
And his Divinity is never so precious to me
That I do not at all times
Feel it in all my limbs,
So that I can never cool down.
Why should I be concerned with what the angels feel?

(pp. 46–7)

(iv) Concerning the orchard, the flower, and the singing of the maidens

You are like a new bride
Whose only love has left her sleeping,
He to whom she had inclined herself with total trust,
From whom she cannot bear to part ... for even one hour.
When she awakens she can have him no more
Than her senses can bear,
And this causes her to begin her lamentations.
While the youth is not at home with her
She must be very much at one with him.
'I come to you at my pleasure whenever I wish;
If you are modest and still
And conceal your sorrow as best you can,
The power of love will grow in you.
Now I will tell you where I am.
I Myself am in all places and in all things
As I ever was without beginning,
And I await you in the orchard of love
And pick for you the flower of sweet reunion
And ready your bed there
With the pleasurable grass of holy knowledge,
And the bright sun of My eternal Divinity
Will shine on you with the concealed wonder of My delight,
Which you have bred in Me a little secretly.

143

And I lower the highest tree of My Holy Trinity
So that you can pick the green, white and red apples of my gentle humanity;
And the shade of My Holy Spirit shall protect you
From all earthly sorrow,
So that you will forget your heartache.
As you embrace the tree I will teach you the song of the maidens,
The melody, the words and the sweet harmony –
Unintelligible to those
Who are imbued with lasciviousness.
And yet they shall have a sweet exchange.
My love, now begin to sing, and let Me hear how well you can do it.'
'Ah, my beloved, I am hoarse in the throat of my chastity,
But the sweetness of Your kindness
Has cleared my throat so that I now can sing.
So, Lord, Your blood and mine are one, untainted;
Your voice and mine are one, undivided;
Your robe and mine are one, immaculate;
Your mouth and mine are one, unkissed.
These are the words to the song of the voice of love,
And the sweet sound of the heart must linger
Since it was not written by human hands.'

(pp. 54–5)

(v) How a person seeks God

When God seemed alien to a person, she seeks Our Lord, saying: 'Lord, my pain is deeper than the abyss, my heartache more bitter than the world, my fear is taller than the mountains, my yearning is higher than the stars. I can find You nowhere in these things.'

In this misery, the soul became aware of her beloved beside her, and he was like a fair youth, ineffably beautiful. She would have concealed herself, but instead she fell down at His feet, greeting His wounds, which were so sweet that she forgot all her pain and her age. She thought: 'Alas, how gladly I would see His countenance, although then you would have to deprive yourself of the wounds, and how gladly you would hear His words and his longing.'

She rose, dressed and adorned herself in unwavering modesty. He said; 'Welcome, beloved!'

(p. 217)

(vi) *Thus speaks the loving soul to her dear Lord*

If all the world were mine
And were of pure gold,
And if I could at will be here eternally,
Remain the noblest, the fairest,
And the richest queen,
It would all be meaningless to me.
So much rather would I see
Jesus Christ, my dear Lord,
In His heavenly glory.
Think of how they suffer, who wait a long time for Him.

(p. 246)

(b) Gertrude the Great: *Exercises*

(i) *Exercise III, ll. 87–112*

Exercise of marriage and of consecration

Probably intended for the anniversary of a nun's profession.

Who is like you, O my lord Jesus Christ, my sweet love, high and immense and who regards the most lowly things? Who is like you among the powerful, Lord, you who choose the feeblest things in the world? Who is as great as you, who established heaven and earth, you whom the Thrones and Dominations serve, and who wish to take your pleasures with the children of men? How great is your grandeur, king of kings and Lord of powers, who rules over the stars and bring your heart close to that of a man? Who are you who in your right hand hold riches and glory? You are filled with delights, and have a Bride on the earth. O Love, whither do you bend your majesty? O Love, from where do you derive the source of wisdom? Surely from the abyss of misery. O Love, to you alone, to you alone belongs this remarkable and abundant wine, by which the heart of God is overcome and made drunk.

(ii) *Exercise V, ll. 401–23*

Exercise of divine love

Gertrude recommends exercises and meditations for each of the canonical hours.

At Vespers, together with Jesus, your lover, dressed in the armour of love, advance confidently against all temptation, so that, with his grace ever helping and comforting you, you will be able to conquer the world, the flesh and the devil, and triumph gloriously over all temptation. And ask for this

145

through prayer, and through this verse:

O my sweetest Jesus, do not let my feet stumble, you who neither slumber nor sleep, you the guardian of my soul.

O God who is Love, you yourself are my wall and my bulwark. Those who in this world can stand firm in trial, they will know what shelter has been prepared for them in your peace, to shade them from the heat and protect them from the rain. Ah, now behold and look upon my battle: you yourself have shaped my fingers for the fight. Let an army come to fight against me, my heart will not fear, for you my sure rampart and my strong tower will be with me, both within and without.

Where is my enemy, if you are helping me? Let him advance upon me, if you fight before me! Through your glance alone you reveal to me, and you lay bare the machinations of Satan, and in one breath your Word dissipates them before me. If my enemy flings me down a thousand times, falling upon your right arm so dear to me, I will embrace that arm and kiss it with all my heart, and, protected by you, defended by you, marching out unwounded from the midst of the fight, I shall stand firm.

(iii) The Herald of Divine Love, Book 2: ch. 10

Fear of writing

It seemed to me so unfitting to write down all these things, that I could not manage, in this respect, to resolve the conflict in my conscience, and thus I kept putting it off until the Feast of the Exaltation of the Holy Cross; on that day during Mass I had resolved to apply myself to other thoughts. But the Lord restored my spirit with these words: 'Certainly, you should know that you will never escape from the prison of the flesh until you have repaid every last farthing.' And I had been thinking that I had repaid all these gifts of which I speak, if not through writing, at least verbally, but the Lord confuted me with those words which, that very night I had heard read at Matins: 'If the Lord had taught his doctrine only for the sake of those who were then living, there would only be his sayings, and not the Scriptures, but yet it is on account of the Scriptures that many are now saved.' And the Lord added: 'I want to have in your writing a clear, incontrovertible witness to my divine loving kindness, through which I shall benefit many souls, in this Last Age.'

Then, very cast down in myself, I began to consider how difficult, nay impossible, it would be for me to find the expressions and the words which could make everything that had been said to me comprehensible to the human intellect, without risk of scandal. In order to remedy my pusillanimity swiftly, the Lord seemed to pour down upon my soul like a powerful torrent of rain. Under the violence of the downpour, in my human wretchedness, like a fragile, tender plant, cowering and beaten down, I could not drink anything in, except for a few very significant expressions which my intellect alone could never have found. Thus, even more overwhelmed, I asked what all this might lead to.

Then your gracious loving kindness, my Lord, with its customary sweetness, lightened my burden and refreshed my soul with these words: 'Since you think you cannot profit from this inundation, I shall press you to my divine Heart, so that my influence will act on you slowly and gently with repeated inspiration, according to your capacity to bear it.'

Lord God, since you completely fulfilled this promise, I recognise its truth! For four days, each morning, at the most suitable time, you inspired me with part of what I have written above, with so much clarity and sweetness, that it was possible for me to write down effortlessly things which I did not clearly know, just as if I had known them by heart for a long time. You moderated this however, so that, when I had written down a suitable portion for the day, after that no effort on the part of my own intelligence could produce for me a single word; yet on the next day they would come to me in such abundance and so easily. Thus you disciplined and restrained my impetuosity, since, as Scripture teaches, one ought not to become so attached to the active life that one neglects the contemplative. Thus in your constant zeal for my salvation, you let me rejoice in the sweet embraces of Rachel at times without my being deprived of the glorious fecundity of Leah; in the wisdom of your love may I achieve both active and contemplative to your satisfaction.

(iv) The Herald of Divine Love, Book 2: ch. 16

Visions of the Infant Jesus

On the most holy day of your Nativity, I took you from the crib, a weak little baby swaddled in bands, and pressed you to my breast, bringing together all the bitterness of your childhood troubles, like a bouquet of myrrh between my breasts, and sharing the divine grapes of sweetness, offered and pressed to slake the most intimate thirst of my soul. Even as it seemed to me that I could never receive a better gift, since it pleases you often to add to your past gifts an even more noble gift, you yourself augmented the superabundance of your saving grace, in the way I shall describe.

The following year, in fact on the same feast-day, during the mass 'Dominus dixit', I received you from the womb of the Virgin Mother, in the form of a little baby, so weak and delicate that I cradled you at my breast for a while; it seemed to me that I felt again some of the compassion which, before the feast, had made me pray particularly for a certain soul in affliction.

But I must admit that, even in receiving such a great favour, alas, my piety did not have sufficient ardour; whether this was because of your justice, or my negligence, I do not know. However, in the end it was your wisdom combined with your grace which arranged things so that I should be conscious of my unworthiness, and tremble at my negligence in letting my sluggardliness divert me into vain thoughts. Whatever the case, you alone can answer for me, oh Lord my God. . . .

Then on the day of the most sacred Purification, while the procession was commemorating how you chose to be led to the temple like a victim, you, our salvation and our redemption, while they were singing the anthem 'Cum inducerent', the Virgin, your mother, took back her baby, the blessed fruit of her womb from me, with a severe expression, as if to reproach me for not properly taking care of you, the joy and honour of her immaculate virginity. Remembering that, by the grace derived from you, she is given to sinners for their reconciliation and to the desperate for their hope, I said to her, 'Mother of tenderness, have you not received the very source of mercy, your son, in order to obtain grace for those who need it, and in order to cover our innumerable faults with your unsurpassed charity?'

Finally, and more clearly than the day, I was shown that you cannot hold back the abundance of your sweetness when, the next year, on the same holy day, you favoured me with a similar gift to the year before, but greater still, as if I had merited the gift of the previous year by my great and diligent devotion to you; however, in fact I really now merited, not a new gift, but rather a just punishment for having wasted the first. Yet, during the reading of the Gospel, at the words: 'Peperit Filium suum primogenitum' (She brought forth her first-born Son) your immaculate mother, with her unsullied hands presented you to me, the son of her virginity, beloved child, who with all your strength, were stretching towards my embrace. And I alas, all unworthy, I received you, darling baby, as you clasped your little arms around my neck. And by the sweet breath exhaled from your blessed mouth by your sweet spirit, I felt myself so strengthened and vivified that, from then on, let my soul bless you forever, Lord my God, and all that is within me praise your name.

And as your blessed mother prepares to swaddle you, I shall ask to be wrapped with you too, so that even the slight obstacle of a linen cloth should not separate me from you, whose embraces and kisses are infinitely sweeter than honey. And thus I understand that you are wrapped in the all-white swaddling of innocence and secured with the golden ties of charity, and that, to be swaddled and bound with you, it is necessary for me to strive constantly for purity of heart and charitable works.

6 LETTERS OF SAINT CLARE OF ASSISI

Text from: *Francis and Clare: The Complete Works* (1982), ed. R. J. Armstrong and I. Brady, London: SPCK, pp. 199–202.

Clare of Assisi *c.* 1193–1253 was born into a wealthy merchant family in Assisi. When she first heard Francis preach is unknown, but in 1212, in part to avoid a proposed marriage, she sought Francis's help and received the tonsure. Despite her relatives' forceful objections, Clare was given refuge in a nearby convent and she eventually settled at the Church of San Damiano, which Francis had had restored, and was soon joined by other women, including her sister Agnes. Thus the 'Poor Ladies' of Assisi became recognized as followers of Francis, the 'Poor Man' (Il Poverello) of Assisi. Clare had to struggle, first against a papal ordinance against founding any new women's orders, and then to gain the right to create her own Rule for the Poor Ladies, based on the Rule of Francis's friars, with its emphasis on perfect poverty. It was not until two days before her death that Clare finally secured papal approval of her Rule. Clare was ill for much of her life; possibly extreme ascetic practices were to blame, although her sensible remarks to Agnes of Prague below on the subject would seem to suggest otherwise.

Clare had initially been attracted by the Franciscan ideal of perfect poverty and ministry to the poor and Francis himself seems to have envisaged her leading a group of women in helping the poor and sick. Such a life was not possible for women within the Church – in particular women could not decently beg for alms as the Friars did, and gradually Clare came to accept the limitations of enclosure, although she refused to give up the ideal of poverty. The women 'made a little money by spinning and by making altar linens, and grew a few vegetables in their garden, but they remained very poor' (Moorman 1968: 35). Petroff (1986: 231–5) gives a stirring account of Clare's struggles to keep alive the Franciscan ideal.

Blessed Agnes of Prague was born in 1203, daughter of Ottokar, king of Bohemia and Queen Constance of Hungary. Agnes was sought as a bride for his son by Emperor Frederick II, and some years later, he himself wanted to marry her. Agnes came under the influence of the Friars Minor who visited Prague, and she founded a church, friary and hospital for them. In 1234 she entered the convent, and began to write to Clare, whom she longed to emulate in the Franciscan way of life. Agnes remained in the convent for the rest of her life, dying at the age of 79. This letter comes from *c.* 1238; Agnes wanted clarification of the Poor Ladies' rules about fasting as she was seeking approval of a similar Rule for her own foundation from the Pope. Clare's reply shows an intimate knowledge of the Bible, from which many of her phrases are drawn, a poetic evocation of the beauties of contemplation, and practical advice on the subject of fasting. The stress laid on the virtues of poverty and humility is typical of Clare's preoccupation with holding fast to the apostolic ideals of her mentor, Francis.

Third letter

To the lady [who is] most respected in Christ and the sister loved more than all [other] human beings, Agnes, sister of the illustrious king of Bohemia, but now the sister and spouse of the Most High King of heaven: Clare, the most lowly and unworthy handmaid of Christ and servant of the Poor Ladies: the

149

joys of redemption in the Author of salvation and every good thing that can be desired.

I am filled with such joys at your well-being, happiness, and marvellous progress through which, I understand, you have advanced in the course you have undertaken to win the prize of heaven. And I sigh with such happiness in the Lord because I know you see that you make up most wonderfully what is lacking both in me and in the other sisters in following the footprints of the poor and humble Jesus Christ.

I can rejoice truly – and no one can rob me of such joy – because I now possess what under heaven I have desired. For I see that, helped by a special gift of wisdom from the mouth of God Himself and in an awe-inspiring and unexpected way, you have brought to ruin the subtleties of our crafty enemy and the pride that destroys human nature and the vanity that infatuates human hearts.

I see, too, that by humility, the virtue of faith, and the strong arms of poverty, you have taken hold of that incomparable treasure hidden in the field of the world and in the hearts of men with which you have purchased that field of Him by Whom all things have been made from nothing. And, to use the words of the Apostle himself in their proper sense, I consider you a co-worker of God Himself and a support of the weak members of His ineffable Body. Who is there, then, who would not encourage me to rejoice over such marvellous joys?

Therefore, dearly beloved, may you too always rejoice in the Lord. And may neither bitterness nor a cloud [of sadness] overwhelm you, o dearly beloved Lady in Christ, joy of the angels and crown of your sisters!

> Place your mind before the mirror of eternity!
> Place your soul in the brilliance of glory!
> Place your heart in the figure of the divine substance!
> And transform your whole being into the image of the Godhead Itself
> through contemplation!
> So that you too may feel what His friends feel
> as they taste the hidden sweetness
> which God Himself has reserved
> from the beginning
> for those who love Him.

Since you have cast aside all [those] things which, in this deceitful and turbulent world, ensnare their blind lovers, love Him totally Who gave Himself totally for Your love. His beauty the sun and moon admire; and of His gifts there is no limit in abundance, preciousness, and magnitude. I am speaking of Him Who is the Son of the Most High, Whom the Virgin brought to birth and remained a virgin after His birth. Cling to His most sweet Mother who carried a Son Whom the heavens could not contain; and yet she carried Him in the little enclosure of her holy womb and held Him on her virginal lap.

Who would not dread the treacheries of the enemy of mankind, who, through the arrogance of momentary and deceptive glories, attempts to reduce to nothing that which is greater than heaven itself? Indeed, is it not clear that the soul of the faithful person, the most worthy of all creatures because of the grace of God, is greater than heaven itself? For the heavens with the rest of creation cannot contain their Creator. Only the faithful soul is His dwelling place and [His] throne, and this [is possible] only through the charity which the wicked do not have. [He Who is] the Truth has said: 'Whoever loves me will be loved by My Father, and I too shall love him, and We shall come to him and make our dwelling place with Him.'

Therefore, as the glorious Virgin of virgins carried [Christ] materially in her body, you, too, by following in His footprints, especially [those] of poverty and humility, can without any doubt, always carry Him spiritually in your chaste and virginal body. And you will hold Him by Whom you and all things are held together, [thus] possessing that which, in comparison with the other transitory possessions of this world, you will possess more securely. How many kings and queens of this world let themselves be deceived! For, even though their pride may reach the skies and their heads through the clouds, in the end they are as forgotten as a dung-heap!

Now concerning those matters which you have asked me to clarify for you: which are the specific feasts our most glorious Father Saint Francis urged us to celebrate in a special way by a change of food, feasts of which, I believe you already have some knowledge – I propose to respond to your love.

Your prudence should know then that, except for the weak and the sick, for whom [Saint Francis] advised and admonished us to show every possible care in matters of food, none of us who are healthy and strong should eat anything other than Lenten fare, either on ferial days or on feast days. Thus, we must fast every day except Sundays and the Nativity of the Lord, on which days we may have two meals. And on ordinary Thursdays everyone may do as she wishes, so that she who does not wish to fast is not obliged. However, we who are well should fast every day except on Sundays and on Christmas.

During the entire Easter week, as the writing of Saint Francis tells us, and on the feasts of the Blessed Mary and of the holy Apostles, we are not obliged to fast, unless these feasts occur on a Friday. And, as I have already said, we who are well and strong always eat Lenten fare.

But our flesh is not bronze nor is our strength that of stone. No, we are frail and inclined to every bodily weakness! I beg you, therefore, dearly beloved, to refrain wisely and prudently from an indiscreet and impossible austerity in the fasting that I know you have undertaken. And I beg you in the Lord to praise the Lord by your very life, to offer to the Lord your reasonable service and your sacrifice always seasoned with salt.

May you do well in the Lord, as I hope I myself do. And remember me and my sisters in your prayers.

5

WOMEN AND POWER

INTRODUCTION

[King Sigibert of the Franks] sent messengers loaded with gifts to Spain and asked for the hand of Brunhild, the daughter of King Athanagild. This young woman was elegant in all that she did, lovely to look at, chaste and decorous in her behaviour, wise in her generation and of good address.... She was, of course, an Arian, but she was converted by the bishops sent to reason with her and by the king who begged her to accept conversion. She accepted the unity of the blessed Trinity and was baptized with the chrism. In the name of Christ she remains a Catholic.[1]

(Gregory of Tours 1974: 221–2)

When he [Chlothar II] saw her [Brunhild], he said: 'O enemy of the Lord, why have you done so many evil things and how have you had the temerity to kill so many of the royal family?' Then the army of the Franks and Burgundians united in shouting that the very wicked Brunhild deserved death. Then King Chlothar had her lifted onto a camel and paraded through all the army. Then she was tied to the hooves of unbroken horses and torn limb from limb. Finally she died; her only grave was the fire and her bones were consumed. After establishing peace, the king went home.

(*Liber Historiae Francorum* 1974: 96)

Was Queen Brunhild of the Franks the near-saintly figure whom Gregory depicts, or was she rather the villainess whom Chlothar II, Fredegund's son, rightly put to death to end her reign of terror? The partiality and bias of medieval sources is nowhere more clearly demonstrated than in contemporary accounts of powerful women. As

[1] Brunhild was still alive when Gregory was writing; she died in 613.

Pauline Stafford writes about queens in the early Middle Ages, what shapes the text about the powerful woman is: 'every possible form of bias and distortion … malicious gossip, political propaganda, deliberate suppression of facts, inadequate knowledge, blatant anti-feminism, even simple lies' (Stafford 1983: 3).

For the queen to commission her own account of her life, such as the *Encomium Emmae* (written in praise of Emma, wife of both Æthelred and Cnut of England), is no better guarantee of 'truthfulness', as the modern reader understands it, for the *Encomium* has the propagandist aim of furthering the claim to the throne of Emma's son by Cnut, Harthacnut. It suppresses Emma's first marriage to Æthelred, as if to imply that Edward and Alfred, her sons by Æthelred, are sons of Cnut (Stafford 1983: 3). The texts which tell us about powerful women must be interrogated closely, for, although the information from writers such as Gregory and Bede purports to be history, medieval chroniclers understood history in terms of patterns and types. Nowhere is stereotyping more apparent than in the accounts of women in this period. Thus the rule of Ermengarde, daughter of the Marquis of Tuscany, who governed northern Italy in the tenth century is indicted as a 'pornocracy' by the poet Liutprand of Cremona:

> the cause of her power, shameful though it be even to mention it, was that she carried on carnal commerce with everyone, prince and commoner alike…. Ermengarde's beauty, in this corruptible flesh, roused the fiercest jealousies among men: for she would give to some the favours she refused to others.

> (cited from Wemple 1987: 148)

Liutprand's indictment is self-contradictory: logically, Ermengarde cannot have slept with everyone *and* also have refused her favours to certain men. If the woman wields power for ends which the writer approves, then she is an Esther, a Judith and ornament of her people; if she uses her power, however effectively, for ends with which the writer has no sympathy, she is a Jezebel (a list of queens so characterized in Stafford 1983: 21), and deserves no better than the horrific fate meted out to Brunhild.

Definitions

Women held both power and authority in different areas and at different times in the medieval period. The distinction between power and authority is important. To adapt the classic distinction made by Max Weber, power is: 'the probability that one actor within a social relationship will be in a position to carry out his own will, despite resistance'; when 'power rests on the notion that an individual has the "right" to impose his will, and when it is exercised within a hierarchy of roles, it is defined as "authority"' (Lamphere 1974: 99). Thus a Merovingian queen, such as Fredegund, might have the *power*, in terms of forcefulness of character and personal access to treasure, to order assassins to attack her rivals, or to seize and torture Parisian housewives; later Carolingian queens had *authority* over the running of the palace. Setting the level of taxes on agricultural products was seen as part of the domestic arrangements, and, according to Hincmar of Reims, the queen would oversee the royal treasury, freeing the king to concentrate on military activity (Stafford 1983: 99).

Nor must we discount 'influence' when considering the relations of medieval women to power: 'to bring about a decision on another's part to act in a certain way, because it is felt to be good for the other person, ... and for positive reasons, not because of sanctions which might be imposed' (Lamphere 1974: 99–100). The activities of the king's mistress are often analysed in these terms – see the description of Lady Mede in *Piers Plowman* (Langland 1978: 17), construed as a satirical portrait of Edward III's mistress, Alice Perrers. But by the fourteenth century Froissart depicts the queen herself as using her femininity to persuade her husband to act against his first inclinations, as we see in excerpt 5 below. It would be misleading to suggest that, by the fourteenth century, such strategies were the only way in which women could exercise power in public. However, the institutional authority of the queen had declined from the heyday of the 980s when queen regents ruled most of Europe, from Italy across Germany to the Baltic, over England and over France (Stafford 1983: 141).

The early period

In the early part of the period, as Christian missionaries spread northwards and westwards among the Germanic tribes, women in this area seem to have shared some authority with men. Tacitus (AD 98) tells us that 'they [the Germanic tribes] believe that there resides in women an element of holiness and a gift of prophecy; and so they do not scorn to ask their advice, or lightly disregard their replies' (Tacitus 1948: 108). Tacitus was not writing an anthropological study of the Germanii, for his chief aim was to contrast the decadent mores of contemporary Rome with the purity and nobility of the barbarian tribes. But his depiction of Germanic women as counsellors chimes with the adage from the Old English poem *Maxims I* on the relationship between a noble husband and wife: '[A woman shall] know how to give advice to him, both of them together, holding authority in the fortress' (*Anglo-Saxon Poetic Records* 1936: 159–60). We cannot build too much on these sketchy references, but Bede's accounts of English royal couples, together with the custom of enthronement, where king and queen sat side by side on formal occasions (Hollis 1992: 152), and the later ritual of consecrating the queen (Stafford 1990: 62), all point to a concept of queenly authority, even if the notion of complete Germanic egalitarianism cannot be sustained. The queen's authority always derived from the king, mediating between him and his warriors in ritual and treasure-giving: she had no status of her own (Enright 1988).

Christian queens were particularly charged with the conversion of pagan husbands. Clotild, who converted her husband Clovis, king of the Franks (Gregory of Tours 1974: 29–31), had some success and was credited with the conversion of the nation. The Frankish princess Bertha of Kent and her daughter Æthelburg, queen of Edwin of Northumbria, were the recipients of letters from Popes Gregory and Boniface respectively, urging them to their Christian duty in this regard. Bede credits neither queen with any particular success, preferring to ascribe the royal conversions to the preaching skills of the Christian missionaries (Hollis 1992: 218).

Women's power, as in most periods of history, derived from two related sources: family and wealth. Status was bestowed by father and husband; thus a wife might be repudiated if a more politically advantageous match could be made with a more influential family. The serial marriages of Robert II ('Robert the Pious' who ruled France from 996 to 1031) illustrate his progression from concubine to well-born but infertile wife, to a second wife who gave him sons, but whom he repudiated in order to return to the first wife after the succession had been assured (Duby 1983: 75–85). In the late sixth century, Merovingian kings were given to marrying slave girls – Fredegund started her career thus, as her daughter Rigunth tauntingly reminds her (chapter 3, excerpt 1 above) – but other kings were more anxious about their wives' status. By the ninth century the need to find a bride to match one's rank – while avoiding contravention of the Church's consanguinity laws – had become near-impossible in France (Duby 1983: 78). As we have seen, this gave kings a convenient excuse for ridding themselves of unsatisfactory wives by suddenly and zealously applying the consanguinity laws. Some kings, such as Otto II of Germany, sought a way out of the kinship maze by marrying further afield: Otto's bride was Theophanu, daughter of the Byzantine emperor (d. 991). The position of a foreign bride, far from her own kin, could be difficult; Theophanu came into conflict with her forceful mother-in-law Adelaide, when she became regent of the Ottonian Empire after her husband's death (Ennen 1989: 2–6). Eventually the two women reached a *modus vivendi*, but Odilo of Cluny still refers to her as 'that Greek woman' in his Life of Adelaide (Stafford 1983: 3). Sixty or so years later the monk Othlo of Emmeram records a vision in which a nun sees Theophanu in torment dressed in burning rags, regretting that she had omitted to do penance for wearing fine clothes, for such extravagance had not been regarded as sinful in her own country (*Patrologia Latina* 146: col. 373). Some brides were resourceful enough to escape being sent in marriage to a foreign land: Hadwig, niece of Otto I, was betrothed to Constantine of Byzantium, but when a Greek painter came to paint her portrait for her betrothed she pulled a face 'so full of hatred for the marriage', according to the Chronicle of the monastery of St Gall, that neither the painting nor the marriage came to anything. Hadwig stayed in her own land and married a Swabian noble instead (Ennen 1989: 83–4).

The economic basis of power is crucial to our understanding of women's status in the medieval period. We saw in chapter 1 how women's lives were shaped by the varying bride-price, morning-gift and dowry arrangements current in their particular society, and in the laws governing the acquisition, alienation and bequeathing of their property. Women might gain spiritual power by becoming saints if they were in a position to grant land for religious purposes; the lives of many royal women demonstrate a choice of sanctity over queenly authority. Anglo-Saxon rulers would often retire to monasteries at the end of their reigns, while Radegund of Poitiers, who was anyway proving to be a rather unsatisfactory queen, was allowed to take the veil by her husband Lothar I (Gregory of Tours 1974: 168; Stafford 1983: 99). There is a clear connection between the capacity of royal women in France and Anglo-Saxon England to endow monastic houses, and the establishment of double monasteries, where an abbess – often herself of royal blood – ruled over nuns and monks. Stephanie Hollis argues that the notion of the queen's overlordship of monastic houses stems from the model of joint rule by king and queen which she thinks obtained in Germanic societies (Hollis 1992: 208–9). In other countries, queens might alienate part of their dowry land for monastic purposes: Adelaide of Germany had a long struggle with her son Otto and his wife Theophanu, and later with Theophanu alone to assert her right to do this. Royal families did not necessarily oppose monastic foundations: part of the royal woman's responsibility was to watch over the land's monastic foundation: 'tribal gods, dynastic saints and the royal dead watched over the world of early medieval kings' (Stafford 1983: 120). And the queen's maintenance of the shrines and royal mausoleums was an important part of her duties. In the early medieval period, many queens were able to attain sainthood as an alternative to exercising their secular power (Schulenberg 1978: 118).

Women and arms

Among the aristocracy, the tenth and eleventh centuries saw a growing number of women emerging as chatelaines. They held landed property and were responsible for providing military manpower and for the administration of justice in their domains. From the disorders of the Viking period onwards the chatelaine was expected to defend garrisons when the king or lord was absent elsewhere, almost as an extension of her domestic duties. The wives of Crusaders, whose husbands and male kin might be absent for a decade or so, usually held authority over their husbands' domains. The lady was mostly engaged in maintaining the status quo however, rather than undertaking any new initiatives (McNamara 1989: 26–37). The chatelaine might sometimes succeed in repelling attack without recourse to arms: native intelligence and an understanding of male psychology could save the day. The Empress Berengaria was caught unawares by a Muslim force at Toledo in 1139 when her husband, Alfonso VII, was elsewhere. Berengaria averted the attack by declaring that there was no honour in winning a castle from ladies. To emphasize the extreme femininity of the garrison's occupants, she and her ladies put on their finery and withdrew to the summit of the castle where they played musical instruments until the discomfited attackers withdrew (Dillard 1984: 15). In the fifteenth century, the women of the Paston family in East Anglia had to defend one of their manors against armed attack in the absence of their menfolk who were in London. Writing to her husband in 1448, Margaret Paston comes straight to the point:

> Right worshipful husband, I recommend myself to you and pray you to get some crossbows, and some windases [devices for bending crossbows] to bend them with, and some quarells [crossbow-bolts]; for your buildings here are so low that no one can shoot out from them with a long bow, however much we have need of it. I suppose you could get such things from Sir John Fastolf if you sent to him. And also I would like you to get two or three short pole-axes to defend the doors with, and as many padded jackets as you can.
>
> (*Paston Letters* 1958: 9)

(Defence was not the only thing on Margaret's mind; she goes on to ask in the same letter for a pound of almonds and a pound of sugar.)

Women did not necessarily restrict themselves to defence: Æthelflæd of the Mercians took the initiative in establishing anti-Viking coalitions with neighbouring rulers (Wainwright 1990: 51); Richilde of Hainault was captured fighting at the battle of Cassel in 1071. Contemporary chroniclers found nothing out of the ordinary about such women, though later medieval writers view both Æthelflæd and Richilde as prodigious, even as transgressive in their actions – a thirteenth-century chronicler interprets Richilde's presence on the battlefield as evidence that she was practising sorcery (McLaughlin 1990: 194, 200). Thus there is some historical evidence for women actually taking to the field themselves: Gaita, wife of Robert of Guiscard, a Norman adventurer, successfully halted a rout among her husband's men: 'as they continued to run, she grasped a long spear and charged at full gallop against them. It brought them to their senses and they went back to fight.' Anna Comnena, who gives us this account, compares Gaita to 'another Pallas, if not second Athena' (Anna Comnena 1969: 147). Gaita was acting in an exceptional, emergency situation here, but McLaughlin argues that women's direct participation in fighting declined as warfare ceased to be organized on a domestic basis, that is, under a lord and his troop of retainers (McLaughlin 1990). Nevertheless, even Christine de Pizan, who herself wrote a treatise on military tactics, advised the noblewoman to familiarize herself with weapons and to make sure her castles were well garrisoned (Christine de Pizan 1985: 129). Women may never have fought as a matter of course, but writers throughout the period relished the depiction of fighting women, whether valkyries like the Norse Brunhild, the Amazon queens of the histories of Troy (Owen 1993: 148–52), or cross-dressing female knights such as Silentius/Silentia, the hero(ine) of the *Roman de Silence*

(*Silence* 1992). Unlike the fighting women of non-western traditions, the career of the European woman warrior ends in domesticity or death (Weigle 1992: 347; Larrington 1992: 156).

The Amazon story was inherited from classical sources, but the shield-maiden and female knight have their genesis in this period. Some scholars suspect that there were actual Viking women warriors (Clover 1986; 1993: 367); Joan of Arc provides an attested historical instance of a fighting woman (though Joan claimed never to have taken life). However, the writers who elaborated the stories of valkyries, female knights and maiden kings were intrigued by the notion of the fighting woman as an inversion of the normal and natural and enjoyed exploring the imaginative possibilities of the motif. For a knight to discover that the brave opponent he had been fighting against was a woman added sexual piquancy: a favourite scene is the death of the Amazon queen Penthesilea in the Troy histories. Achilles kills her in ignorance of her sex, then weeps over her beauty (Owen 1993: 148–52). The failure of the fighting woman, either accidentally killed by superior male skills or recognized and domesticated, confirmed the natural, God-given order. Men were dominant and women subordinate; any reversal of this position could only be temporary.

The later period

Women lost their power bases at different times for a number of reasons. They were still able to acquire power within the family, and in times of conflict – when male mortality was very high – often inherited large dominions. Contemporary writers engaged with the troubling figure of the heiress in varying ways: a stock figure of medieval romance is the king's only daughter, who must be won, despite rival suitors and the king's opposition, if the hero is to achieve maturity and prosperity. Anxieties about the imbalance of status inherent in the marriage of the heiress to a man of lower status are explored in the Norse 'maiden-king sagas' in which the arrogant queen typically scorns and tortures her suitors before she is humbled, often brutally, and agrees to make a match with the saga's hero (Kalinke 1990).

Changes in dowry customs and inheritance laws weakened the queen's position in the High Middle Ages.

A queen might still influence a husband or son, and his bureaucracy, or as the surviving parent she might be trustee with the power of regent during the minority of her son. But neither her office itself, nor her inheritance rights and marriage portion sustained her position. Royal women, except those who could claim the right of primogeniture in the event they had no brothers, lost authority.

(Stuard 1987: 163)

159

Eleanor of Aquitaine (*d.* 1204) was perhaps the last medieval woman ruler to exercise the kind of authority common in the early period. She inherited more than a quarter of modern France, a possession which she kept under her own control during her two marriages to the French king Louis VII and the English Henry II. Eleanor accompanied Louis on the First Crusade, giving rise to scandalous rumours about her relationship with her uncle, Raymond, ruler of Antioch; her marriage with Louis was never to recover, though it is probable that, had Louis appointed her Regent of France, Eleanor would have been content to stay behind. Eleanor's adventures in the East quickly became the stuff of legend: an anonymous author in Reims, writing in the year 1260, spins a splendid tale of how Eleanor fell in love with Saladin, leader of the Saracens, and was on the point of turning apostate and eloping with him when Louis was alerted by one of the queen's appalled maid-servants (Owen 1993: 105–7). In the early part of Henry's reign Eleanor often acted as his regent in England while he was abroad maintaining the Crown's French territories. Later the couple became estranged through Eleanor's encouragement of her sons' political ambitions. After Henry's death Eleanor emerged as a political force to be reckoned with, protecting Richard I's interests in England while he was at the Crusades. When he was taken prisoner on his way home she was largely responsible for raising his ransom. When she married Henry II, Eleanor found he intended simply to add her territory to the other Crown lands. Although she took particular pains to try to ensure that one of her younger sons should rule independently over Aquitaine after her death – installing Richard as duke while he was still the second son – only John, king of England, outlived her. John was unable to retain control over the distant duchy, however, and the French king Philip Augustus regained Aquitaine soon after Eleanor's death.

Royal women thus lost authority as the role of the queen was redefined. Richenza (*d.* 1141), wife of Lothar of Süpplingenberg, was the last German empress to sign her own decrees (McNamara 1989: 27). Opportunities for exercising informal power also diminished in comparison with the early period, for the noblewoman had always been able to participate in public life to some extent through her kin connections. Now, however, royal courts began to institute echelons of trained civil servants to administer affairs of state, staffed by men educated in arts or law at the universities. Kin connections could work to a woman's disadvantage as well: the sad story of Leonor López de Córdoba who, from the age of 8 spent nine years as a political prisoner, losing her father and brothers because of her family's affiliation to the overthrown monarch Pedro I of Castile, bears witness to the vicissitudes which an innocent woman might suffer (Amt 1993: 158–63).

Church reform limited the noblewoman's power to intervene in Church affairs as lay patronage (the right of rulers to appoint to ecclesiastical positions) was withdrawn, and the close alliances of queen and bishop so often depicted by Bede and Gregory of Tours were no longer advantageous to the Church (Hollis 1992: 165–9) (Fig. 10). Nevertheless, in the later medieval period aristocratic women

Figure 10 The seal of the Queen's College, Oxford, depicting the founder
Queen Philippa, wife of Edward III. Reproduced by kind permission of the
Fellows of the Queen's College.

continued to administer their estates as dowagers, or their dowry property in
second marriages, often with the assistance of counsellors and estate officials,
much as Christine de Pizan describes in excerpt 7 below (Archer 1992).

Women from other social classes also found their participation in political
structures restricted as the household became marginalized as a unit of economic
and political significance in the developing towns. In the northern cities of Bruges,
Ghent, Cologne and Frankfurt in the late medieval period, women were excluded
from the exercise of public power as it became concentrated in the hands of guilds
and associations of artisans, precisely because women were identified with the
family, a unit no longer significant in urban politics. Aristocratic women retained the
power deriving from the family for longer: Martha Howell points to the irony whereby
'Margaret of Burgundy could have governed the Low Countries and ... Catherine
Sforza ruled Milan precisely at the time when not a single one of the successful
craftswomen and merchants of Cologne or Frankfurt or Bruges even sat on their
town councils' (Howell 1988: 54).

In rural communities women had less opportunity than their fathers and brothers
to take part in the processes of justice and contract law; Judith Bennett shows how
landholding women appear in the court rolls of the English village of Brigstock –
buying and selling property, answering complaints and pursuing litigation – chiefly
in adolescence or in widowhood; married women were invariably represented by
their husbands (Bennett 1988: 18–36). Unmarried women, then, were expected to
discharge their legal responsibilities to the court, just as a man would be, but they

could never hold the important public offices of reeve, aletaster or juror. Bennett's summing up of the Brigstock findings could serve as a neat summary for the status of women in post-1000 Europe: 'the extension of public power to women when convenient, and their exclusion from political authority no matter how inconvenient, might apply to medieval English women generally.... Medieval women, in short, were often powerful but they were never authoritative' (Bennett 1988: 29). Similar evidence exists from other countries: in medieval Norway, for example, it has been calculated that roughly 20 per cent of families must have had only daughters to inherit, yet women still never held public office. Landholding widows were allowed to send a male relative to represent them at the local assembly, a provision which implies that they had the right to attend in person if they wished (Ormøy 1988: 176).

By the end of the medieval period women had lost many of the rights they had enjoyed in the years before 1000. As ever, birth or marriage into a powerful family bestowed informal power; possession of land and money before marriage and during widowhood conferred legal rights which disappeared on marriage. Participation in public affairs had become a near-impossibility for women of all classes, except where influence might be effected behind the scenes, in the role of royal wife, mistress, or as queen mother. Under any other circumstances a woman could not speak or act in the public domain, unless she had authority derived from God. As we have seen in chapter 4, from the twelfth century onwards both nuns and secular women increasingly turned towards the divine to give meaning to their lives. Female mysticism, which peaked in the fourteenth century, mainly concerned itself with the interior life, but Hildegard of Bingen in the twelfth century, and St Birgitta [Bridget] of Sweden and St Catherine of Siena in the fourteenth century all commented vigorously upon church and state politics, writing to the Pope and to secular rulers to persuade them of the error of their ways (Obrist 1984: 228–32; Berrigan 1984: 252–65). These women were authorized to speak by their visionary experiences of the divine and their interventions were textual, grounded in traditions of prophecy and mystic revelation. In the later medieval period women did not involve themselves directly in political and military action, with the exception of one of the most intriguing figures of the period, Joan of Arc.

Joan's authority came directly from her 'voices': St Michael, St Catherine of Alexandria and St Margaret of Antioch, who dispatched her on her impossible-seeming mission to regain France for the Dauphin, later Charles VII, and who continued to instruct her throughout her campaigns and her trial. Essential to both her initial success and her final destruction were two factors: the 'voices' and her cross-dressing. Joan's account of the voices was such as to convince those she met of the rightness of her mission, from the provincial governor, Robert de Baudricourt (who paid for her first horses and gave Joan her first sword and retainers) to the Dauphin himself. Joan's cross-dressing not only allowed her to live and fight beside men without danger of sexual violence but also, in its very transgressiveness, marked her out as 'other'. Marina Warner explains its significance thus:

> Through her transvestism, she ... could transcend her sex; she could set herself apart and usurp the privileges of the male and his claims to superiority. At the same time, by never pretending to be other than a woman and a maid, she was usurping a man's function but shaking off the trammels of his sex altogether to occupy a different, third order, neither male nor female, but unearthly, like the angels whose company she loved.
>
> (Warner 1981: 145–6)

The questions of dress and whether the voices were saintly or diabolical were central issues at Joan's trial: at her recantation she agreed to resume female clothing and denies her voices: 'I Joan, called the Maid, ... confess that I have gravely sinned, in pretending deceitfully to have had revelations from God and his angels, saints Catherine and Margaret' (Duby and Duby 1973: 137). Joan signed her recantation on Thursday, 24 May, but, on the following Monday, the inquisitors entered Joan's cell to find her once more in male clothes. Asked if she had heard her voices since the preceding Thursday, she answered that she had, adding that she had only denied the voices previously 'for fear of the fire'. The recording clerk notes 'Responsio mortifera' – a fatal reply – in the margin of his notes (Warner 1981: 141). On the following Wednesday she was burned at the stake.

Joan was not an orator or rhetorician: the surviving letters dictated by her (see excerpt 8 below) are blunt and forceful in the extreme. Her life was lived through symbols, signs and ritual; the visual and oral. Yet, just like Fredegund, eight centuries previously, our understanding of Joan is entirely dependent on contradictory texts, those of her trial for heresy, written to show her guilt, and of her rehabilitation, in which evidence pointing to her sanctity was eagerly noted. Contemporaries too found Joan hard to interpret: to Christine de Pizan, she was a heroine, the answer to France's prayers, and she celebrated Joan in her last poem, *Ditié de Jehanne d'Arc*, as France's saviour:

> Oh! What honour for the female sex! It is perfectly obvious that God has special regard for it when all these wretched people who destroyed the whole Kingdom – now recovered and made safe by a woman – something that five thousand men could not have done – and the traitors have been exterminated. Before the event they would have scarcely believed this possible.
>
> (Christine de Pizan 1977: 46)

The Bourgeois de Paris, who was an adherent of the Burgundians, enemies of Joan and the Dauphin, took quite a different view of her: writing of the Armagnac faction's failed assault on Paris he comments: 'a creature in the form of a woman

... was with them and who was called La Pucelle – what it was God alone knows!' (Duby and Duby 1973: 14). So too, for us – and like the other historical women discussed here – Joan and her medieval sisters remain, in the end, unknowable.

1 FREDEGUND

Texts: II, III and V from Gregory of Tours (1974) *The History of the Franks*, transl. L. Thorpe, Harmondsworth: Penguin, pp. 297–8, 303–4, 390–2; I and IV are from the *Liber Historiae Francorum*, translations taken from J. Martínez Pizarro (1989) *A Rhetoric of the Scene: Dramatic Narrative in the Early Middle Ages*, Toronto: Toronto University Press, pp. 81–2 and 10. Excerpt VI adapted from the *Liber Historiae Francorum* (1974) transl. L. Bachrach, Lawrence, Kans.: Coronado Press, pp. 90–1.

Queen Fredegund (*d.* 597) was a former slave and wife of King Chilperic, ruler of the Franks, whose kingdom, Neustria, was centred on Soissons, in northern France. Our information about her is drawn from the two sources cited here: the two authors Gregory of Tours (*d.* 594) and the early eighth-century author of the *Liber Historiae Francorum*, taking different views of Fredegund. Gregory had much to do with Fredegund: at one point (Gregory of Tours 1974: 316–23) he is brought to trial accused of slandering her, a charge of which he is cleared. The author of the *Liber Historiae Francorum* is less partisan: although he laces his history with some colourful anecdotes about Fredegund, he seems to admire her enterprise. For him the villainess of the period is Brunhild, whose death is recounted above. Gregory ends his *History* before Fredegund's death, while the author of the *Liber Historiae Francorum* records her burial in the basilica of St Vincent at Paris. Christine de Pizan's verdict on Fredegund is judicious: 'Although she was cruel, contrary to the natural disposition of women, nevertheless, following her husband's death, with great skill this lady governed the kingdom of France which found itself at this time in very great unrest and danger' (Christine de Pizan 1982: 33).

I
How Fredegund brings about a separation between King Chilperic and his wife Audovera

Fredegund is Audovera's servant and King Chilperic's concubine. The scene is set at the christening of Audovera and Chilperic's newborn daughter. Audovera forgets the prohibition of marriage between the parents and godparents of a child at that time.

The bishop arrived, and no lady could be found to receive the little girl from the font. Fredegund said to Audovera: 'We shall never find one so fine as you to receive her. Therefore receive her yourself.' Hearing this, the queen received her from the holy font. When the victorious king came home, Fredegund went out to meet him and said: 'Praised be God that our lord the king is victorious over his enemies. A daughter has been born to you. With whom will my lord the king sleep tonight, since my lady the queen is godmother to your daughter Childesinda?' He said: 'If I may not sleep with her, I shall sleep with you.' As the king entered his hall, the queen came towards him with the little girl, and he said to her: 'You have done a terrible thing through your simple-mindedness; from now on you can no longer be my wife.'

II
The dysentery epidemic

Martínez Pizarro points out the dissimilarity between Fredegund's pious speech here and her other utterances in the *History of the Franks*, explaining why she sounds like a sermonizing bishop: 'she is acting out a scene of repentance; her words echo the texts used by medieval preachers to bring their audience to a realization of guilt, and to make them see their misfortunes as punishment for past crimes.' Her language is 'suited to what she says, but not what she is' (Martínez Pizarro 1989: 98).

In these days King Chilperic fell ill. When he recovered, his younger son, who had not yet been baptized in the name of the Holy Ghost, was attacked in his turn. They saw that he was dying and so they baptized him. He made a momentary recovery, but then Chlodobert, his older brother, caught the disease. When their mother Fredegund realized that he too was at death's door, she repented of her sins, rather late in the day, it is true, and said to the king: 'God in his mercy has endured our evil goings-on long enough. Time and time again He has sent us warnings through high fevers and other indispositions, but we have never mended our ways. Now we are going to lose our children. It is the tears of paupers which are the cause of their death, the sighs of orphans, the widows' lament. Yet we still keep on amassing wealth, with no possible end in view. We still lay up treasures, we who have no one to whom we can leave them. Our riches live on after us, the fruits of rapine, hated and accursed, with no one left to possess them once we are gone. Were our cellars not already overflowing with wine? Were our granaries not stuffed to the roof with corn? Were our treasure-houses not already full enough with gold, silver, precious stones, necklaces and every regal adornment one could dream of? Now we are losing the most beautiful of our possessions! Come, then, I beg you! Let us set light to all these iniquitous tax-demands! What sufficed for King Lothar, your father, should be plenty enough for our exchequer, too.' As she said this, the queen beat her breast with her fists. She ordered to be placed before her the tax-demands which had been brought back by Mark from her own cities [given as her morning-gift], and she put them on the fire. She spoke to the king a second time. 'What are you waiting for?' she asked. 'Do what you see me doing! We may still lose our children, but we shall at least escape eternal damnation.' King Chilperic was deeply moved. He tossed all the files of tax-demands into the fire. As soon as they were burnt, he sent messengers to ensure that no such assessments should ever be made again.

Meanwhile their youngest son wasted away before the onslaught of the disease and finally died.

III
The stepson

After the death of their sons, King Chilperic and his wife spent the month of October in mourning in the forest of Cuise. Then, at the suggestion of Fredegund, Chilperic sent his son, Clovis, to Berny, in the hope that he would die of the same disease. The epidemic which had killed Clovis's brothers was still raging there in all its intensity, but he did not catch it. The king moved to Chelles, his estate near Paris. After a few days he ordered Clovis to join him there. I will now tell you in full detail how Clovis met his death.

While Clovis was staying with his father on the estate at Chelles, he began to boast in a childish way. 'Now that my brothers are dead,' he kept saying, 'the entire kingdom comes to me. The whole of Gaul is mine to command; fate has made me heir to the entire country. My enemies are now in my power and I can do to them whatever I choose.' He also made some unforgivable remarks about his stepmother, Queen Fredegund. She came to hear of this and was terrified. Not long afterwards someone approached the queen and said: 'It is through Clovis's treacherous behaviour that you sit there deprived of your sons. He has fallen in love with the daughter of one of your women-servants, and it is through the mother's magic arts that he has encompassed their death. I warn you, you can expect no better fate yourself, now that you have lost the hope through which you were to have reigned.' The queen was greatly frightened. She was still in a state of nervous depression because of her recent loss, and she worked herself up into a fury. She took the girl on whom Clovis had cast sheep's eyes and had her thrashed. Then she ordered all her hair to be cut off, and had her tied to a stake which was stuck up outside Clovis's lodging. The girl's mother she had bound and subjected to torture, until she forced her to admit that the charges against her were true. All this she reported to the king, adding a few details of her own. Then she demanded her revenge on Clovis.

The king was just setting off for the hunt. He ordered Clovis to be brought before him in secret. When he arrived, the king commanded that he should be seized and manacled by Duke Desiderius and Duke Bobo. He was stripped of his weapons and his clothes, and paraded before the queen in rags and with his arms bound. She ordered him to be kept in custody, for she wanted to find out if the events had really happened as she had been told, whose advice Clovis had been following, at whose encouragement he had acted as he did and who were his most intimate friends. He denied everything else, but he admitted that he possessed many close associates. Three days later the queen gave orders that he should be taken across the River Maine, with his arms still bound. He was kept under close surveillance on an estate called Noisy-le-Grand. While he was a prisoner there he was murdered by a stab with a knife. They buried his body immediately. Messengers were sent off to the king to announce that Clovis had stabbed himself with his own hand; and they added the confirmatory detail that the knife with which he had struck the blow was still in the wound. Chilperic accepted their report: the queen kept egging him on, but in my opinion it was the king who had delivered Clovis up to death and yet he wept no tear. The young prince's household was dispersed. His mother [Audovera] was murdered in the most cruel fashion. His sister was tricked by Fredegund's servants and persuaded into entering a nunnery, where she has become a religious and where she remains to this day. All their property was purloined by the queen. The woman who had given evidence against Clovis was condemned to be burnt alive. As she was dragged off to the stake, the poor creature started to admit that she had lied. Her confession availed her nothing: she was bound to the stake and set alight while still alive.

IV
The death of Chilperic

Queen Fredegund was beautiful, extremely cunning, and given to infidelity. The mayor of the palace was then Landeric, a clever and resourceful man of whom the queen was very fond, for he was her partner in adultery. One day, early in the morning, the king was preparing to ride with a hunting party from his estate at Chelles, near Paris, but since he loved his wife very much he returned from the stables to her chamber in the palace. She was in the room, washing her hair with water. The king, coming from behind, struck her on the buttocks with a stick. She, thinking it was Landeric, said, 'What are you doing, Landeric?' Looking back, she saw that it was the king and became very frightened. The king, extremely unhappy, left and went hunting. The queen then called Landeric and told him everything that had happened with the king, adding: 'Think, therefore, of what you should do, for tomorrow we shall be subjected to dreadful tortures.' Landeric, feeling wretched and moved to tears, said, 'On an evil hour did my eyes see you! I do not know what I should do, for terrors beset me on every side.' And she replied: 'Do not fear. Listen to my advice. Let us do as I say and we shall not die. When day is over and in the evening the king comes back from hunting, let us send someone out to kill him, and let it be proclaimed that Childebert, the Austrasian king [Chilperic's nephew], has plotted this against him. Once the king is dead, we shall reign together with my son Chlothar.'

V
Widowhood

Meanwhile the widowed Queen Fredegund arrived in Paris. She took with her that part of her treasure which she has secreted within the city walls, and she sought sanctuary in the cathedral, where she was given protection by Bishop Ragnemod. The remainder of her treasure, which had been left behind in Chelles and which included the golden salver which Chilperic had recently had made, was confiscated by the treasury officials, who lost no time in joining King Childebert, he being in Meaux at the time.

Queen Fredegund took the advice of her supporters and sent messengers to King Guntram [Chilperic's brother]. 'Let my lord come and take charge of his brother's kingdom,' she said. 'I have a tiny baby, whom I long to place in his arms. At the same time I shall declare myself his humble servant.' King Guntram wept bitterly when he heard of his brother's death. As soon as his mourning was over, he summoned his army and marched on Paris. He had already taken up his quarters within the city walls when his nephew, King Childebert, arrived from another direction.

Next some envoys come to Guntram from Childebert, asking him to share the kingdom with him. Guntram refuses.

The envoys departed. A second set of messengers then arrived from Childebert to ask King Guntram to surrender the person of Queen Fredegund. 'Hand over the murderess,' they said, 'the woman who garrotted my aunt, the woman who killed first my father, then my uncle and who put my two cousins to the sword.' 'We will consider all these matters at an assembly which we propose to hold,' answered King Guntram, 'and so decide what is to be done.' He had taken Fredegund under his protection, inviting her frequently to eat with him, and promising that he would see that she came to no harm. One day, when they were eating at the same table, the queen rose and begged to be excused, but Guntram asked her to stay. 'Won't you have something more to eat?' he asked. 'You must excuse me,' answered Fredegund. 'I beg you to do so, my lord, for what happens so frequently to women has happened to me, and I am pregnant again.' Guntram was astonished when he heard this for he knew that four months earlier she had borne a son. All the same, he let her go.

Childebert's charges against Fredegund were founded, according to Gregory and the author of *Liber Historiae Francorum*. The child referred to here never materializes; Fredegund's motive, other than to keep Guntram guessing, remains obscure.

VI
Fredegund's battle strategy

When Fredegund heard this [sc. the approach of the Austrasian army under Childebert] she assembled an army with Landeric and the other Frankish leaders. When they arrived at Berny Rivière, she gave out lavish presents and mobilized them to fight against their enemies. Saying that very soon a large army of Austrasians would come against them, she devised this plan and put it before the Franks, saying: 'Let us approach them by night and have our men carry lights before us, and hold tree branches in their hands and have little bells tied to their horses so that the vigilant sentries of the enemy won't be able to recognize us. At dawn, we will attack and perhaps we will defeat them completely.' This counsel was accepted.

When the plan had been formed, they agreed a day on which they should assemble for battle in a place called Droisy in the Soissons area. Just as Fredegund had counselled, they set out at night ready for battle, with the men in the front rank holding branches. Carrying young King Chlothar, they rode as far as Droisy when, however, the Austrasian guards saw all the tree branches before the Frankish line. When the guards heard the bells tinkling, one said to his companion: 'Wasn't there a field there yesterday, and over there, so how do we see a forest there now?' His companion laughed and said: 'You were drunk then, and now you are crazed. Can't you hear those are the bells of our horses, grazing by the forest?' Then dawn broke and, with a blast of trumpets, the Franks charged the sleeping Austrasians and Burgundians. Together with Fredegund and young Chlothar, they killed most of the army, innumerable men of all ranks. Gundobald and Wintrio just evaded capture by running away. Landeric chased Wintrio, who escaped on a very fast horse. Fredegund and the army advanced on Reims, and ravaged the Champagne district.

2 SIGRID THE STRONG-MINDED

Text from: Snorri Sturluson (1941) *Heimskringla: Oláfs saga Tryggvasonar,* ed. B. Að albjarnason, Islenzk Fornrit 26, Reykjavík: Hid Islenzka Fornritafelag, pp. 287–9, 309–10, 341, 349. Transl. C. Larrington.

Sigrid was queen over territory in Sweden. The events recounted here unfold between 993 and 1000. How far the story of Sigrid and Olaf may have any historical basis, how much it is shaped by, or even a reworking of, the story of Sigurd the Dragon-Slayer is a matter for dispute among Norse scholars. Most probably, as Preben Meulengracht Sørensen (Sørensen 1993a: 20) suggests, the saga-author borrows the pattern from heroic poetry for interpretative reasons, that is: in order to explain the meaning of the historical events. The four-way model of the vengeful woman and husband as instrument of vengeance, the erring former lover and his innocent wife recurs frequently in Norse: see Heinrichs (1986) for detailed examination of this theme.

I
Dealings with Harald of Grenland

Harald of Grenland was king in Vestfold, as was mentioned before. He married Asta, the daughter of Gudbrand kula. One summer, when Harald went on a Viking expedition in the Baltic to get treasure for himself, he came to Sweden. Olaf the Swede was king at that time. He was the son of Eirik the Blessed-with-Victory and Sigrid, daughter of Skoglar-Tosti. Sigrid was then a widow and owned many large farmsteads in Sweden. And when she heard that Harald of Grenland, her foster-brother, had landed in Sweden a short distance away, she sent messengers to him to invite him to a feast. He did not delay, and set out with a large company of men. He was warmly welcomed. The king and the queen sat in the seats of honour and drank together during the evening, and his men were given a splendid feast. That night when the king went to sleep, the bed was tented over with furs, and provided with gorgeous coverlets. There were very few people present in the room. And when the king was undressed and had got into bed, then the queen came to him and poured out drink for him herself and persuaded him to drink a great deal and was very merry. The king became completely drunk, and so did she. Then he fell asleep, and the queen also went to sleep. Sigrid was the wisest of women, and prophetic about many things. Again the next day there was another splendid feast. And it came about, as always happens when people have been very drunk, that the next day most of them are rather cautious about drinking. But the queen was merry, and she and the king talked a great deal together. She said that she did not value the possessions and property which she held in Sweden any the less than his crown and possessions in Norway. When she said this, the king became downcast and rather displeased, and got ready to set off, but the queen was extremely cheerful and sent him on his way with magnificent presents. Harald went back to Norway in the autumn, stayed at home during the winter, and seemed rather miserable. The next summer he went back to the Baltic with his men, and set course for Sweden, and sent a message to Queen Sigrid, that he wanted to meet her. She rode down to meet him and they spoke together. He quickly broached the question of whether Sigrid would marry him. She said that it would be shameful for him and that he was already well married, and that marriage was a good match. Harald said that Asta was a good, talented woman – 'but she is not as well-born as I am'. Sigrid said, 'It may well be that you are better born than she is. But I think rather that the luck of both of you depends on your staying with her.' They did not exchange many more words before the queen rode away. King Harald was then rather gloomy. He decided to ride up country and see Sigrid again. Many of his men tried to dissuade him from this, but none the less he went with a great company of men, and came to the farmstead which the queen ruled over. The same evening another king arrived there. He was called Vissavald, who had come from the east, from Kiev. He intended to ask for Sigrid's hand. It was arranged that both the kings should be accommodated in a large and ancient hall, with all their men. And there was no shortage of drink there that evening, so strong that they all became dead-drunk and the bodyguards and the night-watch fell asleep. Then Queen Sigrid attacked them in the night both with fire and with weapons. The hall burned down with all the men who were inside, and those who came out were struck down. Sigrid said that she would discourage petty kings from coming from other countries to woo her. After that she was called Sigrid the Strong-minded.

> Sigrid had known that Harald was destined to be the father of St Olaf, the future king and patron saint of Norway (reigned 1015–30). Sigrid thus had hoped to secure a promise of marriage from Harald when they first met and to become the saint's mother. By the time Harald returned the following year, Asta, his wife, was already pregnant with the saint, born posthumously to Harald. Harald made up his mind too late as far as Sigrid was concerned, and she lost all interest in him.

II
Dealings with Olaf Tryggvason

Queen Sigrid the Strong-minded stayed on her estates in Sweden. That winter King Olaf [Tryggvason, king of Norway from 995 to 1000] sent men to Queen Sigrid to open the question of marriage, and she accepted his suit, and the matter was decided with a betrothal. Then King Olaf sent Queen Sigrid the great gold ring which he had taken from the temple door at Hlathir, and this was reckoned to be a magnificent treasure. The meeting to arrange the wedding was to be held the next spring at the river, at the boundary [between the kingdoms]. And this ring, which King Olaf had sent to Queen Sigrid, was very greatly praised by everyone. The queen had with her her smiths, two brothers. And when they handled the ring and weighed it in their hands, they spoke privately to one another, and the queen called them to her and asked what they thought was so funny about the ring. She said that they should tell her publicly what they had found. They said that the ring was counterfeit. Then she had the ring broken up, and they found brass in it. Then the queen was furious and said that Olaf would play her false in more matters than this one.

The same winter King Olaf went up to Ringerike and converted the people. Asta Guthbrands-daughter married a man called Sigurd the Sow, shortly after the death of Harald of Grenland. He was the king in Ringerike. Sigurd was the son of Halfdan and he was the son of Sigurd Brushwood, son of King Harald Fairhair. Olaf [the future saint] was with Asta at that time,

171

her son by Harald of Grenland. He was brought up in his youth with his stepfather, Sigurd Sow. When King Olaf Tryggvason came to Ringerike to preach Christianity, then Sigurd Sow was baptized, as was Asta his wife, and Olaf her son, and Olaf Tryggvason became godfather to Olaf Haraldsson. He was then three years old. King Olaf went then out to the Vík area and spent the winter there. It was the third winter that he was king over Norway.

Early in the spring King Olaf went east to Konungahella to the meeting with Queen Sigrid. And when they met they discussed that matter which had been talked of in the winter, that they should get married, and the negotiations were going promisingly. Then King Olaf said that Sigrid should accept baptism and the true faith. She said: 'I am not going to abandon that faith which I hold and my family have held before me. But I don't mind if you believe in whatever god you please.' Then King Olaf became very angry and immediately shouted, 'Why should I want to marry you, you dog of a heathen?' and struck her in the face with the glove which he was holding. Then he stood up and so did she. Then Sigrid said, 'That may well bring about your death.' Then they parted. The king went north to the Vík and the queen east into Sweden.

Sveinn forkbeard, king of Denmark, was married to Gunnhild, daughter of Burizlaf, king of the Wends. But at this time, which we have now reached, the news was that Gunnhild took sick and died, and a little later King Sveinn married Sigrid the Strong-minded, daughter of Skoglar-Tosti, and the mother of Olaf, king of Sweden. Then a great affection sprang up, because of this connection, between the two kings and Eirik the earl, son of Hákon.

As was written earlier, King Sveinn Forkbeard had then married Sigrid the Strong-minded. Sigrid was very hostile to King Olaf Tryggvason and this was the cause: that Olaf had broken his betrothal with her and struck her in the face, as was mentioned earlier. She egged on King Sveinn to go to war with King Olaf Tryggvason, and said that there was sufficient justification to fight King Olaf, for he had slept with Thyri, the king's sister, 'without your permission, and none of your kinsmen would ever have put up with that'. Queen Sigrid often spoke in this vein, and eventually her persuasion was such that King Sveinn decided to carry out this plan. And early in the spring King Sveinn sent men east to Sweden to see King Olaf of Sweden, his relation-by-marriage and to Earl Eirik and told them that King Olaf of Norway had called up an army and intended to go to Wendland in the summer. He also sent a message that the king of the Swedes and the earl should go abroad and come to meet King Sveinn and they should go to war in alliance against King Olaf. And the king of the Swedes and Earl Eirik got ready for this journey and called up a large fleet of ships from Sweden, and the army went south to Denmark, and when they got there, King Olaf Tryggvason had already sailed east.

Thyri had been sent to Wendland to marry Burizlaf on the understanding that she would inherit Gunnhild's property, but the marriage lasted only a week. Thyri ran away and took refuge in Norway where she married Olaf Tryggvason instead. Olaf sets off for Wendland because he had been egged on by Thyri to recover the property she owned there. The army catches up with Olaf and he is killed in a mighty battle at Svöld (1000). The victors divide up Norway amongst themselves.

3 ANNA DALASSENA AND IMPERIAL POWER

Text from: Anna Comnena (1969) *The Alexiad*, transl. E. R. A. Sewter, Harmondsworth: Penguin, pp. 118–21.

Anna Comnena was a Byzantine princess, daughter of Emperor Alexius of Constantinople and the Roman Empire which, at the time at which Anna is writing, stretched as far as the border with Hungary in the west, taking in Dubrovnik, Bulgaria and Greece. In the east, it extended into Turkey, encompassing the southern shore of the Black Sea, and as far east as Ephesus. Anna was born in 1083, the eldest of her parents' seven children and died some time after 1148. She was intended as the wife of Constantine Ducas, son of the previously deposed emperor and rightful heir to the throne, who was sharing the throne as junior partner with Alexius. Anna had thought that she and Constantine would rule jointly after her father's death, but when her younger brother John was 4 or 5 years old, he was declared heir, and Anna's marriage to Constantine called off. It is likely that the feud between Anna's grandmother, Anna Dalassena, described below, and the Ducas family made the match impossible. In 1097 Anna Comnena married Nicephorus Bryennius, son (or possibly, grandson) of her father's old rival. The marriage seemed happy enough, by Anna's account, lasting forty years and producing four children. Anna embarked on the *Alexiad* some thirty years after her father's death in 1118. The work is naturally highly laudatory of her father, but, perhaps unusually, evidences a strong grasp of military tactics and interest in the technology of contemporary warfare. Highly educated, Anna knew something of science, astrology and medicine; she wrote poetry, which has not survived. Her admiring portrait of her famous grandmother is typical of the character sketches which Anna includes in her history; typical also is her vagueness about the whispering campaign conducted against Anna Dalassena.

The reader may be surprised by the honour conferred upon his mother by the emperor in this matter, since he yielded her precedence in everything, relinquishing the reins of government, as it were, and running alongside as she drove the imperial chariot; only in the title of emperor did he share with her the privileges of his rank. And this despite the fact that he had already passed his boyhood years and was of an age which in the case of men like him is particularly susceptible to the lust for power. Wars against the barbarians, with all their attendant trials and tribulations, he was prepared to face himself, but the entire administration of affairs, the choice of civil magistrates, the accounts of the imperial revenues and expenditure he left to his mother. At this point the reader may well censure him for transferring the government of the empire to the *gynaeconitis* [women's quarters], but had he

173

known this woman's spirit, her surpassing virtue, intelligence and energy, his reproaches would soon have turned to admiration. For my grandmother had an exceptional grasp of public affairs, with a genius for organization and government; she was capable, in fact, of managing not only the Roman Empire, but every other empire under the sun as well. She had vast experience and a wide understanding of the motives, ultimate consequences, interrelations good and bad of various courses of action, penetrating quickly to the right solution, adroitly and safely carrying it out. Her intellectual powers, moreover, were paralleled by her command of language. She was indeed a most persuasive orator, without being verbose or long-winded. Nor did the inspiration of the argument readily desert her, for if she began on a felicitous note, she was also most successful in ending her speeches with just the right words. She was already a woman of mature years when she was called upon to exercise imperial authority, at a time of life when one's mental powers are at their best, one's judgement is fully developed and knowledge of affairs is widest – all qualities that lend force to good administration and government.... In the past, when Anna Dalassena was still looked upon as a younger woman, she had impressed everyone as 'having an old head on young shoulders'; to the observant her face alone revealed Anna's inherent virtue and gravity. But, as I was saying, once he had seized power my father reserved for himself the struggles and hard labour of war, while she became so to speak an onlooker, but he made her sovereign and like a slave said and did whatever she commanded....

Not only was she a very great credit to her own sex, but to men as well; indeed, she contributed to the glory of the whole human race. The women's quarters in the palace had been the scene of utter depravity ever since the infamous Constantine Monomachos [reigned 1042–55] had ascended the throne and right up to the time when my father became emperor had been noted for foolish love intrigues, but Anna effected a reformation; a commendable decorum was restored and the palace now enjoyed a discipline that merited praise. She instituted set times for the singing of sacred hymns, stated hours for breakfast; there was now a special period in which magistrates were chosen. She herself set a firm example to everybody else, with the result that the palace assumed the appearance rather of a monastery under the influences of this really extraordinary woman and her truly saintly character; for in self-control she surpassed the famous women of old, heroines of many a legend, as the sun outshines all stars. As for her compassion for the poor and her generosity to the needy, no words could do justice to them. Her house was a refuge for penniless relatives, but no less for strangers. Priests and monks she honoured in particular: they shared her meals and no one ever saw her at table without some of them as guests. Her outward serenity, true reflection of character, was respected by angels but terrorized even the demons, and pleasure-loving fools, victims of their own passions, found a single glance from her more than they could bear; yet to the chaste she seemed gentle and gay. She knew exactly how to temper reserve and dignity; her own reserve never gave the impression of harshness or cruelty, nor did her tenderness seem too soft or unrestrained – and this, I fancy, is the true definition of propriety: the due proportion of warm humanity and strict moral principle. She was by nature thoughtful and was always evolving new ideas, not, as some folk whispered, to the detriment of the state; on the contrary they were wholesome schemes which restored to full vigour the already corrupted empire and revived, as far as one could, the ruined fortunes of the people.

4 ALVILD THE PIRATE

Text: Saxo Grammaticus (1980) *A History of the Danish People*, transl. P. Fisher and H. Ellis-Davidson, 2 vols, Woodbridge, Suffolk: Boydell Press, vol. I, Book VII, pp. 210–12.

Saxo was a Danish monk writing in Latin *c.* 1200. His *Gesta Danorum* starts in legendary times, and draws on many native Scandinavian traditions. The first nine books of the *Gesta Danorum* depict the powerful and active women of the heathen past, usually critically, unless they are those 'who by manly virtues have aided men' (Strand 1980: 357). Strand 1980 is a full study of Saxo's treatment of women in the text.

The story goes that in the same period Sivard, king of Götaland, had two sons, Vemund and Osten, and a daughter Alvild, who almost from her cradle displayed such true modesty that she had her face perpetually veiled by her robe to prevent her fine looks arousing anyone's passions. Her father kept her apart under very close supervision and gave her two poisonous snakes to rear, intending that these reptiles should act as protectors of her chastity when eventually they had grown to full size. No one could easily pry into her bedroom when entry was blocked by such a dangerous barrier. He also decreed that anyone who tried to get in unsuccessfully should at once be decapitated and have his head impaled on a stake. When fear was applied to young men's forwardness it checked their heated fancies.

Then Alf, Sigar's son, believing that the more perilous an enterprise the more brilliant it was, declared himself a suitor. He was told to subdue the creatures which kept guard by the girl's room, for the terms of the decree dictated that only their vanquisher should enjoy her embraces. To aggravate their ferocity towards him he wrapped his body in a pelt wet with blood. Draped in this he soon approached the confining doors where, grasping a bar of red-hot steel in a pair of tongs, he thrust it down the viper's gaping throat and laid it lifeless on the floor. Next, as the other snake swept forward in a rippling glide, he destroyed it by hurling his spear straight between its open fangs. But when he asked for the victor's earnings according to the words of the agreement, Sivard answered that he would only take as his son-in-law the man his daughter had chose freely and genuinely.

As the girl's mother was the only one to grudge the suitor's petition, she examined her daughter's heart in an intimate conversation. When the princess warmly praised her wooer's excellence, the mother abused her bitterly, saying she had lost all sense of shame and been won by baited looks; she had not formed any proper judgement of his virtue, but, gazing with an unprincipled mind, had been tickled by his enticing appearance.

Once Alvild had been prevailed upon to despise the young Dane, she changed into man's clothing and from being a highly virtuous maiden began to lead the life of a savage pirate. Many girls of the same persuasion had enrolled in her company by the time she chanced to arrive at a spot where a band of pirates were mourning the loss of their leader, who had been killed fighting. Because of her beauty, she was elected the pirate chief and performed feats beyond a woman's courage.

Alf undertook many fatiguing voyages in her pursuit until, during winter, he came across the fleet of the Blakmanni. At that time of the year the running waters solidified so that a vast pack of ice gripped their vessels and, however strongly they rowed, they could make no progress. Since the prolonged cold guaranteed the prisoners a fairly safe footing, Alf ordered his men to test the frozen bight of the sea after putting on brogues [a kind of overshoe]; if they dispensed with slippery shoes, he said, they could dash over the icy surface with a better balance. As the Blakmanni supposed they had prepared their heels for a speedy flight, they came in to do battle; however, they could only make a lurching advance, for the smoothness beneath their soles gave their feet an unsteady hold. Since the Danes were able to move across the ice-bound deep more securely, they crushed their adversaries, who could only totter along.

After this victory they steered towards Finland. It so happened that when a party was sent into a narrow gulf to reconnoitre, they had discovered the harbour occupied by a handful of ships. Alvild had sailed before them with her fleet into the same confined inlet. Immediately she caught sight of unfamiliar craft in the distance, with rapid rowing she shot off to encounter them, judging it wiser to burst on an enemy than lie waiting for him. Though his companions were warning him not to attempt a larger number of vessels with his own, Alf replied how intolerable it would be if anyone reported to Alvild that his purposeful course was upset by a few boats in his path; it would be wrong to let such a petty circumstance smirch the fine record of their enterprises. The Danes were filled with astonishment when they found what graceful, shapely-limbed opponents they had.

When the sea-fight started, young Alf leapt on to Alvild's prow and forced his way up to the stern, slaughtering all who resisted him. His comrade Borkar struck off Alvild's helmet, but seeing the smoothness of her chin, realized that they ought not to be fighting with weapons but kisses; they should lay down their hard spears and handle their foes more persuasively. Alf was overjoyed when, beyond all expectation, he had presented to him the girl he had sought indefatigably over land and sea despite so many perilous obstacles. He laid hands on her more lovingly and compelled her to change back into feminine clothing; afterwards she had a daughter by him, Gurith. Borkar married Gro, Alvild's attendant, who bore him a son called Harald.

In case anyone is marvelling that this sex should have sweated in warfare, let me digress briefly to explain the character and behaviour of such females. There were once women in Denmark who dressed themselves to look like men and spent almost every minute cultivating soldiers' skills; they did not want the sinews of their valour to lose tautness and be infected by self-indulgence. Loathing a dainty style of living, they would harden body and mind with toil and endurance, rejecting the fickle pliancy of girls and compelling their womanish spirits to act with a virile ruthlessness. They courted military celebrity so earnestly that you would have guessed they had unsexed themselves. Those especially who had forceful personalities or were tall and elegant embarked on this way of life. As if they were forgetful of their true selves they put toughness before allure, aimed at conflicts instead of kisses, tasted blood, not lips, sought the clash of arms rather than the arm's embrace, fitted to weapons hands which should have been weaving, desired not the couch but the kill, and those they could have appeased with looks they attacked with lances.

5 QUEEN PHILIPPA AND THE BURGHERS OF CALAIS

Text from: P. Strohm (1992) *Hochon's Arrow: The Social Imagination of Fourteenth-Century Texts*, Princeton, N.J.: Princeton University Press, p. 100.

Edward III of England has been angered by the stubborn resistance of the people of Calais in France to his army, and demands that six prominent burghers be handed over to him. Despite their pleas for mercy, he orders them to be beheaded. His queen, Philippa of Hainault, intervenes, working her influence through her submissive posture (mentioned twice), her extreme pregnancy (also mentioned twice), and through the opportunity it gives the king of combining the kingly qualities of justice and mercy. See Strohm (1992: 99–105) for a suggestive analysis of this scene's place in the 'history of sentiment', and the development of the notion of the queen as intercessor. Strohm also points out that in actuality Philippa was either not yet, or only just, pregnant, when Calais surrendered (Strohm 1992: 102 n.6); the pregnancy is exaggerated for effect.

Then the noble queen of England, who was extremely pregnant, humbled herself and besought his pity so tenderly that she could not be withstood. The valiant and good woman threw herself on her knees before the king her lord and said, 'Ah, my dear lord, since I passed over the sea in great peril, as you well know, I have asked nothing of you, nor demanded any favour. Now I pray you humbly and ask of you a favour for the son of the blessed Mary and for your love of me, that you show a merciful disposition to these six men.' The king waited a moment before speaking and looked at the good woman his queen who was so very pregnant and besought him so tenderly on her knees. And he softened his heart, and his anger abated, and when he spoke he said, 'Ah, my lady, I would have much preferred that you be anywhere than here. You have prayed so forcefully that I would not dare to refuse the favour which you ask of me.'

6 A NOBLE LADY KNOWN TO CHRISTINE DE PIZAN

Text from: Christine de Pizan (1982) *The Book of the City of Ladies*, transl. E. J. Richards, New York: Persea Press, pp. 211–12.

In her dialogue with Christine, Lady Rectitude lists a number of Christine's contemporaries who have distinguished themselves. Note the theatrical and public nature of the gesture of the Dame de la Rivière.

And even without going back to look for historical examples, how many other examples of the generosity of ladies from your own time could be mentioned! Was not the generosity great which was shown by the Dame de la Rivière, named Marguerite, who is still alive, and was formerly the wife of Monsieur Burel de la Rivière, first chamberlain of the wise King Charles? On one occasion among others it happened that this lady, as she was always wise, valiant, and well-bred, was attending a very fine celebration which the duke of Anjou, later king of Sicily, was holding in Paris. At this celebration there were a large number of noble ladies and knights and gentlemen in fine array. This lady, who was young and beautiful, realized while she watched the noble knights assembled there, that a most noteworthy knight of great fame among those then living, named Emerion de Poumiers, was missing from this company of knights. She, of course, allowed that this Sir Emerion was too old to remember her, but his goodness and valiance made the lady remember him, and she felt there could be no more beautiful an ornament for such an assembly than so noteworthy and famous a man, even if he were old, so she inquired where the missing knight was. She was told that he was in prison in the Châtelet in Paris because of a debt of five hundred francs that he had incurred during his frequent travels in arms. 'Ah!' said the noble lady, 'What a shame for this kingdom to suffer a single hour of such a man imprisoned for debt!' Whereupon she removed the gold chaplet which she was wearing on her rich and fair head and replaced it with a chaplet of periwinkle on her blond hair. She gave the gold chaplet to a certain messenger and said, 'Go and give this chaplet as a pledge for what he owes, and let him be freed immediately and come here.' This was done and she was highly praised for it.

7 THE WAY OF LIFE OF THE WISE PRINCESS

Text from: Christine de Pizan (1985) *The Treasure of the City of Ladies*, transl. S. Lawson, Harmondsworth: Penguin, pp. 59–62.

Prudence, as I have said before, will advise the wise princess how her life should be ordered, and as a result she will adopt the following way of life. She will rise quite early every day and address her first words to God, saying, 'Lord, I beseech thee to guard us this day from sin, from sudden death and from all evil mischance, and also protect all our relatives and friends. To those who have passed on, pardon, and to our subjects, peace and tranquillity. Amen, Pater Noster.' She will say such additional prayers as her devotion may prompt her to, but she will not insist on having a great attendance of servants around her. (The good and wise Queen Jeanne, the late wife of King Charles V of France, followed this course when she was alive. She rose every morning before daylight, lit her candle herself to say her prayers, and did not allow any woman of hers to get up or to lose sleep on her account.)

When the lady is ready she will go to hear her Masses, as many as accord with her devotion and as time and leisure will permit her. For there is no doubt that this lady, to whom great powers to govern are entrusted, will merit the trust that many lords have, and have had, in their wives when they see that they are good and prudent and they themselves have to go away to be occupied elsewhere. The husbands give them the responsibility and authority to govern and to be head of the council. Such ladies are more to be excused in the eyes of God if they do not spend so much time in long prayers as those who have more leisure, nor do they have less merit in attending conscientiously to public affairs than those who occupy themselves more with prayers (unless they intend to devote themselves to the contemplative life and leave the active life).

But as I have said before, the contemplative life can manage quite well without the active, but the good and proper active life cannot function without some part of the contemplative. This lady will have such a good, orderly system that as she leaves her chapel there will be some poor people at the door to whom she herself with humility and devotion will give alms from her own hand, and if any deserving petitions are made to her, she will hear them kindly and give a gracious reply. She will not detain those that she can deal with quickly, and she will therefore increase her alms and also her great renown. If she perhaps cannot consider all the requests that are made to her, certain gentlemen will be appointed to hear them. She will wish them to be charitable and work quickly, and she herself will watch over their conduct.

When she has done these things, if she has responsibility of government, she will go to the council on days when it is held. There she will have such a bearing, such a manner and such an expression when she is seated in her high seat that she will indeed seem to be the lady and mistress over all, and everyone will hold her in great reverence as their wise mistress with great authority. She will conscientiously hear the proposals that are put forward and listen to everyone's opinion. She will be so attentive that she will grasp the principal points and conclusions of matters and will note carefully which of her counsellors speak better and with the best deliberation and advice, and which seem to her the most prudent and intelligent. And she will also note, in the diversity of opinions, which causes and which reasons most stir the speakers. In this way she will attend to everything, and when someone comes to her to speak on a subject or to reply, according to the circumstances, so wisely will she consider the matter that she cannot be thought simple or ignorant. If she can find out in advance what someone is going to propose and what the ramifications of it may be, and if she can with wise counsel think of a suitable reply, it is all to the good. Furthermore, this lady will establish a certain number of wise gentlemen who will sit on her council, who she will deem good, loyal, virtuous and not too covetous. A great many princes and princesses are put to shame by counsellors filled with covetousness, for according to their own inclinations they incite and encourage those whom they counsel. Inevitably, those who indulge in such vice counsel neither well nor loyally, neither to the profit of their souls nor to the honour of their bodies, and so the prudent lady must inquire whether they lead virtuous lives. She will be counselled every day by these gentlemen at a certain hour about the necessary matters that she has to deal with.

After the morning council she will have her midday meal, which ordinarily and especially on solemn days and on feast days will be in the hall, where the ladies and maidens are seated, and other suitable persons ranked according to their position at court. There she will be served in a manner befitting her rank, and while the plates are still on the table (according to the fine old custom of queens and princesses) she will have a gentleman at hand who will speak of the deeds of some good deceased person, or will speak on some excellent moral subject or tell stories of exemplary lives. No dispute will be conducted there. After the tables have been taken up and grace has been said, if there are any princes or lords present, if there are any ladies or damsels or other visitors around her, then she will receive each of them in such honour as is fitting so that everyone will feel contented. She will speak to them in a thoughtful manner, with a pleasant expression; to the elderly people in a more serious manner, to the young people in a different and merrier one. And if one happens to say or to hear any amusing thing or any merriment she will know how to contain it with such a pleasant manner that everyone will say that she is a gracious lady and one who well knows her manners in all places.

After the spices have been taken and it is time to retire, the lady will go to her chamber, where she will rest for a short while if she feels the need to. Then afterwards, if it is a weekday and she has no other more important occupation with which to avoid idleness, she will take up some work, and she will have the women and girls around her to choose freely whatever she likes from all respectable kinds of merriment, and she herself will laugh with them and divert herself in private gatherings so unconstrainedly that they will all praise her great liberty and indulgence and they will love her with all their hearts. She will be occupied like this until the hour of vespers, when she will go to hear them in her chapel if it is a feast day and if no weighty business prevents her, or otherwise she will say them without fail with her lady chaplain. After doing this, if it is summer, she will go off to amuse herself in a garden until suppertime, walking up and down for her health. She will wish that if any persons need to see her for any reason they be allowed to enter and she will hear them. At bedtime she will pray to God. And that concludes the schedule of the ordinary day of the prudent princess living in good and holy occupation.

8 JOAN OF ARC

Text from: G. and A. Duby (1973) *Les Procès de Jeanne d'Arc*, Paris: Gallimard, pp. 33–4, 126–7, 185. Transl. C. Larrington.

Joan was born in Domrémy, in what is now northern France, in 1412 or 1413. Inspired by the voices of Saints Michael, Margaret and Catherine, in 1429 she went to the aid of the Dauphin of France, later Charles VII, who was seeking to recover the northern part of the kingdom from the English, and from the Burgundians who recognized Henry VI of England as king. Initial success, the relief of Orléans, the crowning of Charles at Reims and the recognition of Charles as king by various cities formerly under Burgundian sway was followed by a failed assault on Paris, and a truce was declared. Early in 1430 Joan was captured at Compiègne and handed over to the ecclesiastical authorities for trial. The trial began in January 1431 and lasted until May; Joan was burnt. In 1450 and 1452 inquiries were held into her trial and sentencing; in 1455–6 the verdict against her was rescinded. Although the case for Joan's canonization was placed before the Vatican in 1869, it was not until 1920 that she was finally made a saint. Excerpt I is a text of the letter Joan sent at the beginning of her mission, warning her enemies that they cannot succeed against her; the phrases in square brackets are those which Joan later denied using. Excerpt II is from the University of Paris's findings against her in her trial. Excerpt III comes from the inquiry of 1452, when evidence that Joan had died as a good Christian was beginning to be gathered.

I
Joan's letter to the English, Poitiers, 22 March 1429

Jesus Maria

King of England, and you Duke of Bedford, who call yourself regent of the kingdom of France, you William de la Pole, count of Suffolk, Lord John Talbot, and Thomas Lord Scalles, who call yourself lieutenants of the said Bedford, do right in the eyes of the King of Heaven. Return to the [Maid], who is sent by God, the King of Heaven, the keys of all the towns which you have seized and ravaged in France. She has come here by God's will to re-establish the blood royal. She is quite ready to make peace, if you will submit to her, and depart from France, and make compensation for the damage you have caused, and return the moneys which you have received in all the time that you have held them [sc. the towns].

And as for you, archers, soldiers, gentlemen, and all others who are besieging Orléans, depart in God's name to your own country. And if you do not, expect to hear news from the Maid who will shortly make you see great damage to yourselves.

King of England, if you do not do thus, I am [general] in this war and I assure you that wherever I find your people in France I shall fight them, and pursue them, and expel them from here, whether they will or not. And if they do not wish to obey, I shall have them all killed. I am sent here by God, the King of Heaven, to fight them [body for body], and to expel them from all France. And if they are willing to obey, I shall be merciful to them. So do not think of remaining there longer, for you shall by no means hold the kingdom of France, by God, the King of Heaven, son of the Virgin Mary. But Charles, the true heir, shall hold it, for God, the King of Heaven, wishes it so. And to him it is revealed through the Maid, that very soon he will enter Paris, in good and fine company. And if you do not wish to believe this news sent to you by God and by the Maid, I warn you that wherever we find you, we will go against you and attack you. And there we shall make a greater affray than there has ever been in the kingdom of France in the last thousand years. And believe resolutely that the King of Heaven will send such forces to the Maid that neither you nor your soldiers will be able to overcome her, nor the people of her army. And through these blows we shall see who has the greater right.

And you, Duke of Bedford, who lay siege to Orléans, the Maid asks you not to bring about your own destruction. And if you obey her, you will come to see that the French will do the most beautiful deed that has ever been done for the sake of Christianity.

And I ask you to answer me if you desire to make peace in the city of Orléans, where we hope to be very shortly, and if you do not do so, recollect the great injuries you will suffer.

Written this Tuesday of Holy Week.

The 'most beautiful deed ever done for the sake of Christianity' may refer to a plan for a joint crusade to liberate Jerusalem.

II
From the condemnation of Joan by the University of Paris in 1431

You, Jeanne, you have said that, since the age of thirteen, you have experienced revelations and the appearance of angels, of St Catherine and St Margaret, and that you have very often seen them with your bodily eyes, and that they have spoken to you. As for this first point, the clerks of the University of Paris have considered the manner of the said revelations and appearances, the aim and the content of that which was revealed, and the quality of the person. Having considered all that was to be considered, they have declared that all the things mentioned above are lies, falsenesses, misleading and pernicious things and that such revelations are superstitions, proceeding from wicked and diabolical spirits.

Item: you have said that your king had a sign by which he knew that you were sent by God, for St Michael, accompanied by several angels, some of which having wings, the others crowns, with St Catherine and St Margaret, came to you at the chateau of Chinon. All the company ascended through the floors of the castle until they came to the room of your king, before whom the angel bearing the crown bowed. And once you said that when your king received this sign he was alone; on another occasion you said that the crown, which you call the sign, was given to the Archbishop of Reims, who gave it to your king in the presence of several lords and princes, whom you named. As for this matter, the clerks say that it is not in the least probable, but it is rather a presumptuous lie, misleading and pernicious, a false statement, derogatory of the dignity of the Church and of the angels....

Item: you have said that, at God's command, you have continually worn men's clothes, and that you have put on a short robe, doublet, shoes attached by points; also that you have had short hair, cut around above the ears, without retaining anything on your person which shows that you are a woman; and that several times you have received the body of Our Lord dressed in this fashion, despite having been admonished to give it up several times, the which you would not do. You have said that you would rather die than abandon the said clothing, if it were not at God's command, and that if you were wearing those clothes and were with the king, and those of your party, it would be one of the greatest benefits for the kingdom of France. You have also said that not for anything would you swear an oath not to wear the said clothing and carry arms any longer. And all these things you say you have done for the good and at the command of God. As for these things, the clerics say that you blaspheme God and hold him in contempt in his sacraments; you transgress Divine Law, Holy Scripture and canon law. You err in the faith. You boast in vanity. You are suspected of idolatry and you have condemned yourself in not wishing to wear clothing suitable to your sex, but you follow the custom of Gentiles and Saracens.

III

Evidence of Isembard de la Pierre, an Augustine friar who was close to Joan in her final days, given to the 1452 inquiry

An Englishman, a man-at-arms, who hated her very much and who had sworn that he would place a faggot on Jeanne's pyre with his own hands, as he did so and heard Jeanne call on the name of Jesus, in her last moments, was struck into a trance, and, as if in ecstasy, was taken into a tavern, near the Old Market, so that he might recover with the help of a drink. And after eating with a friar of the preaching orders, the Englishman confessed – the witness heard him – through this friar who was also English, that he had sinned gravely and that he repented of what he had done to the said Jeanne, for he thought that she was a good woman; for, as it seemed to him, this Englishman had seen, as Jeanne gave up the ghost, a white dove flying away in the direction of France. He said also that, after the meal, on the same day, the officer came to the convent of the said preaching friars and said to the witness and to Brother Martin Ladvenu that he was very afraid that he was damned, for he had burned a holy woman.

6

EDUCATION AND KNOWLEDGE

INTRODUCTION

Around the year 1400 an unusual event occurred in the Polish town of Krakow. A young woman, who had come into an inheritance, disguised herself as a man and spent two years as a student at the University's Faculty of Arts. A model student, she was on the verge of obtaining the bachelor's degree when she was unmasked by an observant soldier. Taken before a judge and asked her motive in disguising her sex, the young woman answered simply: 'Amore studii' (For the love of learning). She chose to be sent to a convent where she rose to be abbess in charge of the other nuns and, adds the narrator of this incident, she was said to be living yet (Shank 1989: 190–7).

Stories of women's cross-dressing in order to obtain knowledge, usually about the Christian religion, are frequent in the legends of early saints (Brown 1988: 156–9), and the Polish tale has certainly been subjected to a degree of narrative shaping to make it conform to such models. However, there are verifiable historical details in the account which suggest that the anecdote was indeed based on a true story. As an illustration of the hunger of many women in the later Middle Ages for access to the institutions of learning forbidden to them on the grounds of their sex, it could scarcely be bettered.

Although one of the most studied books of the Middle Ages, Aristotle's *Metaphysica*, began with the often-quoted text, 'Omnes homines naturaliter scire desiderant' (All humans naturally desire knowledge), this thirst for knowledge and intellectual curiosity on women's part was usually construed as reprehensible. Women are as 'instable and mobile as a leaf on a tree shaken by the wind,' wrote the Spanish moralist Francisco Ximenez; 'women's bodies are limp and unstable, and so women are unstable and unsteady in desire and will,' reasoned Giles of Rome (Casagrande 1992: 86–7). The anti-feminist tradition chose to analyse women's intelligence in terms of quick-wittedness and cunning, as the numerous fabliaux in which a woman saves her skin by quick thinking bear out (Blamires 1992: 130–47).

Moreover, the injunction of St Paul against women teaching (I Timothy 2: 11–12) made attendance at a university and the taking of a degree (essentially a licence to teach) a pointless exercise; women would never be permitted to put their acquired learning to any such practical use. Nevertheless women throughout the medieval period showed themselves adept at both teaching and learning outside the academy, absorbing all that Christian learning could offer and reinterpreting both traditional dogma and their experiences as women in their own educational writings.

Formal learning

Opportunities for formal education for women varied greatly throughout the period. At different times girls might be educated chiefly in the home, by their mothers, nurses or tutors; as boarders in convents or as day-pupils at convent schools; or in city elementary and grammar schools. In Anglo-Saxon England, the educational standards of the nunneries and double houses were the equal of the monasteries. It was to the Abbess Hildelith and her nuns at Barking in Essex that Aldhelm dedicated his treatise *De Virginitate* in the late seventh century, written in a Latin which is, as Christine Fell says, 'notoriously difficult and complex' (Fell 1984: 109). Aldhelm clearly regarded his readership as capable of appreciating his style, as his introductory remarks (excerpted below) indicate (Fig. 11). The letters of the women who corresponded with the Anglo-Saxon bishop Boniface (*c.* 675–754) on his mission to Germany in the 730s show that they had been taught Latin from Aldhelm's writings, and English women's houses provided many of the books which Boniface needed for the religious foundations he established in Germany (Fell 1984: 109–16). Christine Fell has suggested that King Alfred's late ninth-century educational reforms sketched in his Preface to the *Cura Pastoralis*, proposing the teaching of vernacular literacy with instruction in Latin for the more advanced, were aimed at young people of both sexes (Fell 1984: 100).

Nor, it seems, was learning in the convents restricted solely to the reading of Scripture. The Italian poet Fortunatus took up residence in Poitiers in the sixth century and exchanged poetry with the abbess of the convent of Sainte-Croix, the redoubtable Radegunde (Gregory of Tours 1974: 168, 526–31). Rumours of this literary relationship caused Abbess Caesaria of Arles to write to Radegunde in admonition, fearing lest the study of the Bible might be suffering in the convent, but the correct and polished Latin of Baudonivia, a Sainte-Croix nun who wrote the *Life of St Radegunde*, seems to indicate that the composition of poetry was not necessarily inimical to educational studies (Dronke 1984a: 28–9, 86).

In Carolingian France Charlemagne ordered the establishment of a network of town and monastic schools, in which no distinction was made at the elementary level between boys' and girls' curricula. Children would learn to read from the Psalter, usually learning large portions by heart, and to write on wax tablets – script

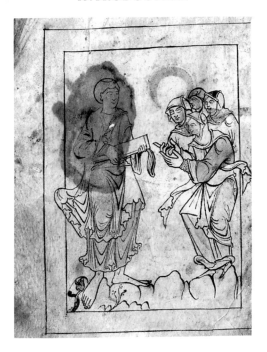

Figure 11 Aldhelm presents his work *Carmen de Virginitate* to Abbess Hildelith of Barking, for whose nuns the poem was written. From a manuscript of the Carmen from Christ Church, Canterbury, *c.* 1000. MS Bodl. 577. iiv–1r. Bodleian Library, Oxford.

which could easily be erased. Singing was taught to every child, not the musically gifted alone, for singing had an important mnemonic function. The calculation of the calendar was also taught, although the intricacies of the ecclesiastical calendar, in particular the method for calculating the date of Easter, were reserved for secondary schools. The abacus was introduced from Mozarabic Spain in the ninth century, revolutionizing the teaching of arithmetic (Riché 1976: 463–8; 1989: 227).

Those who progressed to secondary school would learn Latin grammar from Donatus and Priscian's textbooks. Fables, proverb collections and the compilation of wise sayings, *The Distichs of Cato* – a book, incidentally, used to teach Latin in Scotland until the Second World War (Pálsson 1985: 12) – were the first Latin texts which the young scholar would read. Once Latin was mastered, both written and spoken (for children were encouraged to speak Latin in class and at recreation alike), the students would advance through the subjects of the *trivium*: grammar, dialectic (which we would call logic), and rhetoric; and the *quadrivium*: arithmetic, music, geometry and astronomy. Those with special skills would be encouraged in drawing; in addition, girls would learn to embroider and sew.

With the decline of the nunneries in England in the twelfth and thirteenth centuries, educational standards in convents fell dramatically. Strict rules of enclosure hampered the nuns' access to teachers and women's foundations were able to attract fewer bequests and donations which might be spent on books (Power 1922). The developing universities attracted teachers away from the monasteries, and the nunneries suffered even more drastically (Legge 1950: 51). Educators could no longer rely on the religious woman's knowledge of Latin and instructive texts were now most likely to be written in the vernacular. Thus the author of *Ancrene Wisse* (c. 1225), a handbook for three sisters living as recluses in western England, paraphrases in his English text each of the quotations from the Vulgate which he cites as authorities in his work (Millett and Wogan-Brown 1990: 110–49). The collapse of Latin learning among women may have facilitated the development of vernacular literature in England, for, as Bella Millett points out, the recluse was expected to read as part of her daily routine, and her solitude would prevent her having anyone read to her, whether in Latin or English. An ex-nun might be able to read Latin, but the woman who took up the life of the recluse from the secular world would be likely only to be able to read the vernacular, like most noble women. Thus a demand for vernacular religious texts was created (Millett 1993).

In continental Europe standards in the convents remained higher for longer. Héloise (1101–64) was educated in the convent of Argenteuil near Paris and already had a formidable reputation for learning before Peter Abélard was engaged as her private tutor; when she herself became an abbess, Abélard provided, at her request, a Rule for her order which stressed the importance of study – of Latin, Greek and even Hebrew, a language which Abélard claims Héloise knew well. Those noble girls who were destined to become nuns might be admitted to convents when they were as young as 5 years old and thus were educated in the Bible, the writings of the Fathers, and most importantly in the Latin language from a very early age. Such an education seems to have afforded women thinkers a particular confidence in their intellectual powers. Caroline Bynum argues that the German mystics Gertrude the Great (*d.* 1291) and Mechthild of Hackeborn (*d.* 1298 or 1299), both childhood oblates, evince a striking lack of anxiety about their position as women writers and mystics, in contrast to their contemporary Mechthild of Magdeburg (*d.* 1282 or 1297). Gertrude and Mechthild of Hackeborn had spent their entire lives subject to female authority, instructed by female teachers and protected from the sense of worthlessness and self-doubt engendered by life in the patriarchal world outside the convent, which is apparent in Mechthild of Magdeburg's writings, for she had entered the convent relatively late in life (Bynum 1982: 252–5).

Secular education

Until the thirteenth century there was no great difference between the education of noblemen and women in England and on the Continent, for men were destined to become knights (*milites*), not intellectuals (*clerici*). Girls learned to ride so that they might join in the hunt, and the term *virago* (literally: one who acts like a man) was not yet a term of opprobrium (Riché 1989: 294–6). Throughout the Middle Ages churchmen felt that a modicum of education was desirable for women; they might thus learn the articles of faith, be able to read prayerbooks and psalters and benefit from instructive stories which would keep them modest and chaste. Moreover, the education of women had been sanctioned by no less an authority than Jerome in his letter on the education of Pacatula (Jerome 1893: 258–9). However, many authorities saw no reason for the ordinary woman to learn how to write, for the activities of reading and writing were far less closely linked than in modern educational thinking (Clanchy 1993: 193–5). Ladies of the high aristocracy were deemed to require more advanced education for purely practical reasons: they might be called upon to administer large estates in their husbands' absence. One extremist – Philippe de Novare – however argues that all women should be kept illiterate on the grounds that they would thus avoid being drawn into illicit correspondence with lovers (Shahar 1988: 155).

In the late Middle Ages, those aristocratic girls not destined to take the veil might be taught to read the vernacular by their mothers or nurses, before they were sent to be educated in convents, or went to court to learn etiquette and deportment. As the opportunities for them to learn Latin diminished, women came to foster a culture of the vernacular within the home, both for their religious and recreational reading, and for teaching their children. Girls would be taught the alphabet and elementary reading skills at the age of 6 or 7; the mother's role as teacher of the daughter is captured in the iconography of fourteenth- and fifteenth-century Books of Hours where St Anne is depicted teaching the Virgin Mary to read (Bell 1989: 134–61) (Fig. 12). Fifteenth-century Italian moralists felt that mothers could safely be entrusted with the initial religious education of their children, following the principles in Jerome. Mothers should teach children their first prayers and correct them for their failings (Vecchio 1992: 133–4).

By the late fourteenth century some bourgeois girls were able to attend grammar or cathedral schools, which were usually single-sex; the Polish woman of the anecdote recounted above is reported to have attended grammar school; as early as the thirteenth century schools for girls existed in the cities of Flanders. Ida of Nivelles, a Cistercian nun, attended a mixed municipal Latin school; Beatrijs van Tienen, a girl from a patrician family who later became a Cistercian abbess, went to a Latin school from the age of 7 (Opitz 1992: 297–8). These city schools taught reading and writing of the vernacular and the basic tenets of religion; those in Paris were subject to the Cantor of the Cathedral of Notre Dame and are known to have had female teachers as well as male. Often husband and wife would set up a school together, as in Bamberg in southern Germany, where the city regulations stipulated such an arrangement for coeducational schools (Opitz 1992: 298). Exceptionally, the fourteenth-century chronicler Froissart recalls attending a mixed elementary school in Valenciennes in France, where he made considerable efforts to ingratiate

Figure 12 St Anne teaches the Virgin to read (the letters in the book spell 'Domine' (Lord)). From a Book of Hours (Use of Sarum) *c.* 1325–50. MS Douce 231 fols. 2v–3r, Bodleian Library, Oxford.

himself with his female classmates and where Latin was taught, but Latin was not generally found on the elementary school curriculum (Shahar 1990: 215).

Traditional knowledge

Women of the peasant class (the vast majority of European women, of course) were unable to gain formal education of any sort. We should not imagine them as invincibly ignorant, however, for they would be likely to have learnt much from their mothers and grandmothers, passed down in oral form; the network of female friendships discussed above in chapter 2, a woman's 'gossips', her goddaughters and their mothers would have shared their information and experience. Only one woman in a circle needed to be able to read – or be read to – in order to pass on information disseminated through texts to others, as Felicity Riddy's account of the Duchess of York repeating the devotional works she had heard read to her over supper to her gentlewomen shows (Riddy 1993: 110). Nor did the advent of Christianity occlude all earlier forms of knowledge and practice. In northern Europe women seem to have been literate in runic script before Christian literacy arrived, as references in Old English poetry – 'The Husband's Message' (*Anglo-Saxon Poetic*

Records 1936: 225–7) and the Icelandic sagas seem to indicate (*Egils saga* 1933: 245; *Poetic Edda* 1969: 77, 79). Rune-inscribed wooden slips excavated from the medieval quarter of Bergen in Norway indicate that as late as the thirteenth century both sexes would use runes to communicate messages ranging from love charms to notes calling husbands home to dinner (Liestøl 1963). There is no reason to suppose that women were not skilled in oral genres – some poems composed by women in skaldic metre survive from tenth-century Norway (see chapter 7 below), while saga accounts depict women decoding these complex verses (Jesch 1991: 161–8; Harris 1991).

Women would not only have learned from older women how to run the household, but also how to heal the sick, using charms and herbal remedies. Such knowledge was increasingly regarded with suspicion as medicine began to be institutionalized in university medical faculties; in the later medieval period men sought to exclude women healers from exercising their trade and to establish a monopoly over all medical practices except childbirth (Green 1989; Amt 1993: 108–12). Although in some early texts knowledge of charms and soothsaying is not incompatible with Christianity (see excerpt 3 below), by the end of our period, accusations of witchcraft were beginning to be levelled at women who were skilled in traditional forms of wisdom and healing methods (Kieckhefer 1988: 194–200). We have few records of individual peasant women from later in the period, and thus it is difficult to generalize about how far they were familiar with Christian doctrine. In the evidence which Joan of Arc gives at her trial, she asserts that she had learned her Pater Noster, Ave Maria and Credo from her mother – 'and from no-one else except her mother'. It seems likely that Joan formed her other religious views, in particular her devotion to the Virgin Mary and the sacred name of Jesus, from listening to the preaching of mendicant friars (Duby and Duby 1973: 26–7, 29–30).

Learning about women

Formal education disseminated particular views about women, traditions which were inherited from the classical world and biblical sources. The orthodoxy concerning women was broadly misogynistic (see Blamires (1992) for a wide-ranging anthology of misogynist texts and Bloch (1991) for an idiosyncratic analysis of medieval misogyny), but it would be a mistake to categorize the thinking of the entire period as unequivocal in this regard. In the early twelfth century in particular, the attention of canon lawyers such as Gratian (who compiled the important body of ecclesiastical law, the *Decretum*, around 1140) turned to marriage and sexual relations while new thinking about the nature of the individual was making headway in the schools (Benton 1982; Morris 1987). Fresh doctrines of the relation between the sexes were assayed. Hugh of St Victor (1096–1140) advances this interpretation of the creation of woman:

She [Woman] is made from the man's side in order to show that she is created for the delight of companionship, nor did she happen to be created from the head where she would be seen to dominate, to the damnation of the man, nor from the feet, made subject in servitude. She was made therefore not as mistress, not as slave but as companion to the man; created not from the head, not from the feet, but from the side.

(Patrologia Latina 175, col. 284)

However, this formulation was soon abbreviated: the observation that woman was not created from the head, and so ought not to dominate man became a commonplace of misogynist writing while the rest of the text was discarded, exemplified by Jacques de Vitry (Blamires 1992: 145). Peter Abélard (1079–1142) in *Letters* 2 and 6 celebrates women's faith and power to move God: 'because the sex of woman is weaker, their virtue is more pleasing to God and more perfect' (Blamires 1992: 235). In a highly untraditional comment Abélard suggests that Christ need not have been born from a woman at all, but deliberately chose the weaker body. Thus Christ consecrated female genitals more by his birth than he consecrated male genitals by his circumcision (Blamires 1992: 236; Ferrante 1975: 24). However, such relatively liberal thinking made little headway against the universal dissemination of anti-women writing at all cultural levels. We find few examples of women protesting the orthodox view of women: Héloïse exemplifies the educated woman who internalizes the beliefs that marriage and child-rearing are inimical to the intellectual (see excerpt 5 below) and that women are fundamentally inferior to men, even though she seems to have been at least as intellectually able as her lover Abélard. Of the women writers of the period it is only Christine de Pizan who takes issue with the custom of educating sons, not daughters, and who robustly defends both women's ability to profit from education and their absolute right to education for the development of the human spirit (Christine de Pizan 1982: 52–4, 85–9).

Since medieval formulations posited woman as signifying the material, against man as the spiritual, learned accounts of women's bodies, the very sites of their materiality, are of particular interest. Aristotle (384–322 BC) was the main source for the understanding of female physiology, mediated through early physicians such as Soranus and Galen, and the sixth-century encyclopaedist Isidore of Seville (Laqueur 1990: 25–52 and Cadden 1993 sketch the transmission of Aristotelian anatomy through the period). With the new access to Greek learning in the twelfth century, Aristotle's authority became even more entrenched. Traditional belief had a powerful hold even over the intellectually curious: late thirteenth-century dissectionists in Bologna 'found' that the uterus was indeed divided into seven chambers, just as they had been led to believe. 'Thus the benefits of experiment were minimal, an object-lesson in the "theory-ladenness" of scientific observation'

(Thomasset 1992: 53). Complementing the scientific theories of female physiology are some medical writings by women, giving accounts of their own physical nature. Hildegard of Bingen's *Causae et Curae* is a description of female sexuality which, although rooted in medieval humour theory and composed by a woman who herself had had no sexual experience, is soundly based, at times even poetic. The best known gynaecological writings of the period are those of Trota or Trotula, a female physician who practised in Salerno in Italy in the late eleventh or twelfth centuries (Benton 1985; Ferrante 1984; Green 1989). Although her existence was long in doubt, she has now been securely identified as the author of only one work in Latin: a cluster of texts preserved in compilations became attached to her name, and present an interesting combination of contemporary medical orthodoxy, empirical observation and traditional herbal lore (Amt 1993: 98–108).

Women as teachers

The earliest educational text from the period is the work of a woman; as early as 841–3 Dhuoda composed a Latin instruction for her son, synthesizing an enormous list of sources both classical and contemporary (Dronke 1984a: 36–54; Marchand 1984; Amt 1993: 123–9; and see p. 83 above). A woman called Ingunn is recorded as teaching Latin to the boys at the cathedral school in Hólar, northern Iceland in the eleventh century (Clover 1993: 386). The idea of women as teachers is a natural extension of the responsibilities of motherhood and nurturing; thus, as we see below, even recluse women seem to have been in the habit of teaching young girls, much as Ælred of Rievaulx may have deprecated the distraction from the work of contemplation.

In the later Middle Ages several writers took on the task of composing manuals of instruction for women in both practical and ethical matters. Anxious fathers – the Knight of the Tour-Landry (*c.* 1371) – or elderly husbands – the Ménagier de Paris (*c.* 1392) (Power 1928; 1986: 96–119), the Florentine author Francesco di Barberino (*d.* 1348) – or wise and experienced ladies such as Christine de Pizan produced handbooks which combined tips for good household management with guidelines for appropriate behaviour towards one's husband, his guests, his family and one's servants.

Popular as such works seem to have been (as a professional writer, Christine is unlikely to have written a treatise for which there was no demand), women, in particular those from the rising bourgeoisie, still hankered after the learning which their brothers acquired as of right. Héloise's study with Peter Abélard ended in personal disaster for both teacher and student, and may have functioned as a warning to other women (one wonders what conclusions Christine de Pizan might have drawn from the story). By the close of the period, however, earliest in northern Italy, but spreading rapidly northwards, the new humanism, with its penchant for speculative thinking and its motto 'Dare to Know' began to challenge the theocentric preoccupations of conventional scholastic thinking, a wisdom epitomized by the classical and Pauline aphorisms 'Know thyself' and 'Seek not to know the highest' (Ginzburg 1990: 60–75). It became possible to envisage the pursuit of knowledge for its own sake, even to the point of concluding a Faustian bargain with the Devil (see excerpt 8 below), as an ambition to which women might not only aspire, but in which they might even succeed. We can identify around twenty women among the Italian humanists at the beginnings of the Italian Renaissance, and by the sixteenth century, Erasmus was advocating that the education of the woman should never cease; even after marriage she should continue to cultivate her intellectual interests (King 1984: 56–90; Bainton 1984: 117–38). The case for women's education would have to be made over and over again in the centuries which follow; as men felt themselves to be challenged and threatened by women's study, propaganda about the 'unfeminine' nature of the learned woman began to be disseminated. It may, however, be possible to conclude, as Joan Ferrante does (Ferrante 1984: 34–5), that the medieval period is one in which the achievements of the educated woman 'can command the respect and attention of the male establishment' without further qualification.

1 THE LEARNING OF ANGLO-SAXON NUNS

Texts from: (a) Aldhelm (1989) *The Prose Works*, transl. M. Lapidge and M. Herren, Cambridge: D. S. Brewer; (b) and (c) Boniface (1940) *The Letters of Saint Boniface*, transl. E. Emerton, New York: Columbia University Press; repr. Octagon, 1973, pp. 59–61 and 64–5.

Aldhelm (born *c.* 640, died *c.* 709), sometimes described as the 'first English man of letters', was abbot of Malmesbury, and later bishop of Sherborne. He wrote a number of works in both prose and poetry; in both forms his Latin is complex, obscure, crammed with neologisms and highly ornate. His treatise in praise of virginity, *De Virginitate*, was written for the Abbess Hildelith and her nuns at the double monastery of Barking in Essex. The monastery had been founded *c.* 650 and Hildelith was its second abbess. The date of the text is uncertain, possibly 675–80. Even when allowance is made for Aldhelm's rhetorical flourishes, it seems that the learning among the work's dedicatees, in theology and patristics, as well as grammar and rhetoric, must have been remarkable.

Winfred, later known as Boniface, was born in the western part of the kingdom of Wessex around 675. He entered the monastery at Exeter at the age of 7 and eventually became abbot, but at the age of 40 he decided to join the missionary efforts to convert the North German tribes. With a commission from the Pope, and with some support from the king of the Franks, Charles Martel, he was able to found a diocesan base in Hessen, and eventually established a number of further dioceses eastwards from the Rhine. A number of English women, notably Leoba, Eadburg and Bucge, were among Boniface's correspondents and Leoba herself joined the German mission and became abbess of a foundation at Bischofsheim. Eadburg, abbess of Thanet, is asked to send him a particularly ornate copy of the Epistle of St Peter. As Christine Fell comments, 'It is interesting that among the dozens of requests for books which he [Boniface] sent constantly to all his English contacts, the request for a really finely executed piece of work goes to Eadburg's scriptorium' (Fell 1984: 113).

(a) Aldhelm addresses the nuns of Barking at the beginning of *De Virginitate*

To the most reverend virgins of Christ, [who are] to be venerated with every affection of devoted brotherhood, and to be celebrated not only for the distinction of [their] corporeal chastity, which is [the achievement] of many, but also to be glorified on account of [their] spiritual purity, which is [the achievement] of few: Hildelith, teacher of the regular discipline and of the monastic way of life; and likewise Justina and Cuthburg; and Osburg too, related [to me] by family bonds of kinship; Aldgith and Scholastica, Hidburg and Berngith, Eulalia and Thecla – [to all these nuns] unitedly ornamenting the Church through the renown of their sanctity, Aldhelm, dilatory worshipper of Christ and humble servant of the Church, [sends his] best wishes for perpetual prosperity.

Some time ago, while proceeding to an episcopal convention accompanied by brotherly throngs of associates, I received most pleasurably what had been written by your Grace to my humble self and, with my hands extended to the heavens, I took care joyously to extend immense thanks to Christ on behalf of your welfare. In your writing not only were the ecclesiastical compacts of [your] sworn vows – which you had pledged with a solemn promise – abundantly clear, but also the mellifluous studies of the Holy Scriptures were manifest in the extremely subtle sequence of your discourse.

And when, reading aloud the individual texts of your letters, I had scanned [them] with the keen gaze of [my] eyes and had thought them over with a certain natural curiosity about hidden things – as, it is said, is innate in me – and had very much admired the extremely rich verbal eloquence and the innocent expression of sophistication, then, I say, the governor of lofty Olympus and the ruler of heaven rejoices with an inexpressible exultation on seeing, thus, the catholic maidservants of Christ – or rather adoptive daughters of regenerative grace brought forth from the fecund womb of ecclesiastical conception through the seed of the spiritual Word – growing learned in divine doctrine through [the Church's] maternal care....

For just as the swarm [of bees], having left in companies and throngs the restricted openings of the windows and the narrow entrance-halls of the beehive, pillages the beautiful meadows of the countryside, in the same way your remarkable mental disposition – unless I'm mistaken – roaming widely through the flowering fields of Scripture, traverses [them] with thirsty curiosity, now energetically plumbing the divine oracles of the ancient prophets foretelling long in advance the advent of the Saviour with certain affirmations; now, scrutinizing with careful application the hidden mysteries of the ancient laws miraculously drawn up by the man [Moses] who is said to have cruelly smitten the Memphitic realm [Egypt] with ten most savage afflictions of plagues ...; now, exploring wisely the fourfold text of the evangelical story [the four Gospels], expounded through the mystical commentaries of the catholic fathers and laid open spiritually to the very core and divided up by the rules of the fourfold ecclesiastical tradition according to *historia, allegoria, tropologia* and *anagoge*; now, duly rummaging through the old stories of the historians and the entries of the chroniclers, who by their writing have delivered to lasting memory the chance vicissitudes of times gone by; now, sagaciously inquiring into the rules of the grammarians and the teachings of experts on spelling and the rules of metrics [as they are] measured out into accents [and] times, fitted into poetic feet, broken up into cola and commata – that is, into pentimemeres and eptimemeres – and indeed, divided individually into a hundred kinds of metre.

> *Historia, allegoria, tropologia* and *anagoge* are the traditional methods of fourfold exegesis, used to uncover all the possible meanings in biblical texts. They are summarized in the mnemonic couplet 'Littera gesta docet, quid credas allegoria / Moralis quid agas, quo tendas, anagogia' (The literal teaches of events, the allegorical what you should believe, the moral what you should do, where you are going (i.e. the doctrine of the Four Last Things: heaven, hell, death and judgement), the anagogical).
> Cola and commata: plurals of 'colon' and 'comma' referring respectively to a larger 'limb' and a smaller 'clause' of a sentence or strophe; pentimemeres and eptimemeres: group or colon of verse consisting respectively of five or seven half feet.

(b) The young Leoba writes to Boniface (*c.* 732)

To my revered master Boniface, bearing the insignia of the highest office, most dear to me in Christ and bound to me by ties of kinship, I, Leoba, least of the servants of those who bear the easy yoke of Christ, wish enduring health and prosperity.

I beg you graciously to bear in mind your ancient friendship for my father, Dynne, formed long ago in the West Country. It is now eight years since he was called away from this world, and I ask your prayers for his soul. I recall to your memory also my mother, Æbbe, who, as you know, is bound to you by ties of blood. She lives a life of suffering, bowed down by grievous illness. I am the only daughter of my parents and, unworthy though I be, I wish that I might regard you as a brother; for there is no other man in my kinship in whom I have such confidence as in you. I have ventured to send you this little gift, not as if it deserved even a kindly glance from you but that you may have a reminder of my insignificance and not let me be forgotten on account of our wide separation. May the bond of our true affection be knit ever more closely for all time. I eagerly pray, my dear brother, that I may be protected by the shield of your prayers from the poisoned darts of the hidden enemy. I beg you also to be so kind as to correct the unskilled style of this letter and to send me, by way of example, a few kind words which I greatly long to hear.

I have composed the following verses according to the rules of poetic art, not trusting to my own presumption, but trying only to exercise my little talents and needing your assistance. I have studied this art under the guidance of Eadburga, who still carries on without ceasing her investigation of the divine law.

Farewell, and may you live long and happily, making intercession for me.

> The omnipotent Ruler who alone created everything,
> He who shines in splendour forever in His Father's kingdom,
> The perpetual fire by which the glory of Christ reigns,
> May preserve you forever in perennial right.

(c) Boniface writes to Eadburga asking her to make him a copy of the Epistle of St Peter in letters of gold (c. 735)

To his most reverend and beloved sister, the Abbess Eadburga, Boniface, humble servant of the servants of God, sends heartfelt greetings of love in Christ.

I pray to Almighty God, the rewarder of all good works, that He will repay you in the heavenly mansions and eternal tabernacles and in the choir of the blessed angels for all the kindnesses you have shown me, the solace of books and the comfort of the garments with which you have relieved my distress.

And I beg you further to add to what you have done already by making a copy written in gold of the Epistles of my master, St Peter the Apostle, to impress honour and reverence for the Sacred Scriptures visibly upon the carnally minded to whom I preach. I desire to have ever present before me the words of him who is my guide upon this road. I am sending by the priest Eoban the materials for your writing.

Do then, dearest sister, with this petition of mine as you have always done with my requests, so that here also your works may shine forth in golden letters for the glory of our heavenly Father. I pray for your well-being in Christ, and may you go on upward to still greater heights of holy virtue.

2 THE TEACHING OF GIRLS

Text from: Ælred of Rievaulx (1971) *Treatises and the Pastoral Prayer* I, Cistercian Fathers 2, Kalamazoo, Mich.: Cistercian Publications, pp. 49–50.

Ælred of Rievaulx (for whose life see p. 128 above) wrote a short treatise *De Institutione Inclusarum* (About the Institution of Recluses) for his sister who had decided to retreat from the world as a recluse. The treatise comprises Ælred's views on the 'Outer Rule' (the minutiae of the recluse's dress, diet and way of life), the 'Inner Rule' (the interior disposition of the recluse towards God), and a series of meditations to assist the recluse in her contemplation. The Latin text, from which the extract below is taken, was composed between 1160 and 1162. The treatise was translated into Middle English in two versions: one deals only with the latter half of the original, the second, dating from the mid-fifteenth century, translates the whole work but with drastic abbreviation and omission. The passage cited below is one which was curtailed in translation: the Middle English reads simply: 'Be war also that thou be not occupied in techynge of children. For somme recluses ther ben that thorugh techinge of children turnen her celles in-to a scole-house: doo not so' (Ælred 1984: 3–4); a similar warning is found in the thirteenth-century *Ancrene Wisse* (Millett and Wogan-Browne 1990: 140–1).

Never allow children access to your cell. It is not unknown for a recluse to take up teaching and turn her cell into a school. She sits at her window, the girls settle themselves in the porch; and so she keeps them all under observation. Swayed by their childish dispositions, she is angry one minute and smiling the next, now threatening, now flattering, kissing one child and smacking another. When she sees one of them crying after being smacked she calls her close, strokes her cheek, puts her arms around her neck and holds her tight, calling her 'My own baby girl, my own pet'. There before her very eyes, even though she may not yield to them, the recluse has worldly and sensual temptations, and amid them all what becomes of her continual remembrance of God?

3 A WISE WOMAN PROPHESIES

Text translated from: 'Eiríks saga in rauda' (1935) in *Eyrbyggja saga*, ed. E. O. Sveinsson and M. Thordarson, Islenzk Fornrit 4, Reykjavík: Hid Islenzka Fornritafelag, pp. 206–9.

'Eiríks saga in rauda' (Eric the Red's Saga) is more accurately the story of a young woman, Gudrid, rather than the saga of the discoverer of Greenland himself. Gudrid journeys with her father from Iceland to the new colony of Greenland, where she marries a son of Eric the Red. After his death in an epidemic and a prophetic encounter with his ghost, Gudrid marries an Icelander and takes part in the short-lived attempt to colonize Vinland (America), where, incidentally, she gives birth to Snorri, the first non-Native American. The family return to Iceland where Gudrid is the ancestor of Icelandic bishops, a lineage which includes St Thorlak, the patron saint of Iceland, whose future birth is signalled in this extract as the bright ray of light which the seeress sees. The saga was probably composed in the later thirteenth century, well after the events of which it tells; these occur in the late tenth/early eleventh century. The pagan practices depicted in this extract cannot therefore be regarded as historical, although some details in the description of the sybil, notably her sex and her position on a raised platform, do correspond with what is known of such figures in Scandinavia. Striking too is the absence of any authorial condemnation of Gudrid for participating in a pagan rite. Her father's disapproval is manifested by his refusal to stay on the farm while the divination takes place, but Gudrid's status as the foremother of bishops and saints remains uncompromised.

At that time there was a great famine in Greenland; people were not able to catch very much when they went out hunting, and some people were lost altogether. There was a woman in the settlement called Thorbjorg; she was a seer and known as 'the little sybil'. She had had nine sisters, and all of them were seers, but she was then the only one still alive. It was Thorbjorg's custom in the winter to go to feasts and those who invited her most were those who were curious to know what their fates were or how the year would go; and since Thorkel was the farmer of greatest standing there, it was felt that it was up to him to find out when the famine which had now come over them might be relieved. Thorkel invited the prophetess to his farm, and she was made welcome there, according to the custom for receiving such women. A highseat was prepared for her and a cushion placed upon it; it had to be filled with chicken feathers. And when she came in the evening with the man who had been sent to fetch her, this is how she was dressed: she had a dark-blue cloak with a drawstring at the neck and precious stones decorating it all the way down to the bottom; she had glass beads around her neck, and a black lambskin hood on her head, lined with white catskin. She had a staff in her hand and on top was a knob; it was inlaid with brass and there was a jewel on the knob; she had a belt of touchwood [a kind of tree-fungus] around her waist and on it a great purse in which she kept her magic charms which she needed for her divination. She wore hairy calfskin shoes on her feet with long thongs and with great tin buttons on the end of them. On her hands she had catskin gloves, and they were white inside and furry. And when she came in, it seemed advisable to everyone to greet her politely. She received their greetings as her humour took her. Thorkel the farmer took her by the hand and led her to the seat which had been prepared for her. Thorkel asked her to look over the family and the household. She said very little about anything. The trestle-tables were taken down in the evening and now should be told what the prophetess ate: porridge of kid's milk and a dish made of the hearts of all the kinds of animal which were available. She had a brass spoon and a knife mounted in walrus-tusk, with a double ring of copper about it, and the point was broken. And when the tables had been cleared, Thorkel went up to Thorbjorg and asked how the household there struck her and what her feelings were about the state and the fortunes of the people there, and how quickly she might be able to tell him what he had asked her, and what everyone was very eager to know about. She said that she could not prophesy anything until the next day, when she had slept on things overnight.

And in the morning of the following day she was brought the equipment which she needed to perform *seid* [a particular kind of magic]. She asked for the help of some women who might know that spell which is necessary to *seid*, a spell called Vardlokkur [Defending Ring]. But no such women could be found. They asked around the farm to see if anyone knew it. Then Gudrid said: 'I am neither wise in magic nor a seer, but Halldis, my foster-mother, taught me that song in Iceland, which she called Vardlokkur.' Thorkel said, 'You are lucky to know that.' She said, 'There is one drawback, that I don't want to assist with this for I am a Christian.' Thorbjorg said: 'It may well be that you will be a great help to the people here, and you will be no worse a woman than you were before; but it is with Thorkel that I leave the matter of getting me what I need.' Thorkel now brought pressure to bear on Gudrid and she said that she would do as he wished. Then the women made a ring around the dais, and Thorbjorg sat up on high. Gudrid recited the spell so beautifully and so well that no one who was there had ever heard the poem spoken with a lovelier voice. The seer thanked her for her recitation and said that she had now brought many spirits there who had enjoyed listening to the spell so well performed, 'and before they would not come near us nor pay any attention to us. And now many things have become plain to me which before were concealed both from me and from other people. And I can tell you this, Thorkel, that this famine will not last any longer than for this winter, and when spring comes, so the weather will improve. The sickness, which has been hanging over us for a long time, will also depart, more quickly than people might expect. And I shall reward you, Gudrid, for the help which you have offered us here, for your fate is now as clear as day to me. You will make a match here in Greenland, and it will be a most honourable one, though it will not last long for you, for your course lies back towards Iceland, and you will have there great and splendid descendants, and from your family tree there shines one ray more brightly than I can easily bear to look at; now farewell and the best of luck to you, daughter.'

Afterwards people went up to the wise-woman and each one asked what he was most curious to know: she gave promising accounts of the future, and indeed this proved to vary little from what she forecast. Next someone came to fetch her from another farm, and she went away. Then Thorbjorn [Gudrid's father] was sent for, since he had not wanted to stay in the place while such sorcery was performed.

4 WOMEN'S PHYSIOLOGY

Text from: P. Dronke (1984) *Women Writers of the Middle Ages*, Cambridge: Cambridge University Press, pp. 175–8, 180–1.

Hildegard of Bingen (1098–1179) was born into a noble German family, the youngest of ten children; vowed to God by her parents, she was enclosed with a recluse aunt at the age of 8 near Disibodenberg on the Rhine; other women came to join them and a new foundation grew up. From her earliest years she experienced visions and was often subject to serious illness – the two tendencies seem to be interconnected. In 1136 she was elected abbess of Disibodenberg and her literary career began. Hildegard wrote three long works: *Scivias* (The Way to Knowledge), the *Liber Vitae Meritorum* (Book of Life's Merits) and *Liber Divinorum Operum* (Book of Divine Works) recounting and analysing her visions. She also wrote two medical treatises, *Physica* and *Causae et Curae*; the latter treating the physiological and psychological from a woman's point of view for the first time in western history. Hildegard was also an accomplished poet and musician; she composed a collection of song sequences, *Symphonia Harmoniae Caelestium Revelationum* (Symphony of the Harmony of Celestial Revelations) (see chapter 7 below) and *Ordo Virtutum* (The Order of the Virtues), a morality play which she later set to music. Other writings include commentaries on the Gospel, the Rule of St Benedict and the Athanasian Creed, an invented language (*Litterae Ignotae*) with a 900-word glossary and some saints' Lives.

The following passages are taken from the medical treatise *Causae et Curae*. They demonstrate that Hildegard's knowledge is based on orthodox medical thought, in particular the theory of the humours; nevertheless, the virgin nun takes a straightforward and non-judgemental view of the workings of the female body, making no reference to Christian notions of the sinfulness of sexual activity (Newman 1987: 121–55; Dronke 1984a: 171–83). Hildegard was in correspondence with a number of women who sought her advice about both spiritual and health matters (Flanagan 1989: 165–71); thus, although her personal experience is limited, the women to whom she wrote and spoke may have provided her with the joyous, even lyrical, description of sexual intercourse given in the first extract.

On intercourse

When a woman is making love with a man, a sense of heat in her brain, which brings forth with it sensual delight, communicates the taste of that delight during the act and summons forth the emission of the man's seed. And when the seed has fallen into its place, that vehement heat descending from her brain draws the seed to itself and holds it, and soon the woman's sexual organs contract and all the parts that are ready to open up during the time of menstruation now close, in the same way as a strong man can hold something enclosed in his fist.

When God created Adam, Adam experienced a sense of great love in the sleep that God instilled in him. And God gave a form to that love of the man, and so woman is the man's love. And as soon as woman was formed God gave man the power of creating, that through his love – which is woman – he might procreate children. When Adam gazed at Eve, he was entirely filled with wisdom, for he saw in her the mother of the children to come. And when she gazed at Adam, it was as if she were gazing into heaven, or as the human soul strives upwards, longing for heavenly things – for her hope was fixed in him. And so there will be and must be one and the same love in man and woman, and no other.

The man's love, compared with the woman's is a heat of ardour like a fire on blazing mountains which can hardly be put out, whilst hers is a wood-fire that is easily quenched; but the woman's love, compared with the man's is like a sweet warmth proceeding from the sun, which brings forth fruits....

But the great love that was in Adam when Eve came forth from him, and the sweetness of the sleep with which he then slept, were turned in his transgression into a contrary mode of sweetness. And so, because a man still feels this great sweetness in himself, and like a stag thirsting for the fountain, he races swiftly to the woman and she to him – she like a threshing-floor pounded by his many strokes and brought to heat when the grains are threshed inside her.

Conceiving male and female children

When the man approaches the woman, releasing powerful semen and in a true cherishing love for the woman, and she too has a true love for the man in that same hour, then a male child is conceived, for so it was ordained by God. Nor can it be otherwise, because Adam was formed of clay which is a stronger material than flesh. And this male child will be prudent and virtuous....

But if the woman's love is lacking in that hour ... and if the man's semen is strong, a male child will still be born, because the man's cherishing love predominates. But that male child will be feeble and not virtuous.... If the man's semen is thin, and yet he cherishes the woman lovingly and she him, then a virtuous female child is procreated.... If the man's semen is powerful but neither the man nor the woman cherish each other lovingly, a male child is procreated ... but he will bitter with his parents' bitterness; and if the man's semen is thin and there is no cherishing love on either side in that hour, a girl of bitter temperament is born.

The blood in every human being increases and diminishes according to the waxing and waning of the moon ... when, as the moon waxes, the blood in human beings is increased, then both men and women are fertile for bearing fruit – for generating children – since then the man's semen is powerful and robust; and in the waning of the moon, when human blood also wanes, the man's semen is feeble and without strength, like dregs.... If a woman conceives a child then, whether boy or girl, it will be infirm and feeble and not virtuous.

The temperaments of women

De sanguinea (About sanguine women)

Some women are inclined to plumpness, and have soft and delectable flesh and slender veins, and well-constituted blood free from impurities.... And these have a clear and light colouring, and in love's embraces are themselves lovable; they are subtle in arts, and show self-restraint in their disposition. At menstruation they suffer only a modest loss of blood, and their womb is well developed for childbearing, so they are fertile and can take in the man's seed. Yet they do not bear many children, and if they are without husbands so that they remain childless, they easily have physical pains; but if they have husbands, they are well.

De flecmatica (About phlegmatic women)

There are other women whose flesh does not develop as much, because they have thick veins and healthy, whitish blood (though it does contain a little impurity, which is the source of its light colour). They have severe features, and are darkish in colouring; they are vigorous and practical, and have a somewhat mannish disposition. At menstruation their menstrual blood flows neither too little nor too abundantly. And because they have thick veins they are very fertile and conceive easily, for the womb and all their inner organs, too, are well developed. They attract men and make men pursue them, and so men love them well. If they want to stay away from men, they can do so without being affected by it badly, though they are slightly affected. However, if they do avoid making love with men they will become difficult and unpleasant in their behaviour. But if they go with men and do not wish to avoid men's love-making, they will be unbridled and over-lascivious, according to men's report. And because they are to some extent mannish on account of the vital force (viriditas, lit. greenness) within them, a little down sometimes grows on their chin.

De colerica (About choleric women)

There are other women who have slender flesh but big bones, moderately sized veins and dense red blood. They are pallid in colouring, prudent and benevolent, and men show them reverence and are afraid of them. They suffer much loss of blood in menstruation; their womb is well developed and they are fertile. And men like their conduct, yet flee from them and avoid them to some extent, for they can interest men but not make men desire them. If they do get married, they are chaste, they remain loyal wives and live healthily with their husbands; and if they are unmarried, they tend to be ailing – as much because they do not know to what man they might pledge their womanly loyalty as because they lack a husband....

De melancolica *(About melancholic women)*

But there are other women who have gaunt flesh and thick veins and moderately sized bones; their blood is more lead-coloured than sanguine, and their colouring is as it were blended with grey and black. They are changeable and free-roaming in their thoughts, and wearisomely wasted away in affliction; they also have little power of resistance, so that at times they are worn out by melancholy. They suffer much loss of blood in menstruation, and they are sterile, because they have a weak and fragile womb. So they cannot lodge or retain or warm a man's seed, and thus they are also healthier, stronger and happier without husbands than with them – especially because, if they lie with their husbands, they will tend to feel weak afterwards. But men turn away from them and shun them because they do not speak to men affectionately, and love them only a little. If for some hour they experience sexual joy, it quickly passes in them. Yet some such women, if they unite with robust and sanguine husbands, can at times, when they reach a fair age, such as fifty, bear at least one child. . . . If their menopause comes before the just age, they will sometimes suffer gout or swellings of the legs, or will incur an insanity which their melancholy arouses, or else backache or a kidney ailment. . . . If they are not helped in their illness, so that they are not freed from it either by God's help or by medicine, they will quickly die.

5 HÉLOISE AND ABÉLARD

Text from: *The Letters of Abélard and Héloise* (1974), transl. B. Radice, Harmondsworth: Penguin, pp. 66–8, 71–2.

Peter Abélard was born in 1079 into a noble Breton family. He arrived in Paris around 1100 where he studied with William of Champeaux before setting up his own rival school. His increasing reputation made him 'a thorn in his teachers' flesh, conscious as he was of his own intellectual superiority, no respecter of persons and revelling in the cut and thrust of debate' (*Letters* 1974: 11). He later went to study theology with Anselm at Laon, but soon fell out with him, and returned to Paris to become head of the Cloister School where he had studied as a young man. In his late thirties, at the peak of his intellectual powers, he undertook to tutor Héloise, the 17-year-old niece of one of the canons of the cathedral. His account of his seduction of his pupil and the passionate affair which developed from it, follows. When the affair was discovered the pair refused to break it off; Héloise became pregnant and gave birth to a son. Abélard now promised her uncle that he would marry Héloise if the wedding could be kept secret, so that his promotion through Holy Orders would not be hindered. Although Fulbert, Héloise's uncle, agreed, Héloise herself refused, for the reasons which Abélard gives in extract (b) below. Eventually she consented to the wedding, and Abélard took her for safekeeping to the convent at Argenteuil where she had been educated as a girl. Fulbert interpreted this action as evidence that Abélard intended to abandon his niece, and had his men break into Abélard's room one night and castrate him. In despair,

Héloise, under pressure from Abélard, took vows and joined the convent, while he entered the Abbey of St Denis.

In 1132, some thirteen years after these dramatic events, Abélard wrote the *Historia Calamitatum* (History of my Misfortunes), recounting his life until that point. It is written for a third person, to comfort him in his own difficulties, but, Peter Dronke suggests, the public nature of the letter is such that it seems likely that Abélard himself arranged for Héloise to be sent a copy. Her reception of the *Historia* initiated a personal correspondence with Abélard; although at one time it was argued that her letters were forgeries, Peter Dronke has demonstrated their authenticity fairly conclusively (Dronke 1984a: 107–43). Abélard's account of the affair makes it plain that he was motivated more by lust than love in his dealings with Héloise; so overwhelming a sexual passion burned in them that, even while Héloise was in retreat at Argenteuil, they made love in a corner of the refectory (see chapter 2 above, p. 54, for Héloise's recollection of their passion). Abélard sounds dispassionate, even heartless, as he reveals the degree of calculation with which he embarked on his seduction; certainly in his letters to Héloise he is ready to recall their physical relationship in terms of disgust and horror, 'the wanton vileness of our former ways'. He plays down any spiritual commitment between them, except in terms of their joint vows to enter the cloister; although, referring to his intentions when they married, he says: 'At the time I desired to keep you whom I loved beyond measure for myself alone, but he [God] was already planning to use this opportunity for our joint conversion from the world' (*Letters* 1974: 149). While Héloise expresses an undiminished love and devotion towards Abélard in her letters, it is clear that Abélard wants only to use Héloise's love for him to urge her towards excellence in her spiritual life; he is anxious to convert whatever he may once have felt for her into concern for her spiritual well-being. Héloise outlived Abélard by some twenty years; his body was brought to the foundation of the Paraclete which he had founded for her, and eventually both bodies were buried together at St Denis. They now rest in the Père Lachaise cemetery in Paris.

(a) Abélard's account of his affair with Héloise

There was in Paris at the time a young girl named Héloise, the niece of Fulbert, one of the canons, and so much loved by him that he had done everything in his power to advance her education in letters. In looks she did not rank lowest, while in the extent of her learning she stood supreme. A gift for letters is so rare in women that it added greatly to her charm and had won her renown throughout the realm. I considered all the usual attractions for a lover and decided she was the one to bring to my bed, confident that I should have an easy success; for at that time I had youth and exceptional good looks as well as my great reputation to recommend me, and feared no rebuff from any woman I might choose to honour with my love. Knowing the girl's knowledge and love of letters I thought that she would be all the more ready to consent, and that even when separated we could enjoy each other's presence by exchange of written messages in which we could speak more openly than in person, and so need never lack the pleasures of conversation.

All on fire with desire for this girl I sought an opportunity of getting to know her through private daily meetings and so more easily winning her over; and with this end in view I came to an arrangement with her uncle, with the help of some of his friends, whereby he should take me into his house, which was very near my school, for whatever sum he liked to ask. As a pretext, I said that my household cares were hindering my studies and the expense was more than I could afford. Fulbert dearly loved money, and was moreover always ambitious to further his niece's education in letters, two weaknesses which made it easy for me to gain his consent and obtain my desire: he was all eagerness for my money and confident that his niece would profit from my teaching. This led him to make an urgent request which furthered my love and fell in with my wishes more than I had dared to hope; he gave me complete charge over the girl, so that I could devote all the leisure time left me by my school to teaching her by day and night, and if I found her idle I was to punish her severely. I was amazed by his simplicity – if he had entrusted a tender lamb to a ravening wolf it would not have surprised me more. In handing her over to me to punish as well as to teach, what else was he doing but giving me complete freedom to realize my desires, and providing an opportunity, even if I did not make use of it, for me to bend her to my will by threats and blows if persuasion failed? But there were two special reasons for his freedom from base suspicion: his love for his niece and my previous reputation for continence.

Need I say more? We were united, first under one roof, then in heart; and so with our lessons as a pretext we abandoned ourselves entirely to love. Her studies allowed us to withdraw in private, as love desired, and then with our books open before us, more words of love than of our reading passed between us, and more kissing than teaching. My hands strayed oftener to her bosom than to the pages; love drew our eyes to look on each other more than reading kept them on our texts. To avert suspicion I sometimes struck her, but these blows were prompted by love and tender feeling rather than anger and irritation, and were sweeter than any balm could be. In short, our desire left no stage of love-making untried, and if love could devise something new, we welcomed it. We entered on each joy the more eagerly for our previous inexperience, and were the less easily sated.

(b) Héloise's arguments against marriage for the philosopher

But apart from the hindrances to such philosophic study, consider, she said, the true conditions for a dignified way of life. What harmony can there be between pupils and nursemaids, desks and cradles, books or tablets and distaffs, pen or stylus and spindles? Who can concentrate on thoughts of Scripture or philosophy and be able to endure babies crying, nurses soothing them with lullabies, and all the noisy coming and going of men and women about the house? Will he put up with the constant muddle and squalor which small children bring into the home? The wealthy can do so, you will say, for their mansions and large houses can provide privacy and, being rich, they do not have to count the cost nor be tormented by daily cares. But philosophers lead a very different life from rich men, and those who are concerned with wealth or are involved in mundane matters will not have time for the claims of Scripture or philosophy.

6 WOMEN'S EDUCATION AND CHRISTINE'S OWN EXPERIENCE

Text from: Christine de Pizan (1982) *The Book of the City of Ladies*, transl. E. J. Richards, New York: Persea Press, pp. 153–5.

Christine's life is detailed in chapter 1 above (p. 31). *The Book of the City of Ladies* is Christine's response to the misogynist attitudes which she encountered time and time again in her reading, a history of women's contribution to western civilization, and an energetic protest against the unthinking adoption of anti-feminist clichés by male writers. The book is a debate between Christine herself and three allegorical figures, the ladies Reason, Rectitude and Justice, who together construct a city out of the stories of exemplary women, providing an alternative women's history as a protection against male calumny.

Following these remarks, I, Christine, spoke: 'My lady, I realize that women have accomplished many good things and that even if evil women have done evil, it seems to me, nevertheless, that the benefits accrued and still accruing because of good women – particularly the wise and literary ones and those educated in the natural sciences whom I mentioned above – outweigh the evil. Therefore, I am amazed by the opinion of some men who claim that they do not want their daughters, wives, or kinswomen to be educated because their mores would be ruined as a result.'

She [Rectitude] responded, 'Here you can clearly see that not all opinions of men are based on reason and that these men are wrong. For it must not be presumed that more necessarily grow worse from knowing the moral sciences, which teach the virtues, indeed, there is not the slightest doubt that moral education amends and ennobles them. How could anyone think or believe that whoever follows good teaching or doctrine is the worse for it? Such an opinion cannot be expressed or maintained. I do not mean that it would be good for a man or a woman to study the art of divination or those fields of learning which are forbidden – for the holy Church did not remove them from common use without good reason – but it should not be believed that women are the worse for knowing what is good.'

Here Rectitude recounts the stories of Hortensia and Novella, two learned, modest and chaste women.

'Thus not all men (and especially the wisest) share the opinion that it is bad for women to be educated. But it is very true that many foolish men have claimed this because it displeased them that women knew more than they did. Your father, who was a great scientist and philosopher, did not believe that women were worth less by knowing science; rather, as you know, he took great pleasure from seeing your inclination to learning. The feminine opinion of your mother, however, who wished to keep you busy with spinning and silly girlishness, following the common custom of women, was the major obstacle to your being more involved in the sciences. But just as the proverb already mentioned above says, 'No one can take away what Nature has given', your mother could not hinder in you the feeling for the sciences which you, through natural inclination, had nevertheless gathered together in little droplets. I am sure that, on account of these things, you do not think you are worth less but rather that you consider it a great treasure for yourself; and you doubtless have reason to.'

And I, Christine, replied to all of this, 'Indeed, my lady, what you say is as true as the Lord's Prayer.'

7 THE FOOLISHNESS OF FASHION

Text adapted from: *Book of the Knight of the Tour-Landry* (1971), transl. William Caxton, ed. M. Y. Offord, EETS SS2, Oxford: Oxford University Press, pp. 38–40.

What is known of the life of the Knight of the Tour-Landry is given above in chapter 1 (p. 30). The French text tells us that he began to write his book of instruction for his daughters in 1371. Geoffroy de La Tour-Landry and his wife Jeanne de Rougé, who came from a rich and powerful Breton family, had three daughters, for whose edification the treatise was composed. The *Book* contains a number of anecdotes, exempla and fabliaux illustrating the Knight's views as to how women should behave; one of the most attractive sections is the debate between the Knight and his wife (see above chapter 2, pp. 72–4). As well as rehearsing well-known exempla of saintly women, the Knight often draws conclusions from his own experience, as in this extract in which he discusses the dangers of following fashion too closely. The *Book* became widely known; its usefulness as a manual of instruction for young ladies is attested by the translations both into German and into English. Caxton translated the *Book* into English in 1483 and published it in 1484. Six copies of Caxton's book have survived to the present day.

Fair daughters, I pray you not to be the first to wear new styles or fashions, and that rather you should be the last and wait the longest, and especially the new fashions of women from foreign countries. For I shall tell you now about a debate between a baroness who lived in Guyenne, and of the Lord of Beaumont, the father of the present Lord, who was a wise and subtle knight. This lady reproached him concerning his wife, and said: 'Fair cousin, I have come from Brittany and have seen my fair cousin, your wife, who is not arrayed or adorned as are the ladies of Guyenne, or those of many other places. For the furred borders of her garments and of her hoods are not big enough, according to the fashion which is now worn.' Then the knight answered her: 'Madam, since she is not arrayed according to your fashion and her fur borders seem too narrow, and you blame me for this, you may be certain that you shall not blame me for it any longer. For I shall have her arrayed as quaintly and as nobly as you or any other is, and even more so. For you have only half of your garments and your hoods trimmed outside with grey fur and ermine, but I shall have her even better arrayed. For I shall have all her kirtles and hoods made with fur outside and she shall be better furred than you or any other.' After this he said: 'Madame, do you think that I do not want my wife to be arrayed like the good ladies of the country, for truly I do, but I do not want her to give up the fashion of good women and of honourable ladies in France and of this country, who do not wear the fashions of the mistresses nor of the lovers of the Englishmen, or of the military companies. For these are the ones who first had these fashions in Brittany and Guyenne, with these great fur borders, and these open-sided gowns. For I was there at that time and saw it, and I think that those who array themselves so are ill-counselled and ill-advised, to follow the fashion of those kind of women who brought it here, even if the princess and other English ladies, who have adopted it after a long time, can wear it if they wish. But I have heard from wise men that every good lady and woman ought to follow the fashion and the state of the good ladies and women of their country, and the common fashion of the country to which they belong. And that they are wisest who are the last to take up such novelties and new fashions. And thus by renown the ladies of France and these border regions are accounted the best ladies that there are and the least blamed.' And these words were said in front of many people, at which the lady thought herself foolish and didn't know what to answer. And then many of them began to murmur and said among themselves that she would have done better to have kept quiet and said nothing.

And therefore, my fair daughters, this is a good example to follow and keep average estate and the fashion of the good ladies of the country and the ordinary people of the realm that they are of. That is to say, the fashion which the good ladies commonly follow, and that is a noble thing. For those who follow a fashion which has come with strange women and from other countries, they are more mocked and scorned than those who follow the fashion of their own country as you have heard, as of the good knight who was wise and had great self-possession in reproving the lady. And know for certain, those who first put on and follow the new fashions are scorned and mocked. But God have mercy on us on this day after some have heard of any new fashion or novelty of gown or array shall never rest until they have a copy of it, and they say to their husband or lord every day: 'Such a thing and such would become me well and it is very fair, I pray you that I may have it'. If their lord or husband says to her: 'My love, if someone who has it is considered as wise as someone who doesn't have it', she then will say: 'So what if they don't know how to dress themselves, what has it to do with me, since such a one has it, I may have it too, and wear it as well as she does?' And I say to you that they shall find so many reasons that they must needs have their way, but this sort of woman is not accounted the most wise, or the most knowledgeable, but they most have their hearts set on worldly pleasure. I do not speak against the ladies and the demoiselles who can do what they wish, for I do not intend to say anything, if I realize it, against their estate, for it does not appertain to me, nor does it become me to do anything but honour and obey them as far as it is in my power, nor do I intend to speak against them in this book, but to my own daughters, women and servants, to whom I may speak as it pleases me and according to my will.

8 SELLING ONE'S SOUL FOR KNOWLEDGE

Text from: E. Colledge (ed. and transl.) (1965) *Medieval Netherlands Religious Literature*, New York: London House and Maxwell, pp. 195–8, 204–6.

The play *Marika* or *Mary of Nijmeghen* has been attributed to Anna Bijns, a fourteenth- or fifteenth-century poet from Antwerp. The play is an early variant of the Faust legend with a female protagonist who sells her soul to the Devil in return for instruction. After seven years of keeping company with the Devil, astonishing people in taverns with her rhetoric and ability to perform complex mathematical calculations, Mary repents of her life, and, with great difficulty, succeeds in doing penance and saving her soul. As Elizabeth Petroff points out, by learning from the Devil and having sexual relations with him, Mary is in effect a witch, even though the play does not present her as such (Petroff 1986: 349). The Devil's interest in the liberal arts, crowned by necromancy – literally the power to summon the dead, as in the *Aeneid*, but generally understood in the medieval period as the art of summoning and controlling spirits (Kieckhefer 1988: 152–75) – rather than theology, corresponds to satirical commonplaces about the scholar, exemplified by Chaucer's Doctor of Phisik, whose 'studie was but litel on the Bible' (Chaucer 1988: 30).

Mary is the ward of her uncle, Sir Gilbert, a priest. She is sent on an errand to a nearby town and advised to stay overnight with her aunt. The aunt refuses to let her in the house, accusing her of promiscuity, and Mary sets off home in a state of rage and despair, when the Devil appears before her.

MARY: God, help! Why am I so terrified? What is happening to me? I hardly can account for myself, but since I set eyes on this man, how faintly my heart is beating.

DEVIL: Pretty child, do not fear any harm or sorrow. I shall do you no injury nor trouble you. But I promise you that if you will act by my advice and come with me, you may be sure that before long I shall make you a lady of ladies.

MARY: Friend, I am sitting here almost out of my mind, so upset and so discomposed by the scolding words that I have had to endure without any fault of mine – 'whore, slut, bitch' – that I would as gladly entrust myself to the Devil as to God, for I sit here half mad.

DEVIL: By Lucifer, I cannot lose! She has swallowed down her draught of wrath, and now sits as if turned to stone by despair. I need not complain, for I may well hope to win. Pretty child, let me ask you if you will be my friend?

MARY: Who are you, friend?

DEVIL: A Master of Arts, and I never fail in what I undertake.

MARY: It is all the same to me whom I go with: I'd as soon go with the worst as with the best.

DEVIL: If you would give your love to me, I would teach you the arts as no one else could: the seven liberal arts, rhetoric, music, logic, grammar, geometry, arithmetic and alchemy, all of which are most important arts. There is no woman upon earth so proficient in them as I shall make you.

MARY: You seem indeed to be a man full of art. Who are you then?

DEVIL: What does that matter to you? It would be better for you not to ask me who I am. I am not the best of my family, but no one could love you better than I.

MARY: What is your name, friend?

DEVIL: One-eyed Moenen; and I have lots of good friends who know me well.

MARY: You are the Devil out of hell.

DEVIL: Whoever I am, I shall always be good to you.

MARY: I feel no fear of you, no terror or horror. Though Lucifer himself were to come up out of hell, I should not run away from him. I am not touched by any fear.

DEVIL: Well, my pretty, let us not waste time. If you will come with me and truly do my will, I shall teach you everything which you can possibly think of, as I told you before; and you will never again be without riches and jewels and money.

MARY: That is well said, but whilst we are now talking, before you and I are joined in friendship, teach me the seven liberal arts, for I take great delight in all such things. You will teach them to me, won't you?

DEVIL: You can trust me for that! I shall teach you everything you need to know.

MARY: Necromancy, that is a fine art. My uncle knows a lot about it, and sometimes he does marvels which he gets out of a book. I do not think that he has ever failed. They say he can make the Devil crawl through a needle's eye whether he likes it or not. That is an art that I would like to learn.

DEVIL: Pretty innocent, everything which I know is at your disposal, to make you happy; but I never learned necromancy, which is a very complicated and difficult art, in which are many dangers. If you were beginning to recite a spell with your pretty red lips, and you were to forget a word or a letter, so that you could not at once say the right thing to the spirit whom you had conjured, he would break your neck straight away. You can see how dangerous it is, my pretty flower.

MARY: If that is the case, I shall not begin it: I do not want to learn anything which could kill me.

DEVIL: Ah ha! that has put her off the scent! The idea of her wanting to learn necromancy! If she had learned necromancy, the danger would be in case she were to call up all hell and put them in danger, and even to exercise her powers over me if she chose, or get me into some tight place. I teach her necromancy? Not likely! I shall do what I can to make her forget the idea. Now listen to what I shall teach you, my pretty love, if you will just give necromancy up.

MARY: What else shall I learn?

DEVIL: I'll tell you now. I shall teach you all the languages in the world, so that the whole world will honour and pay tribute to you, for you have no idea what an achievement this is, then, because you also know the seven liberal arts, you will be high in every man's esteem.

MARY: The sorrows which oppress me lessen as I listen. I shall be most obedient to your will, if you will do this.

SELLING ONE'S SOUL FOR KNOWLEDGE

Mary changes her name because of the Devil's antipathy to the name of the Virgin. Now called Emma, she has finished her education; she and the Devil visit a tavern in Antwerp.

EMMA: Moenen, dear, would it be through geometry if I were able to count exactly how many drops of wine there are in a pot?

DEVIL: Yes dear, but have you remembered how to do it? That was something I taught you yesterday.

EMMA: That is true, indeed, and you also taught me logic, and I have remembered all that as well.

A DRINKER: Friend, what is that your wife says? Can she really calculate exactly how many drops of wine went into this pot? I have never heard anything to equal it.

DEVIL: That is nothing to some of the things she can do. You never saw the like of her in all your life. She understands all the seven liberal arts, astronomy and geometry, arithmetic, logic and grammar, music and rhetoric, the most ancient of them all. She could hold her own against the cleverest scholar who studied in Paris or Louvain.

SECOND DRINKER: My good friend, I beg you to allow us to see or hear something of her skill.

FIRST DRINKER: Yes, please, and I will buy you each a pint of wine, and I swear that if anyone tried to interrupt you, we shall fight them for you, if they give you trouble.

DEVIL: The poem you made up yesterday when we were walking in the High Street at noon, say that for them.

EMMA: Please excuse me. I am a very dull scholar at rhetoric, much as I should like to practise it, so as to master all the seven liberal arts; it requires more than industry for rhetoric which is an art which must come of its own accord. All the other arts can be learned by application and instruction, if one will work hard at them, but rhetoric is to be esteemed above them all. It is a gift of the Holy Spirit, and though one finds many ignorant creatures who despise it, that gives great sorrow to lovers of rhetoric.

SECOND DRINKER: Well, my dear, how many times do you want us to ask you?

FIRST DRINKER: Recite something for us that you know: It is only for fun, and we shall be satisfied, and then I shall recite something too.

213

EMMA: Then be quiet, and I shall sing you a song as well as I can; rhetoric has to be listened to and taken in, so do not let us have any chattering.

(*declaims*) O rhetoric, o true and lovely art, I who have always esteemed thee above all, I lament with grief that there are those who hate you and despise you. This is a grief to those who love you. Fie upon them who do so, for I wholly despise them. But for those who support you, life is full of hurt and sorrow. Ignorant men are the destruction of art.

They say in the proverb that through art grows the heart, but I say that it is a lying fable, for should some great artist appear, those who are unskilled and know not the first thing about art will make their opinion prevail everywhere, and artists will be reduced to beggary. Always it is the flatterer who is preferred, and always artists suffer such harm, and ignorant men are the destruction of art.

Fie upon all crude, coarse, common minds, trying to measure art by your standards: everyone should pay honour to pure art, art which is the ruler of many a pleasant land. Honour be to all who are the promoters of art, fie upon the ignorant who reject art, for this is why I proclaim the rule that ignorant men are the destruction of art.

Prince, I will devote myself to art, and do everything in power to acquire it. But it is to all lovers of art a sorrow that ignorant men pay so little honour to art.

A crowd gather to hear this poem, and Moenen causes a brawl in which two men are killed. The couple stay in Antwerp for six years and, by Emma/Mary's later admission to the Pope, cause more than two hundred deaths.

7

WOMEN AND THE ARTS

INTRODUCTION

Should I also tell you whether a woman's nature is clever and quick enough to learn speculative sciences as well as to discover them, and likewise the manual arts? I assure you that women are equally well-suited and skilled to carry them out and to put them to sophisticated use once they have learned them.

(Christine de Pizan 1982: 83–4)

Medieval women may, as Lady Reason tells Christine above, have been as well-suited to artistic production as any man, but the evidence for this contention is hard to come by today. Many of the artefacts which women must have created have been lost over time: embroidery and textile work, pottery, sculpture and metalwork. Other artistic endeavours such as dance or musical performances are lost at the moment they are completed: how Adelina the 'joculatrix' mentioned in the Domesday Book came by her surname is now impossible to discover – the term may mean 'singer' or 'entertainer' (Fell 1984: 54–5).

The modern distinctions between crafts and art, or artistry and work, were not so clear-cut for medieval people. The creation of pottery is one area where decorative and utilitarian functions overlap, while, in the early period, the decoration of some household objects, combs for example, with runic script may have had a magical as well as a decorative or identifying function. The distinction between creative 'literature' and 'writing', in the absence of our highly developed systems of publishing, distributing and reviewing written texts, is also less tenable. Writers were conscious of the moral dimension of their writing: Langland in *Piers Plowman* agonizes over the life of the poet which he has chosen, even though his poetic creation is directed towards social and religious reform (Langland 1978: 135; Schmidt 1987: 5–20), while, in his famous 'Retractions' appended to *The Canterbury Tales*, Chaucer appears to revoke those of his writings which did not have an overt moral purpose (Chaucer 1988: 328). The Church distrusted fictional writings – Chaucer's Parson cites St Paul, who 'repreveth hem that weyven [turn aside from] soothfastnesse / And tellen fables and swich wrecchednesse' (Chaucer 1988: 287) – unless they pointed a moral or a spiritual truth. Yet those writers who did wish to write in fictional modes developed a number of strategies for circumventing this prescription: to this women were no exception, though, as we shall see below, they often faced gender-specific difficulties when they came to create texts.

Applied arts

Medieval European women were certainly involved in making textiles, tapestries, carpets and hangings, typically in family-centred businesses. Their identities, and the nature and extent of their participation, are often hidden in the documentary records, since women were usually not members of the guilds who upheld technical standards and controlled the markets. No guild statutes from the embroiderers of fourteenth-century London survive, but women were certainly both apprentices and mistresses in the craft. Elis Mympe, a London embroiderer, was taken to court in 1369 by a father whose daughter Alice had been apprenticed to her for five years, during which time Elis had both mistreated her and failed to provide for her. Records from 1330 show that the three counterpanes made for the churching of Queen Philippa needed 112 workers: 70 men paid fourpence ha'penny a day and 42 women paid three and a quarter pence a day. The two artists or designers who headed the project earned eight and a quarter, and six and a quarter pence per day respectively (Staniland 1991: 49, 28). We cannot tell how the work was divided up between the sexes; that women were paid less than men is not surprising, and should not lead us to conclude that their work was necessarily easier or less skilled. Embroidery was by no means a matter for professionals: the work of the first Serbian woman writer, Yephimia (excerpt 7 below), was embroidered on a pall for a prince's coffin.

Women worked in metal too: an early twelfth-century Spanish silver cross with figures in relief, now in the Metropolitan Museum of Art, New York, proclaims that its maker was the goldsmith and sculptor Sancia Guidosalvi, for scattered across its surface are letters proclaiming this fact and dedicating the work to the Redeemer (Frugoni 1992: 407).

Painting

Women were also painters and illuminators. In response to the women of classical times whom Lady Reason lists in the passage above, Christine tells of a lady she knows:

> I know a woman today, named Anastasia, who is so learned and skilled
> in painting manuscript borders and miniature backgrounds that one
> cannot find an artisan in all the city of Paris – where the best in the

world are found – who can surpass her, nor who can paint flowers and details as delicately as she does, nor whose work is more highly esteemed, no matter how rich or precious the book is. People cannot stop talking about her. And I know this from experience, for she has executed several things for me which stand out among the ornamental borders of the great masters.

(Christine de Pizan 1982: 85)

Anastasia is clearly a professional artist, and it has been suggested that Christine herself may have run a kind of atelier producing manuscripts for clients, subcontracting Anastasia to do the illumination (Willard 1984: 45–6). Elsewhere women artists are hard to locate. In the convents some nuns both copied and illuminated their work. The Codex Sintram–Guta, now kept in Strasburg, is dated at 1154 and is the result of a collaboration between the priest Sintram and a nun Guta (Fig. 13). The portrait of a quite different nun, also named Guta, appears in a manuscript from the later twelfth century, inside an initial 'D', with the motto 'Guta peccatrix mulier

Figure 13 Guta, a nun, on the Virgin's left and Sintram, the priest and canon, on the Virgin's right, collaborators on the Codex Sintram–Guta *c.* 1154. Strasburg, Bibliothèque du Grand Séminaire, Cod. 37, fol. 4. © Inventaire Général/SPADEM 1974.

Figure 14 Thamar, an illustrious classical figure, paints the Virgin Mary while her male assistant grinds the colours. From a 1402 copy of Boccaccio's *De Mulieribus Claribus*, Bibliothèque Nationale MS 12420 fol. 86. © Bibliothèque Nationale de France, Paris.

scripsit et pinxit hoc librum' (Guta, a sinful woman, wrote and painted this book). A twelfth-century Psalter, now in the Walters Gallery, Baltimore, shows a female illuminator whose name is given as Claricia, swinging gaily in the hoop of an initial 'Q'; she is fashionably dressed with wide, flowing sleeves and long, unbound hair. Alexander (1992: 20) argues that the context suggests a warning against gossip directed at a specific Claricia rather than a female self-portrait, but other scholars (e.g. Frugoni 1992: 402–3) are happy to accept Claricia as a real woman – Miner (1974: 12) plausibly identifies other work in the same manuscript by the artist.

Later in the period we find a husband-and-wife team working on a fifteenth-century Book of Hours: an inscription tells us that Alanus copied the book and his wife illuminated it, while Margriete Sceppers and Cornelie van Wulfschkercke have been identified as illuminators in the late fifteenth and early sixteenth centuries in Bruges (Alexander 1992: 155). In thirteenth- and fourteenth-century Bologna there were many women miniaturists and calligraphers: in 1279 Allegra, wife of Ivano, promised a Carmelite friar that she would copy an entire bible for him (Frugoni 1992: 400). Juttchen the puppet-painter is frequently cited in the Frankfurt records from 1484 onwards (Ennen 1989: 205). Historical documents suggest that wives worked alongside their husbands in family painting businesses, though Paul Binski thinks that their role was closer to that of the apprentice, mixing colours and fetching materials, rather than that of creative artists in their own right. Hence the well-known picture of Thamar (Fig. 14), inventor of painting, with her male apprentice grinding pigment, from a French translation of Boccaccio's *De Mulieribus Claribus* (About Famous Women) (one of Christine's sources for *The City of Ladies*) derives its piquancy from its inversion of the usual state of affairs in an artist's atelier (Binski 1991: 9–10).

Music

The noble girl was expected to be able to play a musical instrument of some kind and to sing to entertain her immediate household. The Ménagier de Paris approves his young wife dancing and singing, but only in a private capacity:

And know that I am pleased rather than displeased that you tend rose-trees, and care for violets, and make chaplets, and dance, and sing: nor would I have you cease to do so among our friends and equals, and it is but good and seemly so to pass the time of your youth, so long you neither seek nor try to go to the feasts and dances of lords of too high rank, for that does not become you, nor does it sort with your estate, nor mine.

(Power 1928: 42)

Few young women would possess the virtuoso talents of the young Isolde in excerpt 6 below. Professional female musicians also existed: Christine Fell points out that the terms 'fiddler', 'singer' and 'leaper' all have feminine forms in Old English, though these usually appear in Latin glosses (Fell 1984: 54) and women are depicted playing instruments in manuscript illuminations both in Anglo-Saxon England and in later continental sources. In late medieval Frankfurt there were female lute and cymbal players, pipers, fiddlers and bellringers (Ennen 1989: 205). Secular musical skill was by no means an innocent pastime for many contemporary moralists; Isolde's playing made 'hearts grow full of longing' and one thirteenth-century manuscript warns:

> just as a hunter holds with a string or with a net a trained bird that sings and flaps its wings as if it were free, so the devil leads a minstrel-maiden who knows all the songs to dance to so she can drag other girls into the circle.
>
> (Frugoni 1992: 395)

The best evidence of women's musical activity comes from convents. In the convent at Helfta, ruled over by Gertrude of Hackeborn, Mechthild, the abbess's sister, was the chantress or choirmistress and earned the nickname 'The Nightingale of God' (Gertrude 1993: 9). Gertrude herself describes how she tried to sing and concentrate on Jesus at the same time:

> Moreover, I could see that you were sweetly affected when I began to chant in Choir, exerting all my powers to sing and fixing my attention on you at each note, like a singer who has not yet learned the melody and follows it carefully in the book.
>
> (Gertrude 1993: 116)

Gertrude's predecessor in German convent life, Hildegard of Bingen, composed a cycle of over seventy songs, together with a musical play, the *Ordo Virtutum* (Play of the Virtues). The songs are liturgical in character, and many are written for specific feasts of saints, such as that for St Ursula, quoted below. Hildegard's music is preserved in two manuscripts, though the songs are arranged in a different order in each (Flanagan 1989: 106–40). How much music meant to Hildegard is illustrated by the extract from the letter to the prelates of Mainz, cited below, in which Hildegard not only reproaches the Church authorities with their interdiction of music in the community, but also provides a theologically sound justification for the centrality of music to human worship, and demonstrates its divinely ordained nature.

Hildegard's play is a kind of morality play: Dronke suggests plausibly that it was based on the well-known *Psychomachia* of Prudentius (Dronke 1970: 169–70), while Hozeski (1972) speculates that Hildegard may have known the works of Hrotsvit of Gandersheim. There is no record of the play's being performed, though Flanagan suggests that the letter of Abbess Tengswindis (or Tengswich) of Andernach in which she politely enquires of Hildegard as to the truth of the rumour that on feast days Hildegard's nuns adorned themselves with 'rings, veils and tiaras studded with symbolic images' (Dronke 1984a: 165) may arise from a garbled account of the performance of the play (Flanagan 1989: 138).

Art and community

Arts then could flourish in the convent environment, provided that the aim of the artistic activity was to praise and illuminate the glory of God. While lay sisters performed the mundane tasks of cleaning and food preparation, the nuns had, between attendance at Divine Office, leisure for embroidering church vestments, copying and illuminating manuscripts, or composing hymns and musical sequences. In other female communities, such as the beguinages of the Low Countries, the communal organization of daily life enabled some women to write at considerable length, not simply accounts of visions or mystical experiences, but fully fledged poetical works, drawing on the secular and courtly love-lyric styles they had been brought up with. Both Mechthild of Magdeburg (see pp. 142–5 above) and Hadewijch wrote religious poetry within the beguine environment.

Beyond the religious community, courts provided some opportunities for a few women to write creatively, giving them access to networks of patronage. Christine de Pizan is depicted in various manuscripts presenting her finished works to her patrons: Isabeau of Bavaria, Jean, Duc de Berry, the Dukes of Burgundy. Other patrons included Louis of Orléans, the English Duke of Salisbury, the Count of Marche and the Duke of Milan. Christine's writing career was reasonably long, while, in the stormy politics of late fourteenth- and early fifteenth-century France, the lives of her patrons tended to be short, so there is nothing unusual about her frequent changes of patron. Both Chaucer, who could not live on his income as a civil servant, and Machaut, who had, like Christine, a succession of patrons, had to devote some of their time to being professional courtiers in order to secure their livelihoods (Willard 1984: 163–4). Marie de France too seems to have written by royal command: her *Lais* are dedicated to a 'noble reis' (noble king), usually identified with Henry II of England, while her *Fables* are dedicated to a certain Count William.

Throughout the period, noble women too operated as patrons of literary activity: Marie de Champagne's late twelfth-century circle at Troyes, where Chrétien de Troyes flourished, is the best known. Caxton describes how Duchess Margaret of Burgundy encouraged him in the publication of the first English book in 1476, *The History of Troyes*, even assisting him in his initial translation difficulties (Blake 1969: 46–9). The rhetoric of the troubadours, though ostensibly asking only for honour and the lady's love, looks beyond the lady to the source of her social and economic power, the lord, and, in effect, asks for patronage. Financial metaphors both conceal and reveal the complex notions of status with which the poetry plays, especially in the verse of the poets of bourgeois, as opposed to noble, origins (Kay 1990: 119–27).

A woman did not need to be rich or noble to inspire a work of art. The lavishly illuminated St Albans Psalter was created for the early twelfth-century English recluse Christina of Markyate. The forty full-page pictures are followed by a translation of Gregory the Great's justification of the use of pictures in religious practice: they enable the illiterate to 'read by seeing' – by meditating on the pictures (Clanchy 1993: 191). It has been suggested that both the illustrations and the other texts included in the codex – the Life of St Alexis, who persuaded his wife to chastity on their wedding night, for example, just as Christina avoided consummating her own marriage – echoed Christina's own interests and life-story (Holdsworth 1978: 185–95).

Women writers/women authors

Access to textuality

Women who wished to compose texts have always faced the problem of finding the time away from domestic responsibilities. The professional writer requires assistance: the opening of *The City of Ladies* (excerpt 8 below) makes clear how Christine de Pizan is dependent on the labour of her mother as housekeeper for the time to work as a professional writer, and we have seen above how the convent and the beguine community, in so far as they freed women from domestic labour, were productive environments for the creation of texts.

In addition to this perennial difficulty, medieval women faced other historically contingent restrictions on their access to textuality. Chapter 6 has indicated the limited extent to which women became literate in their own vernaculars, let alone in Latin, across the period, and how the skills of reading (which many women were able to do) and of writing were regarded as separate. In twelfth-century England, for example, a well-educated noble lady would be expected to be able to read three languages: Latin, French and English, but writing was a skill for scribes, who earned their living by it (Clanchy 1993: 194). In the convents, even after the learning of Latin had declined, nuns were usually literate, or – as in the case of Mechthild of Hackeborn, whose *Book of Special Grace* was written by two fellow nuns, one almost certainly Gertrude the Great – it was not difficult to find a compliant scribe. In Mechthild's case it seems rather that it was the author's modesty and reticence, rather than the difficulty of finding a willing scribe, that delayed the writing of her book until Mechthild was in her fifties (Gertrude 1993: 11).

If a woman in secular life, who could not herself write, wished to commit her text to parchment, she needed to find someone (almost invariably a man, and a cleric) who was willing to write for her. Many of the outstanding mystical writers of the fourteenth and fifteenth centuries thus depended on a confessor, a spiritual intimate, to write for them: Angela of Foligno dictated her autobiography to her uncle and confessor, Fra Arnaldo over a period from 1290 to 1296; Catherine of

Siena's spiritual director eventually became her biographer; Umiltà of Faenza could read and write Latin herself, but nevertheless preferred to dictate to one of her disciples (Petroff 1986: 236–9). Mechthild of Magdeburg is anxious about the deficiencies of her style:

> Now, I lack the German language, and I have no command of Latin, so if this has any merit to it, I cannot take the credit, for there was never such a worthless dog who did not readily come to his master when enticed with a white roll.
>
> (Mechthild 1991: 33)

How far the scribes were instrumental in shaping the discourse they took down is impossible to determine from the surviving texts. For some modern readers the peculiar conditions of production of some medieval women's texts have been difficult to come to terms with. Perhaps naively, some readers have hoped to be able to gain access to a pure and unmediated medieval mind and thus are doomed to frustration. Hirsh (1975) argues strongly against the notion that the voice we hear in the *Book of Margery Kempe* can in any sense be called 'Margery's'; rather he believes that we distinguish the voice and interpretative comments of the scribe in many parts of the text. Marion Glasscoe, among many other scholars of Margery, rejects this view, arguing that the *Book* must be read as a totality, authorized by Margery, and written by a scribe who has a clear idea of the limitations of his own role in creating the work (Glasscoe 1993: 285–6; Boffey 1993: 162–4).

The Italian mystics were charismatic enough to be assigned literate male confessors who supported their efforts to produce texts. Few medieval women writers had an uncomplicated relation to their writings, as Margery Kempe's account of her difficulties in getting her *Book* written (excerpt 9 below) indicates. Margery was eventually successful, once the reluctance of her chosen scribe and the machinations of the Devil were overcome, and her *Book* came into being as an authentic record of her experiences. There may have been many other women writers or authors whose texts became separated from their historical progenitors. In excerpt 4 below Marie de France alludes to her anxiety that some clerk may claim her *Fables* as his own; thus Marie is careful to embed her authorial imprimatur in all her texts which have survived: the *Fables*, the *Lais*, and her translation of the *Espurgatoire de St Patrick*. Whether women may have been responsible for some of the vast body of anonymous medieval writings is an open question (Boffey 1993: 165–6). Alexandra Barratt has suggested that the early Middle English debate poem 'The Owl and the Nightingale' may originate from the nunnery at Shaftesbury and has also speculated that the late fourteenth-century courtly poems 'The Flower and the Leaf' and 'The Assembly of Ladies' might have been composed by a woman (Barratt 1987a; 1987b). Where the persona of an anonymous poem is presented as female, and without irony, it is hard, as Barratt points out, to see what the usefulness of assuming a male author may be (Barratt 1992: 17).

Women writers may very well have chosen to remain anonymous because of the twin problems of intention and authority. The problem of intention has been discussed above and its results are plain: with the exception of Christine de Pizan and Marie de France, no secular imaginative texts of any length by medieval women authors survive. Perhaps because there was no tradition of women composing secular poetry – Christine cites only Sappho as a woman poet in the secular tradition (Christine de Pizan 1982: 67–8) – perhaps because poetry was an art, reliant on rhetorical skills which very few women had the opportunity to learn, it is not until beyond the end of our period that we find a text like 'Queen Elizabeth's Hymn to Venus' (Barratt 1992: 275–7). Women might compose love-lyrics – the *trobairitz* are a case in point – in certain courtly environments, but considerations of modesty and the difficulty of finding a subject position from which to speak, as we saw in chapter 2 above, must have inhibited many women from composing. Although romances were very popular with women readers – after devotional texts they were the biggest single generic group of works in English women's possession (Meale 1993: 138–43) – there are no known women writers of romance except, once more, for Marie.

Authority

How dared a woman write? The nun of Barking who translated Ælred's *Life of Edward the Confessor* into French around 1163 asks those who hear this 'romance' not to despise it because the translation was done by a woman (Clanchy 1993: 268). In the shorter version of her *Revelations of Divine Love*, Julian of Norwich too draws attention to her unworthiness as a woman to address her fellow Christians; however, she goes on to assert the irrelevance of her gender to her message, and, in the longer version, she strikes out all reference to her sex:

> But God forbid that you should say or take it so that I am a teacher, for I mean not so, nor I meant never so. For I am a woman, ignorant, feeble and frail.... But because I am a woman, should I therefore believe that I should not tell you of the goodness of God, since that I saw in that same time that it is his will that it should be known?
>
> (Julian 1978: 47–8)

Even Hrotsvit of Gandersheim, a self-proclaimed 'Mighty Voice' (one meaning of her name) feels that she has to apologize for her audacity in gender-specific terms in the Preface to her *Legends*:

> Though metrical composition seems difficult and arduous for women, frail as we are, I, relying only on the help of the ever-merciful grace on

224

high, never on my own strength, decided to harmonize the songs in this trifling work in dactylic measures.

(cited from Dronke 1984a: 65)

Dronke shows, however, that even as Hrotsvit makes these traditional assertions about feminine inadequacy, she is demonstrating her mastery of the form she has chosen – the metre she uses is the hexameter, the heroic metre, and 'the heroic was a masculine prerogative' (Dronke 1984a: 66). Notwithstanding Dronke's persuasive analysis of Hrotsvit's growing self-confidence as she subverts the pagan comedies of Terence to Christian ends, transforming his 'shameless unchaste actions of sensual women' into 'the laudable chastity of holy maidens', such self-deprecating remarks about the inadequacy of the female writer might be multiplied almost indefinitely from women of the period.

In part, the writer of either sex suffered from anxiety about authority. Medieval teaching and learning was based on the analysis of the words of those wise men whom tradition – the Church, the classical world, courtly patronage systems – had certified as 'auctoritates' (Minnis 1988: 9–15). To speak or write in the expectation that others would listen or read was to set oneself up as an 'auctor'. Authorizing strategies thus had to be found: the argument that one was writing to instruct in morality, or to educate through commentary on, or making new versions of, 'authorized' material was one effective means of circumventing the inhibition. Other writers – the later medieval women mystics are a good example – referred to God as their authorization. Mechthild of Magdeburg suggests that her writings are causing her to be persecuted (Mechthild 1991: 55–6), but nevertheless it is the will of God that she should continue in her work.

The problem of authority was compounded for women by the injunction of St Paul that women should neither preach nor teach: 'Let the woman learn in silence with all subjection. But I suffer not a woman to teach, nor to usurp authority over the man, but to be in silence' (I Timothy 2: 11–12). Women thus had to be doubly careful in their choice of authorizing strategies: a straightforward appeal to the authority of the divine Word was ruled out. Margery Kempe, accused by the Archbishop of York for contravening precisely this text, argues that she is merely speaking of divine things rather than preaching herself, and she substitutes a different authority: the woman who recognizes Jesus's divinity: (Luke 11: 27–8; Kempe 1940: 126). Women did have one *auctor* of their own: an exception to St Paul's rule whose case was often argued in the schools was Mary Magdalen. She was the first to learn of Christ's Resurrection and ran to tell the good news to the other disciples. Mary was thus authorized by Christ to spread the word: in the apocryphal stories about her Mary is said to have sailed with Lazarus and Martha to the south of France where she preached Christianity to the population and converted a heathen prince (Haskins 1993: 88, 121). Although Margery has a particular fondness for Mary Magdalen, it is the saint's life as a sexual woman before her conversion, rather than her authorization as preacher, which attracts her.

Appeal to divine authority was an effective strategy for women when they were writing of their own religious and mystical experiences, if they were orthodox in their convictions and if they were able to convince their confessor or bishop of the validity of their testimony. Nor should we underestimate the importance of the 'writerly community', the knowledge and support which one woman writer could gain from another. The community could be a literal and spatial one, such as the convent of Helfta, so productive of women's writing in the cases of Gertrude and the two Mechthilds. In other instances women encouraged one another by letter: Elisabeth of Schönau (1129–65) corresponds with Hildegard of Bingen; since Hildegard has papal authorization for her prophecies and visions, Elisabeth gains a kind of authority by proxy for her own writings (Clark 1992). Elisabeth's writings impart a strong impression of her own consciousness of being part of a community of sisters who support her in her spiritual endeavours (Petroff 1986: 141); her reputation as a writer for women is confirmed by Mechthild of Magdeburg, who reports that Elisabeth passed swiftly into heaven because, God says:

> she is and was a messenger to the unholy women who sat in the castles, steeped in lasciviousness, wrapped in pride and constantly surrounded by vanity that by rights they should have descended into the abyss. Many women followed her example as far as they could and would.
>
> (Mechthild 1991: 162–3)

Virginia Woolf famously remarked: 'we think back through our mothers if we are women' (Woolf 1977: 72–3). Margery Kempe finds such mothers, such authorization in the lives of Dorothea of Montau, Marie of Oignies and Birgitta of Sweden as relayed to her through the texts they left behind and the stories which circulated about them. Margery's individual style of mysticism: her remaining in the world, her tears and her visions are authenticated by the women who preceded her (Kempe 1940: 39, 143, 152–3; Stargardt 1985; Glasscoe 1993: 281–5), as well as by Julian of Norwich whom she consults about her spiritual experiences (Kempe 1940: 42; Glasscoe 1993: 291–2). The tradition of female sanctity, however slight, and the solidarity and support of the female community thus could function as authorization for some women writers.

Other women were able to write as translators, as re-presenters of pre-existing texts. The nun of Barking alluded to above was only one of a number of convent women who translated or made versions of saints' lives from Latin into the vernacular (Wogan-Browne 1993), while in later Middle English writing Juliana Berners, who composed a treatise on hunting, based on two different French sources (Barratt 1992: 232–3), Margaret Beaufort, and Eleanor Hull c. 1394–1460 were all translators from French. The action of translation allowed a self-effacement on the part of the writer: she became a mediator rather than an 'auctor' or originator. It is noticeable that these women were translating from

French into English rather than from Latin or Greek: it was not until the humanist movement of the sixteenth century that women like Margaret More, Thomas More's daughter, or Katerina Jagellonica, queen of Sweden who wrote in seven different languages, or Margaret Peutinger of Germany, who detected errors in Erasmus, were equipped to move easily between the vernacular and the classical languages (Bainton 1984).

Christine de Pizan, as so often the exception which proves the rule, was as much a translator/compiler as an original author. As a professional writer, and rather like a modern journalist, Christine was prepared to turn her hand to whatever writing needed to be done, whether asked for a book of moral instruction for the Dauphin, a book on political principles, or the biography of a deceased French king. Embarking on a treatise of military tactics, the *Livre des Fais d'Armes et de Chevalerie* (Book of the Feats of Arms and Chivalry), Christine is more than usually conscious of the disadvantages of being a woman writer; strategically she invokes Minerva, Roman goddess of war: 'Lady and high goddess, may it not displease you that, I a simple woman, in no way comparable to your greatness in reputed knowledge, should dare to speak of such an institution as that of arms' (cited from Willard 1982: 183). Nevertheless, Christine succeeds not only in amalgamating material from Latin and French sources but also in incorporating material from conversations with certain of her contemporaries who were themselves military strategists, though the latter are not named. The result is a wholly new work which was clearly regarded as valuable: Caxton translated it for Henry VII in 1489 (Willard 1982: 183).

Representation and self-representation

The representations of women which the woman reader or listener encountered in her readings were not all as stereotyped as the wicked women which Christine de Pizan discovers in the pages of Mathéolus (excerpt 8 below). Although the anti-feminist stereotype was so well established as to become a commonplace of literary debate (see Blamires 1992 for numerous examples), along with the temptresses, villainesses, nagging wives, and malevolent old women the woman reader was also exposed to models of virtuous women. These were primarily to be found in saints' lives, where the capacity for mere women to surpass men in saintliness and endurance was a cause for wonder and emulation (Bynum 1982: 203–9, 259–61; Bloch 1991: 67–8), or in histories, in which good and bad queens, such as Fredegund or Brunhild and the saintly Clotild in Gregory of Tours (see chapter 5 above), or the wicked Northumbrian queen Jurmenburg and the virginal Æthelthryth in Eddius's *Life of Wilfrid* are instructively contrasted (Hollis 1992: 165–72). The range of images of women was greater than the virgin/whore stereotypes often cited as delimiting the range of representations in medieval literature. The heroines of romances are often resourceful and courageous:

Nicolette of the French 'chantefable' 'Aucassin and Nicolette' is far more determined, talented and impressive than the rather feeble Aucassin. Nicolette is able to escape from prison; Aucassin languishes in a dungeon until he is released. Nicolette journeys in disguise to find her lover in order to bring about a happy denouement; Aucassin pines for his lady, but cannot muster the energy or resolve to fetch her himself ('Aucassin and Nicolette' 1971). Isolde, in Gottfried's *Tristan* is the equal of Tristan in devising strategems; the notion of the 'strong woman' has become a cliché of Icelandic family saga study (Frank 1973; Jochens 1986), and even the sexually voracious, nagging and lying heroine of the fabliau is accorded respect for her cunning in a tight spot (Hines 1993; Burns 1993a; 1993b). Nor are women simply motivated by sexual passion or their own best interests: in the German poem 'Das Frauenturnier' ('The Ladies' Tournament') (dated to just before 1300) noble women, left to their own devices while their men are away at peace negotiations, decide, after some debate, to dress as knights and joust under male names in order to win honour for themselves. On their return, the knights praise their ladies, but forbid them from jousting again. One girl whose father is too poor to engage in chivalry takes the name of the duke of the region; she emerges as the winner of the tournament and wins a rich dowry and noble husband from the duke (Westphal-Wihl 1989). While the women about whom the female audience learned were by no means naturalistic portrayals of 'real women', nevertheless medieval representations of women did offer a range of behaviours, attitudes and ways of inhabiting the social role of 'woman' which was neither stereotyped nor coercive.

The strong impetus towards self-effacement of the woman writer, discussed above, gives little scope for writing 'as a woman', for self-representation in texts by women writers. Certain writers, working in personal and subjective genres, such as the *trobairitz* whose poetry is discussed above in chapter 2, take pains to emphasize, as opposed to ignoring or effacing, their unnatural position as speaking women, the *trobairitz* often display a consciousness of the lack of 'fit' between their own feelings and the rhetoric of the male-developed discourse of courtly love: sometimes they flaunt their refusal to play the part of silent textual object; at others they express anxiety about the impropriety of taking the initiative. Castelloza expresses both views in different poems (Rieger 1992: 520–1, 540–1). Other women, like the bold Welsh woman poet Gwerful, write in order to fill the lack of texts expressing female experience; her poem on the female genitals (above pp. 71–2) humorously makes clear the 'gaps and absences' as Macherey calls them (Eagleton 1976: 34–5) that male discourse, by its very partiality, must leave.

Christine de Pizan takes up a self-consciously writerly position both in the *Book of the City of Ladies*, and in the 'Quarrel of the Rose' – the debate about the merits and demerits of Jean de Meung's continuation of Guillaume Lorris's *Roman de la Rose*. Christine seems to have initiated the debate in a conversation with a friend,

Jean de Montreuil, who later sent her a letter praising the poem. Gontier Col, a scholar at the royal court, also became involved in the debate, as did Jean Gerson, Chancellor of the University of Paris. Christine's objections to the *Roman de la Rose* can be summarized as: her dislike of the impropriety of the language – its sexual frankness; her suspicion that Meung was urging an intellectual basis for free love; and her disgust at the representation of women, particularly the notorious Vieille (the Old Woman who is one model for the Wife of Bath), in the poem. Supporters of the *Roman* leapt to its defence; one, Pierre Gontier, a canon of Notre Dame, addresses Christine with condescension. Speaking of her criticism of the *Roman*, he exclaims: 'O most foolish presumption! O word too soon issued and lightly spoken from the mouth of a woman to condemn such a man', while Jean de Montreuil, in the heat of the quarrel compares her with 'the Greek whore who dared to write against Theophrastus'. Charity Willard argues that Christine's objections were not directed against the poem as a whole, but only against certain parts of it, and were produced in reaction to its inflated reputation (Willard 1984: 73–89). Nevertheless, for modern readers who wish to claim Christine as a proto-feminist, 'revolutionary ... profoundly feminist' as her translator describes her (Christine de Pizan 1982: xxviii), Christine's moralistic and conservative position in the 'Quarrel' cannot easily be set aside: while Sheila Delany's 1990 article is a useful corrective to such ahistorical and romantic notions, at the same time it demonstrates the futility of analysing Christine's writings in terms of modern ideas of 'political correctness'.

Women's language: écriture féminine

Whether women can, do and should use language in distinctively different ways from men has been a preoccupation of modern French feminist theory (Moi 1985: 102–63 provides a good overview). Virginia Woolf argues that the sentence is not fundamentally a female form, that its shape is uncomfortable for women, and that for women to write freely, new forms must be found (Woolf 1977: 73–5). French feminist theory has suggested that women's language might be plural, unstructured, free-flowing, playing with a multitude of meanings, emotional. The implications of this theory for the investigation of past women's writing have yet to be worked out: if women's language is a transhistorical phenomenon, rooted in universal forms that are present in the prelinguistic Semiotic Order, as Kristeva (1980) proposes, then medieval women's writings too should be found to display such features. Moreover, the identification of anonymous poetry as 'masculine' or 'feminine' writing may reveal a wider participation by women in the production of medieval texts than has hitherto been thought. The enterprise is a difficult one: *écriture masculine* or *féminine* cannot simply be mapped onto 'male author' and 'female author'; men can imitate *écriture féminine*; women, especially those taught by men to an advanced level in the masculinized educational system, such as

Héloise, learn successfully to use and deploy male styles and arguments. 'Master Heinrich, you are amazed at the masculine style of this book? That surprises me. I am far more concerned about the fact that I, a sinful woman must write,' writes Mechthild of Magdeburg (Mechthild 1991: 139–40). Patricia Belanoff has attempted a Kristevan reading of two Old English 'women's poems' (see pp. 53–4 above for 'Wulf and Eadwacer'), suggesting that the ambiguities, polysemy, diffuseness of structure and emotionality of these two poems fits with modern theories of feminine writing (Belanoff 1990). The argument is an attractive one, but finally the suspicion that the subject of the poems – a woman's loss of her lover and her bleak situation – is what produces the emotionality, and that a context of no longer recoverable legend is responsible for the ambiguities undermines the argument. The poems certainly display the features noted: that these could not be produced by a male poet representing himself in a female persona remains unproven.

Yet the writing of many medieval women does show common features, stylistic traits which are not exclusive to women, but typical of them. The erotic mysticism of Hadewijch and Mechthild of Magdeburg is paralleled in Henry of Suso, yet more women mystics than men adopt the feminized position. Images of melting, deliquescence, ecstasy almost to the point of orgasm can be found in men writers (Robertson 1993: 153); Julian of Norwich's exploration of the Motherhood of Christ is found in earlier men's writing, as Caroline Bynum has shown (Bynum 1982: 110–46). However, much fruitful work is being generated by explorations of Kristeva's (1980) and Irigaray's (1985) ideas of the bodily: that medieval women can and do 'write out of their bodies'. Margery Kempe's understanding of her identity and her calling is inscribed in her bodily practices of weeping and sobbing, and in seeing Christ and the saints, long before her experience becomes text (Lochrie 1991: 23–46; Harding 1993: 173–4); other female mystics, as we saw in chapter 4 above, used their bodies to produce signs of holiness which signified God's love in this world as surely as letters on a page signified this meaning: 'they insistently proclaimed their inalienable right to invent a different tongue, one that enlisted the body as sensory support in the creation of a "total" language whose syntax incorporated shouts, tears, and silence as well as words' (Régnier-Bohler 1992: 432–3). Laurie Finke calls attention to the dream of Leoba, the eighth-century Anglo-Saxon nun (see above, p. 196), in which she sees a purple thread drawn out of her mouth:

> when she took hold of it with her hand and tried to draw it out there was no end to it; and as if it were coming from her very bowels, it extended little by little until it was of enormous length.
>
> (Talbot 1954: 212)

An aged nun interprets the thread as signifying the divinely authorized words which she might use to teach and preach both inside her own community and outside in the German missionary field (Finke 1992: 79).

'Art for Art's sake' – that late nineteenth-century rallying cry – would have been anathema to the medieval women artists we have encountered here. For them, artistic expression, whether in things created by their own hands or else in their own words, was always subordinated to a higher purpose. Most often it was the glory of God, his divine love and its operation in the human and fallen world, which inspired these women; very frequently it was love of humanity and the desire to instruct or to share experiences which provided the motivation. Throughout, even where women do not intend to place themselves at the centre of the stage or the text, the problems which they sought to solve, as Peter Dronke writes, cause them to 'look at themselves more concretely and more searchingly than many of the highly accomplished men writers who were their contemporaries' (Dronke 1984a: x). Although to attempt to recuperate the 'real medieval woman', even from the kind of texts to which Dronke refers here, must inevitably be a hopeless enterprise, yet through the writings by, for and about medieval women which this book has presented, we may have illuminated some sense of our own, and their, historical contingency, their sameness and their Otherness, the forces which shaped their lives and identities, and the continuities and disjunctions between then and now.

1 THE FIRST WESTERN DRAMATIST: HROTSVIT'S *DULCITIUS*

Text from: K. Wilson (1984) *Medieval Women Writers*, Manchester: Manchester University Press, pp. 54–7.

Hrotsvit seems to have lived between 935 and 1000 and was a canoness in the convent of Gandersheim in Germany, 'a small, proudly independent principality ruled by women' (Dronke 1984a: 55). Hrotsvit was the first known poet in Germany, and the first person to write drama in Europe since classical times. She wrote eight sacred legends in verse, six dramas in rhymed prose, two historical poems or epics, three lengthy prose prefaces and a number of shorter works. *Dulcitius* seems to have been written *c.* 962, when she was already well known as a poetess. She was, as she tells us, familiar with the comedies of Terence, and tries to use comic techniques for Christian purposes – evil is thwarted with comic inevitability in some of her plays. We do not know exactly how her plays were staged, if at all, whether they were performed as a kind of 'dramatic reading', punctuated with mime, or whether some more elaborate performance was possible. Her *Prefaces* show her anxiety and modesty about daring to write, but, wittily and with much humour, she is proud of herself for daring to go where others have not gone before.

Dulcitius is the story of three sisters, Agapes, Hirena and Chionia, who are martyred for their faith by Governor Dulcitius. Before he has them killed, Dulcitius visits them in their prison quarters with the intention of raping them, but God protects the sisters through a novel trick. The dialogue is written in rhymed and rhythmic prose; the translator has indicated where the speech pauses and rhyming phrases coincide.

DULCITIUS:	Bring forth, soldiers, the girls you hold sequestered.
SOLDIERS:	Here they are whom you requested.
DULCITIUS:	Wonderful, indeed, how beautiful, how graceful, how admirable these little girls are!
SOLDIERS:	Yes, they are perfectly lovely.
DULCITIUS:	I am captivated by their beauty.
SOLDIERS:	That is understandable.
DULCITIUS:	To draw them to my love, I am eager
SOLDIERS:	Your success will be meagre.
DULCITIUS:	Why?
SOLDIERS:	Because they are firm in faith.
DULCITIUS:	What if I sway them by flattery?
SOLDIERS:	They will despise it utterly.
DULCITIUS:	What if with tortures I frighten them?
SOLDIERS:	Little will it matter to them.
DULCITIUS:	Then what should be done?
SOLDIERS:	Consider carefully.
DULCITIUS:	Under guard they must be held in the inner room of the workshop in whose vestibule the servants' pots are kept.
SOLDIERS:	Why there?
DULCITIUS:	So that I may visit them often at my leisure.
SOLDIERS:	At your pleasure.
DULCITIUS:	What do the captives do at this time of night?
SOLDIERS:	Hymns they recite.
DULCITIUS:	Let us go near.
SOLDIERS:	From afar we hear their tinkling voices clear.
DULCITIUS:	Stand guard before the door with your lantern but I will enter and satisfy myself in their longed-for embrace.
SOLDIERS:	Enter. We will guard this place.
AGAPES:	What is that noise outside the door?
HIRENA:	That wretched Dulcitius is coming to the fore.
CHIONIA:	May God protect us!
AGAPES:	Amen.
CHIONIA:	What is the meaning of this clash of pots, utensils, and pans?
HIRENA:	I will check. Come here, please, and look through the crack!
AGAPES:	What is going on?
HIRENA:	Look, the fool, the madman so base, he thinks he is enjoying our embrace.
AGAPES:	What is he doing?
HIRENA:	Unto his lap he pulls the utensils, he embraces the pots and pans, giving them tender kisses.

CHIONIA: Ridiculous!

HIRENA: His face, his hands, his clothes   are so soiled, so filthy and so loath,   that with all the soot that clings to him, he looks like an Ethiopian.

AGAPES: It is only right   that he should appear in sight   as he is in his mind: possessed by the fiend.

HIRENA: Wait! He prepares to leave. Let us watch how he is greeted,   and how he is treated   by the soldiers who wait for him.

SOLDIERS: Who is coming out?   A demon without doubt!   Or rather, the devil himself is he,   let us flee!

DULCITIUS: Soldiers, where are you taking in flight?   Stay! Wait! Escort me home with your light!

SOLDIERS: The voice is our master's tone   but the look the devil's own. Let us not stay!   Let us run away!   The apparition will slay us!

DULCITIUS: I will go to the palace and complain,   and reveal to the whole court the insults I had to sustain.

DULCITIUS: Guards, let me into the palace,   I must have a private audience.

GUARDS: Who is this monster vile and detestable?   Covered in rags torn and despicable?   Let us beat him,   from the steps let us sweep him;   he must not be allowed to enter.

DULCITIUS: Alas, alas, what has happened?   Am I not dressed in splendid garments? Don't I look neat and clean?   Yet anyone who looks at my mien loathes me as a foul monster. To my wife I shall return,   and from her learn   what has happened. But there is my spouse,   with dishevelled hair she leaves the house,   and the whole household follows her in tears!

WIFE: Alas, alas, Dulcitius, my lord, what has happened to you? You are not sane; the Christians have made a laughingstock out of you.

DULCITIUS: At last now I know –   this mockery to their witchcraft I owe.

WIFE: What upsets me, what makes me sad,   is that you were ignorant of all that passed.

DULCITIUS: I command that those insolent girls be led forth, and that they be stripped of all their clothes publicly,   so that in retaliation for ours, they experience similar mockery.

SOLDIERS: We labour in vain;   we sweat without gain.   Behold, their garments remain on their virginal bodies, sticking to them like skin. But he who ordered us to strip them snores in his seat,   and cannot be woken from his sleep.   Let us go to the emperor's court and make a report.

DIOCLETIAN: It grieves me greatly to hear how Governor Dulcitius fared, that he has been greatly deluded, so greatly insulted, so utterly humiliated. But these vile young women shall not boast with impunity of having made a mockery of our gods and those who worship them. I shall direct Count Sissinus to take due vengeance.

2 SOME NORSE WOMEN POETS

Texts from: J. Jesch (1991) *Women in the Viking Age*, Woodbridge, Suffolk: Boydell Press, pp. 164–5, 166–7.

(a) Jorunn *skaldmey* (the female poet)

We know nothing about Jorunn. We only know of her existence because this poem is preserved in *Heimskringla*, the history of the Norwegian kings written by the Icelander Snorri Sturluson. By the year 900 King Harald Fairhair had united Norway under his rule, and had a good number of sons to succeed him. Even before his death, the sons had started to compete for power and influence, and battles broke out between them. Eric Bloodaxe was fast gaining pre-eminence over his brothers when Halfdan the Black, another brother, attacked him. A showdown between Halfdan and his father was averted through the mediation of the poet Guttorm Sindri, who composed poems in praise of both parties, and refused to take any reward for his verse, except for the two warring kings to make peace. Jorunn's poem is composed in response to this event, praising the poet's achievement. The imagery is complex, playing with the traditional vocabulary used to denote warriors and battle in Old Norse. Jorunn is well aware of the paradoxical nature of her undertaking: instead of exalting deeds in battle, she is celebrating the absence of battle; the poet Guttorm is described as 'the enemy of rings' (i.e. one who gives them away) and the 'battle-tree', yet he is fighting for peace. As Jesch points out, Jorunn's poem 'cunningly makes use of the traditional language and preoccupations of skaldic verse to subvert its more usual subject matter' (Jesch 1991: 165). The style of both poems is typical of Norse skaldic verse: the poetry is ornamented by 'kennings', traditional formulations in which a warrior may be allusively described as, for example, 'a tree of weapons', a ship as 'the plank of the sea-king', and a sword as 'the wound-sea's reed'.

Halfdan! I'm told Harald Finehair heard
about those deeds of darkness,
and that poem seems darksome to
the adventurer of the blade.   [warrior]
The ruler let weapons redden
in the blood of the rascal crowd,
the folk endured the king's anger
and many a house fell in flames;

because the powerful king
of warriors prepared to rejoice
when the quickeners of death dared   [warriors]
to blot with blood the wound-sea's reed.   [wound-sea = blood;
                                                    reed of blood = sword]

Where do equally battle-quick
chieftains two know greater honour,
grandeur granted the destroyers
of the planet of the prow-boss,   [shield]
than was given the firs of gold   [men]
by toughminded kings because of
the praise of clearsighted Sindri?
The trouble of princes ceased.

The enemy of rings performed   [generous man]
Harald's potent panegyric;
Guttorm got from the sovereign
good pay for recited poem;
the battle-tree ended bloodshed   [man, warrior]
between truly successful kings;
the armies of the two princes
had prepared for the storm of swords.   [battle]

(b) Steinunn the poetess

Steinunn was an Icelandic woman who lived at the time of the Conversion to Christianity
(c. 1000). These two verses refer to the misadventure of Thangbrand, a Christian
missionary who had been shipwrecked on his way back to Norway to report on the
success of his mission to King Olaf Tryggvason. In these verses Steinunn treats the
shipwreck as a victory by the pagan god Thor over the god of the missionary, Christ, who
has failed to protect his servant. Like Jorunn, Steinunn subverts a common motif of
skaldic poetry, in which the difficult and dangerous sea-journey of the hero is celebrated,
to poke fun at the failure of Thangbrand's voyage.

Thórr altered the course of Thangbrand's
long horse of Thvinill, he tossed and   [ship]
bashed the plank of the prow and smashed
it all down on the solid ground;
the ski of the ground of Atall   [ship]
won't later be buoyant on the sea
since the baleful gale caused by him
splintered it all into kindling.

235

The killer of ogresses' kin	[Thórr]
pulverized fully the mew-perch	[mew-perch bison = ship]
bison of the bell's guardian	[bell's guardian = priest]
(the gods chased the steed of the strand);	
Christ cared not for sea-shingle	[sea-shingle stepper = ship]
stepper when cargo-boat crumbled;	
I think that God hardly guarded	
the reindeer of Gylfi at all.	[ship]

3 HILDEGARD AND MUSIC

Texts from: (a) Peter Dronke (1984) *Women Writers of the Middle Ages*, Cambridge: Cambridge University Press, pp. 197–8; (b) Gothic Voices, directed by C. Page (1986) *A Feather on the Breath of God: Sequences and Hymns by Abbess Hildegard of Bingen*, London: Hyperion CD 66039, accompanying booklet, pp. 6–7, 14–16.

Hildegard's music has enjoyed an enormous revival of interest in the last two decades. Music was an integral part of the Divine Offices which the nuns at the Rupertsberg performed several times a day. In 1178 Hildegard permitted a nobleman who was apparently under Church interdiction to be buried in the grounds of the community. Hildegard knew that, although the dead man had once been excommunicated, he had been reconciled with the Church before his death. However, the prelates of Mainz, acting in the name of the archbishop who was away in Italy, condemned Hildegard for burying an excommunicate, and demanded his exhumation. Hildegard refused, and as a result the whole community was itself placed under interdiction; the nuns were not permitted to sing Divine Office, hear Mass or participate in the Eucharist. Hildegard wrote to the prelates defying them. She refused to permit the desecration of the nobleman's grave as a matter of conscience, and went on to warn the prelates of the seriousness of their actions. Music, in Hildegard's understanding, is not simply a pleasurable activity, it is divinely ordained, and those who forbid it do so at their peril. The situation was resolved only six months before Hildegard's death in 1179 when the archbishop, writing from Rome, permits the ban to be lifted if witnesses to the dead man's repentance can be produced.

(a) Letter to the prelates of Mainz

I also beheld something about the fact that, obeying you, we have till now ceased to celebrate the Divine Office in song, reading it only in a low voice: I heard a voice from the living light tell of the diverse kinds of praises, of which David says in the Psalms: 'Praise him in the call of the trumpet, praise him on psaltery and lute, praise him on the tambour and in dancing, praise him on strings and on organ, praise him on resonant cymbals, praise him on cymbals of jubilation – let every spirit praise the Lord!'

In these words outer realities teach us about inner ones – namely how, in accordance with the material composition and quality of instruments, we can best transform and shape the performance of our inner being towards praises of the Creator. If we strive for this lovingly, we recall how man sought the voice of the living spirit, which Adam lost through disobedience – he who, still innocent before his fault, had no little kinship with the sounds of the angels' praises. . . .

But in order that mankind should recall that divine sweetness and praise by which, with the angels, Adam was made jubilant in God before he fell, instead of recalling Adam in his banishment, and that mankind too might be stirred to that sweet praise, the holy prophets – taught by the same spirit, which they had received – not only composed psalms and canticles, to be sung to kindle the devotion of listeners; but also they invented musical instruments of divers kinds with this in view, by which the songs could be expressed in multitudinous sounds, so that listeners, aroused and made adept outwardly might be nurtured within by the forms and qualities of the instruments, as by the meaning of the words performed with them.

Eager and wise men imitated the holy prophets, inventing human kinds of harmonized melody (organa) by their art, so that they could sing in the delight of their soul; and they adapted their singing to [the notation indicated by] the bending of the finger-joints, as it were recalling that Adam was formed by the finger of God, which is the Holy Spirit, and that in Adam's voice before he fell there was the sound of every harmony and the sweetness of the whole art of music. And if Adam had remained in the condition in which he was formed, human frailty could never endure the power and the resonance of that voice. But when his deceiver, the devil, heard that man had begun to sing through divine inspiration, and that he would be transformed through this to remembering the sweetness of the songs in the heavenly land – seeing the machinations of his cunning going awry, he became so terrified that . . . he had not ceased to trouble or destroy the affirmation and beauty and sweetness of divine praise and of the hymns of the spirit. So you and all prelates must use the greatest vigilance before stopping, by a decree, the mouth of any assembly of people . . . singing to God . . . you must always beware lest in your judgement you are ensnared by Satan, who drew man out of the celestial harmony and the delights of paradise. . . .

And because at times, when hearing some melody, a human being often sighs and moans, recalling the nature of the heavenly harmony, the prophet David, subtly contemplating the profound nature of the spirit, and knowing that the human soul is symphonic, exhorts us in his psalm to proclaim the Lord on the lute and play for him on the ten-stringed psaltery: he wants to refer his lute, which sounds lower, to the body's control; the psaltery, which sounds higher, to the spirit's striving; its ten chords, to the fulfilment of the Law.

(b) Hildegard's lyrics

Hildegard's lyrics are composed in apparently simple language, yet the words are rich in association. Hildegard draws not only on the Bible, but also on the language and concepts of her own visions (see p. 134 above). The first of these hymns is dedicated to the Virgin Mary, the second to St Ursula, a British princess who, together with 11,000 companions (the number is probably a copyist's mistake), was martyred at Cologne.

Ave generosa – ymnus de Sancta Maria
Hail, noble one – hymn of Saint Mary

Hail, girl of a noble house,
shimmering
and unpolluted,
you pupil in the eye of chastity,
you essence of sanctity,
which was pleasing to God.

For the heavenly potion
was poured into you,
in that the Heavenly word
received a raiment of flesh in you.
You are the lily that dazzles
whom God knew before all others.

O most beautiful
and delectable one:
how greatly God delighted in you!
in the clasp of His fire
He implanted in you so that
His son might be suckled by you.
Thus your womb
held joy,
when the harmony of all Heaven
chimed out from you,
because, Virgin, you carried Christ
whence your chastity blazed in God.

Your flesh has known delight,
like the grassland touched by dew
and immersed in its freshness;
so it was with you,
o mother of all joy.
Now let the sunrise of joy be over all Ecclesia
and let it resound in music

238

for the sweetest Virgin,
Mary compelling all praise,
mother of God. Amen.

O Ecclesia – de undecim milibus virginibus
O Lady Church – of the eleven thousand virgins

O Ecclesia,
your eyes are like sapphire,
your ears the Mount of Bethel,
your nose
like a mountain of myrrh and incense
and your mouth is like the sound
of many waters.

In a vision of true faith
Ursula loved the Son of God
and rejected betrothed and world alike;
she gazed at the sun
and implored the most beautiful youth
saying:

'With a great desire
I have desired to come to you
and rest with you in the marriage of Heaven,
running to you by a new path
as the clouds course in the purest air
like sapphire.'

And after Ursula had said this
this rumour spread amongst the people
And they said:
'In the innocence of girlish ignorance
she does not know what she is saying.'

And they began to play with her
in a great music
until the burden of fire
fell upon her.

Whence they all knew,
for scorn of the world
is like the Mount of Bethel.
And they sensed also

the sweetest odour of myrrh and incense,
because scorn of the world
rises over all things.

Then the Devil
invaded those that were his own,
they that in the bodies of these women
had struck down the noblest qualities.

And all the Elements
heard the great cry,
and before the throne of God
they said:

'O! the red blood
of the innocent Lamb
has streamed out
in the moment of union.

Let all the Heavens hear this!
And let them praise the Lamb of God
with the celestial harmony!
for the throat of the Ancient Serpent
has been choked with these pearls
made of the word of God.

4 MARIE DE FRANCE

Text from: Marie de France (1987) *Fables*, ed. and transl. H. Spiegel, Toronto: Toronto University Press, pp. 257–9, 83–5.

As well as the *Lais*, discussed in chapter 1 above, Marie de France also made a version of some of Aesop's Fables, which she augmented with fabliaux material, typically stories of ingenious wives and stupid peasant husbands and tales with analogues among the folk-tales of a wide range of cultures. Marie's *Fables* are often referred to as translations, but, as Harriet Spiegel points out, the act of versifying, shaping the brisk couplets and witty rhymes which characterize the work, means that the *Fables* should be regarded as a distinctive version: 'Marie did more than put these fables into verse; she made them her own ... she medievalizes her classical fables ... providing a commentary on contemporary life' (Marie 1987: 9). Marie often modifies her fables to sympathize with the female protagonists; in the well-known story of the fox who rapes the she-bear, she makes it clear that the bear who refuses the fox's advances is genuinely upset by his assault, rather than enjoying it, as some other versions of the tale suggest. In the fable given below, her admiration of the sow's quick wits is evident.

(a) Epilogue

To end these tales I've here narrated
And into Romance tongue translated,
I'll give my name, for memory:
I am from France, my name's Marie.
And it may hap that many a clerk
Will claim as his what is my work.
But such pronouncements I want not!
It's folly to become forgot!
Out of my love for Count William,
The doughtiest in any realm,
This volume was by me created,
From English to Romance translated.
This book's called Aesop for this reason:
He translated and had it written
In Latin from the Greek, to wit.
King Alfred, who was fond of it,
Translated it to English hence,
And I have rhymed it now in French
As well as I was competent.
I pray to God omnipotent
To let me to such work attend
And thus to Him my soul commend.

(b) The wolf and the sow

Once long ago a wolf strolled down
A path and chanced to come upon
A sow who was with piglets big.
He hastily approached the pig.
He'd give her peace, he told the sow,
If quickly she'd bear piglets now –
Her piglet babes he wished to have.
With wisdom, the response she gave:
'My lord, how can you hurry me?
When you, so close to me I see,
I cannot bear my young outright;
I'm so ashamed when in your sight.
Do you not sense the implication?
All women suffer degradation
If male hands should dare to touch

At such a time, or even approach!'
With this the wolf hid in retreat
Who'd sought the baby pigs to eat.
The mother pig could now proceed
Who through her cleverness was freed.
    All women ought to hear this tale
And should remember it as well:
Merely to avoid a lie,
They should not let their children die!

5 THE POETRY OF HADEWIJCH

Text from: Hadewijch (1980) *The Complete Works*, transl. C. Hart, New York: Paulist Press, pp. 168–71, 205–7, 344–5.

Hadewijch was a beguine who lived in the mid-thirteenth century in the Low Countries, possibly Antwerp, for one of the manuscripts of her works contains the inscription 'Beata Hadewigis de Antwerpia'. She was the mistress of a beguine group, but was evicted from it and charged with teaching quietism, a doctrine which advocates passive acceptance of whatever happens in the belief that it is God's will. Hadewijch knew Latin and French, as well as her native Dutch, and had been educated in rhetoric, astronomy and music theory, so she may have attended school. We know nothing else about Hadewijch: only that she must have preceded the great Dutch mystic Johannes Ruusbroec (1293–1381) who draws on her work. Hadewijch's poetry is in a tradition which had already been established by Beatrijs of Nazareth and Mechthild of Magdeburg, and which is thought to have originated with St Bernard of Clairvaux, known as *minnemystiek*. This tradition allowed poets, most notably women mystics, to use the erotic and sensual language of contemporary courtly love poetry to describe and evoke their feelings of mystical unity with Christ. Hadewijch's knowledge of French and Latin suggests a courtly upbringing; she sees divine love as a mistress who will lead her through times of rapture and despair to union with Christ.

(a) Poems in stanzas: 16

1 Far and wide we can perceive
The new season:
The birds are in raptures,
While mountain and valley burst into bloom.
All living things
Loose themselves
From the torment of cruel winter.
But it is all over with me
Unless Love quickly
Consoles me for my cruel destiny!

2 Now has my cruel destiny
   Marched its army against me,
   Recruited from every side.
   My highways, but lately free,
   Are heavily occupied.
   Peace is refused me:
   See whether my sad lot can find any counsel?
   If I am led on
   By Love to victory,
   O noble Love, I thank you for it!

3 Love conquers all things:
   May she help me to conquer in my turn!
   And may she who knows every need
   Grant that I may learn
   How hard it is for me
   (Had I the chance)
   To wait for the fruition of Love:
   Cruel reason,
   Which helps against it,
   Introduces confusion in my mental powers.

4 Through Love I can fully conquer
   My misery and exile;
   I know victory will be mine.
   But I have so many misfortunes,
   Which drive me to the verge of death
   Many a time,
   Since Love's arrow first inwardly shot me.
   I am willing to do without everything,
   Until Love wills to place me
   In possession of the magnificence with which she satisfies me.

5 In the days of my youth,
   When Love first fought against me,
   She showed me great advantages –
   Her wisdom, her splendour, her goods, her power.
   When I associated with her,
   And took it upon me
   To pay the full tribute of Love,
   Gladly above all things,
   She bound me to herself in union of love.
   But the storm of happiness now seems fully calmed!

6 Thus Love left me in the lurch
With many things she had promised me,
With many a sweet dainty
By which inexperienced youth was fed.
Choice titbits
With new delight
For which I have gladly suffered all –
I complain and accuse her
With new indignation:
She refuses the happiness that had consoled me.

7 I truly know that Love
Lives, although I thus die often.
Because I know she is living,
I endure everything with joyfulness in play:
Affliction or mercy,
What is evil, or what is good,
I hide them carefully from aliens.
My high-mindedness
Is wise with regard to this:
That Love will compensate with love.

8 To sublime Love
I have given away all that I am.
Whether I lose or win, let all
That is owed her be hers without diminution.
What has happened now?
I am not mine:
She has engulfed the substance of my spirit.
Her fine being
Gives me the assurance
That the pain of Love is all profit.

9 I realize that Love deserves it:
If I lose, if I win, it is all one to me.
What I have most desired,
Since Love first touched my heart,
Was to content her
According to her wish,
As was always apparent:
For I endured
Her blows:
For her sake this was my richest feudal estate.

10 If anyone wishes to content Love,
I counsel him to spare himself in nothing.
He shall give himself totally,
So as to live in the performance of the noblest deeds,
For lovers, secret:
To aliens, unknown,
For they do not understand the essence of Love.
That sweet attendance
In the school of Love
Is unknown to him who never enters there.

However cruelly I am wounded,
What Love has promised me
Remains irrevocably.

(b) Poems in stanzas: 28

1 Joyful now are the birds
That winter oppressed;
And joyful in a short time will be
(We must thank Love for that)
The proud hearts who too long
Have borne their pain
Through confidence in Love.
Her power is so effective
That she will give them in reward
More than they can conceive.

2 He whose wish it is
To receive all love from high Love
Must seek her gladly,
No matter where,
And dare the worst death
If Love destines him for it,
Being always equally bold –
Whatever noble Love commands –
That he may not neglect it
But be ready to perform it.

3 Alas! What then will happen to him
Who lives according to Love's counsel?
For he shall find no one
Who understands his distress.

With unfriendly eyes
Men will show him a cruel look;
For no one will understand
What distress he suffers
Until he surmounts his distress
In the madness of love.

4　The madness of love
Is a rich fief;
Anyone who recognized this
Would not ask Love for anything else:
It can unite opposites
And reverse the paradox.
I am declaring the truth about this:
The madness of love makes bitter what was sweet,
It makes the stranger a kinsman,
And it makes the smallest the proudest.

5　The madness of love makes the strong weak
And the sick healthy.
It makes the sturdy man a cripple
And heals him who was wounded.
It instructs the ignorant person
About the broad way
Whereon many inevitably lose themselves;
It teaches him everything
That can be learned
In high Love's school.

6　In high Love's school
Is learned the madness of Love;
For it causes delirium
In a person formerly of good understanding.
To one who at first had misfortune,
It now gives success;
It makes him lord of all the property
Of which Love herself is Lady.
I am convinced of this,
And I will not change my mind.

7　To souls who have not reached such love,
I give this good counsel:
If they cannot do more,
Let them beg Love for amnesty,

And serve with faith,
According to the counsel of noble Love,
And think: 'It can happen,
Love's power is so great!'
Only after his death
Is a man beyond cure.

High-minded is he
Who becomes so fully ruled by Love
That he can read
In Love's power her judgments on him.

(c) Poems in couplets: 13

What is sweetest in Love is her tempestuousness;
Her deepest abyss is her most beautiful form;
To lose one's way in her is to touch her close at hand;
To die of hunger for her is to feed and taste;
Her despair is assurance;
Her sorest wounding is all curing;
To waste away for her sake is to be in repose;
Her hiding is finding at all hours;
To languish for her sake is to be in good health;
Her concealment reveals what can be known of her;
Her retentions are her gifts;
Wordlessness is her most beautiful utterance;
Imprisonment by her is total release;
Her sorest blow is her sweetest consolation;
Her ruthless robbery is great profit;
Her withdrawal is approach;
Her deepest silence is her sublime song;
Her greatest wrath is her dearest thanks;
Her greatest threat is pure fidelity;
Her sadness is the alleviation of all pain.

We can say yet more about Love:
Her wealth is her lack of everything;
Her truest fidelity brings about our fall;
Her highest being drowns us in the depths;
Her great wealth bestows pauperism;
Her largesse proves to be our bankruptcy;
Her tender care enlarges our wounds;
Association with her brings death over and over;

Her table is hunger; her knowledge is error;
Seduction is the custom of her school;
Encounters with her are cruel storms;
Rest in her is in the unreachable;
Her revelation is the total hiding of herself;
Her gifts, besides, are thieveries;
Her promises are all seductions;
Her adornments are all undressing;
Her truth is all deception;
To many her assurance appears to lie –
This is the witness that can be truly borne
At any moment by me and many others
To whom Love has often shown
Wonders by which we were mocked,
Imagining we possessed what she kept back for herself.
After she first played these tricks on me,
And I considered all her methods,
I went to work in a wholly different way:
By her threats and her promises
I was no longer deceived.

> I will belong to her, whatever she may be,
> Gracious or merciless; to me it is all one!

6 ISOLDE AND HER MUSIC-MAKING

Text from: Gottfried von Strassburg (1960) *Tristan*, transl. A. T. Hatto, Harmondsworth: Penguin, pp. 146–8.

The young hero Tristan from the court of King Mark of Cornwall has killed Morold of Ireland in single combat. During the fight Tristan was wounded with a poisoned sword, and Morold revealed that the only person who could cure it was his sister Queen Isolde of Ireland. After Morold's death, Gurmun, king of Ireland, decrees that any living creature coming from Cornwall to Ireland should be put to death. Tristan, disguised as a wandering minstrel Tantris, makes his way to Dublin, where his plight is brought to the queen's attention. She offers to cure him, in return for tutoring her daughter Isolde in music and courtliness. When his cure is effected, Tristan returns to Cornwall where his praise of his pupil leads King Mark to decide to marry her. Isolde's accomplishments are typical of romance heroines: her education is in courtliness and musicianship, rather than the *trivium* and *quadrivium*. Her ability with languages should be noted, however; it is a common motif in romance that women are more linguistically gifted than men.

From this time on the young princess was constantly under his tuition, and he devoted much time and energy to her. One by one he laid before her for her consideration the best things that he knew, both in book-learning and the playing of instruments, so that she could make her own choice for study as it suited her.

Here is what fair Isolde did. She quickly mastered the pick of his attainments and diligently pursued whatever she took up. The tuition she had already received stood her in very good stead. She had previously acquired a number of refinements and polite accomplishments that called for hands or voice – the lovely girl spoke the language of Dublin, and French and Latin, and she played the fiddle excellently in the Welsh style. Whenever they played, her fingers touched the lyre most deftly and struck notes from the harp with power. She managed her ascents and cadences with dexterity. Moreover, this girl so blessed with gifts sang well and sweetly. She profited from the accomplishments which she had already acquired, and her tutor, the minstrel, much improved her.

Together with all this instruction Tantris engaged her in a pursuit to which we give the name of Bienséance, the art that teaches good manners, with which all young ladies should busy themselves. The delightful study of Bienséance is a good and wholesome thing. Its teaching is in harmony with God and the world. In its precepts it bids us please both, and it is given to all noble hearts as a nurse, for them to seek in her doctrine their life and their sustenance. For unless Bienséance teach them, they will neither prosper nor win esteem. This was the chief pursuit of the young princess; she often refreshed her mind with it and so grew to be courteous, serene, and charming in her ways. Thus the enchanting girl was brought on so much both in her studies and deportment in these six months that the whole land talked of her felicity. Her father the king, too, took great pleasure in it, and her mother was delighted.

Now it often happened when Gurmun was in pleasurable mood or knights from other parts were at court before the throne, that Isolde was summoned to her father in the Palace to while away the time for him and many others with all the polite attainments and pretty ways she knew. Any pleasure she gave her father was pleasure to them all. Were they rich or poor, she was a rapturous feast for their eyes and delight to their ears and hearts – without and within their breasts their pleasure was one and undivided! Sweet and exquisite Isolde, she sang, she wrote, and she read for them, and what was joy to all was recreation for her. She fiddled her 'estampie', her lays, and her strange tunes in the French style, about Sanze and St Denis (than which nothing could be rarer), and knew an extraordinary number. She struck her lyre or her harp on either side most excellently with hands as white as ermine. Ladies' hands never struck strings more sweetly in Lud [London] or Thamise [Thames] than hers did here – sweet, lovely Isolde! She sang her 'pastourelle', her 'rotruenge' and 'rondeau', 'chanson', 'refloit', and 'folate' well, and well, and all too well. For thanks to her, many hearts grew full of longing; because of her, all manner of thoughts and ideas presented themselves. No end of things came to mind, which, as you know, happens when you see such a marvel of beauty and grace as was given to Isolde.

'estampie': a dance played on instruments, often without vocal accompaniment; 'Sanze': possibly Sandde, the saintly father of St David of Wales; 'rotruenge': a rollicking popular dance form with refrain; 'refloit' and 'folate': meaning unknown

7 AN EMBROIDERED PRAISE-SONG

Text translated by Mary Stansfield Popovic (1936), kindly provided by Ivona Ilic, University of Belgrade.

Yephimia was the daughter of the Serbian prince Voihna and was married to the Despot Ugljesa Mrnjavcevic who was killed in the battle of Maritza in 1371. Yephimia was born around 1350 and died sometime after 1405. After her husband's death she sought refuge with Prince Lazar. However, the Turks, under Sultan Murat, invaded his kingdom too, Lazar died in battle and his sons were made to serve in the Turkish army as vassals of Sultan Bayazet. Yephimia, together with Lazar's wife, retired to the monastery of Ljubostinje. Here Yephimia composed the following panegyric to Lazar, embroidering it in silver-gilt on a crimson silk pall for the prince's coffin. The pall, which is 66 by 25 cm, has a border of vine leaves, surrounding the poem, which consists of 26 lines of poetry, each 18 mm high. It can still be seen in the monastery of Ravanica. Yephimia's text is thus not simply a verbal work of art – though in its heartfeltness and rhetorical power it is that – but it also derives its meaning and artistic effectiveness from the purpose of the pall, its physical disposition and the materials in which it is made.

Among the fair things of this world wast thou reared from thy youth up, oh prince Lazar, thou new-made martyr, and the mighty hand of the Lord made thee strong and famous among all the rulers of the earth. Thou didst rule over the land of thy fathers and in all good things didst thou delight the Christian people entrusted to thy hands; with manly heart and pious hopes didst thou go forth against the serpent, the envy of God's church, for thy heart could not suffer to behold the hosts of Ismail ruling in Christian lands; didst thou fail in this, [thou wast resolved] to abandon the crumbling heights of earthly power and, empurpling thyself in thine own blood, unite thyself unto the hosts of the Heavenly King. And thus were thy two desires fulfilled, for thou didst slay the serpent and didst receive from God the martyr's crown. Forget not now, therefore, thy beloved children, whom by thy death thou hast left desolate, while thou art gone hence to the everlasting joys of Heaven; many troubles and sufferings are fallen upon thy beloved children, and their lives are spent in sorrow, for the sons of Ismail rule over them and thy help is sorely needed by us all. Therefore we beseech thee, pray the Ruler of Mankind for thy beloved children and for all [those] who serve them in love and faith, for thy children are compassed about with many ills and those who eat the children's bread have raised great strife against them, and have forgotten, oh martyr, thy goodness unto them. But though thou hast abandoned this life, thou knowest the troubles and sufferings of thy children and as a martyr art free before the Lord; bow the knee to the Heavenly King who has crowned thee with the martyr's crown; beseech him that thy beloved children may pass many years of life in prosperity in accordance with his will; beseech him that the Orthodox Christian faith may stand inviolate in the land of thy fathers; pray that God the Victor may give thy beloved sons, Prince Stephan and Prince Vuk, the victory over all their foes, seen and unseen, for if we have the help of the Lord, we shall render praise and thanks to thee: call George, rouse Demetrius, persuade the Theodores, take with thee Mercurius and Procopius; forget not the forty martyrs of Sebaste, in the place of whose martyrdom thine own beloved sons, Prince Stephan and Prince Vuk, do now contend; pray that they may be given help from God, come thou too to our aid, wherever thou beest. Look upon my humble offerings and magnify them with thy regard, for I offer thee not praise worthy of thee, but only in accordance with my humble powers and therefore I hope for but little reward. But as thou, oh dear my lord and holy martyr, wert ever generous of temporal and passing things, how much more so wilt thou be of those great and everlasting things which thou hast received from God, for thou didst abundantly provide for my bodily needs when I was a stranger in a foreign land. And now I pray thee both that thou wilt preserve me and that thou wilt assuage the bitter storm in my soul and body, Euphemia from her heart offers this to thee, oh blessed saint.

George, Demetrios, the Theodores and the others mentioned are prominent saints in the Orthodox Church.

8 CHRISTINE AND THE PROBLEM OF REPRESENTATION

Text from: Christine de Pizan (1982) *The Book of the City of Ladies*, transl. E. J. Richards, New York: Persea Books, pp. 3–5, 17, 18.

Here Christine recounts how she was inspired to compose *The Book of the City of Ladies* by a chance encounter with a rather obscure misogynist text, the *Lamentations of Mathéolus*, composed around 1300. The book contains the usual commonplaces of medieval misogyny, and Christine uses the encounter to dramatize the woman reader's reaction to seeing herself figured in a text to which she has no right of reply, and whose authority, as a written text, seems to outweigh her own experience of women as by no means universally evil. The allegorical figures of Reason, Rectitude and Justice come to authorize her own writing against the misogynist tradition; Reason traces some of the causes of misogyny. Quilligan (1991: 11–68) is a thoroughgoing examination of Christine's problems with representation, including her own self-representation, authority, and tradition.

(9a) Reading Mathéolus

One day as I was sitting alone in my study surrounded by books on all kinds of subjects, devoting myself to literary studies, my usual habit, my mind dwelt at length on the weighty opinions of authors whom I had studied for a long time. I looked up from my book, having decided to leave such subtle questions in peace and to relax by reading some light poetry. With this in mind, I searched for some small book. By chance a strange volume came into my hands, not one of my own, but one which had been given to me along with some others. When I held it open and saw from its title page that it was by Mathéolus, I smiled, for though I had never seen it before, I had often heard that like other books it discussed respect for women. I thought I would browse through it to amuse myself. I had not been reading for very long when my good mother called me to refresh myself with some supper, for it was evening. Intending to look at it the next day, I put it down. The next morning, again seated in my study as was my habit, I remembered wanting to examine this book by Mathéolus. I started to read it and went on for a little while. Because the subject seemed to me not very pleasant for people who do not enjoy lies, and of no use in developing virtue or manners, given its lack of integrity in diction and theme, and after browsing here and there and reading the end, I put it down in order to turn my attention to more elevated and useful study. But just the sight of this book, even though it was of no authority, made me wonder how it happened that so many different men – and learned men among them – have been and are so inclined to express both in speaking and in their treatises and writings so many wicked insults about women and their behaviour. Not only one or two and not even just this Mathéolus (for the book had a bad name anyway and was intended as a satire) but, more generally, judging from the treatises of all philosophers and poets and from all the orators – it would take too long to mention their names – it seems that they all speak from one and the same mouth. They all concur in one conclusion: that the behaviour of women is inclined to and full of every vice. Thinking deeply about these matters, I began to examine my character and conduct as a natural woman and, similarly, I considered other women whose company I frequently kept, princesses, great ladies, women of the middle and lower classes, who had graciously told me of their most private and intimate thoughts, hoping that I could judge impartially and in good conscience whether the testimony of so many notable men could be true. To the best of my knowledge, no matter how long I confronted or dissected the problem, I could not see or realize how their claims could be true when compared to the natural behaviour and character of women. Yet I still argued vehemently against women, saying that it would be impossible that so many famous men – such solemn scholars, possessed of such deep and great understanding, so clear-sighted in all things, as it seemed – could have spoken falsely on so many occasions that I could hardly find a book on morals where, even before I had read it in its entirety, I did not find several chapters or certain sections attacking women, no matter who the author was. This reason alone, in short, made me conclude that, although my intellect did not perceive my own great faults and, likewise, those of other women because of its simpleness and ignorance, it was however truly fitting that such was the case. And so I relied more on the judgment of others than on what I myself felt and knew. I was so transfixed in this line of thinking for such a long time that it seemed as if I were in a stupor. Like a gushing fountain, a series of authorities, whom I recalled one after another, came to mind, along with their opinions on this topic. And I finally decided that God formed a vile creature when He made woman, and I wondered how such a worthy artisan could have deigned to make such an abominable work which, from what they say, is the vessel as well as the refuge and abode of every evil and vice. As I was thinking this, a great unhappiness and sadness welled up in my heart, for I detested myself and the entire feminine sex, as though we were monstrosities in nature.

(b) Lady Reason accounts for misogynist writing

The causes which have moved and still move men to attack women, even those authors in those books, are diverse and varied, just as you have discovered. For some have attacked women with good intentions, that is, in order to draw men who have gone astray away from the company of vicious and dissolute women, with whom they might be infatuated, or in order to keep these men from going mad on account of such women, and also that every man may avoid an obscene and lustful life. They have attacked all women in general because they believe that women are made up of every abomination. . . .

Other men have attacked women for other reasons: such reproach has occurred to some men because of their own vices and others have been moved by the defects of their own bodies, others through pure jealousy, still others by the pleasure they derive in their own personalities from slander. Others, in order to show they have read many authors, base their own writings on what they have found in books and repeat what other writers have said and cite different authors.

9 BECOMING TEXTUAL: HOW MARGERY GOT HER BOOK WRITTEN

Text adapted from: Margery Kempe (1940) *The Book of Margery Kempe*, ed. S. Meech and H. E. Allen, EETS 212, Oxford: Oxford University Press, pp. 3–5.

In the Proem to *The Book of Margery Kempe*, the scribe traces the hesitation which Margery felt about putting her experiences into textual form, despite the encouragement which she received from various quarters, and the complex process of getting the text written once she had made up her mind to the task. The first scribe, who takes down her words in a mixture of English and German, may have been Margery's reprobate son, whose conversion is described in chapter 3 above (Hirsh 1975: 146); however, as Marion Glasscoe points out, we might expect Margery to identify him if this were the case (Glasscoe 1993: 286). Margery finds a second scribe who at first is reluctant; other hindrances, diabolically inspired, are overcome through Margery's prayers and the *Book* finally comes into being. The problems, both those of her own making, and the practical difficulties which Margery has to overcome to bring her *Book* to fruition are perhaps emblematic of the obstacles which medieval women writers had to surmount.

Some of these worthy and worshipful clerks took it in peril of their souls, and as they would answer to God, that this creature was inspired with the Holy Ghost and commanded her that she get them to write and to make a book of her feelings and revelations. Some offered to write her feelings with their own hands, and she would not consent in any way to this, for she was commanded in her soul that she should not write so soon. And so it was twenty years and more from the time this creature first had feelings and revelations before she had any of them written. Afterward, when it pleased our Lord, he commanded her and charged her that she should have her feelings and revelations written down, and the form of her living, so that his goodness might be known to all the world. Then the creature had no writer who would fulfil her desire nor give credence to her feelings until the time that a man, dwelling in Germany, who was an Englishman by birth and had afterwards got married in Germany and had there both a wife and child, who had good knowledge of this creature and of her desire, moved, I trust, by the Holy Ghost, came to England with his wife and his goods and lived with the aforesaid creature, until he had written as much as she would tell him for the time that they were together. And afterwards he died.

Then there was a priest which this creature had great affection for, and so she communed with him about this matter and brought him the book to read. The book was so badly written that he could scarcely understand it, for it was neither good English nor German, nor were the letters shaped or formed as other letters are. Therefore the priest fully believed that no man could ever read it, unless he had special grace. Nevertheless, he promised her that if he could read it, he would copy it out and write it better with good will. Then there was such evil speaking about this creature and her weeping, that the priest dared not, for cowardice, speak with her, except seldom, nor would he write as he had promised to the aforesaid creature, and so he avoided and deferred the writing of this book well into four years or else more, notwithstanding the fact that this creature begged him for it. At last he said to her that he could not read it, wherefore he would not do it. He would not, he said, put himself in peril by doing it. Then he advised her to go to a good man who had been greatly conversant with him that first wrote the book, supposing that he should best be able to read the book, for he had sometimes read letters written by the other man, sent from beyond the sea while he was in Germany. And so she went to that man, praying him to write this book and never to reveal it as long as she lived, granting him a great sum of goods for his labour.

And this man wrote about a page, and yet it was little to the purpose, for he could not do very well with it, the book was so badly composed and so unreasonably written. Then the priest was vexed in his conscience, for he had promised her to write this book, if he could manage to read it, and had not done his part as well as he might have done, and he asked this creature to get the book again if she could easily do so. Then she got the book again and brought it to the priest with right glad cheer, praying him to do his best and she should pray to God for him and obtain for him grace to read it and write it also. The priest, trusting in her prayers, began to read this book, and it was much more easy, as it seemed to him, than it was before, and so he read over every word to this creature, she sometimes helping where there was any difficulty. This book is not written in order, everything after another, as it was done, but just as the matter came to the creature in mind when it had to be written, for it was so long before it was written that she had forgotten the time and the order when things happened. And therefore she had nothing written down, except what she knew very well to be the truth.

When the priest first began to write this book, his eyes were afflicted so that he could not see to make his letters nor could he see to mend his pen. All other things he could see well enough. He set a pair of spectacles on his nose, and then it was worse than it was before. He complained to the creature about his disease. She said his enemy [the Devil] had envy of his good deed and wanted to hinder him if he could and told him to do as well as God would give him grace to live. When he came again to his book, he could see as well, it seemed to him, as he ever had done, by daylight and by candlelight, and for this reason, when he had written a quire, he added a leaf to it, and then he wrote this proem to express more openly than does the next following, which was written before this.

BIBLIOGRAPHY

Ælred of Rievaulx ((1948) *De Spirituali Amicitia*, ed. J. Dubois, Bruges: Editions C. Beyaent.
———(1971) *Treatises and the Pastoral Prayer* I, Cistercian Fathers 2, Kalamazoo, Mich.: Cistercian Publications.
———(1984) *De Institutione Inclusarum: Two English Versions*, ed. J. Ayto and A. Barratt, EETS 287, Oxford: Oxford University Press.
Aldhelm (1989) *The Prose Works*, transl. M. Lapidge and M. Herren, Cambridge: D. S. Brewer.
Alexander, J. J. A. (1992) *Medieval Illuminators and their Methods of Work*, New Haven and London: Yale University Press.
Amt, E. (ed.) (1993) *Women's Lives in Medieval Europe: A Sourcebook*, New York and London: Routledge.
Andreas Capellanus (1941) *The Art of Courtly Love*, transl. J. J. Parry, New York: Columbia University Press; repr. 1969.
Anglo-Saxon Poetic Records III, 'The Exeter Book' (1936), ed. G. Krapp and E. V. K. Dobbie, London: Routledge.
Anna Comnena (1969) *The Alexiad*, transl. E. R. A. Sewter, Harmondsworth: Penguin Books.
Aquinas, Thomas (1956) *Summa Contra Gentiles*, transl. V. J. Bourke, New York: Doubleday.
Archer, R. E. (1992) '"How ladies ... who live on their manors ought to manage their households and estates": Women as Landholders and Administrators in the Later Middle Ages', in P. J. P. Goldberg (ed.) *Woman is a Worthy Wight: Women in English Society c.1200–1500*, Stroud, Glos.: Alan Sutton.
Archpriest of Hita (1970) *The Book of Good Love*, transl. R. Mignani and M. A. di Cesare, Albany, N.Y.: State University of New York Press.
'Aucassin and Nicolette' (1971) in *Aucassin and Nicolette and Other Tales*, transl. P. Matarasso, Harmondsworth: Penguin Books.
Augustine (1961) *Confessions*, transl. R. S. Pine-Coffin, Harmondsworth: Penguin Books.
Bainton, R. H. (1984) 'Learned Women in the Europe of the Sixteenth Century', in P. Labalme (ed.) *Beyond their Sex: Learned Women of the European Past*, New York: New York University Press.
Bambas, R. C. (1963) 'Another View of the OE "Wife's Lament"', *Journal of English and Germanic Philology* 62, pp. 303–9.
The Bannantyne Manuscript Writtin in Tyme of Pest by George Bannantyne 1568 vol. II (1928), ed. W. Tod Ritchie, Scottish Text Society, NS 22, London and Edinburgh: Blackwood & Sons.

BIBLIOGRAPHY

Barratt, A. (1987a) 'Flying in the Face of Tradition: A New View of "The Owl and the Nightingale"', *University of Toronto Quarterly* 56, pp. 417–85.

——(1987b) ' "The Flower and the Leaf" and "The Assembly of Ladies": Is There a (Sexual) Difference?', *Philological Quarterly* 64, pp. 1–24.

——(ed.) (1992) *Women's Writing in Middle English*, London: Longman.

Bede (1955) *A History of the English Church and People*, transl. L. Sherley-Price, Harmondsworth: Penguin Books.

Beer, F. (1992) *Women and Mystical Experience in the Middle Ages*, Woodbridge, Suffolk: Boydell Press.

Belanoff, P. (1990) 'Women's Songs, Women's Language: *Wulf and Eadwacer* and *The Wife's Lament*' in H. Damico and A. Hennessey Olsen (eds) *New Readings on Women in Old English Literature*, Bloomington, Ind.: Indiana University Press.

Bell, S. G. (1989) 'Medieval Women Book Owners: Arbiters of Lay Piety and Cultural Ambassadors', in J. Bennett *et al.* (eds) *Sisters and Workers of the Middle Ages*, Chicago: University of Chicago Press.

Bennett, J. (1986) 'The Village Ale-Wife: Women and Brewing in Fourteenth-Century England', in B. Hanawalt (ed.) *Women and Work in Preindustrial Europe*, Bloomington, Ind.: Indiana University Press.

——(1987) *Women in the Medieval English Countryside: Gender and Household in Brigstock before the Plague*, Oxford and New York: Oxford University Press.

——(1988) 'Public Power and Authority in the Medieval English Countryside', in M. Erler and M. Kowaleski (eds) *Women and Power in the Middle Ages*, Athens, Ga.: University of Georgia Press.

——(1991) 'Misogyny, Popular Culture, and Women's Work', *History Workshop Journal* 31, pp. 166–88.

——(1992) 'Medieval Women, Modern Women: Across the Great Divide', in D. Aers (ed.) *Culture and History 1350–1600: Essay on English Communities, Identities and Writing*, New York and London: Harvester Press.

Benton, J. (1973 for 1968) 'Clio and Venus: An Historical View of Medieval Love', in F. X. Newman (ed.) *The Meaning of Courtly Love*, Albany, N.Y.: State University of New York Press.

——(1982) 'Consciousness of Self and Perceptions of Individuality', in R. L. Benson and G. Constable (eds) *Renaissance and Renewal in the Twelfth Century*, Oxford: Clarendon Press.

——(ed.) (1984) *Self and Society in Medieval France: The Memoirs of Abbot Guibert of Nogent*, Medieval Academy Reprints for Teaching 15, Toronto: University of Toronto Press.

——(1985) 'Trotula, Women's Problems, and the Professionalization of Medicine in the Middle Ages', *Bulletin of the History of Medicine* 59, pp. 30–53.

Berrigan, J. (1984) 'The Tuscan Visionary: Saint Catherine of Siena', in K. M. Wilson (ed.) *Medieval Women Writers*, Manchester: Manchester University Press.

'Le Bien des Fames' (1989), in G. K. Fiero, W. Pfeffer, M. Allain (eds) *Three Medieval Views of Women*, New Haven and London: Yale University Press.

Biller, P. P. A. (1992) 'Marriage Patterns and Women's Lives: A Sketch of a Pastoral Geography', in P. J. P. Goldberg (ed.) *Woman is a Worthy Wight: Women in English Society c.1200–1500*, Stroud, Glos.: Alan Sutton.

Binski, P. (1991) *Painters*, Medieval Craftsmen Series, London: British Museum Press.

Bishop, J. (1985) 'Bishops as Marital Advisors in the Ninth Century', in J. Kirshner and S. Wemple (eds) *Women of the Medieval World*, Oxford: Blackwell.

Blake, N. F. (1969) *William Caxton and His World*, London: André Deutsch.

Blamires, A. (1992) *Woman Defamed and Woman Defended*, Oxford: Oxford University Press.

Bloch, R. H. (1991) *Medieval Misogyny and the Invention of Western Romantic*

Love, Chicago: University of Chicago Press.

Boase, R. (1977) *The Origin and Meaning of Courtly Love: A Critical Study of European Scholarship*, Manchester: Manchester University Press.

Boccaccio, Giovanni (1993) *The Decameron*, transl. G. Waldman, Oxford: Oxford University Press.

Boffey, J. (1993) 'Women Authors and Women's Literacy in Fourteenth- and Fifteenth-Century England', in C. Meale (ed.) *Women and Literature in Britain 1150–1500*, Cambridge: Cambridge University Press.

Bogin, M. (1976) *The Women Troubadours*, New York and London: Paddington Press.

Bolton, B. (1978) '*Vitae Matrum*: A Further Aspect of the *Frauenfrage*', in D. Baker (ed.) *Medieval Women*, Oxford: Blackwell.

Boncompagno da Signa (1975) *Rota Veneris*, ed. and transl. J. Purkart, Scholars' Facsimiles and Reprints, New York: Delmar.

Boniface (1940) *The Letters of Saint Boniface*, transl. E. Emerton, New York: Columbia University Press; repr. Octagon, 1973.

Brooke, C. (1991) *The Medieval Idea of Marriage*, Oxford: Oxford University Press.

Brooke, C. and Brooke, R. (1978) 'St Clare', in D. Baker (ed.) *Medieval Women*, Oxford: Blackwell.

Brown, J. (1986) *Immodest Acts: The Life of a Lesbian Nun in Renaissance Italy*, Oxford: Oxford University Press.

Brown, P. (1988) *The Body and Society: Men, Women, and Sexual Renunciation in Early Christianity*, New York: Columbia University Press.

Bryant, G. (1984) 'The French Heretic Beguine: Marguerite Porete', in K. M. Wilson (ed.) *Medieval Women Writers*, Manchester: Manchester University Press.

Burns, E. J. (1993a) 'This Prick Which Is Not One: How Women Talk Back in Old French Fabliaux', in L. Lomperis and S. Stanbury (eds) *Feminist Approaches to the Body in Medieval Literature*, Philadelphia, Pa.: University of Pennsylvania Press.

——(1993b) *Bodytalk: When Women Speak in Old French Literature*, Philadelphia, Pa.: University of Pennsylvania Press.

Bynum, C. W. (1982) *Jesus as Mother: Studies in the Spirituality of the High Middle Ages*, Berkeley and Los Angeles: University of California Press.

——(1991) *Fragmentation and Redemption: Essays on Gender and the Human Body in Medieval Religion*, New York: Zone Books.

Cadden, J. (1986) 'Medieval Scientific and Medical Views of Sexuality: Questions of Propriety', *Medievalia et Humanistica* 14, pp. 157–71.

——(1993) *Meanings of Sex Difference in the Middle Ages: Medicine, Science, and Culture*, Cambridge: Cambridge University Press.

Camporesi, P. (1988) *The Incorruptible Flesh: Bodily Mutation and Mortification in Religion and Folklore*, transl. T. Croft-Murray, Cambridge: Cambridge University Press.

Casagrande, C. (1992) 'The Protected Woman', in C. Klapisch-Zuber (ed.) *Silences of the Middle Ages* (*A History of Women in the West* vol. 2), Cambridge, Mass., and London: Belknap Press.

The Chastising of God's Children (1957), ed. J. Bazire and E. Colledge, Oxford: Blackwell.

Chaucer, Geoffrey (1988) *The Riverside Chaucer*, ed. L. Benson, 3rd edition, Oxford: Oxford University Press.

Cherewatuk, K. and Wiethaus, U. (eds) (1993) *Dear Sister: Medieval Women and the Epistolary Genre*, Philadelphia, Pa.: University of Pennsylvania Press.

Chester Mystery Cycle (1974) vol. I, ed. R. M. Lumiansky and D. Mills, EETS SS 2, Oxford: Oxford University Press.

Chojnacki, S. (1988) 'The Power of Love: Wives and Husbands in Late Medieval Venice', in M. Erler and M. Kowaleski (eds) *Women and Power in the Middle*

BIBLIOGRAPHY

Ages, Athens, Ga.: University of Georgia Press.

Chrétien de Troyes (1991) 'Erec and Enide', transl. C. W. Carroll; 'Yvain', transl. W. W. Kibler in *Arthurian Romances*, Harmondsworth: Penguin Books.

Christine de Pizan (1977) *Ditié de Jehanne d'Arc*, ed. and transl. A. J. Kennedy and K. Varty, Oxford: Medium Ævum Monograph 9.

——(1982) *The Book of the City of Ladies*, transl. E. Jeffrey Richards, New York: Persea Press.

——(1985) *The Treasure of the City of Ladies*, transl. S. Lawson, Harmondsworth: Penguin Books.

Clanchy, M. (1993) *From Memory to Written Record: England 1066–1307*, 2nd edition, Oxford: Blackwell.

Clark, A. L. (1992) *Elisabeth of Schönau: A Twelfth-Century Visionary*, Philadelphia, Pa.: University of Pennsylvania Press.

Clark, E. (1991) ' "Adam's Only Companion": Augustine and the Early Christian Debate on Marriage', in R. Edwards and S. Spector (eds) *The Olde Daunce: Love, Friendship, Sex and Marriage in the Medieval World*, Albany N.Y.: State University of New York Press.

Clover, C. J. (1986) 'Maiden Warriors and Other Sons', *Journal of English and Germanic Philology* 85, pp. 34–49.

——(1993) 'Regardless of Sex: Men, Women and Power in Early Northern Europe', *Speculum* 68, pp. 363–87.

Coates, J. (1988) 'Gossip Revisited: Language in All-Female Groups', in J. Coates and D. Cameron (eds) *Women in their Speech Communities*, Harlow: Longman.

Colledge, E. (ed. and transl.) (1965) *Medieval Netherlands Religious Literature*, New York: London House & Maxwell.

Constable, G. (1978) 'Ælred of Rievaulx and the Nun of Watton: An Early Episode in the History of the Gilbertine Order', in D. Baker (ed.) *Medieval Women*, Oxford: Blackwell.

Conway, A. C. (1993) posting on ANSAX-L@wvnvm.earn, 15 October 1993, from caconway@ums1.lan. mcgill.ca..

Cramer, P. (1993) *Baptism and Change in the Early Middle Ages c.200-c.1150*, Cambridge: Cambridge University Press.

Crompton, L. (1980/1) 'The Myth of Lesbian Impunity: Capital Laws from 1270–1791', *Journal of Homosexuality* 6, pp. 11–25.

Cross, C. (1978) ' "Great Reasoners in Scripture": The Activities of Women Lollards 1380–1530', in D. Baker (ed.) *Medieval Women*, Oxford: Blackwell.

Curtius, E. (1953) *European Literature and the Latin Middle Ages*, London: Routledge.

Dafydd ap Gwilym (1982) *Poems*, transl. R. Bromwich, Llandysul, Dyfed: Gomer Press.

Daichman, G. S. (1986) *Wayward Nuns in Medieval Literature*, Syracuse, N.Y.: Syracuse University Press.

Dalarun, J. (1992) 'The Clerical Gaze', in C. Klapisch-Zuber (ed.) *Silences of the Middle Ages (A History of Women in the West* vol. 2), Cambridge, Mass., and London: Belknap Press.

Dante Alighieri (1971) *The Divine Comedy*, transl. J. D. Sinclair, 3 vols, Oxford and New York: Oxford University Press.

——(1969) *La Vita Nuova*, transl. B. Reynolds, Harmondsworth: Penguin Books.

Davies, R. T. (ed.) (1963) *Medieval English Lyrics*, London: Faber.

Delany, S. (1990) ' "Mothers to Think back through": Who Are They? The Ambiguous Example of Christine de Pizan', in S. Delaney (ed.) *Medieval Literary Politics: Shapes of Ideology*, Manchester: Manchester University Press.

Devlin, D. (1984) 'Feminine Lay Piety in the High Middle Ages: The Beguines', in J. A. Nichols and L. Shank (eds) *Distant Echoes: Medieval Religious Women* vol.

259

1, Cistercian Studies Series 71, Kalamazoo, Mich.: Cistercian Publications.

Dhuoda (1975) *Manuel pour mon fils*, ed. P. Riché, Sources Chrétiennes 225, Paris: Editions du Cerf.

Dillard, H. (1984) *Daughters of the Reconquest*, Cambridge: Cambridge University Press.

Dronke, P. (1965–6) *Medieval Latin and the Rise of European Love Lyric*, 2 vols, Oxford: Oxford University Press.

———(1968) *The Medieval Lyric*, London: Hutchinson.

———(1970) *Poetic Individuality in the Middle Ages*, Oxford: Oxford University Press.

———(1984a) *Women Writers of the Middle Ages*, Cambridge: Cambridge University Press.

———(1984b) 'The Provençal *Trobairitz*: Castelloza', in K. M. Wilson (ed.) *Medieval Women Writers*, Manchester: Manchester University Press.

———(forthcoming) 'Andreas Capellanus', *Journal of Medieval Latin* 4.

Duby, G. (1978) *Medieval Marriage: Two Models from Twelfth-Century France*, Baltimore: Johns Hopkins University Press.

———(1983–4) *The Knight, the Lady and the Priest*, transl. B. Bray, New York and Harmondsworth: Peregrine.

———(1992) 'The Courtly Model', in C. Klapisch-Zuber (ed.) *Silences of the Middle Ages* (*A History of Women in the West* vol. 2), Cambridge, Mass., and London: Belknap Press.

Duby, G. and Duby, A. (1973) *Les Procès de Jeanne d'Arc*, Paris: Gallimard.

Eagleton, T. (1976) *Marxism and Literary Criticism*, Berkeley, Calif.: University of California Press.

Egils saga (1933), ed. S. Nordal, Islenzk Fornrit 12, Reykjavík: Hid Islenzka Fornritafélag.

'Eiríks saga rauda' (1935) in *Eyrbyggja saga*, ed. E. O. Sveinsson and M. Thordarson, Islenzk Fornrit 4, Reykjavík: Hid Islenzka Fornritafélag.

Elkins, S. (1988) *Holy Women of Twelfth-Century England*, Chapel Hill, N.C.: University of North Carolina Press.

Ennen, E. (1989) *The Medieval Woman*, transl. E. Jephcott, Oxford: Blackwell.

Enright, M. J. (1988) 'Lady with a Mead-Cup: Ritual, Group Cohesion and Hierarchy in the Germanic Warband', *Frühmittelalterliche Studien* 22, pp. 170–203 .

Fell, C. (1984) *Women in Anglo-Saxon England*, Oxford: Blackwell.

Ferrante, J. M. (1975) *Woman as Image in Medieval Literature*, New York: Columbia University Press.

———(1984) 'The Education of Women in the Middle Ages', in P. Labalme (ed.) *Beyond their Sex: Learned Women of the European Past*, New York: New York University Press.

Finke, L. (1992) *Feminist Theory, Women's Writing*, Ithaca, N.Y.: Cornell University Press.

Finnegan, Sr, M. J. (1991) *The Women of Helfta: Scholars and Mystics*, Athens, Ga.: University of Georgia Press.

Flanagan, S. (1989) *Hildegard of Bingen: A Visionary Life*, London: Routledge.

Flóamanna saga (1987), in *Islendinga sögur* I, ed. Bragi Halldórsson *et al.*, Reykjavík: Svart á Hvítu.

Francis and Clare: The Complete Works (1982), ed. R. J. Armstrong and I. Brady, London: SPCK.

Frank, R. (1973) 'Marriage in Twelfth- and Thirteenth-Century Iceland', *Viator* 4, pp. 474–84.

Frugoni, C. (1992) 'The Imagined Woman', in C. Klapisch-Zuber (ed.) *Silences of the Middle Ages* (*A History of Women in the West* vol. 2), Cambridge, Mass., and London: Belknap Press.

Gertrude of Helfta (1967) *Œuvres spirituelles* I, *Les Exercices*, ed. J. Hourlier and A. Schmitt, Sources Chrétiennes 127, Paris: Editions du Cerf.

——(1968) *Œuvres spirituelles* II, *Le Héraut*, Books I–II, ed. P. Doyère, Sources Chrétiennes 127, Paris: Editions du Cerf.

——(1993) *The Herald of Divine Love*, New York: Paulist Press.

Gilchrist, R. (1994) *Gender and Material Culture: The Archaeology of Religious Women*, London and New York: Routledge.

Ginzburg, C. (1990) *Myths, Emblems, Clues*, transl. J. and A. C. Tedeschi, London: Hutchinson Radius.

Glasscoe, M. (1993) *English Medieval Mystics: Games of Faith*, London: Longman.

Gold, P. S. (1985) *The Lady and the Virgin: Image, Attitude, and Experience in Twelfth-Century France*, Chicago: University of Chicago Press.

Goldberg, P. J. P. (1992) 'Marriage, Migration, and Servanthood', in P. J. P. Goldberg (ed.) *Woman is a Worthy Wight: Women in English Society c.1200–1500*, Stroud, Glos.: Alan Sutton.

Goodich, M. (1985) '*Ancilla Dei*: The Servant as Saint in the Late Middle Ages', in J. Kirshner and S. Wemple (eds) *Women of the Medieval World*, Oxford: Blackwell.

Gottfried von Strassburg (1960) *Tristan*, transl. A. T. Hatto, Harmondsworth: Penguin Books.

Gower, John (1992) *Mirour de l'Omme*, transl. W. B. Wilson, East Lansing, Mich.: Colleagues Press.

Graham, H. (1992) '"A Woman's Work . . .": Labour and Gender in the Late Medieval Countryside', in P. J. P. Goldberg (ed.) *Woman is a Worthy Wight: Women in English Society c. 1200–1500*, Stroud, Glos.: Alan Sutton.

Gravdal, K. (1991) *Ravishing Maidens: Writing Rape in Medieval French Literature and Law*, Philadelphia, Pa.: University of Pennsylvania Press.

Green, M. (1989) 'Women's Medical Practice and Health Care in Medieval Europe', in J. Bennett *et al.* (eds) *Sisters and Workers of the Middle Ages*, Chicago: University of Chicago Press.

Gregory of Tours (1974) *The History of the Franks*, transl. Lewis Thorpe, Harmondsworth: Penguin Books.

Grœnlendinga saga (1935), in *Eyrbyggja saga*, ed. E. O. Sveinsson and M. Thordarson, Islenzk Fornrit 4, Reykjavík: Hid Islenzka Fornritafélag.

Gudmundar saga Biskups (1983), ed. S. Karlsson, Editiones Arnamagnæanæ, Series B vol. 6, Copenhagen: C. A. Reitzels Forlag.

Hadewijch (1980) *The Complete Works*, New York: Paulist Press.

Hanawalt, B. (1986a) *The Ties that Bound: Peasant Families in Medieval England*, Oxford: Oxford University Press.

——(1986b) 'Introduction', in B. Hanawalt (ed.) *Women and Work in Preindustrial Europe*, Bloomington, Ind.: Indiana University Press.

Harding, W. (1993) 'Body Into Text: *The Book of Margery Kempe*', in L. Lomperis and S. Stanbury (eds) *Feminist Approaches to the Body in Medieval Literature*, Philadelphia, Pa.: University of Pennsylvania Press.

Harris, J. (1991) 'The Enigma of *Gísla saga*', in *The Audience of the Sagas* vol. 1, Eighth International Saga Conference Preprints, Gothenburg.

Haskins, S. (1993) *Mary Magdalen: Myth and Metaphor*, London: HarperCollins.

Heinrichs, A. (1986) '*Annat er várt edli*: The Type of the Prepatriarchal Woman' in J. Lindow *et al.* (eds) *Structure and Meaning in Old Norse Literature*, Odense: Odense University Press.

Herlihy, D. (1975) 'Life Expectancies for Women in Medieval Society', in R. T. Morewedge (ed.) *The Role of Woman in the Middle Ages*, London: Hodder & Stoughton.

Herlihy, D. and Klapisch-Zuber, C. (1978) *Les Toscans et leur familles*, Paris: Presse de la Fondation Nationale des Sciences Politiques.

Herolt, Johannes (1928) *The Miracles of the Blessed Virgin Mary*, transl. C. C. Swinton Bland, London: Routledge.

Hildegard of Bingen (1990) *Scivias*, transl. C. Hart and J. Bishop, New York and Mahwah, N.J.: Paulist Press.

Hines, J. (1993) *The Fabliau in English*, London and New York: Longman.

Hirsh, J. (1975) 'Author and Scribe in the *Book of Margery Kempe*', *Medium Ævum* 44, pp. 145–50.

Holdsworth, C. J. (1978) 'Christina of Markyate', in D. Baker (ed.) *Medieval Women*, Oxford: Blackwell.

Hollis, S. (1992) *Anglo-Saxon Women and the Church*, Woodbridge, Suffolk: Boydell Press.

Holloway, J. (1992) *Saint Bride and her Book: Birgitta of Sweden's Revelations*, Focus Library of Medieval Women, Newburyport, Mass.: Focus Texts.

Howell, M. C. (1986) 'Women, the Family Economy, and the Structures of Market Production in Cities of Northern Europe during the Late Middle Ages' in B. Hanawalt (ed.) *Women and Work in Preindustrial Europe*, Bloomington, Ind.: Indiana University Press.

——(1988) 'Citizenship and Gender: Women's Political Status in Northern Medieval Cities', in M. Erler and M. Kowaleski (eds) *Women and Power in the Middle Ages*, Athens, Ga.: University of Georgia Press.

Hozeski, B. (1972) '"Ordo Virtutum": Hildegard of Bingen's Liturgical Morality Play', *Annuale Mediaevale* 13, pp. 45–69.

Hughes, D. O. (1978) 'From Brideprice to Dowry in Mediterranean Europe', *Journal of Family History* 3, pp. 262–96.

Huizinga, J. (1949) *Homo Ludens: A Study of the Play Element in Culture*, London: Routledge.

Irigaray, L. (1985) *Speculum of the Other Woman*, transl. G. C. Gill, Ithaca, N.Y.: Cornell University Press.

Jaeger, S. (1985) *The Origins of Courtliness: Civilizing Trends and the Formation of Courtly Ideals 939–1210*, Philadelphia, Pa.: University of Pennsylvania Press.

Jacquart, D. and Thomasset, C. (1988) *Sexuality and Medicine in the Middle Ages*, transl. M. Adamson, Oxford: Polity Press.

Jerome (1893) *The Letters and Selected Writings of Jerome*, transl. W. H. Freemantle, A Select Library of the Nicene and Post Nicene Fathers of the Christian Church, 2nd series, Oxford: Parker & Co.

Jesch, J. (1991) *Women in the Viking Age*, Woodbridge, Suffolk: Boydell Press.

Jochens, J. (1986) 'The Medieval Icelandic Heroine: Fact or Fiction?' *Viator* 17, pp. 35–50.

Johnston, D. (1991) *Medieval Welsh Erotic Poetry*, Cardiff: Tafol.

Jones, G. (1986) *The Norse Atlantic Saga*, Oxford: Oxford University Press.

Julian of Norwich (1978) *Revelations of Divine Love: The Shorter Version*, ed. F. Beer, Heidelberg: Carl Winter Universitätsverlag.

——(1986) *A Revelation of Love*, ed. M. Glasscoe, Exeter: Exeter University Press.

Kalinke, M. (1990) *Bridal-Quest Romance in Medieval Iceland*, Islandica 46, Ithaca, N.Y.: Cornell University Press.

Karnein, A. (1985) *'De Amore' in volksprachlicher Literatur: Untersuchungen zur Andreas Capellanus-Rezeption im Mittelalter und Renaissance*, Germanisch-Römanisches Monatsschrift 4, Heidelberg: Carl Winter.

Karras, R. (1989) 'The Regulation of Brothels in Later Medieval England', in J. Bennett *et al.* (eds) *Sisters and Workers of the Middle Ages*, Chicago: University of Chicago Press.

Kay, S. (1990) *Subjectivity in Troubadour Poetry*, Cambridge: Cambridge University Press.

Kempe, Margery (1940) *The Book of Margery Kempe*, ed. S. Meech and H. E. Allen, EETS 212, Oxford: Oxford University Press.

Kieckhefer, R. (1988) *Magic in the Middle Ages*, Cambridge: Cambridge University Press.

King, M. L. (1984) 'Book-Lined Cells: Women and Humanism in the Early Italian Renaissance', in P. Labalme (ed.) *Beyond their Sex: Learned Women of the European Past*, New York: New York University Press.

Klapisch-Zuber, C. (1985) *Women, Family, and Ritual in Renaissance Italy*, Chicago: University of Chicago Press.

——(1986) 'Women Servants in Florence during the Fourteenth and Fifteenth Centuries', in B. Hanawalt (ed.) *Women and Work in Preindustrial Europe*, Bloomington, Ind.: Indiana University Press.

——(ed.) (1992) *Silences of the Middle Ages* (*A History of Women in the West* vol. 2), Cambridge, Mass., and London: Belknap Press.

Kleinberg, A. (1992) *Prophets in their Own Country: Living Saints and the Making of Sainthood in the Later Middle Ages*, Chicago and London: University of Chicago Press.

Knight of the Tour-Landry (1971) *Book of the Knight of the Tower*, ed. M. Y. Offord, EETS 30, Oxford: Oxford University Press.

Kowaleski, M. (1986) 'Women's Work in a Market Town: Exeter in the Late Fourteenth Century', in B. Hanawalt (ed.) *Women and Work in Preindustrial Europe*, Bloomington, Ind.: Indiana University Press.

Kowaleski, M. and Bennett, J. (1989) 'Crafts, Gilds, and Women in the Middle Ages: Fifty Years after Marian K. Dale' in J. Bennett *et al.* (eds) *Sisters and Workers of the Middle Ages*, Chicago: University of Chicago Press.

Kristeva, J. (1980) *Desire in Language*, ed. L. S. Roudiez, transl. T. Gora, A. Jardine and L. S. Roudiez, New York: Columbia University Press.

Ladurie, E. (1980) *Montaillou*, transl. B. Bray, Harmondsworth: Penguin Books.

Lamphere, L. (1974) 'Women in Domestic Groups', in M. Z. Rosaldo and L. Lamphere (eds) *Woman, Culture and Society*, Stanford, Calif.: Stanford University Press.

Langland, William (1978) *The Vision of Piers Plowman: A Complete Edition of the B-Text*, ed. A. V. C. Schmidt, London: Everyman.

Laqueur, T. (1990) *Making Sex: Body and Gender from the Greeks to Freud*, Cambridge, Mass.: Harvard University Press.

Larrington, C. (1992) 'Scandinavia', in C. Larrington (ed.) *The Feminist Companion to Mythology*, London: Pandora Press.

Leclerq, J. (1987) 'Solitude and Solidarity: Medieval Women Recluses' in J. A. Nichols and L. Shank (eds) *Peaceweavers: Medieval Religious Women* vol. 2, Cistercian Studies Series 72, Kalamazoo, Mich.: Cistercian Publications.

Legge, M. D. (1950) *Anglo-Norman in the Cloisters: The Influence of the Orders upon Anglo-Norman Literature*, Edinburgh: Edinburgh University Press.

Le Goff, J. (1984) *The Birth of Purgatory*, transl. A. Goldhammer, London: Scholar Press.

Lehmann, R. P. M. (1981) 'Women's Songs in Irish 800–1500', in John Plummer (ed.) *Vox Feminae: Studies in Medieval Woman's Song*, Kalamazoo, Mich.: Medieval Institute Publications.

Lemaire, R. (1989), 'The Semiotics of Private and Public Matrimonial Systems and their Discourse', in K. Glente and L. Winther-Jensen (eds) *Female Power in the Middle Ages: Proceedings from the Second St Gertrud Symposium, Copenhagen, August 1986*, Copenhagen: C. A. Reitzel.

Letters of Abélard and Héloise (1974), transl. B. Radice, Harmondsworth: Penguin Books.

Lewis, C. S. (1965) *The Allegory of Love*, Oxford: Oxford University Press.

L'Hermite-Leclercq, P. (1992) 'The Feudal Order', in C. Klapisch-Zuber (ed.) *Silences of the Middle Ages* (*A History of Women in the West* vol. 2), Cambridge, Mass., and London: Belknap Press.

Liber Historiae Francorum (1974), transl. L. Bachrach, Lawrence, Kans.: Coronado Press.

Liestøl, A. (1963) 'Runer frå Bryggen', *Viking* 27, pp. 5–51.

Lloyd-Morgan, C. (1993) 'Women and their Poetry in Medieval Wales', in C. Meale (ed.) *Women and Literature in Britain 1150–1500*, Cambridge: Cambridge University Press.

Lochrie, K. (1991) *Margery Kempe and Translations of the Flesh*, Philadelphia, Pa.: University of Pennsylvania Press.

Lodge, D. (1988) *Nice Work*, London: Secker & Warburg.

Lucas, A. M. (1983) *Women in the Middle Ages: Religion, Marriage and Letters*, Brighton: Harvester Press.

McDonnell, E. W. (1954) *The Beguines and Beghards in Medieval Culture*, Brunswick, N.J.: Rutgers University Press.

McLaughlin, M. (1990) 'The Woman Warrior: Gender, Warfare, and Society in Medieval Europe', *Women's Studies* 17, pp. 193–209.

McNamara, J. (1989) 'Victims of Progress: Women and the Twelfth Century', in K. Glente and L. Winther-Jensen (eds) *Female Power in the Middle Ages: Proceedings from the Second St. Gertrud Symposium, Copenhagen, August 1986*, Copenhagen: C. A. Reitzel.

Marchand, J. (1984) 'The Frankish Mother: Dhuoda', in K. M. Wilson (ed.) *Medieval Women Writers*, Manchester: Manchester University Press.

Marchello-Nizia, C. (1981) 'Amour courtois, société masculine et figures du pouvoir' *Annales: Economies, Sociétés, Civilisations*, pp. 969–82.

Marie de France (1986) *The Lais of Marie de France*, transl. G. S. Burgess and K. Busby, Harmondsworth: Penguin Books.

——(1987) *Fables*, ed. and transl. H. Spiegel, Toronto: Toronto University Press.

Martínez Pizarro, J. (1989) *A Rhetoric of the Scene: Dramatic Narrative in the Early Middle Ages*, Toronto: Toronto University Press.

Meale, C. (1993) 'Laywomen and their Books in Late Medieval England', in C. Meale (ed.) *Women and Literature in Britain 1150–1500*, Cambridge: Cambridge University Press.

Mechthild of Magdeburg (1991) *Flowing Light of the Divinity*, transl. C. Mesch Galvani, ed. S. Clark, Garland Library of Medieval Literature Series B, vol. 72, New York and London: Garland.

Millett, B. (1993) 'English Recluses and the Development of Vernacular Literature', in C. Meale (ed.) *Women and Literature in Britain 1150–1500*, Cambridge: Cambridge University Press.

Millett, B. and Wogan-Browne, J. (eds) (1990) *Medieval English Prose for Women: Selections from the Katherine Group and 'Ancrene Wisse'*, Oxford: Clarendon Press.

Miner, D. (1974) *Anastaise and Her Sisters*, Baltimore, Md.: Walters Art Gallery.

Minnis, A. (1988) *Medieval Theory of Authorship*, 2nd edition, Aldershot: Wildwood House.

Moi, T. (1985) *Sexual/Textual Politics*, London and New York: Methuen.

——(1986) 'Desire in Langague: Andreas Capellanus and the Controversy of Courtly Love', in D. Aers (ed.) *Medieval Literature: Criticism, Ideology and History*, Brighton: Harvester Press.

Moorman, J. (1968) *A History of the Franciscan Order*, Oxford: Clarendon Press.

Morris, C. (1987) *The Discovery of the Individual 1050–1200*, Medieval Academy Reprints for Teaching 19, Toronto: Toronto University Press.

Mundal, E. and Steinsland, G. (1989) 'Kvinner og medisinsk magi', in H. Gunneng *et al.* (eds) *Kvinnors rosengård: Medeltideskvinnors liv och hälsa, lust och barnafödande*, Stockholm: Centrum för kvinnoforskning vid Stockholms Universitet.

Newman, B. (1987) *Sister of Wisdom*, Berkeley: University of California Press.

Njals saga (1954), ed. E. O. Sveinsson, Islenzk Fornrit 13, Reykjavík: Hid Islenzka Fornritafélag.

Obrist, B. (1984) 'The Swedish Visionary: Saint Bridget', in K. M. Wilson (ed.) *Medieval Women Writers*, Manchester: Manchester University Press.

Oliva, M. (1994) *The Convent and the Community in the Diocese of Norwich from 1350–1540*, Woodbridge, Suffolk: Boydell & Brewer.

Opitz, C. (1992) 'Life in the Later Middle Ages', in C. Klapisch-Zuber (ed.) *Silences of the Middle Ages* (*A History of Women in the West* vol. 2), Cambridge, Mass., and London: Belknap Press.

Origo, I. (1959) *The Merchant of Prato*, London: The Reprint Society.

Ormøy, R. (1988) 'Women as Landholders Seen in the Development of Society in the Norwegian Middle Ages', in K. Glente and L. Winther-Jensen (eds) *Female Power in the Middle Ages: Proceedings from the Second St Gertrud Symposium, Copenhagen, August 1986*, Copenhagen: C. A. Reitzel.

Otis, L. L. (1985) *Prostitution in Medieval Society: The History of an Urban Institution in Languedoc*, Chicago: University of Chicago Press.

Owen, D. D. R. (1993) *Eleanor of Aquitaine: Queen and Legend*, Oxford: Blackwell.

Page, C. (1986) directing Gothic Voices, *A Feather on the Breath of God: Sequences and Hymns by Abbess Hildegard of Bingen*, London: Hyperion CD 66039.

Pagels, E. (1988) *Adam, Eve, and the Serpent*, Harmondsworth: Penguin Books.

Pálsson, H. (1985) *Áhrif Hugsvinnsmála á adrar Fornbókmenntir*, Studia Islandica 43, Reykjavík: Menningarsjödur.

Paston Letters (1958), ed. N. Davis, Oxford: Clarendon Press.

Patrologia Latina (1841–64), ed. J. P. Migne, 221 vols, Paris.

Patterson, L. (1987) *Negotiating the Past: The Historical Understanding of Medieval Literature*, Madison, Wis.: University of Wisconsin Press.

Payer, P. (1984) *Sex and the Penitentials 550–1150*, Toronto: Toronto University Press.

——(1993) *The Bridling of Desire: Views of Sex in the Later Middle Ages*, Toronto: Toronto University Press.

Petrarch (n.d.) *Sonnets for Laura* , transl. G. R. Nicholson, London: Autolycus Press.

Petroff, E. (1986) *Medieval Women's Visionary Literature*, New York and Oxford: Oxford University Press.

Poetic Edda (1969), ed. U. Dronke, Oxford: Oxford University Press.

Power, E. (1922) *Medieval English Nunneries c. 1275–1535*, Cambridge: Cambridge University Press.

——(1928) *The Goodman of Paris: c. 1393*, London: Routledge.

——(1986) *Medieval People*, London: Methuen (first published 1924).

Proverbs of Alfred (1904) ed. W. W. Skeat, Oxford: Clarendon Press.

Quilligan, M. (1991) *The Allegory of Female Authority: Christine de Pizan's Cité des Dames*, Ithaca, N.Y.: Cornell University Press.

Régnier-Bohler, D. (1992) 'Literary and Mystical Voices', in C. Klapisch-Zuber (ed.) *Silences of the Middle Ages* (*A History of Women in the West* vol. 2), Cambridge, Mass., and London: Belknap Press.

Reliquiae Antiquae (1845) vol. II, ed T. Wright and J. Halliwell, London: John Russell Smith.

Riché, P. (1976) *Education and Culture in the Barbarian West*, transl. J. Contreni, Columbia: South Carolina University Press.

——(1989) *Ecoles et enseignement dans le Haut Moyen Age*, Paris: Picard.

Riddy, F. (1993) 'Women Talking about the Things of God', in C. Meale (ed.) *Women and Literature in Britain 1150–1500*, Cambridge: Cambridge University Press.

Rieger, A. (1992) *Trobairitz: Der Beitrag der Frau in der altokzitanischen höfischen Lyrik. Edition des Gesamtkorpus*, Tübingen: Max Niemeyer Verlag.

Robertson, D. W. (1973 for 1968) 'The Concept of Courtly Love as an Impediment to the Understanding of Medieval Texts', in F. X. Newman (ed.) *The Meaning of Courtly Love*, Albany, N.Y.: State University of New York Press.

Robertson, E. (1993) 'Medieval Medical Views of Women and Female Spirituality in the *Ancrene Wisse* and Julian of Norwich's *Showings*', in L. Lomperis and S. Stanbury (eds) *Feminist Approaches to the Body in Medieval Literature*, Philadelphia, Pa.: University of Pennsylvania Press.

Rosaldo, M. Z. (1974) 'A Theoretical Overview', in M. Z. Rosaldo and L. Lamphere (eds) *Woman, Culture and Society*, Stanford, Calif.: Stanford University Press.

Rossiaud, J. (1988) *Medieval Prostitution*, transl. L. G. Cochrane, Oxford: Blackwell.

Saxo Grammaticus (1980) *A History of the Danish People*, transl. P. Fisher and H. Ellis-Davidson, 2 vols, Woodbridge, Suffolk: Boydell Press.

Schmidt, A. V. C. (1987) *The Clerkly Maker: Langland's Poetic Art*, Piers Plowman Studies IV, Woodbridge, Suffolk: D. S. Brewer.

Schulenberg, J. T. (1978) 'Sexism and the Celestial Gynaeceum – from 500–1200', *Journal of Medieval History* 4, pp. 117–33.

——(1984) 'Strict Active Enclosure and Its Effects on Female Monastic Experience (ca. 500–1100)', in J. A. Nichols and L. Shank (eds) *Distant Echoes: Medieval Religious Women* vol. 1, Cistercian Studies Series 71, Kalamazoo, Mich.: Cistercian Publications.

——(1988) 'Female Sanctity: Public and Private Roles, ca. 500–1100', in M. Erler and M. Kowaleski (eds) *Women and Power in the Middle Ages*, Athens, Ga.: University of Georgia Press.

Sedgwick, E. K. (1985) *Between Men: English Literature and Male Homosocial Desire*, London and New York: Columbia University Press.

Shahar, S. (1988) *The Fourth Estate: A History of Women in the Middle Ages*, London: Routledge.

——(1992) *Childhood in the Middle Ages*, London: Routledge.

Shank, M. (1989) 'A Female University Student in Late Medieval Krakow', in J. Bennett *et al.* (eds) *Sisters and Workers of the Middle Ages*, Chicago: University of Chicago Press.

Silence (1992), ed. S. Roche-Mahdi, East Lansing, Mich.: Colleagues Press.

Smith, J. (1978) 'Robert Arbrissel's Relations with Women' in D. Baker (ed.) *Medieval Women*, Oxford: Blackwell.

Smith, R. M. (1992) 'Geographical Diversity in the Resort to Marriage in Late Medieval Europe: Work, Reputation, and Unmarried Females in the Household Formation Systems of Nothern and Sourthern Europe', in P. J. P. Goldberg (ed.) *Woman is a Worthy Wight: Women in English Society c. 1200–1500*, Stroud, Glos.: Alan Sutton.

Snorri Sturluson (1941) *Heimskringla: Oláfs saga Tryggvasonar*, ed. B. Adalbjarnason, Islenzk Fornrit 26, Reykjavík: Hid Islenzka Fornritafélag.

Snow, J. (1984), 'The Spanish Love Poet: Florencía Pinar', in K. M. Wilson (ed.) *Medieval Women Writers*, Manchester: Manchester University Press.

Sørensen, P. M. (1993a) *Fortælling og ære: Studier i islændingesagaerne*, Aarhus: Aarhus Universitetsforlag.

——(1993b) *Saga and Society: An Introduction to Old Norse Literature*, transl. J. Tucker, Odense: Odense University Press.

Spearing, A. C. (1991) 'The Medieval Poet as Voyeur', in R. Edwards and S. Spector (eds) *The Olde Daunce: Love, Friendship, Sex and Marriage in the Medieval World*, Albany, N.Y.: State University of New York Press.

——(1993) *The Medieval Poet as Voyeur: Looking and Listening in Medieval Love*

Narratives, Cambridge: Cambridge University Press.

Stafford, P. (1983) *Queens, Dowagers and Concubines: The King's Wife in the Early Middle Ages*, London: Batsford.

——(1990) 'The King's Wife in Wessex, 800–1066', in H. Damico and A. Hennessey Olsen (eds) *New Readings on Women in Old English Literature*, Bloomington, Ind.: Indiana University Press.

Staniland, K. (1991) *Embroiderers*, Medieval Craftsmen Series, London: British Museum Press.

Stargardt, U. (1985) 'The Beguines of Belgium, the Dominican Nuns of Germany and Margery Kempe', in T. J. Heffernan (ed.) *The Popular Literature of Medieval England*, Knoxville, Tenn.: Tennessee University Press.

Storms, G. (1948) *Anglo-Saxon Magic*, The Hague: Martinus Nijhoff.

Strand, B. (1980) *Kvinnor och män i Gesta Danorum*, Göteborg: Historiska Institutionen.

Strohm, P. (1992) *Hochon's Arrow: The Social Imagination of Fourteenth-Century Texts*, Princeton, N.J.: Princeton University Press.

Stuard, S. M. (1986) 'To Town to Serve: Urban Domestic Slavery in Medieval Ragusa', in B. Hanawalt (ed.) *Women and Work in Preindustrial Europe*, Bloomington, Ind.: Indiana University Press.

——(1987) 'The Dominion of Gender: Women's Fortunes in the High Middle Ages', in R. Bridenthal and C. Koonz (eds) *Becoming Visible*, 2nd edition, Boston: Houghton Mifflin.

Tacitus (1948) *The Agricola and the Germania*, transl. H. Mattingly, rev. S. A. Handford, Harmondsworth: Penguin Books.

Talbot, C. H. (1954) *The Anglo-Saxon Missionaries in Germany*, London: Sheed & Ward.

——(ed. and transl.) (1959) *The Life of Christina of Markyate*, Oxford: Clarendon Press.

Thomasset, C. (1992) 'The Nature of Woman', in C. Klapisch-Zuber (ed.) *Silences of the Middle Ages (A History of Women in the West* vol. 2), Cambridge, Mass., and London: Belknap Press.

Thompson, S. (1978) 'The Problem of the Cistercian Nuns in the Twelfth and Early Thirteenth Centuries' in D. Baker (ed.) *Medieval Women*, Oxford: Blackwell.

Uitz, E. (1990) *Women in the Medieval Town*, transl. S. Marnie, London: Barrie & Jenkins.

Vecchio, S. (1992) 'The Good Wife', in C. Klapisch-Zuber (ed.) *Silences of the Middle Ages (A History of Women in the West* vol. 2), Cambridge, Mass., and London: Belknap Press.

Wainwright, F. T. (1990) 'Æthelflæd, Lady of the Mercians', in H. Damico and A. Hennessey Olsen (eds) *New Readings on Women in Old English Literature*, Bloomington, Ind.: Indiana University Press.

Warner, M. (1976) *Alone of All Her Sex: The Myth and Cult of the Virgin Mary*, London: Vintage.

——(1981) *Joan of Arc: The Image of Female Heroism*, London: Vintage.

Warren, A. K. (1984) 'The Nun as Anchoress: England 1100–1500', in J. A. Nichols and L. Shank (eds) *Distant Echoes: Medieval Religious Women* vol. 1, Cistercian Studies Series 71, Kalamazoo, Mich.: Cistercian Publications.

——(1985) *Anchorites and their Patrons in Medieval England*, Berkeley, Calif.: University of California Press.

Weigle, M. (1992) 'Southwestern Native American Mythology', in C. Larrington (ed.) *The Feminist Companion to Mythology*, London: Pandora.

Wemple, S. F. (1981) *Women in Frankish Society*, Philadelphia, Pa.: University of Pennsylvania Press.

——(1987) 'Sanctity and Power: The Dual Pursuit of Early Medieval Women', in

R. Bridenthal and C. Koonz (eds) *Becoming Visible*, 2nd edition, Boston: Houghton Mifflin.

———(1992) 'Women from the Fifth to the Tenth Century', in C. Klapisch-Zuber (ed.) *Silences of the Middle Ages* (*A History of Women in the West* vol. 2), Cambridge, Mass., and London: Belknap Press.

Wessley, S. (1978) 'The Thirteenth-Century Guglielmites: Salvation through Women', in D. Baker (ed.) *Medieval Women*, Oxford: Blackwell.

Westphal-Wihl, S. (1989) 'The Ladies' Tournament: Marriage, Sex, and Honor in Thirteenth-Century Germany', in J. Bennett *et al.* (eds) *Sisters and Workers of the Middle Ages*, Chicago: University of Chicago Press.

Wierschin, M. (1987) rev. of Karnein, A. (1985) *'De Amore' in volksprachlicher Literatur: Untersuchungen zur Andreas Capellanus-Rezeption im Mittelalter und Renaissance*, *Speculum* 62, pp. 960–3.

Wiesner, M. (1986) 'Early Modern Midwifery: A Case Study', in B. Hanawalt (ed.) *Women and Work in Preindustrial Europe*, Bloomington, Ind.: Indiana University Press.

Wiethaus, U. (1993) 'In Search of Medieval Women's Friendships: Hildegard of Bingen's Letters to her Female Contemporaries', in U. Wiethaus (ed.) *Maps of Flesh and Light*, Syracuse, N.Y.: Syracuse University Press.

Willard, C. C. (1984) *Christine de Pizan: Her Life and Works*, New York: Persea Books.

Wogan-Browne, J. (1993) '"Clerc u lai, muïne u dame": Women and Anglo-Norman Hagiography in the Twelfth and Thirteenth Centuries', in C. Meale (ed.) *Women and Literature in Britain 1150–1500*, Cambridge: Cambridge University Press.

Woolf, V. (1929, repr. 1977) *A Room of One's Own*, London: Grafton.

INDEX

[Literary works are indexed under their author where known.]